New Legal Dynamics
of European Union

JO SHAW

and

GILLIAN MORE

CLARENDON PRESS · OXFORD
1995

Oxford University Press, Walton Street, Oxford OX2 6DP

Oxford New York
Athens Auckland Bangkok Bombay
Calcutta Cape Town Dar es Salaam Delhi
Florence Hong Kong Istanbul Karachi
Kuala Lumpur Madras Madrid Melbourne
Mexico City Nairobi Paris Singapore
Taipei Tokyo Toronto
and associated companies in
Berlin Ibadan

Oxford is a trade mark of Oxford University Press

Published in the United States
by Oxford University Press Inc., New York

British Library Cataloguing in Publication Data
Data available

Library of Congress Cataloging in Publication Data
The new legal dynamics of European Union/[edited by] Jo Shaw and
Gillian More.
p. cm.
Includes bibliographical references.
1. Law—European Union countries. I. Shaw, Josephine. II. More,
Gillian.
KJE949.N49   1995
349.4—dc20   95–41327
[344]
ISBN 0–19–825980–8
ISBN 0–19–826218–3 (Pbk)

1 3 5 7 9 10 8 6 4 2

Typeset by Cambrian Typesetters Frimley, Surrey
Printed in Great Britain
on acid-free paper by
Biddles Ltd, Guildford and King's Lynn

NEW LEGAL DYNAMICS
OF EUROPEAN UNION

Preface and Acknowledgements

It is a truism that all essay collections are the result of collaborative endeavour, involving extensive collaboration and co-operation between editors and contributors. However, it is perhaps even more true about this collection than most. Suggestions for essay titles and abstracts from proposed contributors were gathered together by Jo Shaw, but the book only began to come together at a workshop held at the Europa Institute, University of Edinburgh, in November 1994, organized by Gillian More, where drafts of most of the papers were presented. The outcome of the intensive discussions at this workshop was a friendly, close, and continued collaboration amongst the various contributors, as well as between editors and contributors. In that respect the production of the book has been an invaluable and (we hope) enjoyable learning experience for all involved. For their prompt production of good quality copy and their patient responses to our requests for amendments we would like to thank all our contributors.

We would also like to thank the following people: Willie Paterson for suggesting that the workshop for contributors be held in Edinburgh and for supporting our endeavour; Andrew Scott, acting Director of the Europa Institute, for providing generous financial support for the workshop; Margaret Ainslie for providing administrative and organizational support; Richard Hart of Oxford University Press for supporting the project from the beginning and for making a financial contribution to the workshop; Peter Crowther for initiating and organizing the establishment of an e-mail network which has greatly facilitated communication between participants; John Alder, Head of the Law Department of Keele University, for funding a research assistant; and Linda Veloso for checking the manuscript and bibliography.

Gillian More
Jo Shaw

Table of Contents

List of Contributors

KENNETH A. ARMSTRONG is a Lecturer in Law at Keele University, having previously held a research position based in the European Policy Unit at the University of Manchester. His research interests are currently focused upon the role of institutions in shaping the European Community's policy process.

CATHERINE BARNARD is Jean Monnet Lecturer in Law at the University of Southampton. Her research interests lie in the fields of EC law and labour law. She is author of *EC Employment Law* (Wiley Chancery, 1995).

GRÁINNE DE BÚRCA studied at University College Dublin and the University of Michigan. She is a lecturer at Oxford University and a fellow of Somerville College. Her interests lie broadly in the areas of Criminal Law and European Community Law, and is joint author with Paul Craig of *European Community Law: Text, Cases and Materials* (Oxford University Press, 1995).

DAMIAN CHALMERS studied at Amsterdam and Oxford. Having previously been a Research Officer for the British Institute of International Comparative law and a Lecturer at the University of Liverpool, he is currently a Lecturer at the London School of Economics and Political Science.

PETER CROWTHER was educated at Keele University, Erasmus University, Rotterdam and the University of Oxford. Since 1995 he has worked at the Copenhagen Business School, having previously been a Lecturer in Law at Brunel University. He is currently researching utilities, examining the relationships between different types of corporate governance systems, resulting business strategies, and legal rules.

MICHELLE EVERSON studied at the Universities of Exeter and Saarbrücken, and the European University Institute in Florence, where she completed her PhD. She is currently a researcher at the

Centre for European Legal Policy at the University of Bremen, where she is working on European Citizenship.

LEO FLYNN graduated from the National University of Ireland and the University of Cambridge. He is a Lecturer in Law at King's College, London, having previously taught at the University of Leeds. His teaching and research focuses on EC law, in particular as it relates to State intervention in markets and on equality law.

TAMARA K. HERVEY studied at the Universities of Glasgow and Sheffield and is currently Lecturer in Law at the University of Manchester. She was previously Jean Monnet Lecturer in EC Law at the University of Durham. Her interests include EC sex equality law, the legal protection of minorities, EC constitutional and institutional law, feminist legal method, and comparative law.

IMELDA MAHER, Lecturer in Law, Birkbeck College, University of London, has previously held positions in the University of Warwick and University College, Dublin. Her research interests are EC Law and competition law. She is currently writing a book on the regulation of competition in Ireland.

GILLIAN MORE has held positions as a Lecturer in Law at the Europa Institute, University of Edinburgh and at Keele University. She is currently studying for the English Bar, based at Middle Temple. Her principal field of interest is EC employment law.

COLIN SCOTT is a Lecturer in Law at the London School of Economics and Political Science having previously taught at the University of Warwick. His main fields of research and teaching are utilities regulation, consumer law and public administration. He is currently carrying out research on UK and EC telecommunications regulation and on changes in regulation of public sector bureacracies associated with the development of the New Public Management.

JOANNE SCOTT is a Lecturer in Law at Queen Mary and Westfield College, London, having previously taught at the University of Kent. She is the author of *Development Dilemmas in the EC: Rethinking Regional Development Policy* (Open University Press, 1995).

JO SHAW is Professor of European Law at the University of Leeds, having previously worked at the Universities of Keele and Exeter. Her main fields of research are EC law and Contract Law.

IAN WARD is currently Senior Lecturer at the Centre for Legal Studies, University of Sussex, having taught previously at the Universities of Durham and Iowa. He has been a visiting lecturer at the Catholic University of Portugal and the University of Oslo. His research interests lie in the areas of European law, jurisprudence and comparative law. He is currently engaged in a series of studies relating to the contextual and critical study of European Law.

ELAINE A. WHITEFORD graduated in law from the University of Edinburgh in 1990 and has worked at the Europa Instituut at the Rijksuniversiteit Leiden. She has been a Lecturer in Law at the University of Nottingham since 1995. Her research interests concentrate on the social dimension of the internal market and occupational pensions.

DANIEL WINCOTT is Jean Monnet Lecturer in Law and Politics of European Integration at the University of Warwick. He has published articles on a number of aspects of European integration in journals including *Public Administration*, *West European Politics* and *Democratization*.

List of Abbreviations

AG	Advocate General
AJCL	*American Journal of Comparative Law*
AJIL	*American Journal of International Law*
BB	*Betriebsberater*
BEUC	*Bureau Européen des Unions Consommateurs*
CAP	Common Agricultural Policy
CBI	Confederation of British Industry
CDE	*Cahiers de Droit Européen*
CEE	Charge having an equivalent effect (to a customs duty)
CEEP	European Centre of Enterprises with Public Participation
CITES	Convention on International Trade in Endangered Species of Wild Fauna and Flora
CLJ	*Cambridge Law Journal*
CLS	Critical Legal Studies
CMLR	Common Market Law Review
CRE	Commission for Racial Equality
CTR	Common Technical Regulation
DG	Directorate General
DSB	Dispute Settlement Body
EBLR	*European Business Law Review*
EC	European Community (formerly 'EEC')
ECHR	European Convention on Human Rights
ECJ	European Court of Justice
ECLR	*European Competition Law Review*
ECSA	European Studies Association
EEA	Employment Equality Agency (of the Republic of Ireland)
EEC	European Economic Community (renamed 'EC' by TEU)
EJIL	*European Journal of International Law*
ELR	*European Law Review*
EMU	Economic and Monetary Union
EOC	Equal Opportunities Commission

EOC (NI)	Equal Opportunities Commission (Northern Ireland)
ERPL	*European Review of Private Law*
ETNO	European Public Telecommunications Network Operators' Association
ETSI	European Telecommunications Standards Institute
ETUC	European Trade Union Confederation
ETUI	European Trade Union Institute
EU	European Union
EUI	European University Institute
EUN	European Union National
EuZW	*Europäische Zeitschrift für Wirtschaftsrecht*
Fem. Rev.	*Feminist Review*
GATT	General Agreement on Tariffs and Trade
HRM	Human Resource Management
ICLQ	*International and Comparative Law Quarterly*
IGC	Intergovernmental Conference
IJCLLIR	*International Journal of Comparative Labour Law and Industrial Relations*
ILJ	*Industrial Law Journal*
ILO	International Labour Organization
IO	International Organization
IRJ	*Industrial Relations Journal*
JCMS	*Journal of Common Market Studies*
JEI	*Journal of European Integration*
JEPP	*Journal of European Public Policy*
JLS	*Journal of Law and Society*
JPP	*Journal of Public Policy*
JSWFL	*Journal of Social Welfare and Family Law*
JWT	*Journal of World Trade*
LDF	Legal Defense Fund
LIEI	*Legal Issues of European Integration*
LS	*Legal Studies*
MLR	*Modern Law Review*
NAACP	National Association for the Advancement of Coloured People
NCL	National Consumers' League
NGO	Non-governmental organization
NILQ	*Northern Ireland Legal Quarterly*

NLJ	*New Law Journal*
OECD	Organisation for Economic Co-operation and Development
OJLS	*Oxford Journal of Legal Studies*
ONP	Open Network Provision
Parl. Aff.	*Parliamentary Affairs*
PL	*Public Law*
Pol. Q	*Political Quarterly*
QMV	Qualified Majority Voting
SAP	Social Action Programme
S. Ca. L. Rev.	*Southern California Law Review*
SDA	Sex Discrimination Act
SEA	Single European Act
Stat. L. Rev.	*Statute Law Review*
TCN	Third Country National
TEN	Trans-European Network
TEU	Treaty on European Union
TK	*Tweede Kammer* (second chamber of the Dutch Parliament)
TO	Telecommunications operator
TREM	Trade Related Environmental Measure
UNICE	Union of Industrial and Employers' Confederations of Europe
Va. L. Rev.	*Virginia Law Review*
WTO	World Trade Organization
YBEL	*Yearbook of European Law*

Introduction[1]

JO SHAW

This collection of essays on law and European integration forms part
of a trend towards broadening the focus of legal scholarship in this
field. In this Introduction the antecedents of this trend will be
explored and an attempt will be made to explain and to systematize
the different elements of the new body of legal scholarship
concerning European integration. The descriptive term: 'European
Union legal studies' will be developed. It will be argued that the new
work is the result of a number of different external and internal
pressures, and that the opportunity is now greater than ever before
for lawyers to build up dialogues with other scholars of European
integration. A more sophisticated understanding of the interaction
between law/legal norms and processes of integration/disintegration
(in the various guises in which these terms can be understood)
within all areas of European studies can enrich work on integration
by highlighting the particular empirical and normative visions of
lawyers. The emerging trend also underpins the intellectual
foundations of EC law as a subject of study for lawyers and legal
theorists, and so helps to bridge the gap which existed previously
between legal theory and integration theory. Thus, while few if any
of the essays in this collection would claim the status of contribution
to 'high theory' (of law or integration), they nonetheless help to
prepare the ground for such work through 'middle' or 'lower' order
theorizing (Twining, 1986a: 64). To use Twining's words (1986a:
64), the reader will find in these essays *inter alia*: 'general hypotheses
about legal or law-related phenomena capable of being tested by
empirical methods; . . . prescriptive working theories for various

[1] Many thanks to Kenneth Armstrong, Gráinne de Búrca and Imelda Maher for
helpful comments on a draft of this introduction. Conversations with them and with
others, especially Catherine Barnard and Daniel Wincott, at the ECSA Conference in
Charleston, SC in May 1995 proved invaluable in putting together this brief essay.
However, I take full responsibility for its remaining inaccuracies and infelicities.

kinds of participants in legal processes . . . the systematic exploration at a general level of the relationship between law and at least
the more general aspects of . . . other disciplines relevant to law.'

Of course, critical, theoretical, contextualist, or interdisciplinary
approaches to the European Union legal order are not new.
Important contributions to the development of a distinctive legal
voice in European integration studies have already been made (for
example Weiler, 1981, 1982, 1991; Stein, 1981; Snyder, 1990;
Dehousse and Weiler, 1990; Shapiro, 1992; Slaughter Burley, 1993;
Joerges, 1994 and the literature reviewed therein). This volume
seeks to build upon the existing foundations and to suggest possible
new avenues for research and intellectual enquiry. This introduction
therefore aims to provide some signposts for the links between what,
at first sight, seems a rather disparate collection of essays,
principally from younger scholars working and/or educated in the
United Kingdom. The work presented constitutes some of the first
tentative steps towards the articulation of a new voice for European
Union legal studies. This composite notion focuses on both the
'legal' element and the 'European studies' element. For as this
Introduction will show, the subject of European Union legal studies
is only now emerging as scholars apply not only the tools of legal
scholarship (socio-legal studies, postmodernist theory, critical legal
studies, law in context, etc.) but also the tools of interdisciplinary
scholarship concerning processes of regional integration (comparative politics, international relations, public policy analysis, theories
of institutional behaviour, etc.) to the study of the law/integration
interface.

1. BEYOND THE DOCTRINAL PARADIGM

There is still relatively little published work on EC law which does
not take a predominantly traditional and doctrinal approach. Legal
scholarship on the European Union is only slowly breaking out from
a paradigm of what has been (perhaps inappropriately) termed
'orthodox legal scholarship' (Gava, 1994). Most of this work has
concentrated on the Court of Justice, and its role as a 'motor of
integration' has taken on the role of an assumed intellectual
centrepiece. This is not the place to consider why this has been so
(cf. Shaw, 1996; Alter, 1994) but in this Introduction some key

features of the paradigm are identified, schematically,[2] in order to show how that paradigm continues to shape scholarship concerning the Court of Justice.

The dominant voice has hitherto comprised, first, doctrine-based accounts of the development of the principles underlying the legal order of the EU, which concentrate almost exclusively on the achievements (or failures) of the Court of Justice, and secondly, discussions of substantive fields of EU policy with a similar focus. In such work, legislative processes are understood either as wholly separate from judicial activity or as having no real existence until the Court has exercised its interpretative function. These accounts are not merely neutral statements of a juristic reality about what the law *is*. On the contrary, they are prescriptive and ideological statements about the position of law within the process of European integration, as conceived by most lawyers within the mainstream tradition of EC law scholarship. I have argued elsewhere (Shaw, 1996) that much of that scholarship is sustained by positing an immutable link between law and legal processes, and integration, conventionally if somewhat simplistically, is understood as a process leading towards greater centralization of governmental functions.[3] That link is expressed through the language of 'unity', 'uniformity', and 'effectiveness'. In reality that link is at least partly illusory, since certainly in the post-Maastricht EU there is plenty of empirical evidence[4] to suggest that 'disintegration' (or the sustenance of values inimical to centralization) is alive and well in the legal order. This is unsurprising since the emergence of these dialectical properties in law is directly referable to deeper social and political conflicts which have been played out throughout the post-war history of European integration.

That point is explicitly recognized by Burley and Mattli (1993:44) in their work on the Court, where they argue that '[l]aw functions as a mask for politics', and that the mask operates so well in the context of the EU that many important political outcomes are ultimately

---

[2] These comments probably constitute an unfair oversimplification; scholarly work is rarely, if ever, as one-dimensional as the critic may sometimes benefit from portraying it.

[3] This is based on a definition of integration drawn from Dehousse and Weiler (1990: 246) which requires modulation in the post-Maastricht EU.

[4] See, e.g., the Court's recent case law on Article 30 EC, esp. in relation to environmental questions, discussed in Chalmers' essay below.

debated and resolved within a 'language and logic of law'. In work within the tradition of the paradigm, the existence of the mask is generally not challenged. The role of law and of the Court in feeding integration processes is taken for granted, and frequently overstated. By reference, very often, to the talismanic 'rule of law' the Court's capacity to achieve compliance with its judgments is taken as evidence of its authority. Legal scholarship which does accept the 'policy' element in the Court's role proceeds to overstate the rationality of the Court's decision-making processes, given that it has no 'power of initiative' and must wait for the 'right' cases to come before it (Wincott, 1995b). Finally, there are few attempts to develop alternative conceptions of 'integration' in terms, for example, of shared (legal) values rather than a functional approach to the centralization of governmental functions.[5]

We can begin by identifying three ways in which the essays in this collection depart from a traditional paradigm defined in these terms. One group of essays could be said to be most influenced by the broadening, since about 1970, of the notion of legal scholarship. The last twenty-five years have seen the development of socio-legal studies, critical legal studies, law-and-economics, and a much broader conception of what constitutes legal theory (Lacey, 1995). These essays therefore represent an opening out of the body of EC/EU law—understood in its widest definition to include all manifestations of legal discourse and legal text—to the manifold influences of other disciplines and other methods, and to theories beyond positivist jurisprudence. In that sense, we are concerned here with the position of EU legal studies within law as a discipline. The essays of Ward, de Búrca, Everson, Crowther, Hervey, and Barnard fall most clearly within this strand of thinking, which could also include the essay by More. The second approach develops a perspective on EC law which draws, contextually, upon the insights of European studies scholars in other disciplines, but remains essentially both separate from these disciplines and *about* law. Into that category fall the essays of More (again), J. Scott, Chalmers, Whiteford, Maher, Flynn, and C. Scott. A particular contribution of many of these essays is a focus on the link between policy, ideology, and law.

A final category involves the attempt to create a synthesized

---

[5] I am grateful to Gráinne de Búrca for this point.

explanation of European integration (and disintegration) processes. It does more than draw upon other European studies literatures, but rather seeks self-consciously to locate EU *legal* studies within a much broader interdisciplinary and theoretical context. In other words it 'adds the law to European studies'. Here it becomes evident that the analysis of institutions within the broad framework of comparative politics and public policy, and in particular theories of 'new institutionalism', might currently offer the most fertile ground for understanding the roles of the respective actors within the legal and political processes. The essays by Wincott and Armstrong fall most clearly within this category, but elements of the ideas developed most explicitly by them are also found in the essays of Maher, Flynn, and C. Scott and, in rather different ways, those of Crowther, Whiteford, and Barnard. The latter two essays are concerned, to a greater or lesser extent, with *non-state* actors involved in different legal processes.

These divisions are not intended to be closures but, on the contrary, represent merely a first attempt to explain or structure a new voice within legal studies. A variant upon this categorization has been used to determine the order in which the essays appear, but other divisions and categories could equally have been used. Moreover, it will be apparent that a synthesis, in so far as it has yet emerged, is limited to interactions between legal studies and political science. Legal scholarship should not be drawn into interdisciplinary debate solely with political scientists and international relations scholars. Other dimensions, and work from the other social sciences, can and should be explored. Aside from the work of economists,[6] which is strongly apparent in a number of papers in this collection (for example, C. Scott, Flynn and Crowther), and that of specialists in human resource management and labour relations (More), sociologists, social theorists, geographers, and anthropologists are amongst those who are increasingly turning their attention to the 'phenomenon of Europe'.

---

[6] See in this context esp. the work of Majone (1991, 1992, 1993) on issues of regulation and regulatory federalism. See also the body of work expounding and critiquing theories of regulatory competition: Siebert and Koop, 1990, 1993; Sun and Pelkmans, 1995.

Their work therefore poses challenges to lawyers which call for future exploration.[7]

A caveat to readers: it is not the intention of these essays to offer a comprehensive socio-legal, contextual, or critical survey of the whole field of EC/EU law. In that sense, they are not intended as a substitute for a textbook account, as yet unwritten, within the general parameters described here. It is hoped that readers will be better informed about the state of the governance of the European Union having read the book, but there has been no attempt to provide a coherent and consistent account. For that reason, division of the essays by 'subject' has been eschewed. Nonetheless, all the essays relate to core themes and topical debates within the field of European integration. Many of the essays address general constitutional and institutional questions. There are essays which look at general issues of integration theory (Wincott), the evolution of concepts of federalism and Union (Ward), the application of subsidiarity in practice (Maher), as well as the potential theoretical implications of the concept (Ward), and the emergent notions and indices of European identity and statehood (Ward, Everson). A second subject focus is the continuing process of economic integration, post-1993 and the Treaty of Maastricht, including micro and macro studies of the EU's work in progress (Chalmers, Armstrong, C. Scott, Flynn, J. Scott, Crowther, Hervey). Within the context of economic integration, issues concerned with the movement and status of *persons* raise some of the most important questions today (Everson, Hervey). Likewise the highly topical tensions and challenges to economic integration processes posed by environmentalism emerge as a clear theme in three essays (Chalmers, J. Scott, Crowther). Finally, the recurring debates stimulated by the so-called social dimension is examined in a number of essays (Whiteford, More, Barnard).

Equally, in terms of the focus of the essays on developing a voice for European Union *legal* studies, some of the essays address questions of great currency within the discipline of law: the utility and legitimacy of concepts such as 'rights' (de Búrca, Hervey), the role of pressure groups in legal processes (Barnard, C. Scott, Flynn),

---

[7] E.g. the work on territoriality by Darian-Smith (1995), on the anthropology of the EC by Wilson and Estellie Smith (1993) and contributors, on culture and place by Therborn (1995), on technology and government by Barry (1994), and on race and citizenship by Mitchell and Russell (1994).

the failure of modernist explanations of law and authority (Ward), the crisis of constitutionalism (Chalmers, Everson, Ward), the changing global context of territorially limited systems of law (J. Scott), the public/private and state/market divides and the legitimacy and control of state action (C. Scott, Flynn, Crowther, More), and the role of the 'person' and the 'citizen' in the legal order (Hervey, Everson).

2. EUROPEAN UNION LEGAL STUDIES AND THE COURT OF JUSTICE

There is relatively little concern in the essays in this collection with the juridical evolution of the Union, either at national or Community level, and in particular with interactions between judicial actors. That is not to say that studies of the Court of Justice or of national courts as institutional actors are unimportant. Indeed, the role of the Court is embedded in a number of accounts of policy development, such as those by Armstrong on free movement of goods and C. Scott and Flynn on utilities policies, but with a focus on its interactions with *non-judicial* institutions. The Court also appears as a central player in other essays; Chalmers describes a form of judicial constitutionalism in the context of the single market, de Búrca analyses the role of 'rights-talk' in the Court of Justice, and Hervey challenges the universalism of the Court's language in relation to the free movement of persons. Finally, Barnard presents a case study of the use of the Court by non-state actors. However, an unwillingness to make the Court the centrepiece in emerging work in European Union legal studies may be in part a reaction against the dominance of Court-centred work in EC law scholarship, demonstrating that there is more to EC law than the cases (and indeed the formal 'hard law' legislation).

Ironically, as some lawyers turn away from the Court of Justice in their search to identify the essential place of law in the integration process, political scientists and international relations scholars are increasingly affirming the importance of that institution.[8] The work

[8] The Fourth Biennial International Conference of ECSA, Charleston, SC, 11–14 May 1995 saw a panel of political scientists devoted to analysis of the role of the Court, and in particular its interactions with national courts and national authorities ('The European Court of Justice and the Member States').

of Burley and Mattli (1993; Mattli and Slaughter, 1995; cf. Garrett, 1995), who apply theories of neo-functionalism to explain at least in part the influential role of the Court, have played the key role as a catalyst for such debates. It is also interesting to note that much of the new political science work on the Court shows a marked preference for returning to some of the grand theories of integration, in particular neo-functionalism and, to a lesser extent, inter-governmentalism, at a time when the trend for most political scientists is towards looking at specific policy sectors and policy sectors, eschewing grand, macro-level studies of integration processes (Sbragia, 1992; Marks, 1993). Amongst political science-oriented work on the Court, therefore, the more specific or micro focus of the work of Alter and Meunier-Aitsahalia (1994) and Wincott (1995b and 1995c) on particular policy sectors and the interactions of different policy actors is rather the exception.

The relationship between the general work of political scientists on the Court and the traditional doctrinal paradigm beyond which this essay collection seeks to go—and also, implicitly, to critique—is at best ambivalent. The main source of 'legal wisdom' on law and integration in much political science work is, above all, the original and highly influential analyses by Weiler of the development of Community-based supranationalism (esp. Weiler, 1991). Burley and Mattli, for example, conclude that a 'sophisticated legalist' account of the role of the Court 'in political context' articulated by writers such as Weiler, Lenaerts (1992), and Rasmussen (1986) may ultimately provide the best account. Such accounts are 'legalist' in that they assert the importance of legal realities, such as the primacy and authority of EC law as declared by the Court of Justice (Shapiro, 1981:542), but 'sophisticated' in so far as they recognize countervailing political forces which constitute the context within which the Court must operate (Burley and Mattli, 1993: 76), especially, it might be added, the role of the member states.

Beyond this body of 'sophisticated' work, many political scientists have a tendency to rely upon two other sources of information. First, they make use in a slightly unselective way of the work of leading scholars falling broadly within the doctrinal tradition, such as Arnull, Wyatt, Dashwood, Hartley, and Dagtoglou. They accept these works as statements of authority about the work of the Court as well as accurate snapshots of the Community legal order. Secondly, they turn to the work of members and ex-members of the

Court such as Mancini, Everling, Slynn, and MacKenzie-Stuart, themselves describing (and arguably legitimating) their work and that of their colleagues. A marked feature of most of the legal scholarship relied upon is that it is general in character, in that it focuses in particular on the Court's role in formulating general constitutional propositions about the nature of EC law and on the Court's overall method and sense of self-positioning. It rarely engages with a body of work on substantive EC policy areas which sometimes provides a less positive and more sanguine overall assessment of the contribution of EC law and of the Court in particular, and which exhibits a strong sense of context—political and economic. Important examples are Snyder's (1985) work on the Common Agricultural Policy, Scott and Mansell (1993) and J. Scott (1995) on regional development, Dehousse *et al.* (1992) on regulatory strategies, and Hancher (1992) on utilities regulation, but other authors such as Szyszczak,[9] Gormley,[10] and Weatherill[11] could be cited. Moreover, while anecdotal evidence about the work of the Court 'from the insider' can be interesting and useful in understanding how it works, what its priorities are, and where it 'thinks' its judicial activity is leading the EU, such evidence needs to be treated with a certain cautious distance and objectivity, and it needs to be adequately contextualized and theorized. Golub (1994) provides an example of work which is rich in original insights stemming from the application of the methods of political science, but which suffers from some of the weaknesses of focus identified here.

As a consequence, political science accounts of the Court risk falling into two traps. First, while performing the vital function of alerting a broader community of integration specialists to the intensely important role of the Court as an actor in the integration process, such accounts appear to be providing a theory-based explanation of a traditional paradigm of the law/integration interface which has rhetorical and ideological force, but which is sometimes not borne out in practice (Wincott, 1995c). Secondly, from the perspective of lawyers, the Court is described as a strangely static institution, shorn of the intensity and sense of dynamism which come from its continuing conversations on matters of law with

[9] E.g. Szyszczak, 1994, 1995.   [10] E.g. Gormley, 1985.
[11] E.g. Weatherill, 1994, 1995.

national courts, or with litigating institutions such as the European Parliament and the Commission. For example, descriptions and statistical analyses of the involvement of member states and the Commission in cases on Articles 30–6 EC and/or the mandatory requirements (e.g. Kilroy, 1995) can surely only work when they take into account the political dynamics and context of the evolution of the Court's position, such as the development of the 1992 programme, as well as the particularities which stem the use (or abuse) of Article 30 in cases such as those on Sunday trading (Armstrong, in this volume; Rawlings, 1993). There is thus a danger that political science accounts of the Court can slip into assessments of the Court *without the law*.[12]

My conclusion is that much of the work in this volume would not have been possible without the vital contributions of writers such as Burley and Mattli, which reinforce the extent to which so much scholarship on EC law has developed in isolation from the mainstream of European studies, carrying only an internal self-legitimating reference focused on the 'rule of law' and the the almost mythic qualities of law. They begin the task of bringing closer together 'state-centred' international relations scholars, political scientists concerned with the inputs and outputs of policy processes, and the dominant supranationalist or federalist tradition of legal scholarship. They warn of the dangers of doing 'constitutional law without politics' (Shapiro, 1981: 238).[13] However, this work could itself be strengthened by a greater sensitivity to the specifities of the law and of legal norms, especially of EC law, and by attention to the weaknesses highlighted here (see also Wincott, 1995b and 1995c). In that sense law should be understood in its broadest and most flexible sense, as something rather more than a Benthamite system or order of rules.

3. FROM CONSTITUTIONALISM AND IDEOLOGY TO POLICY-MAKING AND INSTITUTIONALISM

The broad progression of the essays in the collection is from constitutionalism, through ideology, to questions of policy-making

[12] I am grateful to Kenneth Armstrong for this insight.
[13] See the discussion of this question in Wincott's essay below.

and institutionalism. In the first eight essays questions of constitutional destiny, ideology, and policy development dominate. The last seven focus, at different levels, on institutional actors and institutional practices, without necessarily being denuded of all sense of constitutional or ideological context. As there is no clear division between the two groups of essays the book has not been divided into sections, but rather the essays have been ordered so as to offer one type of progression; however, others could equally have been envisaged.

The book opens with an essay by Ward which searches for the destiny of the European Union in postmodernist theory, and in particular the postmodernist identification of identity, difference, and the discourse of self and other as crucial for an understanding of the human condition. Ward concludes by suggesting that 'subsidiarity', as the most ambiguous and ill-defined of the terms which currently describe (West) European constitutionalism, offers the greatest potential for achieving what he sees as the postmodern ambition. De Búrca's following essay has a very different ambition. At one level de Búrca offers a systematization of EU legal texts which address or touch upon the question of fundamental rights, including but not limited to the case law of the Court, by identifying the different contexts in which those rights appear. However, her specific focus is on the function and impact of the *language* of rights, not upon the outcomes of particular cases or the contents of particular measures, and she concludes—against a background awareness of the limitations of rights discourse—that rights language has the potential to enrich the values upon which the EU legal order operates. In that context, a particular interest lies in de Búrca's exploration of other meanings of 'integration', including the Durkheimian sense. A theme shared by Ward and de Búrca at the start of this collection, therefore, is a certain idealism in the search for a higher value or ethic for the European polity and legal order.

The focus of the three essays which follow is the 'market', so often the dominant figure in European studies and especially in EC law. Chalmers' essay is the first explicit attempt by a UK legal academic to assess the impact of theories of economic constitutionalism and German ordo-liberalism upon both the origins of the single market in the Treaties and its subsequent development in the hands of the Court of Justice (cf. Everson, 1995). Everson then seeks out the essence and the legacy of the European 'market citizen', assessing

the claim of the concept of citizenship to an enduring significance
even in the non-statal polity of the European Union. 'Market' is seen
in Hervey's essay in much starker politico-ideological terms, almost
as a 'contaminating' force which ensures that Court case-law feeds
into a dominant *status quo* involving discrimination against and
disadvantage for women, ethnic and national minorities, and other
so-called 'excluded' groups in EC law. The main thrust of this essay
concerns the treatment of third country nationals under the
pervasive and exclusionary discourse of the 'market'.

The remaining three essays with a primary focus on questions of
ideology assess the responses of the various Community institutions
to long-standing socio-economic conflicts and tensions, and the way
in which these are played out in the legal domain. The essays
consider in particular the conflicts between interventionism and
laisser-faire in social and labour law (Whiteford), between protection
of employment and labour market flexibility (More), and between
protection of the environment and global free trade (J. Scott). The
actual or potential institutional role of the Court of Justice, as one
conversant in a debate whose acts might have 'unintended
consequences' (to use the language of new institutionalism) in the
resolution of these conflicts (for example, through its interpretation
of the Acquired Rights Directive as described by More, or through
its refusal hitherto to ascribe direct effect to the GATT in the
internal Community legal order (J. Scott)), highlights the link
between these essays and those which follow.

Armstrong provides a general introduction to theories of institutionalism at the beginning of his essay, which is followed by an
application of ideas of 'historical institutionalism' to the field of the
free movement of goods. His approach requires him to identify and
weave together the respective roles of the Court of Justice and the
Commission, and to indicate the importance of institutions in
policy-making processes. He attempts to show how the choices of
decision-makers are constrained by internal and external factors,
and concludes that many policy solutions are satisfactory rather
than optimal. Armstrong's essay is followed by three which, more or
less explicitly, use similar ideas to explain utilities (especially
telecommunications) regulation (C. Scott, Flynn) and the approach
taken by the Commission to the review of EU legislative activities,
mandated in the aftermath of the introduction of the subsidiarity
principle (Maher). As Maher's essay in particular shows, strong

ideological pressures for reform and change can sometimes be mediated through the specific priorities and demands of the EU institutions and emerge as substantially 'downgraded' bureaucratic practices.

Two final examples of institutional analysis follow, albeit in a very different vein. Barnard's principal focus is an assessment—through the socio-legal literature—of the effectiveness and the measure of 'success' of a litigation strategy pursued by the UK Equal Opportunities Commission. However, her work contributes to our understanding of the range of institutional inputs into EU policy-making at *many levels*, in this case by a public sector actor, but which is independent of the decision-making processes of central government. A different approach to the assessment of the 'choices' of institutions is offered by Crowther, who applies principles of the economics of international taxation to the interrelationship between Articles 12, 92/93, and 95 EC. Using the hypothetical example of a regionally based tax, Crowther concludes that the institutional structure currently operated under the Treaty provides no incentives for a member state to bring a potentially illegal tax policy to the attention of the Commission, so that the benefits of decentralizing the levying of taxes are not in fact realized.

The volume concludes with a novel integrated legal and political analysis of European integration by Wincott, which draws its principal strength from weaving together the operating contexts, learning processes, and policy objectives of the various institutions. Like Armstrong, Wincott carefully pulls together the roles of the Commission and the Court, adding a critical review of the strength of the member states. Wincott's essay performs an important practical function. He explicates, in theoretical terms, questions about the impact and roles of institutions demonstrated empirically in the earlier essays.

In many senses, this final essay can be read as both the beginning and the end of the project which underlies this volume; the reader is invited to read both forwards and backwards through the essays in order to appreciate the different interdisciplinary dynamics which the contributors bring to bear. Thus by juxtaposing the first and last essays of the collection, we can see in sharp relief two (not necessarily mutually exclusive) ways forward for legal scholars working in the field of European integration. We are stretched from the limits of the legal imagination of the text to a point at which an integrated reading of the history of Community and Union through law and other social sciences becomes possible (thereby, of course, opening up the opportunity to create an integrated future). Put crudely, legal research and scholarship can now begin to enquire more self-consciously into two theoretical problematics: 'what is law?' and 'what is integration?' Hitherto, the closed and polemical character of much work on EEC law has meant that scholars have made only a limited and disappointing contribution to the understanding of these questions. They have made even fewer strides towards a synthesis of the two notions. By embracing a broader descriptive notion of European Union legal studies and by providing a platform for work which begins the process of enquiry into these questions, this collection of essays is intended to stimulate debate on these questions and to offer some, so far incomplete, insights into how a future research agenda might shape up.

Identity and Difference:
The European Union and Postmodernism

IAN WARD

This essay argues that the European Union can be best understood as a postmodern text, and perhaps as a postmodern polity. From a textual perspective, the European Union is beset by problems of identity; so also is the field of European legal studies. From a political perspective, the European Union apparently continues to defy objective determination. It does not fit comfortably with any of the familiar modernist theories of law and society. In the first section of this essay I introduce postmodernism. In the second I investigate the theory that the Union is a postmodern text. In the third, I suggest how we might be able to perceive the evolution of the Union as a postmodern polity. The European Union, I suggest in conclusion, can be best described as postmodern in that it defies both a readily identifiable textual identity and a readily determinable political determination.

1. IDENTIFYING POSTMODERNISM

Trying to 'identify' postmodernism is, of course, the ultimately absurd act (Camus, 1975). Postmodernism identifies identification as critical, and also denies its possibility. All that we can do is to identify certain postmodern texts, and thereby certain characteristics, which we may choose to term postmodern. Two names dominate current postmodernist thinking. The first is that of Jean-François Lyotard. In *The Postmodern Condition* Lyotard openly advocated the virtues of postmodernist aesthetics over modernist technology. The former, he suggests, 'reflect' upon and 'respect' the particular, while the latter is engaged in a dehumanizing 'totalizing' of the human condition. Textually, this totalization is revealed in the championing of 'metanarratives' (Lyotard, 1984a). The critique of 'metanarratives', and their denial of the particular, was developed

further in *The Differend*. A 'differend' is determined as an incommen-
surable difference (Lyotard, 1988). The crucial characteristic of
postmodernism is that, in contrast with modernism, it is content
with difference. There is no anxiety to find basic truths which can
serve to determine identity. Postmodernism champions difference.
In *The Differend* Lyotard determines postmodernism as an
innately jurisprudential ambition. The reality of the 'differend'
demands a plurality, or 'multiplicity of justices' (Lyotard, 1984b;
Carroll, 1984). Auschwitz represents a particular symbol for
Lyotard, as in so much postmodern thinking. He suggests that it
represented the ultimate totalizing ambition, and thus the final
negation of the modern humanist ethic. Such totalization, he
affirms, sought to 'silence' the excluded. After Auschwitz, according
to Lyotard, there can only be 'sentences'. Universalist idealism is
dead. In a lecture given in Vienna on the subject of Auschwitz and
Heidegger, Lyotard made one of his rare forays into political
discourse, suggesting that the attempt to 'totalize' a political Europe
shared the same ambition as Hitler, to expunge difference, and to
'silence'. Europe, he implied, was becoming a 'metanarrative',
which he noted was a supreme irony, precisely because the original
impulse behind the European idea was to build a new Europe in
which difference could be respected, and in which there could never
be another Auschwitz (Lyotard, 1993).

The second influential postmodernist is Jacques Derrida. Like
Lyotard, Derrida is most renowned for his championing of the text;
he too suggests that in the postmodern world, following the death of
humanist ethics, there can be only a textual ethic. A postmodern
ethics, he suggests, perhaps most powerfully in *Of Spirit: Heidegger
and the Question*, will respect the textuality of difference. It is one
which empowers the voice of the 'silenced' against the totalizing
ambitions of modernism. For Derrida, as for Lyotard, the epitome of
modern humanism was Hitler's Germany. The epitomic text was
the Freiburg *Rektorat*, Heidegger's tortuous attempt to champion a
universalizing *Geist* in 1933 as a philosophical apologia for Nazism
(Derrida, 1989).[1] Deconstruction of a text, Derrida stresses, is

---

[1] Heidegger retired from active politics shortly after the *Rektorat*, and the extent to
which he consciously realized the errors of his ways and foresaw the terrors of a
totalized politics, or alternatively the extent to which he remained a committed
although frustrated Nazi, is one of the more burning debates in contemporary
philosophy (Wolin, 1991).

merely the prelude to a textual-ethical reconstruction. Concentration on difference and on the particular is thus not nihilistic, as is so often alleged. To the contrary, it is the totalizing impulse of modernism which is nihilistic. Auschwitz was the epitome of modernity and of nihilism. Deconstruction of any text, according to Derrida, will reveal its implicit codes. It will recognize what is identified in the text, and what is silenced and left 'outside' the text. The ambition of the postmodern ethic is to reintroduce the excluded, and to empower the particular (Balkin, 1987).

Again like Lyotard, Derrida sees postmodernism and deconstruction as particularly jurisprudential exercises. The ambition of both (in a sense the only ambition) is to describe justice. In his essay *The Force of Law* Derrida impressed that the 'force' of law is the product of the necessary 'difference' between the 'we' and the 'other': those with voice (and text) and those silenced and powerless. Law is thus a 'differential force'. In aligning textual deconstruction with political power 'differentials', Derrida explicitly approves the textual turn in Critical Legal Studies. His concentration on the 'deconstructibility' of justice, as opposed to the undeconstructibility of law, serves to emphasize still further its ethical component. Law has nothing to do with justice, which is itself an 'obligation' owed to the 'other'. A postmodern jurisprudence, he affirms, is a jurisprudence which forever deconstructs the pretended universalism of any philosophy of law and any constitutional order. A properly critical jurisprudence is the championing of the particular, and a complementary openness to that which lies 'beyond', and which has yet to be realized (Derrida, 1990: 925–33, 945–7, 959–73, 1007–15).

What is of especial interest, for our particular purpose, is that Derrida has written specifically on the question of Europe. In *The Other Heading: Reflections on Today's Europe* Derrida has tried to uncover the semiotics of European studies. What characterizes contemporary Europe, he suggests, is first a failure of identity and secondly a denial of difference. The fulcrum of Derrida's essay is the theme of temporality: the comparison of the Europe of yesterday, today, and tomorrow (Derrida, 1992; Ward, 1994b). The most important characteristic of the European discourse, according to Derrida, is that it is historical. The designers of the modern Europe, he suggests, have failed to take note of its historicity. This is a crucial failing, because the critical tradition in Europe has always been a historical one (Goodrich, 1992). Europe has in the past been defined by its difference, and European culture by its acknowledgement of the 'other'. The Europe of 'yesterday' has always been critical. Europe is a 'plural' idea.

But 'today' something 'unique' is afoot. Europe is being redesigned in such a way as to deny difference. Europe wishes to totalize. The raw politics of today's Europe, he continues, is a 'crisis of memory'. Europe wishes to forget itself. Such an ambition, he suggests, can only result in a failure of identification, because identification can only be mediated through its constituent and historical particular (Derrida, 1992: xvii–xxxii, 3–12, 24–5, 29–32). This crisis has two totalizing textual roots, determined by their ambiguity: *'capitale'* and *'capital'*. The former is cultural dominion, the latter economic dominion. The new European discourse, he suggests, is a discourse of capital and technology, which hopes to 'close off' the future. It is a teleology determined to deny the particular and the possibility of the 'beyond' (Derrida, 1992: 47–55, 69–70). The alternative Europe of 'tomorrow', Derrida suggests (the postmodern alternative) is one of indeterminacy, pluralism, and participatory politics. Only a truly pluralist discourse can subvert the universalizing and centralizing ambitions of political homogeneity. Pluralism will always subvert attempts to establish objective ends of the human condition. The postmodern 'responsibility' demands that we continually define and redefine, such that identity is always present and future, at once universal and particular. Europe is thus both a universal and a particular, determinative of and determined by the 'other' (Derrida, 1992: 22–9, 72–5).

2. IDENTITY AND DIFFERENCE IN THE EUROPEAN UNION

Neither Europe nor European law is well defined. In the only genuinely critical study of European law to date, Francis Snyder concluded that the contradictions in European agricultural law resulted from the particular failure by European lawyers and politicians to define the term 'agriculture'. He made a similar observation regarding the term 'distortion of competition', the indeterminacy of which, he suggested, served to prevent any rational and consistent competition jurisprudence (Snyder, 1990). Another example of jurisprudential ill-definition is proportionality, which

Sophie Boyron has convincingly suggested is a legal concept not only unfamiliar in the UK but also untranslatable in UK jurisprudence (Boyron, 1992).

A further concept, which we like to think is at the heart of our jurisprudence but which in fact serves by its absence to identify UK jurisprudence, is 'right'. Despite many calls for a Bill of Rights in the UK, we have no jurisprudential tradition of 'right'. There are no 'rights' in UK law. We are subjects of the Crown, even if we are now endowed with rights in European law as newly determined citizens of the European Union. Our lack of rights in domestic law is perhaps most pregnant in the area of remedies against the Crown. With the advent of European law this failing is becoming ever more obvious. In the UK currently we have remedies against the Crown, including injunctive relief and even damages, for breaches of 'rights' in European law, but not in domestic law. The position, as one senior member of the bench has recently noted, is 'anomalous and wrong in principle'.[2] Another has suggested that it is at the least an 'unhappy' inconsistency.[3] I would suggest, more strongly, that the discrepancy makes a mockery of any claims that either EC or UK jurisprudence is coherently rights-based (Ward, 1993; 1994a). On a wider scale, a similar accusation of incoherence and inconsistency with regard to 'fundamental rights' in European law as a whole has already been levelled by a number of commentators (Coppel and O'Neill, 1992; Phelan, 1992).

However, the biggest failures of identity in the European Union are constitutional. There has always been a certain ambiguity, if not anxiety, about the self-identification of the European 'Union'. Yet strangely it seems to be an offhand anxiety. For decades there was a European Community. There still is. But now there is also a European Union. This, however, is merely a substitute term. The text that everybody at Maastricht wanted, except the UK and Denmark, was a European Federation, or perhaps Confederation; no one was prepared to say exactly what they wanted. What is connoted by a Union, as opposed to a mere Community? Robert Ladrech suggests that the phrase 'an ever closer Union', which finally replaced the presence of federalism in the original Dutch draft of the Maastricht Treaty, symbolizes the conscious lack of

---

[2] *M* v. *Home Office* [1992] 4 All ER 79, 139.
[3] *In re M* [1993] 3 WLR 433, 448.

identity in the European constitutional order (Ladrech, 1993: 58).
There is, he suggests, a total lack of identity. There is also, he
implies, a 'silence', both constitutional and jurisprudential. Europe
is characterized by a chronic 'underdevelopment of a political
discourse'. The two silences are not coincidental. Rather they both
result from, and at the same time contribute to, not only a lack of
identity but also a lack of interest. Lack of familiarity breeds both
distrust and disinterest (Ladrech, 1993: 57–9).

This problem of identity is thus a constitutional failing.
Maastricht has done nothing to clarify the constitutional position.
The lack of a legal personality or a constitutional identity remains,
as Everling suggests, the overriding weakness of the Union structure
(Everling, 1992). Indeed, as Deirdre Curtin has observed, the
Maastricht 'Union' has served only to retard the identification of a
European Constitution. In her damning critique of Maastricht
Curtin berates the failure to address the problem of constitutional
identity. The 'Union', she suggests, is 'a loose tarpaulin-like
structure . . . suspended artificially and tenously above [the
Community, betraying] more of a *bricoleur*'s amateurism than a
master brick-layer's strive for perfection and attention to detail.'
(Curtin, 1993: 23–4). In her concluding comments, Curtin
eloquently describes the constitutional inadequacies of contemporary Europe:

The result of the Maastricht summit is an umbrella Union threatening to
lead to constitutional chaos; the potential victims are the cohesiveness and
the unity and the concommitant power of a legal system painstakingly
constructed over the course of some 30 odd years . . . The whole future and
credibility of the Communities as a cohesive legal unit which confers rights
on individuals and which enters into their national legal systems as an
integral part of those systems, is at stake. (Curtin, 1993: 67).

Joseph Weiler has suggested two alternative visions which could be
adopted in order to effect a constitutional identity in Europe. The
first is a federal identity, which he terms 'Europe as Unity', and
the second is an intergovernmental identity, which he terms 'Europe
as Community'. Weiler himself clearly favours the latter model. At
present, he suggests, the Maastricht 'Union' cannot be properly
identified with either option. In order for a choice to be made, or
indeed for any constitutional order to be identified in the future, he
emphasizes the urgent need to create a European 'discourse'
(Weiler, 1991). The viability of various federal models has already

been explored on numerous occasions. None of them really work and, as Ladrech suggests, no one now really advocates a federal model for Europe, at least not one which is familiar in contemporary political thought (Ladrech, 1993; Koopmans, 1992; Mutimer, 1989). As Koopmans has re-emphasized, the crucial failing in any mooted federal model is that which pervades contemporary debate surrounding the constitutional jurisprudence of the new Europe as a whole: the question of sovereignty (Koopmans, 1992: 1047–52).

We in the UK are particularly obsessed with sovereignty, and the obsession is not merely jurisprudential. It is around the banner of sovereignty that Euroscepticism rallies its troops. Clearly the European Union requries some degree of transference of constitutional sovereignty. Lord Denning's so-called 'dexterous revolution', in the resolution of *Macarthy's* v. *Smith*,[4] is now seen as a sham (Allen, 1983). The critical question now is rather whether this matters, and what shape a constitutional jurisprudence not founded on sovereignty will take. The need to look outside existing theories of sovereignty has been suggested by an increasingly large number of commentators. Bruno de Witte has suggested that the 'challenge ahead is to make out of the national constitutions building blocks of European unity rather than bulwarks of sovereignty' (de Witte, 1991: 22). As the idea has caught on, the most substantive articulation has been made by Neil MacCormick, who urged us to move 'beyond' sovereignty. In MacCormick's words: 'To escape from the idea that all law must originate in a single power source, like a sovereign, is thus to discover the possibility of taking a broader, more diffuse, view of the law' (MacCormick, 1993: 8).[5]

3. THE EUROPEAN UNION AND A POSTMODERN JURISPRUDENCE

I suggest that the acknowledgment that we must now look 'beyond' sovereignty, and thus modernist jurisprudence, is a recognition that

---

[4] [1979] 3 All ER 325.

[5] See also his comments at 16: 'Taking the view of the sovereign state which I have suggested, or any reasonable variant of its terms, it seems obvious that no state in Western Europe any longer is a sovereign state. None is in a position such that all the power exercised internally in it, whether politically or legally, derives from purely internal sources.

we must look to a postmodern alternative. Certainly Hannah Arendt, in an earlier appeal for a post-war polity 'beyond sovereignty', suggested that such a movement was post-modern, if not postmodern in a contemporary sense (Arendt, 1972). A postmodern jurisprudence is one which can be identified as moving 'beyond' sovereignty and, at least in the UK, into uncharted waters. It thus follows, in postmodern thinking, that such a polity should be better able to respect difference and to represent the interests of the excluded and the 'silenced'. The 'silence' in contemporary European political discourse is a direct result of a perceived failing of democracy. Also, of course, the 'silence' of democracy is a 'silencing' of difference. Democracy is the only protector of difference in the post-modern world.

The question of the alleged 'democratic deficit' in Europe has been thoroughly debated. As Weiler suggests, it will not be possible to create a greater interest in Europe, and thus a greater trust amongst the peoples of Europe, unless there is a 'transformation' in the democratic appearance of Europe (Weiler, 1991: 2403). Shirley Williams has noted precisely the same fact. Priorities in the new European political order are not only to democratize but also to appear to democratize (Williams, 1991). In her critique of Maastricht Curtin suggests that it is apt that the greatest political challenge which faced the politicians, the problem of democratic deficit, resulted in the most obvious constitutional failure. The supposed co-decision procedure, she suggests, goes nowhere near far enough to remedy the situation (Curtin, 1993: 35–9). Philip Raworth is only marginally more positive, noting the many carefully preserved restraints on the Parliament's legislative powers. The problem of identity, he perceptively observes, is at once a problem of difference and of democracy:

This persistence of national particularism reflects a Community consciousness that is lacking or at least in its infancy. Thus, Parliament is as yet an idiosyncratic body incorporating a European identity that is still artificial. This artificiality is well illustrated by the discrepancy between Parliament's enthusiasm for a federal European state, and the more reserved attitude of the national electorates that became apparent during the ratification process of the Maastricht Treaty (Raworth, 1994: 22–33).

Democracy is still largely 'silent' in post-Maastricht Europe, and the failure of identity is the inevitable result of this silence.

It is perhaps fair to say that a substantive postmodern political jurisprudence has yet to establish itself. Postmodernism, as Alan Hunt has suggested, can be better described as 'approaching' or 'confronting' law (Hunt, 1990). The most recent approaches have tended to concentrate on textualism and psychoanalysis. This is only to be expected (Douzinas, Warrington, and McVeigh, 1991). Yet the 'political' import of postmodernism is familiar. The critique of universalism and technology, the pluralism, the advocacy of participatory democracy, the concern for difference and for the excluded, and the 'politics' explicit and implicit in Lyotard and Derrida are of course ideas and concepts which have been championed over the past two decades by the Critical Legal Studies movement. Indeed, a more political postmodern approach cannot be distinguished, in its origins, from CLS. If a genetic association must be suggested, it is that postmodern jurisprudence seeks to go 'beyond' CLS (Douzinas, Goodrich, and Hachamovitch, 1994).

The most concerted attempt to date to present a postmodern political jurisprudence is that of Drucilla Cornell. Cornell has developed her postmodern jurisprudence almost exclusively from Derrida (Cornell, 1992; 1993). Her primary aim is to stress the ethical reconstructive potential of deconstructionism.[6] What she terms the 'philosophy of the limit' is a philosophy which identifies boundaries and moves 'beyond' them so as to acknowledge the discourse of those initially excluded by the 'limits' of modernism. What she ultimately advocates is 'dialoguism' from which can be developed a postmodern 'ethic of citizenship'. It is an expression of pluralism and of participatory democracy, complemented by a conception of identity, which is at once reflectively determinable and fluid, and which, rather than threatening difference, actually nourishes it. A postmodern polity is founded upon difference and upon 'transformative' discursive participation (Cornell, 1992: 59–60, 84–9, 120–37, 145–54).

Another attempt to define the boundaries of a postmodern polity

---

[6] She states: the entire project of the philosophy of the limit is driven by an ethical desire to enact the ethical relation. Again, by the ethical relation I mean to indicate the aspiration to a nonviolent relationship to the Other, and to otherness more generally, that assumes responsibility to guard the Other against the appropriation that would deny her difference and singularity (Cornell, 1992: 62).

has been made by Richard Rorty. Rorty advocates a 'postmodern bourgeois liberalism', constructed by two essential concepts: the reality of political contingency and conversational solidarity. Like Cornell, Rorty suggests that a postmodern liberal polity will be conversationally constructed and will reflect the ethics of a constructively rational community. Such a community, he suggests, always 'respects' difference. Indeed, it is defined by difference. Accordingly Rorty suggests: 'A liberal society is one whose ideal can be fulfilled by persuasion rather than force, by reform rather than revolution, by the free and open encounters of present linguistic and other practices with suggestions for new practices. But this is to say that an ideal liberal society is one which has no purpose except freedom, no goal except a willingness to see how such encounters go and to abide by the outcome' (Rorty, 1989: 60–1).

Such a community will encapsulate a radical decentralization of power. It will, as urged by Rorty, 'revitalize' democracy. Is this the definition of today's Europe, and tomorrow's? Attracta Ingram has suggested that it might be. The key, according to Ingram, is to realize a Union 'founded on liberal justice', which takes us 'beyond' the liberalism of the nation-state. A postmodern liberalism must radically decentralize power from the nation-state and relocate it at its most basic societal level. A European identity can only be effected if national identity is erased. There must then be, she concludes, a 'self-defining European "us" ' (Ingram, 1993: 23).

Can the new Union realize this ambition? The key to whether the European Union is actually postmodern in its political guise, I suggest, lies with that most ill-defined of concepts: subsidiarity. Subsidiarity has been deliberately drafted to be ambiguous. It is a 'constitutional' term which is not supposed to be determinable, at least not objectively. A conceptual text whose ambition is to sow confusion of meanings is a peculiar technology, or so it seems to those of us brought up in a jurisprudential tradition of analytical rigour. Moreover, subsidiarity is particularly important because the establishment of its identity, either as a mechanism for totalization or for respecting the particular, will determine the nature of the European legal and constitutional order. It may be a postmodern incarnation of difference as justice, or alternatively it may turn out to be the technology which will 'silence' the particular.

Significantly, every effort was made at Maastricht to avoid providing any determination. It is immediately apparent that even in the Euro-world of seemingly endless ambiguity and compromise subsidiarity is a peculiar beast. The ambiguities surrounding its possible meaning and its potential effectiveness are considerable. On the latter point, most importantly, in purely political terms the understanding of subsidiarity championed by the UK government is quite different from that accepted by all the other members of the Union. As Anthony Teasdale has observed, to the various heads of government on the continent, convinced that subsidiarity was the mechanism which would affirm the next step in quasi-federal integration, the enthusiasm with which it was championed by the anti-federalist UK government has proved acutely unnerving (Teasdale, 1993).

To date political commentators have been uniformly wary about aligning themselves with either definition of subsidiarity. Teasdale expresses considerable doubt as to whether the UK interpretation is tenable. Although he acknowledges that alternative definitions are feasible, the weight of tradition in European federal thinking, most obviously in Germany, militates against a pluralist determination of subsidiarity. Although it will now be for the European Court to make a determination, he considers the situation 'fatally confused' (Teasdale, 1993: 189–97). As John Peterson has observed, the inclusion of two rival definitions of subsidiarity in the same Treaty text does nothing to aid clear definition. The inclusion of subsidiarity in Article A of the Treaty on European Union, and developed in Article B, suggests that decisions in the Union are to be taken 'as closely as possible' to the citizens. However, he continues, subsidiarity as presented in Article 3B of the EC Treaty, as a procedural device for dividing competences between the Union and its member states, is undeniably federal—and implicitly centralist— in ambition. The reason for the alternative and deeply ambiguous use of subsidiarity at Maastricht is, he suggests, simply the result of political expediency. The ambiguity of subsidiarity 'acted as the glue to keep support for the Maastricht Treaty from becoming unstuck' (Peterson, 1994: 120–1). As yet, however, it remains to be confirmed whether it will be able to fulfil this role.

In its Community guise, subsidiarity will be determined through use and familiarity. A postmodern determination has already been articulated. In Peterson's opinion, a postmodern Europe must seek to identify a fresh determination of subsidiarity, one which is 'beyond' the federalism debate, and which can better effect the postmodern idea of a 'Europe of the Regions' (Peterson, 1994: 118–9, 123–9). Perhaps rather surprisingly some legal commentators have tended to accept more readily such a decentralizing definition of subsidiarity (Toth, 1992; Cass, 1992; Emiliou, 1992). The ready acceptance of subsidiarity as a decentralizing and anti-federalist concept which can better facilitate a pluralist, and thus more participatory democratic Europe is, of course, immanently critical in a strictly jurisprudential sense. Nicholas Emiliou has championed subsidiarity as a mechanism for legal and political 'diversification', albeit as presented in a more identifiably 'co-operative' federal legal structure. Subsidiarity will, he suggests, be the mechanism for 'guaranteeing' the liberty of the new European citizen and for preventing the 'over-extension and overload of the Community system' (Emiliou, 1992: 407). Such is a postmodern ambition.

4. CONCLUSION: THE EUROPEAN UNION AS A POSTMODERN TEXT?

The European Union suffers at all levels, it seems, from an acute failure of identity. It is customary to suggest that this is a negative factor in European studies. But is it? Identity matters to post-modernism. However, more accurately, it is indeterminacy which really matters. Indeterminacy is the cherised idol because it preserves the potential for change and for the empowerment of the excluded. Such an understanding of identity forever preserves difference, and is preserved by it. The European Union is the first political and constitutional order to be created in the postmodern era, at least in western Europe. Community, Union, Federation? It all seems to be infinitely negotiable. Any one, or two, or more, it seems, can exist at the same time. Consciously or not, the boundaries of identification in Europe remain conspicuously fluid, and so in this sense the European Union appears to be an archetypal postmodern polity.

Certainly there is no firm constitutional order in Europe. There is no constitutional document. If the Maastricht Treaty exists instead of a readily identifiable constitution, then it is a document which is overtly non-jurisprudential. Again, this is neither surprising nor necessarily regrettable. It matters less because there is no European jurisprudence. One or two rather distressed and anxious jurists have tried to create one, and failed.[7] The fact remains that there is no jurisprudential tradition in European law. Both constitutionally and jurisprudentially Europe is as yet 'silent'. It is silent because there is nothing with which a jurisprudential comparison can be made. What is familiar to us as a constitution or a jurisprudence is clearly inadequate when cast in a European perspective. 'Europe' is 'different', 'beyond' anything which we can comparatively cite. A European constitution, and a European jurisprudence, will then be particular (Hix, 1994). It will be a postmodern jurisprudence. Indeed, it will be the only postmodern jurisprudence to date. It will, as we have already suggested, be a jurisprudence 'beyond' sovereignty, whether unitary or federal.

This requirement is also urged upon us by Ladrech. With regard to a new postmodern European democratic polity, Ladrech advocates that which was articulated by the former President of the French National Assembly, Laurent Fabius. According to Fabius the ambition of such a polity must be 'to move beyond the traditional forms of community. In this respect the European Community would appear to foreshadow a more general movement. Where our nations are concerned, states are increasingly integrated into wider structures, while nation states at the same time show a growing trend toward devolution' (Ladrech, 1993: 66–7).

The similarity between this statement and the postmodern visions of such as Cornell, Rorty, and MacCormick are striking. As Heller and Feher have recently emphasized, a postmodern politics and a postmodern European polity determines the end of our modernist obsessions with sovereignty and nation-statehood. The postmodern Europe will develop by both greater and lesser centralization (Heller and Feher, 1988). The fluidity of the European identity is only a part of a postmodern polity, and is only of value if it preserves the quality of difference. The two must run together.

It is the sheer weight of difference which continues to identify Europe, as it does any political or legal order. Europe, as Derrida suggests, 'is' difference. The attempt to totalize Europe, whether politically, economically, or jurisprudentially, is destined to fail

---

[7] Most recently Joxerramon Bengoetxea has valiantly, but hopelessly, tried to present an analytic jurisprudence of European Court decisions, in the hope that such will take us 'towards' a European jurisprudence. However, it does tell us a lot about a few cases (Bengoetxea, 1993).

because it tends against the reality of a postmodern politics. This is the paradox of integration. Integration can only be identified by the plurality of disintegration. It is the ambition to do away with difference which is both dangerous and inherently flawed. The nature of the postmodern world and of the postmodern text merely serves to underline the intensely modernist ambition of a 'totalized' and teleologically determinable political 'union'. Integration or disintegration are not, finally, mutually exclusive. There is no choice here. Integration presumes difference. Otherwise there is nothing to integrate. Thus, as Derrida again suggests, paradoxically any sort of European Union will only cease to exist when it has realized a political and cultural 'totalization' of Europe. At present the European Union is defined by its difference. That is its great strength. Moreover, it is this quality which must be cherished if a postmodern Europe is to realize the ambitions which a postmodern politics seeks to effect. A postmodern Europe, textually and politically indeterminate, can champion all the qualities so long advocated by the critical lawyers, and so long denied by the modernist legal discourse. The new Europe could evolve as a Europe of pluralism and participatory democracy, beyond the nation-state and beyond modernism.

The Language of Rights and European Integration

GRÁINNE DE BÚRCA

Dissatisfaction with the concept of rights, and particularly the critique of rights developed over the last few decades, has had little effect on the debate about the role of rights in European Community law. This critique of rights emerged largely within the Critical Legal Studies movement, but has also been developed by feminist, communitarian, postmodernist, and other writers (Kennedy, 1979; Hutchinson and Monahan, 1984; Perry, 1984; Tushnet, 1984; Olsen, 1984; Smart, 1989; Kingdom, 1991; Faraday, 1994; Gaete, 1993). One explanation for its absence from EC law is that the lack of critique is not peculiar to the topic of rights within Community law since, as has been pointed out by various commentators, there has in the past been a notable absence of genuinely 'critical' approaches in Community legal scholarship, and little critical scrutiny of the Community project as a whole (Snyder, 1990: 9–31; Weiler, 1993: 430–433; I. Ward, 1994b).

However, even accepting the broader context of European Community legal scholarship, it is arguable that the reason why the familiar critique of 'rights talk' has not been seriously considered or applied in the context of Community law is that the legal system established by the EC Treaties in the 1950s was heavily market-driven, and that other moral or social considerations were at best of secondary or subsidiary relevance. In the face of the apparently overwhelmingly economic impetus of the Community, the language of fundamental rights offered the potential to articulate and to establish a place for other values.

Perhaps as a result of this, the emergence of the language of rights within the Community's judicial, legislative, and institutional processes was widely welcomed by commentators on Community law. Criticism has on the whole focused on matters such as the 'space' given to rights issues being too small, or that legal developments in the area do not go far enough, that a written catalogue of rights is needed, that too few rights are being protected, or that the 'wrong' rights are being protected (Weiler, 1986, 1987; Schermers, 1990; Clapham, 1990; Lenaerts, 1991; Coppel and O'Neill, 1992; Phelan, 1992). The deeper critique of rights referred to above, which has generally focused on the individualistic and adversarial nature of rights, and which maintains that rights discourse is empty rhetoric, concealing both the exercise of power and the reality of disempowerment, has had little impact in Community law.

In this essay I examine the language of rights as it appears within Community law, and the varying contexts in which it is used, since different observations can be made about these different contexts. I will focus not only on the 'fundamental rights' declared and constituted by the Court of Justice as part of the general principles of Community law but also on the language of rights as more widely used throughout the Community legal system, by the institutions in the legislative process, and in the application of Community law to the member states. This will include not just those rights which have been declared by the Court to have fundamental or 'constitutional' status but also those which are created, conferred, or declared by Community legislation and other measures. Indeed, the legislative rights which are created at Community level generally acquire a form of constitutional status at the national level where they take priority over national law. This also entails consideration of those areas of Community law in which the language of rights has, perhaps surprisingly, figured not very largely, or not at all.

Of particular interest is the issue of why the language of rights has come to be used so widely within these areas of Community law, and why it continues to be expanded and developed by the judicial and political institutions. Two partial explanations are suggested, which focus on how that language is perceived as both a *legitimating* and an *integrating* force. Finally, I shall consider the real impact of that language, and whether a more critical or even sceptical approach is called for.

1. CONTEXTS AND CATEGORIES OF RIGHTS WITHIN COMMUNITY LAW

It is important to be specific about what is understood by 'rights' in Community law, since the vocabulary of rights is very fluid.

Comparison of legislative instruments and decisions of the European Court of Justice, as well as some of the literature on Community law, shows clearly that in EC law rights, and even 'fundamental' rights, can mean very different things. Set out below is a range of different contexts in which issues of rights have arisen in Community law, or rather a range of different usages of the language of rights. Moreover, mention is also made of a number of areas in which this language of rights has so far not been employed. In separating out some of the different usages in this way their actual impact, and the extent to which they perform the suggested functions of legitimation and integration, are more easily ascertainable.

The categories are roughly drawn and clearly they overlap, but the division may nonetheless be useful in considering the general function, scope, and possible impact of these main groups of 'rights' which are claimed to be protected within EC law. Of particular interest, for present purposes, is the very fact that in these different contexts the language of rights is, or in certain cases is not used. The primary focus will be on the use of that language, considering critically the possible reasons for its use, its meaning, and its impact in the context of European integration.

1.1 Economic, commercial, and property rights

The first category includes economic, commercial, and property rights, such as the right to trade, the right to use land, and economic liberty. Examples of these in Community language are mostly found in the case law of the Court of Justice, in which they are deemed by the Court to be fundamental Community rights. They have arisen generally in the context of challenges to *Community* policy, such as *Nold*,[1] *Hauer*,[2] *Internationale Handelsgesellschaft*,[3] or to member state action which is implementing such policy, e.g. *Wachauf* and *Bostock*.[4] As in the case of the next two categories, these have been judicially constituted as EC rights without necessarily having any other formal political or constitutional Community foundation, although the

---

[1] Case 4/73 *Nold* v. *Commission* [1974] ECR 491.

[2] Case 44/79 *Hauer* v. *Land Rheinland-Pfalz* [1979] ECR 3727.

[3] Case 11/7 *Internationale Handelsgesellschaft* v. *Einfuhr- und Vorratstelle für Getreide und Futtermittel* [1970] ECR 1125.

[4] Case 5/88 *Wachauf* v. *Germany* [1989] ECR 2609 and Case C-2/92 *R* v. *Ministry of Agriculture, Fisheries, and Food*, ex p. *Bostock* [1994] ECR I-955.

Court often claims to derive them from other national and
international legal sources.

1.2 'Rights of the defence'

The second category includes what might be called rights of defence,
such as the privilege against self-incrimination, the right to a
hearing, freedom from search and seizure, confidentiality of
information, and protection from excessive penalties. Like the first
category, these rights have been claimed both against the
Community and against member states. Claims that these are
'fundamental rights' have most frequently been made by companies
in the context of the exercise by the Commission of its investigative
and other powers in competition proceedings, e.g. *AM & S*,[5]
Hoechst,[6] *Dow Benelux*,[7] *Al-Jubail*,[8] etc. Again, these have been
declared in the case law of the Court of Justice to be fundamental
rights. Such 'rights of the defence' have also been invoked by
individuals against member states when those states are implementing or restricting Community rules, e.g. *Pecastaing*[9] and *Heylens*.[10]
Recently in *Gallagher*,[11] for example, the English Court of Appeal
sought from the Court of Justice a preliminary ruling on whether
certain rights of the defence of an individual had been properly
protected in deportation proceedings.

1.3 Traditional civil and political liberties

The third category includes traditional civil and political liberties,
often drawn from the rights provisions of the European Convention
on Human Rights (hereinafter ECHR), such as human dignity,
privacy, freedom of expression, and the right to family life. The 1977
Joint Declaration on fundamental rights by the Community

---

[5] Case 155/79 *AM & S Europe Ltd.* v. *Commission* [1982] ECR 1575.
[6] Cases 46/87 and 227/88 *Hoechst AG* v. *Commission* [1989] ECR 2859.
[7] Case 85/87 *Dow Benelux* v. *Commission* [1989] ECR 3137.
[8] Case C-49/88 *Al-Jubail Fertilizer Co. & Saudi Arabian Fertilizer Co.* v. *Council* [1991]
ECR I-3187.
[9] Case 98/79 *Pecastaing* v. *Belgium* [1980] ECR 691. See also case 36/75 *Rutili* v.
Minister for the Interior [1975] ECR 1219.
[10] Case 222/86 *UNECTEF* v. *Heylens* [1987] ECR 4097.
[11] *R* v. *Secretary of State for the Home Department*, ex p. *Gallagher* [1994] 3 CMLR 295.

institutions,[12] the Preamble to the Single European Act and the Treaty on European Union, Article F of the Treaty on European Union, and the frequent Court of Justice references to the European Convention confirm the desire of the Community institutions that these should be seen as part of the Community legal framework. Such rights have also been cited in Community legislation, such as Article 10 of the Convention on Human Rights on freedom of expression in the Preamble to the Broadcasting Directive.[13] Reference to rights of this kind are to be found in the context of challenges to Community acts and policies, e.g. *Stauder* (dignity),[14] *Oyowe and Traore* (freedom of expression),[15] and *X* v. *Commission* (privacy).[16] They also arise in the context of member state policies which are said to interfere with or derogate from Community rules in a way which is alleged to infringe such rights, e.g. *Grogan*[17] and *ERT* (freedom of expression),[18] *Commission* v. *Germany* (right to family life).[19]

1.4 Rights created by Community Legislation

The fourth (and also the fifth) category contains rights which are conferred or created by Community legislation. The fourth category includes principally the express 'treaty-given' rights, such as the rights of free movement for workers, services, and students, the right of non-discrimination on grounds of nationality, and rights of citizenship such as voting. Examples of these are found in Articles 6, 8A, 48, 52, 59, and 127 EC, although they are developed in more detail in secondary Community legislation. These specific Treaty rights can be seen as aiming to protect and to further what are essentially the economic interests of the Community's market actors, but they can also be seen as aiming to extend beyond market rights and to encompass and reflect other social concerns.

---

[12] OJ 1977 C 103/1.   [13] Dir. 89/552, OJ 1989 L 298/23.

[14] Case 29/69 *Stauder* v. *City of Ulm* [1969] ECR 419.

[15] Case 100/88 *Oyowe and Traore* v. *Commission* [1989] ECR 4285.

[16] Cases T-121/89 & T-13/90 *X* v. *Commission* [1992] ECR II-2195, on appeal as Case C-404/92P *X* v. *Commission* [1994] ECR I-4780. See also Case T-10/93 *A* v. *Commission* [1994] ECR II-179.

[17] Case C-159/90 *SPUC* v. *Grogan* [1991] ECR 4685.

[18] Case C-260/89 *Elliniki Radiophonia Tileorassi AE* v. *Dimotiki Etairia Pliroforissis & Sotirios Kouvelas* [1991] ECR I-2925.

[19] Case 249/86 *Commission* v. *Germany* [1989] ECR 1263.

1.5 Social Rights

The fifth category covers what are usually called social rights, such as those expressed in the (non-binding) Community Charter of Fundamental Social Rights for Workers, in Article 119 and the related secondary legislation, in legislation passed under Articles 100, 118A, and 235 of the EC Treaty, and under the Agreement on Social Policy annexed to the Protocol of the Treaty on European Union. Examples are workers' rights on transfer of undertakings, rights to health and safety at work, pregnancy and maternity rights, and equal pay and treatment of women and men in employment matters. With the exception of equal treatment, these are not generally declared to be fundamental rights or principles common to all of the member states, but instead are seen as rights conferred by legislation. Most are conferred by legal instruments other than the treaties. Thus categories four and five, unlike the first three categories, concern rights which are not purely judicially constituted at EC level, but which have some legislative or political pedigree, even if their shape is altered by the Court through its interpretation.

1.6 Rights not yet recognized by Community Law

Many other important issues are generally viewed as human rights concerns, but have not yet been classified or dealt with within Community legal processes or instruments as 'rights issues',[20] although these may emerge in the coming years as the expansion of Community areas of competence continues. Five such areas are considered here.

1.6.1 Immigration and Asylum Rights

A first sphere into which the language of rights has not yet really filtered is that of general immigration and refugee policy. Legislative action by the Union has commenced in this area with the proposal for a decision under Article K.3 TEU to establish a Convention on the crossing of external frontiers of the member

---

[20] On the falsity of the claim that Community rights are universal and of equal application, in particular in relation to race, nationality, and gender, see T. Hervey below.

states.[21] Although at present these issues fall mainly to be dealt with
under the provisions in Article K.9 TEU, and thus on an
intergovernmental basis under the 'third pillar' of the European
Union, they can be brought within the sphere of Community action
under the provisions of Article 100C of the EC Treaty.[22] Even if not
· yet part of current Community rights discourse, issues of immigration and refugee policy are likely eventually to be discussed in terms
of rights, particularly since Article K.2 uses that language by
referring to the ECHR and to the Convention on the Status of
Refugees. Earlier attempts by nationals of states outside the
Community to invoke the language of rights, when their status
under agreements made between the Community and those other
states was being considered, were rejected by the Court of Justice.[23]
Such agreements often create specific limited rights of access to work
and of non-discrimination on grounds of nationality for citizens of
those states, but until recently they were treated differently and less
favourably than similar rights of Community nationals set out in the
EC Treaty. However, in contrast to the restrictive reading of the
rights of a Moroccan national under the EC–Morocco Co-operation
Agreement given by the Advocate General, the Court of Justice in
Kziber brought the scope of the rights in question closer to that of
similar rights accorded to Community nationals.[24] On the other
hand, the language of fundamental human rights is certainly not yet
evident in the context of such Association or Co-operation Agreements, even if the Court has taken a less restrictive approach than
before to the express rights—e.g. to work and to reside—accorded
by such agreements to these 'non-Community' workers.[25]

[21] OJ 1994 C 11/6 and OJ 1994 C 128/346, 350, 358. See also COM (94) 23 for the
Commission's proposals on immigration and asylum policies.
[22] See the proposal for a Council Regulation on visa policy under Art. 100C, OJ
1994 C 11/15 and on a uniform format for visas, OJ 1994 C 238/8. On competence in
immigration policy see Cases 281, 283–85, 287/85 *Germany* et al. v. *Commission* [1987]
ECR 3203.
[23] Case 12/86 *Demirel* v. *Stadt Schwäbisch Gmünd* [1987] ECR 3719.
[24] Case C-18/90 *Office National de L'Emploi* v. *Kziber* [1991] ECR I-199; Case C-58/
93 *Yousfi* v. *Belgium* [1994] ECR I-1353.
[25] See also Cases C-192/89 *SZ Sevince* v. *Staatsecretaris van Justitie* [1990] ECR I-
3461; Case C-237/91 *Kus* v. *Landeshauptstadt Wiesbaden* [1992] ECR I-6781; Case C-
355/93 *Eroglu* v. *Land Baden-Württemberg* [1994] ECR I-5131, on the EC–Turkey
Association Agreement.

1.6.2 The right to freedom from racial discrimination

A second area from which the language of human or fundamental
rights used within Community law has been noticeably absent is
that of race, and of ethnic and minority rights. There have been
various forms of 'soft' law, such as declarations on racism and
xenophobia, but there are as yet no developed Community policies
on race which are backed up by law.[26] The Commission has taken
the view that express competence under the Treaty would be
required before substantive measures could be introduced, since it
stated in its 1994 White Paper on Social Policy that it intends to urge
the adoption of special Treaty powers to combat racial discrimination.[27] However, it does apparently intend to consult on the
adoption of a Code of Employment Practice against racial
discrimination, presumably similar to its Code against sexual
harassment.[28] Similarly, the Court of Justice—which has played the
most prominent role in deeming various rights to be part of
Community law—has not used the language of fundamental rights
in the context of race.[29]

1.6.3 Lesbian and gay rights

Reference to lesbian and gay rights has rarely been made, other than
indirectly in the context of other Community legal issues: e.g. the
right to privacy or human dignity which has been raised in certain
cases concerning AIDS testing.[30] Substantial arguments have been
made to the effect that homosexuality and lesbianism are issues
which fall within Community competence, and therefore that gay
rights should be recognized and actively promoted within
Community law (Waaldijk and Clapham, 1993; Tatchell, 1992: 53;
cf. Bamforth, 1995). The European Parliament, weakest amongst
the institutions in terms of its legal powers, is the institution which

[26] The European Council in 1994 proposed a Consultative Commission to
encourage tolerance and understanding of foreigners and proposed developing a
Union policy on racism and xenophobia.
[27] COM (94) 333, Part IV.   [28] OJ 1992 L 49/1.
[29] See Case 100/88 *Oyowe and Traore* v. *Commission* [1989] ECR 4285, a staff case in
which a claim of discrimination was raised and in which race may have been a factor,
where the Court chose to focus its ruling on freedom of expression.
[30] Cases T-121/89; T-13/90 *X* v. *Commission* [1992] ECR II-2195; Case C-404/92P
X v. *Commission*, [1994] ECR I-4780; Case T-10/93 *A* v. *Commission* [1994] ECR II-
179.

uses the language of rights most widely, and has done so also in the context of gay rights. In its Report on Equal Rights for Homosexuals and Lesbians in the European Community (A3-28/94) the European Parliament's Committee on Civil Liberties and Internal Affairs included a motion for a resolution on Equal Rights,[31] calling for the setting up of a European institution to ensure equal treatment without reference to nationality, religion, colour, sex, sexual orientation, or other differences. It also called on the Commission to present a draft directive on combatting discrimination on the basis of sexual orientation.

1.6.4 Rights for people with disabilities

The claims and interests of people with disabilities do not seem to have attained the same status of 'fundamental rights' protected within Community law, although the Community has asserted competence in the field of disability. In the context of vocational training policy under Article 127 (previously 128) of the EC Treaty, the Council has established three action programmes for disabled people, the most recent—which refers in its Preamble to the Community Charter of Fundamental Social Rights for Workers— having been adopted in 1993.[32] However, although the Council adopted a recommendation in 1986 on the employment of disabled people in the Community, recommending the elimination of negative discrimination and suggesting certain positive action, a recommendation is a relatively weak form of Community soft law which, apart from its indirect interpretive effect, has not been backed up by other measures binding on the Member States.[33] Further, the Court of Justice has touched only indirectly on

---

[31] See the Resolution on Equal Rights for Homosexuals and Lesbians in the EC, OJ 1994 C 61/40.

[32] Council Decision 93/136, establishing what is called 'Helios II', OJ 1993 L56/30. See also Council Decision 93/512, OJ 1993 L 240/42 on a Community technology initiative for disabled and elderly people, on the basis of Arts. 235 and 130A of the Treaty. Although this latter decision goes beyond the scope of vocational training and makes reference to economic and social cohesion, its Preamble refers more to reducing the need for expensive residential and nursing care than to the rights of disabled people.

[33] Council Recommendation 86/379, OJ 1986 L225/43. For another such measure of soft law see Commission Communication on the Social Integration of Disabled People—A Framework for the Development of Community Action, OJ 1981 C 347/14.

disability in its case-law, principally in the context of social benefits for workers under Regulations 1612/68 and 1408/71. Indeed, one possible reading of the Court's ruling in the case of *Bettray* is that disabled people who are in rehabilitative sheltered employment, which is tailored to their needs rather than to the needs of the market, might not constitute 'workers' within the meaning of Article 48 of the EC Treaty, and consequently would share none of the rights granted to workers under Community law.[34]

1.6.5 *Environmental, cultural, and language rights*

Other issues which have gained importance within general human rights discourse have not acquired that status or been discussed in those terms in Community legal vocabulary and instruments, even where those issues fall within Community competence. One example is cultural and language rights, which are generally viewed as group rights rather than individual rights. The language of 'protection' rather than the language of rights has been used here; see for example the reference to protection for minority languages by the Court in *Groener*.[35] Article 128 of the Treaty similarly refers to 'respect' for regional diversity rather than the rights of regions; Article 130R uses 'protecting the quality of the environment' rather than the language of environmental rights, and Article 129 similarly refers to 'human health protection'.

To refer to these 'excluded categories' is not necessarily to argue that they should be considered as fundamental rights within Community law. It is simply to note that these issues have not achieved the same status within Community law, either in legal instruments or in the language of the Court of Justice, as have the 'Community rights' set out in the first five categories. Whether the Community's field of action *should* encompass an explicit programme of human rights protection in areas such as race, sexual orientation, disability, the environment, or culture is another question altogether. The answer to that question depends on broader and more fundamental political and ideological questions about the reason for the Community's existence, what its legitimate aims are, what its role should be, and what the relationship between state or local powers and Community central powers should be.

---

[34] Case 344/87 *Bettray* v. *Staatssecretaris Van Justitie* [1989] ECR 1621.
[35] Case 379/87 *Groener* v. *Minister for Education* [1989] ECR 3967.

However, it is worth noting that since the Community asserts competence in the field of human rights in areas such as those set out in the first five categories above, this raises questions about why other issues and areas which are more widely considered to be 'human rights' concerns are not discussed in those terms within Community law and policy.

2. TWO EXPLANATIONS FOR THE EXPANSION OF RIGHTS IN COMMUNITY LAW

Consideration of the role of rights in Community law generally begins by examining how the terminology of rights, which is not found in the original three Treaties, was introduced into Community law. As a result, the focus of discussion is usually on the challenge to the supremacy of Community law which came first from the German legal system, in which constitutionally recognized rights were allegedly infringed by Community measures. However, the specific historical trigger for the emergence of a vocabulary of rights in Community law is only one part of the picture. It does not fully account for the continuance and expansion of the role of rights within Community law, nor for the fact that the judicial and the political institutions have increasingly brought the language of rights into their decision-making and formalized it in legal instruments. This expansion can be seen in the case-law of the Court, in declarations and recommendations issued by the Council, the Parliament, and the institutions jointly, in the Preamble to the Single European Act and Article F of the common introductory provisions to the Treaty on European Union, as well as in the request by the European Council—acted on subsequently by the Council of Ministers—to refer the compatibility of accession by the Community to the ECHR to the Court of Justice under Article 228.[36]

Bearing in mind the various usages of the language of rights in Community law set out in the categories above, two general reasons for the prevalence of the language of rights within Community legal discourse will now be considered. These two explanations relate to what may be seen as the legitimating force and the integrating force of that language.

[36] See Bull. EU 4-1994, 1.1.4.

2.1 Legitimation

In tracing the emergence of fundamental rights as a subject within
Community law, it has been suggested that the failure in the early
1950s of the European Political Community, with its express
adoption of the rights provisions of the European Convention on
Human Rights, led to the pursuit of a less ambitious European
project (Dauses, 1985). The explicit federalist approach of the early
1950s was replaced by a functionalist and subsequently a neo-
functionalist approach, in other words by a more gradual sector-by-
sector approach to European integration. In this way, the existing
Coal and Steel Treaty was followed by the Atomic Energy Treaty
and the specifically Economic Treaty in 1957.

Partly in keeping with the strategy of the neo-functionalist
approach, a limited spillover effect occurred so that, even without
formal Treaty amendments, some expansion of the powers and
competence of the Community into other areas followed.
Community activity moved beyond specific economic boundaries to
affect various other areas of formerly exclusive member state
competence (Weiler, 1991: 2431–53). Such expansion—perhaps
particularly because some of it came about through judicial action
rather than political consensus—required legitimation. A second
reason for the perceived lack of legitimacy of Community law, in
addition to this extension of competence beyond what appeared to
be the express parameters of the Treaty, was that its law-making
processes were not particularly democratic and lacked accountability (Keeling and Mancini, 1994). Legitimation of the
Community's powers was important not just so that those affected
and regulated by Community law would accept its status and
authority, but also in order that the Community could acquire and
maintain a degree of moral standing in its international relations
and in the eyes of the rest of the world. If the Community was to
fulfil its aspirations and to develop into a single economic bloc and a
unified political power which would take its place on the international stage, it would have to establish a more secure ethical or
moral foundation (Twomey, 1994). In the late twentieth century an
increasingly integrated quasi-federal organization such as the
Community would have to take on board what has been called the
'global human rights constituency'. The international status of

human rights had become such that no state and no developed political entity, especially not such an ambitious emerging supra-national order, could afford to eschew its language or its values.

Thus, for example, the Community in its dealings with non-member states, concerning either aid agreements or association and co-operation agreements, sometimes makes such agreements conditional upon the third country agreeing to improve its 'human rights' record. This has occasionally resulted in the European Parliament using its power of assent to such agreements, by threatening to withhold assent unless a so-called human rights clause is inserted into the agreement. This apparent exportation by the Community of its proclaimed human rights standards would seem to be an assertion of the Community's moral standing in its international relations. The inclusion by the Treaty on European Union of Article 130U(2) on development co-operation in the EC Treaty formalizes this assertion, by declaring that 'Community policy in this area shall contribute to the general objective of developing and consolidating democracy and the rule of law, and to that of respecting human rights and fundamental freedoms'.

Clearly, the very use of the language of rights denotes a certain moral content to Community laws and policies. To be able to point to decisions of the Court which purport to protect fundamental rights, and to legal instruments of the Community's institutions and of the Member States which claim to respect such rights, appears to enhance the status of the European legal order. Whether the use of this language and the formalization of the status of rights in law has any real impact on the nature of the Community, on the way in which law and policy is made, and on the lives of those within the Member States, is of course another question.

2.2 Integration

The concept of rights as an integrating force is a common one, with which many federal societies are familiar. It has been suggested that 'there is hardly anything that has greater potential to foster integration than a common bill of rights, as the constitutional history of the United States has proved' (Cappelletti, 1989: 395); Frowein has expressed the view that 'the question of common values protected by the legal system cannot be avoided if the process of integration is to continue towards the creation of a union to which all citizens feel a common allegiance' (1986: 231) and more recently wrote of 'the shaping of a European identity in the protection of human and fundamental rights' (1990: 358); another commentator has expressed the view that 'talking about human rights may sometimes bestow identity on Community citizens' (Clapham, 1990: 311); and a fourth, writing on the desirability of the adoption of a code of Community rights, has suggested that 'by encapsulating the nature of the legal order which it underpins, a code would create an integrationist *culture* of rights currently lacking at the Community level' (Twomey, 1994: 129).

As with the integrating experience of the Bill of Rights in the US mentioned by Cappelletti, the adoption of a Charter of Rights in Canada has since generated debate over its political purpose, rather than the 'legal' purpose of protecting rights of citizens against government: 'the larger political purpose . . . was to strengthen national unity by providing constitutional support to a new definition of Canadians as a rights-bearing citizenry regardless of location' (Cairns, 1992: 49). Although the comparison between the European Union and Canada clearly has its limits, given the differences between a single federal nation (albeit one with distinct cultural and linguistic traditions and under the perennial threat of disintegration) and the European Union, there are useful similarities to be observed in considering the role of rights in contributing to the creation of an identity across national or provincial barriers. The language of European 'citizenship' has entered official Community vocabulary with the introduction by the Treaty on European Union of Articles 8-8E into the EC Treaty, and if the formal rights conferred on that citizenry are as yet extremely thin, its rhetoric may have considerable force.[37] This formal incorporation into Community law of the language of citizenship, which is currently in vogue on account of its ability to capture the idea of the individual as part of a broader political community

---

[37] It may also prove to have some practical impact. See the argument based on European citizenship in Art. 8 EC to challenge exclusion orders within the UK in Case C-229/94 *R* v. *Secretary of State for the Home Department, ex p. Adams* (judgment of the High Court of 29 July 1994) and *R* v. *Secretary of State for the Home Department*, ex p. *McQuillan*, (judgment of 9 Sept. 1994).

involving reciprocal rights and duties, was evidently a significant ideological move.[38]

So the concept of human and fundamental rights may be seen as capable of providing a moral grounding to a legal order which on its face was established principally to support the pursuit of economic goals, and also to forge an identity which could simultaneously (i) have a cross-national appeal to individuals and to groups within the Community and (ii) emphasize shared or common values already existing within the member states.

This use of rights as an integrating tool can be seen in both the Court's stressing of the 'common constitutional traditions' of the member states and in the adoption by the political institutions of this language in their declarations, and by the member states in later Treaties such as the Single European Act and the Treaty on European Union. The emphasis on shared or common values is shown by the fact that many of the provisions and principles invoked are drawn from agreements which all member states have signed, such as the ECHR and the Council of Europe's European Social Charter. The European Parliament—the institution most vocal in its call for greater legitimation of the Community's legal and political system, especially since, being a democratically elected institution, an increase in parliamentary powers is likely to form part of any such reform—frequently calls for accession to the ECHR, and in 1989 adopted its own Declaration of Human Rights.[39]

The use of the idea of common constitutional traditions has been variously described as a 'comparative phenomenological approach' (Cappelletti, 1989: xiv) or a '*ius gentium*' approach (Barrington, 1992: 259), and it can be seen to have both a descriptive and a prescriptive function: it claims to draw on rights and principles which exist and which are recognized in constitutional traditions, and on the other hand it elevates these into general principles of Community law and in so doing aims to forge a 'common law' or perhaps a 'common bill of rights' for the European Community and, in turn, for its member states.

---

[38] Cappelletti suggested that European peoples would be unlikely to agree on an enforceable Community charter of rights until such day as 'the French, the English and all the others regard themselves as being citizens of the Community, with rights as such' (Cappelletti, 1989: 381–2).   [39] OJ 1989 C 120/51.

3. ASSESSING THE REALITY: THE IMPACT OF THE LANGUAGE
OF RIGHTS ON EUROPEAN INTEGRATION

The themes of integration and legitimation are connected, in that
the idea of fundamental rights is likely to have little success in
contributing to the creation of a political allegiance and a sense of
identity across the Community unless it is seen to be of some real
value. In considering whether the creation of a vocabulary of rights
has in fact had a practical, beneficial impact within the Community
it is necessary to think about what it means to say that rights are
protected. In a legal context this generally means that instruments
exist which declare that certain values are recognized by law as
'rights', which are to be protected or advanced, with the result that
those who feel aggrieved may pursue a claim through legal processes
by relying upon the notional right. It would be difficult, if not
impossible, to assess whether the lives of those whose rights are said
to be protected is improved, but perhaps the important practical
question in so far as Community law is concerned is whether the
values which these fundamental rights purport to represent are
actually reflected in the course and in the results of the Community's
political and judicial processes, and whether they prevail over other
very different values (usually 'market' values) which are also central
to Community policy.

Given that the express concerns of the three original Treaties were
largely economic, the enunciation of a broad range of fundamental
rights within Community law, drawn from various constitutional
sources and human rights treaties, certainly holds out the promise
that the pursuit of economic and other powerful interests will not
always prevail over other fundamental human concerns. Although
this promise may create for the Community, as an aspiring political
and international actor, a better ethical and constitutional profile,
however, the success of the Community project depends not just
upon its external and international stature but also upon a
substantial degree of internal commitment from its participant
states and populations. It is from this point of view that the
integrating influence of the concept and language of fundamental
rights is crucial.

One of the familiar claims of the developed critique of rights, to
which reference was made at the beginning of this paper, is that

whilst the language of rights lends legitimacy to power and to law it is purely rhetorical and has little real impact. The question which this claim raises in the Community context is whether the appeal to common Community fundamental rights is empty rhetoric with little substantive impact, so that rather than creating 'an integrationist culture of rights' or 'bestowing identity on Community citizens' its effect is negligible and may even be disintegrating. A related aspect of the critique is that whilst the rhetoric of rights may have symbolic force, such language often conceals the unfairness of the *status quo*. Further, it is argued that what purport to be universal rights may benefit principally the powerful rather than the disempowered. Whether these criticisms are borne out in the Community context cannot be answered precisely, only in a broadly impressionistic manner. However, a general consideration of the issues arising from the various groups or categories of rights set out above might suggest some tentative answers.

3.1 Rights as an integrating or a divisive force?

Consider initially the invocation of those rights categorized in the first three groups above, when claims are being made *against* the operation of *Community* policies. These groups included commercial and property rights, rights of the defence, and traditional substantive civil rights. The methodology used by the Court of Justice in the case of *Hauer*,[40] in which reference was made to property rights derived from a comparative analysis of member state constitutions and the ECHR, shows the integrating potential of the language and the concepts used. The reference to 'common constitutional traditions' emphasizes that the member states are the source of these rights, and the reference to the ECHR and to other international agreements signed by all member states in cases such as *Nold*,[41] *Internationale Handelsgesellschaft*,[42] *Al-Jubail*,[43] and *Dow Benelux*,[44] invokes an image of consensus and of shared values. Further, the context in which these concepts are being invoked is that of a challenge to Community action, with the result that Community policies appear to be required to conform to the rights and common traditions of the member states. The same is

[40] *Supra* n. 2.   [41] *Supra* n. 1.   [42] *Supra* n. 3.
[43] *Supra* n. 8.   [44] *Supra* n. 7.

particularly evident of the 'rights of the defence' in group two, when pleaded against the actions of a powerful and unelected Commission. The use of the language of procedural rights and the derivation of these concepts from 'the legal interpenetration of the member states', to quote the terminology of the Court of Justice in *AM & S*,[45] clearly expresses the ideal of integration. The context in which this ideal is expressed is attractive to the member states and to the interests which are affected by Community law, since it appears to curb Community powers by reference to rights deriving from national sources.

When the same language of rights described in those three groups is used in the context of challenges to member state action, on the other hand, the methodology becomes more problematic. In this context, the rhetorical appeal to common constitutional traditions may lose its force, if the state in question does not share the particular conception of the right in issue. Such problems have arisen in diluted form in situations like that of *Pecastaing*,[46] in the *German Housing* case,[47] and in *Wachauf*,[48] in which the right in issue is not contested, but there are some differences amongst states as to their particular requirements in a specific context. More serious tensions may arise where the flexibility of the language of rights used by the Court conceals very stark differences amongst member states as to the concrete realization of a constitutional right or principle 'common to the member states'. Freedom of expression may be said to be a fundamental right to which all member states subscribe in the ECHR and within their own constitutional framework, but the question of freedom of expression within Community law for commercial broadcasting companies in *ERT*,[49] for advertising associations in *Bond*,[50] for video distributors in *Cinéthèque*,[51] or for pregnancy counselling and abortion information

---

[45] *Supra* n. 5.   [46] *Supra* n. 9.   [47] *Supra* n. 19.
[48] *Supra* n. 4.

[49] *Supra* n. 18. See also *R* v. *Secretary of State for the National Heritage*, ex p. *Continental Television BV* [1993] 2 CMLR 333. Questions on Dir. 89/552, which refers in its Preamble to Art. 10 of the ECHR, have been referred as Case C-327/93, OJ 1993 C 211/19 to the Court of Justice, in the context of a dispute over the transmission of pornography.

[50] Case 325/85 *Bond Van Adverteerders* v. *Netherlands* [1988] ECR 2085.

[51] Cases 60 & 61/84 *Cinéthèque* v. *Fédération Nationale des Cinemas Français* [1985] ECR 2605.

services in *Grogan*[52] has anything but an integrating force in the Community (Clapham, 1990: 311).

The language of rights used in the context of the fourth group above—mostly Treaty-given rights—can equally cause controversy. While it seems clear that to confer the status of fundamental rights on some of the central aims of the Community may give them added legal weight and rank, this is also a divisive technique in view of the economic focus of these aims and their expansive nature. The clash of Community and national values, to which the promotion of market-oriented Treaty rights of free movement has given rise, has been well documented elsewhere (Phelan, 1992; Coppel and O'Neill, 1992). However, the issues and the apparent clash of values are not always clear-cut. It may be that the use of the language of fundamental rights in the context of some of these Treaty-given rights is partly intended to express the existence of other values, rather than simply market values, alongside (and perhaps in tension with) the Community's single market aims. In other words, the free movement of workers and their families may be partly constructed as a social right rather than purely as a market-integrating technique; this is also the case of the principle of non-discrimination in access to education. Moreover, the right to equal pay may be also a social and moral right rather than purely a means of equalizing the conditions of competition for employers. However, although to recognize the possibly complex nature of such Treaty rights may acknowledge their social and moral dimension in addition to their market-integrating thrust, it does not resolve the tensions which may exist between the different state and Community values. For example, even if the tension is not between a purely commercial Community right to buy a medical service and a national constitutional right to life but between the latter and a human right in Community law to personal autonomy or to receive information, an undeniable tension and potential for divisiveness still exists. Whatever the nature of the tension, it cannot be said that the expression of Treaty rights as fundamental Community rights has a clearly unifying and integrating effect.

In the fifth category above, the language of rights is used in relation to Community primary and secondary legislation which creates what are usually referred to as social rights. In so far as they

---

[52] *Supra* n. 17.

are contained in Community legislation which is applicable to the member states, they generally acquire constitutional status at the national level. The integrating potential of rights in this context is evident when some of the effects of Community sex discrimination law and employment law are considered. The benefits derived from such legislation, and the language of rights used, have had appeal for constituencies which cross state boundaries. Groups representing women's or workers' interests, for example, can mobilize and pursue action at a Community-wide level, transcending national frontiers.[53] On the other hand, pulling against the unifying potential of Community social rights is their tendency to give rise to resistance and dissent on the part of member states—particularly the United Kingdom—which question the scope of the Community's legislative competence in the sphere of social policy. A further challenge to the integrating potential of such social rights may arise from the cross-Community groups on which rights are said to be conferred if, for example, it is felt that the harmonizing process across the member states will lead to a lowest common denominator approach rather than to the enhancement of existing rights.

It is evident even from such very general observations that the language of rights has both integrating and divisive potential. The appeal to common constitutional traditions and the appeal to individuals and international groups expresses a unifying ideal. The promotion of single market freedoms as fundamental rights also pushes in the direction of market integration. However, these tendencies are in tension with the divisive effect of the appeal to rights, especially when member state policies which express very different values are undermined, or when the articulation and creation of Community rights are seen to impinge on what is considered to be primarily a matter of state competence.

On a Durkheimian analysis, law exists largely as the expression or visual symbol of an underlying organic social solidarity. Organic solidarity existed, in Durkheim's view, in a society which was interdependent and which shared the values reflected in the law (Durkheim, 1893). The process in the Community sometimes appears as the reverse, in which an attempt is being made to *create* solidarity through law, by declaring common principles and rights

---

[53] See the suggestion that the process of European integration offers similar advantages for homosexual and lesbian interest groups (Tatchell, 1992: 12).

in the hope that these will influence the legal systems of the member states as an integrating force. In legislating for the concept of European citizenship it is hoped to encourage the people of one member state to feel a sense of common cause with those in another. Clearly, however, there may be a danger in the attempt to express and create uniform rights and values where in reality there is diversity. Pahl has criticized the Community's concern with social cohesion, and argued that its desire to ensure the same social rights across the member states as a means to European integration is based on the assumption that social consensus is self-evidently a good thing, as well as 'on the further assumption that such cohesion and consensus already exists at the nation state level' (Pahl, 1991: 358). However, it is possible that the Community's appeal to common values and to uniform rights does not necessarily assume or rely on the existence of cohesion at national or local level, since the appeal of rights to specific groups (women, workers, etc.) across national boundaries may have a certain integrating effect Community-wide, without there being a consensus nation-wide on any given issue. Equally, people living in Northern Ireland, for example, might seek to identify themselves through the idea of European citizenship as a way of transcending the conflict of national identities.

It is true that the exposure of national divisions and fractures does not necessarily undermine the overall degree of cohesiveness or commitment to a measure of integration within the European Community. Indeed it has been argued in the context of the United States that 'the very act of summoning "community" through a language of rights may expose the divisions within the community . . . rights then can be understood as a kind of language that reconfirms the difficult commitment to live together even as it enables the expression of conflicts and struggles' (Minow, 1990: 309). However, despite the undoubted force of the economic interdependence of the European Community's member states, the degree of political commitment to a European society—as compared with that within the United States, for example—remains rather weak. It may be that if too great a gulf opens up between the values expressed in Community law and policy and those which underpin the different cultural, legal, and political systems of the different member states a crisis point may be reached and the 'commitment' to a European society undermined.

3.2 The social impact of rights

The question of whether the Community's uses of the language of
rights is more divisive than integrating is connected with the
question of the social impact of these uses. It has been suggested
already that the themes of integration and legitimation are
connected, in that rights discourse may lose some of its appeal if it is
not seen to be of some benefit to those it purports to protect.

It is immediately apparent from considering the cases categorized
above that rights in Community law are often invoked not by
individuals but by corporate applicants and other powerful entities.
This is certainly clear in the case of the rights classified in the first
and second groups—economic and property rights and rights of the
defence. These cases are not examples of the invocation of rights to
protect the interests of the disempowered. On the other hand, even
though the language of rights was adopted in such cases by the
Court of Justice, this did not often deliver the desired outcome, since
the economic and property rights were said not to be absolute or
unconditional (see *Nold, Internationale Handelsgesellschaft*, and *Hauer*
above). This observation might reinforce one of the central claims of
rights critics, that the invocation of rights tends to be of rhetorical
value rather than of practical benefit. By contrast, however, in
several of the cases involving rights of the defence, although these
were generally pleaded on behalf of large companies suspected of
engaging in anti-competitive practices, some of the Court's rulings
did involve curtailment of excessive or oppressive investigatory
powers of the Commission.

In the context in which they have been used, not against the
Community but against member states which have acted to restrict
the exercise of a Community rule or policy, the 'rights of the defence'
in the second category do sometimes appear to have afforded a
measure of concrete benefit and protection for individuals rather
than for corporate interests, in the face of inadequate processes for
challenging restrictive state action—e.g. *Pecastaing*,[54] *Johnston* v. *Chief
Constable of the RUC*,[55] *Heylens*,[56] and more recently possibly *Adams*[57]

---

[54] *Supra* n. 9.
[55] Case 222/84 *Johnston* v. *Chief Constable of the Royal Ulster Constabulary* [1986] ECR
1651.   [56] *Supra* n. 10.   [57] *Supra* n. 37.

and *Gallagher*.[58] However, even in the context of the rights in the third category (traditional civil and political liberties such as those in the ECHR) which are generally considered to be 'human rights', it is apparent that those invoking the language of rights are often not the oppressed minorities or individuals as might be expected. This can be seen from the various cases which have involved freedom of expression for advertising or commercial television companies, or pleas invoking the 'privacy of the dwelling' for businesses resisting investigation into anti-competitive practices. On the other hand, the vocabulary of rights has proved advantageous to the relatively disempowered in contexts such as the *German Housing* case[59] and *Stauder*.[60] There has also been a measure of success where individual administrative acts (rather than general legislative measures) of the Community have been challenged for infringing such rights, for example in the cases involving the right to privacy in the context of HIV testing,[61] or freedom of expression in the context of journalists' posts.[62]

Similarly mixed conclusions can be drawn from observing the results of claims to treaty-given rights such as freedom of movement, set out in the fourth category. Although it is obvious that these are essentially aimed at market integration, and thus the language—particularly that relating to free movement of goods and services—is most often invoked to the advantage of commercial organizations, this is also a context in which the language has been of benefit to the less advantaged. In particular, in the context of workers in Article 48 of the EC Treaty, the self-employed in Articles 52 and 59, and prospective students under Article 127 the translation of Community economic freedoms into the language of individual human rights has yielded some benefits. As suggested above, the language of citizenship in Article 8 *et seq* may also prove to be of more than symbolic effect in the future.

Finally, with regard to the social rights categorized in section 2.5 above, this has perhaps been the area in which the language of rights has yielded most substantive benefit for the relatively disadvantaged, and where its rhetorical force has been accompanied by certain practical gains. Paradoxically, of course, these rights are said to be less 'fundamental' (apart from the principle of equal treatment between

---

[58] *Supra* n. 11.   [59] *Supra* n. 19.   [60] *Supra* n. 14.
[61] *X* v. *Commission, supra* n. 16.   [62] *Oyowe and Traore, supra* n. 15.

men and women in employment matters, which has been accorded
symbolic status as a fundamental right) and since they are created
by legislation or are expressed in instruments such as the 1989 Social
Charter they are not accorded constitutional status at Community
level, and are vulnerable to simple alteration.

4. CONCLUSION

Even this brief glance at the range of contexts in which rights
appear in Community law shows that very mixed conclusions
emerge. The language of rights affords a means of introducing a
range of different values—other than predominantly market
values—into the Community's legal and policy-making processes. It
offers a means to develop a moral and ethical foundation for the
Community, and to contribute to the development of a sense of
European identity and a commitment to a European society, in a
way which may further the process of political integration. Equally,
however, it is possible for the language of rights in Community law
to paper over deep national divisions and cultural differences, to
suggest a moral content to Community policies which in reality
further essentially market goals, and to hold out the promise of
protection for human rights whilst actually delivering little of
practical benefit to individuals as opposed to corporations and legal
persons.

A more fundamental criticism of the language of rights, however,
which cannot be answered merely by pointing to the positive or
beneficial effects of the invocation of rights in specific contexts, has
been that the language and the nature of rights is adversarial and
uncompromising, pitting interests against each other in a competition in which the successful right will 'trump' the loser. On the other
hand, it may be said in partial response to this criticism that whilst
the language of rights is clearly oppositional and generates
counterclaims which force a comparison of competing claims, the
approach taken in Community law tends to be less extreme than
that associated with classical liberal rights discourse in which one
right will trump another. The development of a concept of
proportionality within Community law has generated a balancing
approach to rights claims, which may facilitate compromise to a

greater extent than the form of rights-absolutism associated with American jurisprudence.[63]

Finally, one of the most fundamental criticisms levelled at the use of a vocabulary of rights is that the very concept of rights, with its individualizing language and practices, is incompatible with a genuinely participatory democracy. Perhaps this is a criticism which, at the present stage of legal and political development, is least apposite in the context of the Community. The criticism presupposes a fully developed and functioning democratic system in which different interests can be heard and mediated through the political processes, and in which the legalization of interests through the language of rights would undermine and obstruct those processes. However, the European Community's political system remains elitist, largely undemocratic, and beyond the influence of large sections of the population which comprises it. In this context, rather than undermining the democratic process, it is possible that the language of rights has an empowering effect in giving voice to interests which are largely excluded from the political processes and which might not otherwise be heard.

Sweeping generalizations to the effect that 'human rights are fully protected in Community law' on one hand, or that 'the fundamental rights protected in Community law are purely market rights' on the other, do not present an accurate picture. There is a certain amount of confusion over exactly what is meant by fundamental rights in Community law, given the many distinct contexts in which such language is used. The influence and impact of that language on the nature of Community law, on those whose interests it claims to protect, and on the process of integration, is complex. As is evident from the various categories suggested above, much depends on the nature of the 'right' in issue, and on the exact context in which it is invoked or discussed. It is necessary in any given context to evaluate these different features, and to consider the impact of the use of rights in that particular situation.

The language of rights could introduce a richer set of values into Community law and contribute to the development of a better Community. However, a strong scepticism should be exercised in

---

[63] For a recent defence of rights discourse, see J. Tweedy and A. Hunt (1994). For more qualified support for the possible usefulness of rights as tools for social change, see D. Herman (1993).

respect of its rhetoric, of its tendency to conceal differences in power and status and to benefit mainly the powerful. The dangers of declaring consensus where there is none, and of promising change where none is delivered should be heeded. Awareness of the many different ways and contexts in which the language of rights is used in Community law will enable an ongoing critical evaluation of its significance and its role in the process of European integration.

The Single Market: From Prima Donna to Journeyman[1]

DAMIAN CHALMERS

After the failure of the European Defence Community, the Beyen proposals suggested that economic integration should precede full vertical political integration, and that the establishment of a common market should be the starting point for such a process (Milward, 1992: 185–190). Since then the concept of the common market has been the touchstone for the regeneration and consolidation of the European integration process. The original Treaty of Rome saw the establishment of the common market by 1970 as merely setting the foundations for something grander, an 'ever closer union among the peoples of Europe'. The related concept of the internal market and the psychological impact of '1992' were used in the mid 1980s to release the Community from the sclerotic condition into which it had descended, and as an impulse for the Single European Act. More recently, as the exercise of Community competence has been increasingly questioned and scrutinized, the single market has been used as the rock behind which the Community legislator can partially escape the encroachment of the principle of subsidiarity.[2]

For a lawyer the principal dilemma posed by the single market is that it is a concept whose outer limits require constant redefinition. The definition in Article 7A EC of an 'area without internal frontiers in which the free movement of goods, persons, services and capital is ensured in accordance with the provisions of this Treaty' appears,

---

[1] The author would like to thank participants at a seminar at the Copenhagen Business School on 14 November 1994, where an earlier draft of this paper was presented, and also Razeen Sally for providing many useful references on ordoliberalism. The text, and any errors therein, are nevertheless the author's exclusive responsibility.

[2] EC Commission, Communication to the Council and Parliament, 'The Principle of Subsidiarity', SEC(92) 1990, 8; according to the Commission, any matter covered by the imperative of free movement falls within the exclusive powers of the Community.

on its face, simple enough. Yet complexities arise from its
paradoxical nature. On one hand, the concept relies upon specific
Articles of the Treaty for its concrete manifestation.[3] On the other, it
is frequently used as a source of interpretation for the development
of all Treaty provisions,[4] suggesting that it is more than just a sum of
its parts.

It is suggested that the concept was initially heavily influenced by
the ordoliberal philosophy of the Freiburg school, with the result
that the single market began to develop increasingly the qualities of
an economic constitution. The reliance on ordoliberalism as a
predominant source of reasoning served as a rationale for the
constitutional qualities of the EC legal order, the institutional reach
of the single market, and its normative content. Such reasoning, it is
suggested, with its presumption of a unitary economic order and
its functional appearance, served to obfuscate the public choice
dilemmas exposed by economic integration. When the integration
process was relatively undeveloped the inherent tensions were less
evident, yet as the process deepened they became increasingly
exposed. Faced with these tensions, it is argued, the response of the
Court has more recently been to move away from ordoliberalism
towards a system based on a series of segregated parallel legal
orders, each structured according to its own internal points of
reference. The result has been a redefinition of the single market in a
manner which has diminished its scope and made it less seminal to
the development of the integration process.

1. ORDOLIBERALISM AND THE SINGLE MARKET

The influence of the ordoliberal tradition of the Freiburg School has
been seminal in this century.[5] It has been instrumental in the
determination of the constitutional framework which governs both
the Federal Republic of Germany and the European Community
(Gerber, 1994b: 59–75). Whilst ordoliberalism encompasses a broad

---

[3] Joined Cases C-78–83/90 *Compagnie Commerciale de l'Ouest* v. *Receveur Principal des Douanes de la Pallice Port* [1992] ECR I-1847.

[4] E.g. Cases 80 & 81/77 *Ramel* v. *Receveur Principal des Douanes* [1978] ECR 927.

[5] The most interesting works in English on ordoliberalism are Peacock and Willgerodt, 1989a and 1989b.

school of thought, at the root of this tradition is the premise that in the modern world economic systems have to be *created* rather than left to grow (Eucken, 1950: 84). The reason for this is that, left unguided, complex and contradictory pressures will develop within the economic system resulting in dysfunction, and spasmodic and disruptive state intervention (Eucken, 1950: 82–4). Ordoliberalism is predominantly a humanist tradition. Unlike its sister neoliberalism, the constitutional order it requires should reflect the ethical and political views of society. It should therefore go beyond 'supply and demand' (Barry, 1989: 118). Ordoliberals therefore considered that markets had to be instituted by a 'general political decision' which would reflect these values and would be expressed through an economic constitution (Sally, 1994: 463). State power, as its rationale was to further the interests of society (as expressed in this constitution), would thus both be constrained by and flow from these principles (Tumlir, 1989: 133). Ordoliberalism suggests, however, that societal choice as to the content of the economic constitution is subject to ideological and structural constraints.

The ideological constraints are that the constitution must protect the market economy. The rationale is not so much that the market economy will often lead to the optimum allocation of resources, but that economic freedoms, which form the basis of a transaction economy, are as integral to the protection of human dignity, and as indicative of a free society, as political freedoms (e.g. Petersmann, 1992: 17), which are themselves liberal in nature and which therefore underscore individual economic freedoms. A corollary of these freedoms was that there was equality between transactors, and transactions were voluntary in nature. For ordoliberals this was essential, as the obverse of these rights was economic power. Such power, whether private or public, had to be controlled. Hence there was a need for strong competition authorities, if the freedom and equality integral to these rights were to be secured (Tumlir, 1989: 137).

The other key feature of ordoliberalism was its systemic analysis. Walter Eucken, in many ways the intellectual pioneer of ordo-liberalism, suggested that within any society two complementary but incompatible economic *orders* (*Ordnungen*) will exist: the *trans-action* order based on exchange and the *centrally administered* order based on direction (Eucken, 1950: 118). Each order would be judged according to different criteria. The transaction order would use the criteria of competition; the centrally administered order, other external criteria. Yet as the principles of each order were an intrinsic part of that order, the principles of one could not be applied to the other without destruction of the latter (Gerber, 1994b: 42–3). This was not to say that no society could have both a transaction order and an administered one, but merely to indicate that they had to be distinguished (Eucken, 1950: 231).

Such a distinction is present in the EC Treaty. Whilst the system created by the EC Treaty is essentially a transaction one, elements of a centrally administered economy are present. The genesis of Article 90(2) EC[6] was that some member states, notably Italy and France, argued at its inception that the public sector should be immune from the rigours of the competition and trade provisions (Page, 1982: 20). Further exceptions have been created by the Court of Justice. The first is in relation to activity regarded as criminal in all member states. Such activity now seems to fall outside the remit of the single market.[7] A more substantial exception is the case of 'mixed goods', goods or services which are provided free or sold at below their cost of production, usually in the public interest. Examples are education, health, and transport. Such activity is clearly susceptible to abuse through the incidence of 'free riders' who consume these goods irrespective of the economic costs involved. The Court of Justice has consistently and repeatedly held that public sector activity, which is financed principally out of the public purse with public interest objectives in view, does not fall within an exception to the Treaty rules but lies outside the ambit of the Treaty free movement and competition provisions altogether. Activities as diverse as public sector education,[8] air traffic control,[9] and criminal rehabilitation schemes[10] have all been found to fall

---

[6] Article 90(2) EC provides an exemption from the Treaty strictures for undertakings entrusted with the operation of services of a general economic interest or having the character of a revenue producing monopoly where the application of the Treaty would obstruct the performance of their duties.

[7] Case C-275/92 *HM Customs and Excise* v. *Schindler* et al. [1994] ECR I-1039; Case C-324/93 *R* v. *Secretary of State for the Home Department*, ex p. *Evans*, Opinion of Advocate-General Lenz of 4 Oct. 1994. More cryptic is Case 294/82 *Einberger* v. *Hauptzollamt Freiburg* [1984] ECR 1177.

[8] Case 263/86 *Humbel* v. *Belgium* [1988] ECR 5365. See also Case C-109/92 *Wirth* v. *Landeshauptstadt Hannover*, judgment of 7 Dec. 1993.

[9] Case C-364/92 *SAT Fluggesellschaft mbH* v. *Eurocontrol* [1994] ECR I-43.

[10] Case 344/87 *Bettray* v. *Staatsecretaris van Justitie* [1989] ECR 1621.

outside the Treaty on these grounds, even though the activity in
question in each individual case appeared to constitute economic
activity for the purposes of the Treaty.

Ordoliberalism has also had considerable implications for the
institutional structure of the European Community. At a horizontal
intra-Community institution level, the Court of Justice is consigned
a central role in economic policy-making. Courts, with their
autonomy and their language of rights, are seen to offer the greatest
institutional security to individuals and are thus central to the
attainment of both the humanist and economic aims of ordoliberalism
(Petersmann, 1991; 1992). In this respect ordoliberalism shows a
faith in courts as regulators which would not be shared by all today.
In particular, it may be questioned whether courts, based on
essentially bipartisan procedures, with only limited participatory
rights, and with officials at their helm who have a narrow, albeit
very developed, form of expertise, are really suitable fora for the
resolution of questions which draw on a number of disciplines and a
variety of interests (Fuller, 1978/79; Allison, 1994).

Ordoliberalism has had implications not only for the horizontal
institutional structure of the Community but also for its vertical
structure. For ordoliberals the development of an effective international order was dependent upon the presence of effective national
legal orders (Petersmann, 1991: 38; Curzon, 1989: 180). This
resulted from the bottom-up nature of their philosophy: namely that
the historical origins of society were and, in essence, should be a
private law society (Tumlir, 1989: 131–3; Röpke, 1989: 68–70).
Within a transnational system these values should permeate both
national and transnational systems, as values lie at the basis of any
society. Conformity with these values results in a convergence of
both institutional and transnational behaviour. This, in turn, results
in an institutional compression, as these values act to create
elements of a unitary legal system (Petersmann, 1991).

Within the European Community the traditional principle used to
guide institutional behaviour—both Community and national—has
been that of 'market unity', which although it has been referred to
explicitly on more than one occasion,[11] is, it will be argued, implicit

[11] On the linkage see Case 14/68 *Walt Wilhelm* v. *Bundeskartellamt* [1969] ECR 1;
Cases 80 & 81/77 *Ramel Sarl* v. *Administration des Douanes* [1978] ECR 927; Case 13/77
INNO v. *ATAB* [1977] ECR 2115; Case C-359/92 *Germany* v. *Council* [1994] ECR
I-3681.

in much of the Court's other reasoning. 'Market unity' requires: 'adequate mobility of whatever it is supplied in the markets in question and non-discrimination in the sense that neither sellers or buyers are influenced by the origin or destination of what is being bought or sold' (Machlup, 1977: 2).

The principle, it has rightly been observed, is the economic manifestation of the principle of political indivisibility, found in several member state constitutions. This requires that the jurisdiction be characterized by unity and indivisibility of territory, organization, and policy (Barents, 1990: 13–14). The single market therefore has the comprehensive features of an economic constitution but also institutional intervention in the economy both flows from and is constrained by the concept in the same manner as with an 'economic constitution' (van der Esch, 1970: 303; Barents, 1990: 9).

One therefore finds evidence of an express link between the single market and the normative qualities of the Community legal order. In *Costa*,[12] a rationale granted for the supremacy of Community law was that variations in the executive force of Community law in different member states would breach Article 7 EEC (now Article 6 EC), the non-discrimination principle. Whilst this is not exclusively a market principle it is nonetheless necessary to the workings of the market, a point made more recently. Advocate General Lenz in *Faccini Dori*[13] argued that the single market required that directives be capable of horizontal direct effect on the grounds that private operators in states which had not transposed directives would otherwise be placed at a competitive advantage over operators in other member states. The market being a rationale for the constitutional qualities of EC law also serves to condition the latter's normative qualities. This has been most evident in the field of pre-emption, the doctrine whereby member states are precluded from engaging in independent activity in a field exhaustively regulated by Community legislation. Such a principle is clearly a *sine qua non* of a single market. Competitive distortions and restrictions on trade will continue to exist if member states are free to maintain additional laws over and above Community ones. The Court has therefore repeatedly stated the link between pre-emption and the common

---

[12] Case 6/64 *Costa* v. *ENEL* [1964] ECR 585.
[13] Case C-91/92 *Faccini Dori* v. *Recreb* [1994] ECR I-3325.

market and the principle of free movement.[14] The principle thus safeguards both the integrity of the single market and the autonomy of the Community legislature (van Empel, 1992: 14).

Ordoliberal influences can also be seen as a catalyst for the development of substantive constitutional rights. The development of general principles of law and fundamental rights as an integral part of Community law was not simply necessary as a *quid pro quo* for the acceptance of the constitutional qualities of EC law by national courts. The sovereign nature of the EC Treaty also meant that the single market was the pre-eminent objective for all institutional behaviour within the European Community. Following ordoliberal reasoning, if the market was to be willed and coherent, and if such an objective was to be reached, it was important that institutional behaviour be constrained by certain fundamental principles. Of particular importance in this respect are individual economic freedoms such as the right to trade, own property, and pursue business activities.[15] Whilst the Court was constrained by Article 222 EC, which requires national systems of property rights to be left intact, its development of the other individual economic freedoms have therefore arisen as much from systemic as from institutional concerns. The jurisprudential basis for this argument is that the economic freedoms referred to above have been developed out of general principles of law. It has been observed that the funda-mentality of principles[16] differentiates them from rules (Schermers and Waelbroeck, 1991: 27; Lauwaars, 1990: 366–7). Principles rarely present practical solutions to individual solutions—the rights which stem from them serve that role—but rather form part of the structure of the legal system. Breach of these principles brings into question the legal system itself (Dauses, 1985: 406). The principle upon which these individual economic freedoms are based, these

---

[14] E.g. Case 136/78 *Auer* [1979] ECR 452; Case 60/86 *Commission* v. *UK* [1988] ECR 3921; Case 195/84 *Denkavit Futtermittel GmbH* v. *Land Nordrhein-Westfalen* [1985] ECR 3181; Case 158/88 *Commission* v. *Ireland* [1990] ECR I-2367; Case C-169/89 *Gourmetterie Van Den Burg* [1990] ECR I-2143; Case C-41/93 *France* v. *Commission* [1994] ECR I-1829.

[15] Case 4/73 *Nold* v. *Commission* [1974] ECR 491; Case 44/79 *Hauer* v. *Rheinland-Pfalz* [1979] ECR 3727; Case 265/87 *Schräder* v. *Hauptzollamt Gronau* [1989] ECR 2237; Joined Cases C-90 & 91/90 *Neu* v. *Secrétaire d'Etat à l'Agriculture et à la Viticulture* [1991] ECR I-3617; Case C-44/89 *Von Deetzen* [1991] ECR I-5119.

[16] On the nature of principles within the Community legal order see Case 43/75 *Defrenne* v. *SABENA* [1976] ECR 455.

unitary Community freedoms, is that of market unity. This is a principle which appears from the relevant judgments to be independent of any express EC Treaty provision.

Ordoliberalism has also played an axiomatic role in determining the reach of the single market. The first mechanism was Articles 100 and 100A EC, which provide the explicit legal basis for Community action to secure the establishment and functioning of the single market. It has been argued persuasively that it is possible to have a single market without recourse to the notion of 'distortion of competition', simply by the removal of direct restrictions on movement of factors of production (Siebert, 1989; Siebert and Koop, 1993). Whilst this may leave room for regulatory competition, the extent of this phenomenon is questionable, and in any event its advocates argue that it is not socially undesirable. Be that as it may, the Court has rejected such a view, identifying the single market instead as an area in which no distortions of competition are brought about by differences in national legislation.[17] Such distortions cannot be eradicated, however, without harmonization of budgetary, countercyclical, monetary, fiscal, and social policies—in fact any public intervention which either stimulates or restricts supply or demand. Defining the single market in such terms transforms it from an end in itself, albeit an unstable one, into a platform for economic union and even, eventually, total economic integration.[18] It therefore equates the single market with an economic constitution, in so far as it suggests all economic activity must be brought within its remit.

A second role of any economic constitution is to act as a prism through which values, other than market values, are to be incorporated into the market order. Unlike neoliberals, ordoliberals believed that the market would work for social policy aims not only through its efficiency but also through its respect for human dignity (Lenel, 1989: 28; Müller-Armack, 1989: 84). Integral to this within

---

[17] E.g. Cases 91 & 92/79 *Commission* v. *Italy* [1980] ECR 1090; Case C-300/89 *Commission* v. *Council* [1991] ECR I-2867; Case C-202/88 *Commission* v. *France* [1991] ECR I-1223. On the limits of the harmonization process see Advocate General Jacobs in Case C-359/92 *Germany* v. *Council* [1994] ECR I-3698.

[18] A link explicitly recognized in Opinion 1/91 *Draft Treaty on a European Economic Area* [1991] ECR I-6079 where the aim of the Treaty was held by the Court, prior to the Treaty on European Union, to be both the establishment of an internal market *and an economic and monetary union*, despite there being no explicit provisions to that effect at the time.

the Community has been the development of the *ratione materiae* of the single market: persons, goods, capital, and services. These have all become emasculated within the concept of 'economic or gainful activity'.[19] This latter concept is triumphalist in nature. In defining the outer edges of the Community constitutional order, the concept of economic activity has been used as a means of extending the ambit of individual provisions.[20] Furthermore, the Court has used a functional test and has refused arguments that a particular activity may be cultural, for example, if it considers that there is a kernel of economic activity within the activity in question.[21] Whilst providing the illusion that the single market provides a functional, amoral backdrop[22] the concept is intrinsic to the establishment of an ordoliberal order. It serves to ensure that the values which form the backdrop for the analysis of such activity are couched in the language of economics. Measures to protect values which economists would term market externalities can be introduced through the harmonization of laws process, in so far as disparities in national or regional protection of these values distort competition. Provision is thus made for a social market rather than a neoliberal economy through the introduction of these external values, yet these values are introduced into the system in a manner which essentially protects the market and avoids too severe a weakening of the competitive order.[23]

One also finds within the Court's approach to the single market traces of the 'plywood' effect endemic to ordoliberal reasoning, whereby the private law nature of society causes all public actors to be bound by certain unitary principles. A parallel style of reasoning to that which delimits the behaviour of Community institutions has been used to prescribe the behaviour of the member states. The most

---

[19] See Case 53/81 *Levin* v. *Staatssecretaris van Justitie* [1982] ECR 1035 in respect of workers, Case C-2/90 *Commission* v. *Belgium* [1993] 1 CMLR 365 in respect of goods, Case C-275/92 *Schindler supra* n. 7 in respect of services. It is implicitly relevant to capital which requires the object to be a means of legal payment before it can be viewed as capital: Case 7/78 *R* v. *Thompson* [1978] ECR 2247.

[20] See notably Joined Cases 286/82 & 26/83 *Luisi & Carbone* v. *Ministero del Tesoro* [1984] ECR 377 where the Court stated, *contra legem*, that Art. 59 EC included the right to receive services as its object was to 'liberalize all gainful activity not covered by the other EC Treaty provisions'.

[21] E.g. Case 155/73 *Sacchi* [1974] ECR 409.

[22] Case C-159/90 *SPUC* v. *Grogan* [1991] ECR I-4685; Case C-275/92 *Schindler supra* n. 7.

[23] Case 6/72 *Europemballage Corporation and Continental Can* [1975] ECR 495.

notable example of this is the *Dassonville* formula, which is the backdrop for the jurisprudence on Article 30 EC. The frequent use of the formula, and the controversy over its usage and its interpretation,[24] should not conceal the fact that similar styles of reasoning have been used elsewhere, notably in the fields of services[25] and public undertakings.[26] The formula suggests that any measure which, actually or potentially, directly or indirectly, is capable of hindering trade, *prima facie* conflicts with Article 30 EC.[27] On a literal reading, it therefore outlaws any public measure which impinges on the market unless that measure is justified in the public interest. It therefore has strong parallels with the development of the doctrine of proportionality in nineteenth century German administrative law, whereby the principle was seen as a way of emphasizing the presumption of individual freedom, the marginal and exceptional nature of government intervention, and hence the need for the control of the latter (Schwarze, 1992: 688).

It has been argued elsewhere that, the Community being a system of partial integration, this reasoning is essentially rhetorical in nature and has therefore tended to obfuscate rather than to clarify (Chalmers, 1993; Wils, 1993). The normative manifestation of the *Dassonville* formula is, however, the *non-discrimination* principle. The clearest linkage between that principle and the theme of market unity was drawn in *Keck*,[28] where the Court stated:

However, contrary to what had previously been decided, the application to products from other Member States of national provisions restricting or prohibiting certain selling arrangements was not such as to hinder directly or indirectly, actually or potentially, trade between Member States within the meaning of the *Dassonville* judgment . . . provided that those provisions applied to all affected traders operating within the national territory and provided that they affected in the same manner, in law and in fact, the marketing of domestic products and those from other Member States.

[24] See the references to the literature by Advocate-General Tesauro in Case C-292/92 *Hünermund* v. *Landesapothekerkammer Baden-Württemberg*, Judgment of 15 Dec. 1993.

[25] Case C-76/90 *Säger* v. *Dennemeyer* [1991] ECR I-4221; Case C-154/89 *Commission* v. *France* [1991] ECR I-659; Case C-275/92 *Schindler supra* n. 7.

[26] Joined Cases C-46/90 & C-93/91 *Procureur du Roi* v. *Lagauche & Others*, Judgment of 27 Oct. 1993.

[27] Case 8/74 *Procureur du Roi* v. *Dassonville* [1974] ECR 837.

[28] Joined Cases C-267 & C-268/91 *Criminal Proceedings against Keck and Mithouard* [1993] ECR I-6097.

There are good reasons for this linkage. The principle is unique in its coverage in Community law. Unlike the *Cassis de Dijon* line of reasoning it binds not just the host state and the Community institutions but also the home state. Exports are therefore subject to it as well as imports.[29] It is universal in nature in that any public action which affects competitive conditions within the Community is subject to it. Secondly, although the principle has recently been applied rather formalistically,[30] its socio-economic function is not to ensure fairness but to protect comparative advantage (Schwarze, 1992: 602–5; Chalmers, 1994: 397).[31] It therefore performs the same function as the principle that the state may not intervene in the market place in a manner which compels, encourages, or reinforces anti-competitive conduct (Gyselen, 1994: 55).[32] Any state intervention, in so far as it is selective, can be said to be anti-competitive. The principle therefore provides the Court with a very sensitive instrument to control the integration process. As any regulation is potentially discriminatory the rigour with which the Court will apply the principle will depend upon the extent of integration it desires and the heaviness of regulatory touch it considers desirable within the single market.[33] Whilst no legal base is required for national measures, the width of the non-discrimination principle has therefore resulted in a version of the doctrine of conferred powers applying to national measures.[34] Not only is the coverage of the principle universal but, by requiring all institutions to observe

---

[29] Case 15/79 *Groenveld* v. *Produktscap voor Vlees en Vlees* [1979] ECR 3409; Case C-49/89 *Corsica Ferries* [1989] ECR 4441.

[30] See Case C-320/93 *Ortscheit* v. *Eurim-Pharm*, Judgment of 10 Nov. 1994, where a German advertizing regime that treated imports and domestic markets in a differential manner was found to discriminate against imports, despite Advocate-General Gulmann noting in his Opinion of 16 June 1994 that it did not do so in a manner that placed imports at a competitive disadvantage.

[31] Joined Cases 32-33/58 *SNUPAT* v. *High Authority* [1959] ECR 127.

[32] Case 267/86 *Van Eycke* v. *ASPA* [1988] ECR 4769.

[33] Although the Court has recently taken a more relaxed view of what measures it considers to be anti-competitive, it has not suggested that such measures fall outside the ambit of review of Art. 5, 85, 86, and 90 EC. See Case C-2/91 *Meng* [1993] ECR I-5171; Case C-153/93 *Federal Republic of Germany* v. *Delta Schiffahrts- und Speditionsgesellschaft mbH* [1994] ECR I-2557; Case C-379/92 *Peralta* [1994] ECR I-3453.

[34] This doctrine states that an institution has only those powers which are conferred upon it, expressly or implicitly by its constituent documents: Lauwaars, (1972: 56–9).

certain values, their legitimacy is made dependent upon the furtherance of those values.

2. THE REAPPRAISAL OF MARKET UNITY BY THE COURT

The institutional reasons why analogies between the EC Treaty and an economic constitution have begun to falter have been examined elsewhere (Reich, 1994: 459; Joerges, 1994). It is argued, however, that the reason why ordoliberalism no longer provides a suitable model for analysis of the Court's work is that it assumes too rigid and too discrete a separation of the market. Market integration can only be considered as a discrete topic if it is assumed that a distinction can be drawn between market integration and policy integration. In other words, it must be assumed that a dichotomy can be drawn between state intervention in the economy which occurs at frontiers and other forms of state intervention, and that the principal block on trade is state intervention at frontiers. There is no evidence to suggest that such a premise holds true (Pelkmans, 1980: 340–1; Pelkmans and Robson, 1987). Any theory of economic integration is therefore intimately bound up with theories on the function of the state within the modern economy. In this respect state intervention can have two broad functions within a market economy. The *allocative function* is essentially concerned with efficiency, as it requires the state to correct market failure or compensate for its effects. It can require a stabilization role, in that states may have to take countercyclical, budgetary, monetary, or fiscal measures to control the economy. It also involves a regulatory role, as the state will, at the very least, have to create a system where property rights are respected and contracts enforced. In exercising its *distributive functions*, on the other hand, the state is addressing broader concerns of equity and social justice (Musgrave, 1989).

The first challenge which integration poses for the exercise of these functions is that a uniform regime, even a highly regulated one, is likely to be insufficiently sensitive to both local milieux and local resources, as a result of the diversity in geographical and economic circumstances found in the Community (Rehbinder and Stewart 1985: 5). Risk regulation within the single market therefore requires flexibility in the institutional structures rather than rigid uniformity (Dehousse *et al.*, 1992: 20). This flexibility, in turn, is likely to throw up the kind of competitive distortions which the single market is supposed to eradicate.

The second paradox is the 'Frankenstein' effect. Whilst the development of flanking policies might be necessary both for the effective functioning of the single market and in order to render its consequences socially acceptable (Pelkmans and Robson, 1987: 189) these policies can, in turn, subsume the single market. For the principles which run through these policies can, in certain instances, run counter to those of the single market. This is not simply to state that certain goods, which are dangerous to public health, for example, should be outlawed throughout the single market, but extends wider. For certain policies, such as regional, educational, environmental, national security, and cultural policy have a spatial constituent, to the extent that their development requires different rules to be applied to the local environment than those applied to the Community environment. For example, environmental principles dictate that waste be disposed of as close to the source of production as possible. This would predicate a local market in waste but not a Community one. Educational and linguistic policies would require preference to be given to people speaking a certain language. In many cases this will be tantamount to preferring people from the local region. Respect for cultural diversity would require that cultural artefacts are not plundered from one region and moved to another. Whilst limits imposed by certain policies, such as consumer protection, which arguably do not have a spatial element, merely qualify the type of single market on offer, these latter policies run more overtly contrary to the single market, in that they predicate a differential treatment of activity based on region, race, or nationality.

These tensions are likely to increase proportionately to the increase in the rate of integration. Reconciliation has traditionally been attempted through the principle of proportionality.[35] Intervention by Community institutions was constrained by that principle, as was member state action restricting the exercise of the four economic freedoms. The principle does not involve the Court

---

[35] Formally, national measures taken under the 'mandatory requirements' doctrine to protect interests not recognized in the express exceptions in the Treaty must apply indistinctly to domestic products and imports: Case 113/80 *Commission* v. *Ireland* [1981] ECR 1625.

performing some impossible balancing act, namely weighing the value of the interest being protected against the value of the economic freedom being restricted. It allows the institution in question to determine the level of protection, but any measure taken must be both effective and the least restrictive of individual economic freedoms necessary to secure its objective.[36]

Whilst allowing a margin of local autonomy the language of economic rights was thrust to centre stage in areas of policy, where it can be argued that their influence should at best be marginal (Chalmers, 1993: 274). The consequence is an overextension of the principle, an overextension not aided by the dichotomy which the proportionality principle draws between ends and means, whereby the ends sought by policy-makers or administrators are not controlled but the means used are vigorously controlled. This assumes, often falsely, that such a dichotomy is possible. It also presumes, often very falsely, that policy-makers are able to predicate with some certainty the efficacy of the instruments used. The literature is thus full of examples of case-law of the Court being criticized for a misapplication of the proportionality principle, the judgments in *Danish Bottles*[37] (Jadot, 1990: 426; Krämer, 1993: 122; Demiray, 1994: 91) and *Campus Oil*[38] (Gormley, 1985) being two of the more famous examples.

There are clear signs that the influence of ordoliberalism is on the wane. The most obvious example is the amendments brought in by the Treaty on European Union. The tasks of the Community are no longer simply the establishment of a common market and harmonization of national economic policies. Beside the establishment of an economic and monetary union, they include all the activities set out in Articles 3 and 3A EC. The single market and economic convergence are no longer the predominant objectives of the EC Treaty but merely the first among equals in a whole series of other objectives. The explicit purpose of the Treaty is now the establishment of a series of seperate legal orders. These include a transaction order but they also include, *inter alia*, an environmental order, a cultural order, a social order, and an educational order. These

---

[36] E.g. recently Case C-131/93 *Commission* v. *Germany* [1994] ECR I-3315.
[37] Case 302/86 *Commission* v. *Denmark* [1988] ECR 4607.
[38] Case 72/83 *Campus Oil* v. *Minister for Energy* [1984] ECR 2727.

orders being of equal importance, there is no reason to suppose that action taken to further one must necessarily accommodate itself fully to the demands of another. In *German Bananas*[39] the Court noted: '. . . the institution of a system of undistorted competition is not the only objective mentioned in Article 3 of the Treaty which also provided *inter alia* for the establishment of a common agricultural policy.'

These amendments merely recognized a trend towards increased segregation of the Community into a series of parallel orders, each based on its own series of values, which has been developed most extensively in the field of legal basis. Formally, horizontal policies such as culture, health, consumer protection, and environmental protection take subject to the explicit legal bases for the single market, Articles 100 EC and 100A EC.[40] This formal hierarchy has been overturned by the Court's reworking of the requirement that the legal basis for a measure be dependent upon its aim and content.[41] Initially this served as a 'guarantee' ensuring that choice of legal basis was not decided purely upon institutional compromise, but that it was correlated to the measure in question and subject to judicial review (Barents, 1993: 92). More recently it has been used to reassert an egalitarianism between legal bases. The correct legal basis will depend upon where the centre of the measure falls. Thus even if the measure as a whole overlaps between two legal bases, if it falls predominantly with the remit of the 'subservient' legal basis, it should be based upon that competence even if the ancillary aims and content of a measure could normally justify its being based upon a 'predominant' legal basis.[42] Only in the rare instance where the Court will adjudge that a measure is equally centred upon two legal bases will the formal hierarchy apply.[43] The *principles*, which characterize and differentiate these policies, serve as the point of delimitation. The Community legislative institutions predicate these

---

[39] Case C-280/93 *Commission* v. *Germany* [1994] ECR I-4973.

[40] Case C-300/89 *Commission* v. *Council (Titanium Dioxide)* [1991] ECR I-2867; Case C-62/88 *Greece* v. *Council* [1990] ECR I-1527; Case C-405/92 *Etablissements A. Mondiet* v. *Société Armement Islais* [1993] ECR I-6133.

[41] E.g. Case 45/86 *Commission* v. *Council* [1987] ECR 1493.

[42] Case C-70/88 *Parliament* v. *Council (Chernobyl)* [1991] ECR I-4529; Case C-155/91 *Commission* v. *Council (Waste Directive)* [1993] ECR I-939; Case C-187/93 *Parliament* v. *Council (Waste Shipment)* [1994] ECR I-2857.

[43] E.g. Case C-300/89 *Titanium Dioxide supra* n. 40.

principles. Notwithstanding that a measure may severely affect the functioning of the single market they can arrange for it to be founded upon a legal basis other than Articles 100 or 100A EC. As the Community turns its attention increasingly away from establishment of the single market towards risk regulation, this prerogative is likely to be asserted ever more frequently.

The development of segregated legal orders required that a parallel approach be adopted by the Court to risk regulation by the member states. Any measures which contribute towards policies in areas of mixed competence should be treated by the same terms of reference as Community measures. In *Belgian Waste*[44] the Court found that a Wallonian measure banning the storage, tipping, or dumping of non-Wallonian waste in Wallonia was not discriminatory, as waste produced in Wallonia was distinguishable from waste produced outside of Wallonia, on the grounds that its disposal posed less dangers to the environment. It thereby revealed a willingness to abandon the criteria of comparative advantage, namely those of economic substitutability, and to base its decision on the question of whether the two comparators would do equal damage to the environment. Despite doubts about the clarity of the judgment (Gerardin, 1993: 148; Hancher and Sevenster, 1993: 362) the willingness to resort to criteria of environmental protection indicates the development of a nascent hierarchy of norms. Where conflicting pressures of environmental protection and economic integration cannot be resolved the Court will opt for protection of the environment. A 'variable geometry' of norms is therefore developing which will depend on both the phenomenon addressed and the approach taken by the member state or the Community institution towards its regulation.

The backdrop against which these policies are set no longer being that of market integration, the predominant criteria against which they are assessed have altered. These policies must still respect individual economic freedoms because the latter constitute fundamental rights within the Community legal order. Yet as the purpose of these policies is not to facilitate comparative advantage or liberalize trade it cannot be argued that they must always be the least restrictive of trade *per se* or always respect the non-discrimination principle, in so far as it aims to secure trade

---

[44] Case C-2/90 *Commission* v. *Belgium*, [1992] ECR I-9.7.92; [1993] 1 CMLR 365.

liberalization. The test is eased as it shifts from requiring measures to be the least restrictive of individual freedoms to merely declaring measures to be illegal where they are 'patently unsuited' to the objective pursued.[45] Measures taken are only likely to be deemed disproportionate where the burdens imposed upon individuals are manifestly excessive. The fetters have been considerably eased.

It was observed earlier that the constitutional qualities had developed at least in part out of the exigencies of the market order. Correspondingly, these alternate systems have developed their own constitutional qualities. Pre-emption, for example, is not so indispensable. It is perfectly possible to have a Community consumer, environmental or health policy which provides only for minimum standards[46] and allows member state autonomy over and above those. The Court has therefore been perfectly willing either to interpret Community legislation in a manner which leaves member states greater autonomy[47] or to allow member states to derogate from Community legislation where the reasons for derogation are considered legitimate.[48]

Similar arguments can be made with regard to the principle of subsidiarity. Whilst this principle underlies all Community law it has been more prominent within certain of these orders because it only acts to prevent the Community legislating in areas of mixed competence.[49] The delimitation between areas of Community exclusive competence and that of mixed competence is again founded upon the principles of the measure in question. In the view of the Commission, for example, if the purpose of the measure is to secure free movement it falls within an area of exclusive competence.[50] The result is a series of legal orders whose constitutional qualities and whose institutional balance will be increasingly dependent upon the constitutive principles which determine their boundaries.

---

[45] Joined Cases 279 etc./84 *Rau* v. *Commission* [1987] ECR 1069.

[46] E.g. Art. 118A(3) EC, 129(A)3 EC, 130T EC.

[47] Case C-11/92 *R* v. *Secretary of State for Health*, ex p. *Gallagher Ltd., Imperial Tobacco Ltd. and Rothmans International Tobacco Ltd.* [1993] ECR I-22.6.93.

[48] Case C-28/89 *Commission* v. *Germany* [1991] ECR I-583.

[49] Art. 3B(2) EC.

[50] EC Commission, 'The Principle of Subsidiarity', SEC(92) 1990. On implementation of this document see EC Commission, 'Report to the European Council on the Application of the Subsidiarity Principle', COM(94) 533.

3. CONCLUSION

In a 'political economy' the suggestion that one can have economic indivisibility without political indivisibility is intellectually dishonest and smacks of the empire-building that has been so forcefully criticized (Rasmussen, 1986). These recent trends, on that ground, are to be accorded a qualified welcome. The language of ordoliberalism has resulted, however, in a symbiotic link between the concept of the single market and the jurisdiction and authority of the Court of Justice. Unlike most other areas of EC policy, where the Court is dependent upon initial legislative intervention, it is granted primary jurisdiction over the single market by the provisions in the EC Treaty which secure the economic freedoms central to the latter. Whilst in many states the concept of an economic constitution has developed subsequent to that of a political constitution, the paradox of the European Community is that the converse is true. The language of economic constitutionalism has been more extensively articulated than that of civil and political freedoms. If this base were eroded very real dilemmas would be posed for the future jurisdiction and authority of the Court of Justice, and it might be that the integrationist cause will in future need strong legislators rather than strong judges.

The Legacy of the Market Citizen

MICHELLE EVERSON

Agh (1994: 108) has recently observed that 'all historical dramas start with the presentation of the dramatis personae, the chief actors of social life'. Bearing that message in mind, this essay on recent developments within the European Union will study two main actors: the 'market citizen' and the 'Union citizen'.

The market citizen is a well known player on the European stage and consequently poses few problems for academic analysis. According to one very early definition of the term (Ipsen, 1972) the part is strictly limited, solely encompassing the role of the individual European as a '*homo economicus*' (Agh, 1994: 108). Thus, whilst market citizens or *Marktbürger* (Ipsen, 1972: 187) were drawn from amongst the ranks of the nationals of the EC member states, such nationals were only to be regarded as fully fledged market citizens when 'acting as participants in or as beneficiaries of the common market'. In this way they were to be 'reached by' Community norms and legislation (Ipsen, 1972: 102).

The Union citizen, by contrast, is a newcomer to Europe who presents an inordinate challenge to coherent research. Something of the playwright's craft seems, in this particular case, to have been overlooked. The contours of the character are at best vaguely sketched and its substance is as yet indistinct. While it is clear that the status of Union citizenship is intended to contrast with that of market citizenship, there remains an amount of general uncertainty as to exactly which social or political consequences the concept may entail. Introduced by the bold assertion in Article 8(1) of the amended EC Treaty that 'Citizenship of the Union is hereby established', the status of Union citizenship extends automatically to *all* nationals of member states of the European Union, regardless of whether they are economically active.[1] The core of the new concept, however, remains that same right of mobility which

---

[1] Art. 8(1) EC: 'Every person holding the nationality of a Member State shall be a citizen of the Union' (introduced by the Treaty on European Union).

historically attached to the market citizen. Political rights, traditionally seen as central to the institution of citizenship, are correspondingly restricted and appear 'only as a secondary issue' (d'Oliveira, 1994: 147).

Although the exact nature of Union citizenship may now seem to be nebulous, it is nevertheless a progressive concept. Article 8E EC mirrors the general dynamism of the Maastricht Treaty in its creation of a mechanism whereby the substantive content of the institution might be developed in step with the general fleshing out of the Union. Alternatively, in the analysis of one commentator, Union citizenship is quite simply a 'futures market' (d'Oliveira, 1994: 147).

The question of what the character of Union citizenship might be would thus appear to be a normative one. In other words, rather than follow a narrative approach and detail the *existing* nature of this citizen, a more constructive strategy would be to concentrate on what this status should *become*. That is the ultimate aim of this essay. However, caution is appropriate. Rather than indulge in the construction of grand philosophical schemes, a pragmatic and restricted path will be followed. The central issue will thus be whether the concept of the market citizen has created any particular problems which require urgent attention (or correction) via the medium of the institution of the Union citizen.

1. THE UNCERTAIN STATUS OF THE UNION CITIZEN

1.1 Legal Certainty

The uncertainty which attaches to the status of the Union citizen is not entirely attributable to difficulties of legal interpretation. On the contrary, Articles 8 to 8E of the EC Treaty (introduced by the Treaty on European Union) contain a relatively clear index of the rights of the Union citizen.

As regards the question of inclusion, the Treaty is explicit in its recognition of the continued competence of the member states to determine who is a citizen of the Union. Thus, while Article 8(1) EC confirms that '[e]very person holding the nationality of a Member State shall be a citizen of the Union', annexed to the Treaty is a declaration clearly stating that 'the question whether an individual possesses the nationality of a Member State shall be settled solely by reference to the national law of the Member State concerned'. Notwithstanding this residual acknowledgment of the abiding sovereignty of the member states of the Union, any person fortunate enough to be a citizen of the Union is favoured with a series of rights which he or she may enforce against the Union, rather than its component member state units.

As stated above, central to this inventory is the right 'to move and reside freely within the territory of the Member States'.[2] On the political front, Union citizens will benefit first from 'the right to vote and to stand as a candidate at municipal elections in the Member State' in which they reside, and secondly, Union citizens can vote and stand for election to the European Parliament, even those residing in a member state other than their own.[3] In addition, Article 8D EC encapsulates the right of citizens to petition the European Parliament and to apply to the (not yet established) Ombudsman's office with any grievance regarding maladministration within Community institutions or bodies.[4] This catalogue is crowned by the citizen's 'entitlement' to '. . . protection by the diplomatic or consular authorities of any Member State . . .' in any third countries where his or her own country is not represented. Such diplomatic solicitude is to be offered '. . . on the same conditions of the nationals as other Member States'.

One slight barrier to clear legal interpretation is said to be posed by the 'scattering' of further rights of citizenship throughout the Union Treaty (d'Oliveira, 1994: 133). However, these various rights are easily correlated, the most important among them being readily identified as that of civil rights. Such rights arise from the explicit acknowledgment in Article F.2 TEU of the Union's recognition of the European Conventions for the Protection of Human Rights and Fundamental Freedoms 'as general principles of Community Law'.

1.2 Conceptual Obscurity

The major problem is therefore not of law but of political philosophy. In other words, while there is a degree of certainty as to how this citizen may be constituted in legal terms, there is

---

[2] Art. 8A EC.   [3] Art. 8B EC.
[4] With the exception of the Court of Justice and the Court of First Instance.

nevertheless doubt as to his or her political or social relevance within the Union.

In conventional academic language, the partner role to that of the *homo economicus*, is that of the *homo politicus* (Agh, 1994: 108). Alongside their economic activities individuals are also expected to play a part in the social and political life of the society in which they reside. The institution which has above all others been developed and refined to nurture and protect this function is that of citizenship. The citizen, being 'both governor and governed' (Gunsteren, 1994: 36), supposedly possesses the requisite sovereignty to master his own environs and to stamp her own character upon them. Is this new Union citizenship then such a vehicle, consciously designed to afford the 'sovereign Union citizen' the opportunity to dictate the pattern of social and political life in the Union?

Ultimately, it appears that this question must be answered in the negative. However, consider first the possibility of contributing to 'society'. One is immediately required to ask to which particular society Union citizenship pertains. The notion of 'one' citizenship common to all 'Europeans' seems to suggest that there be 'one' European society. However, the continuing sovereignty of the member states in the determination, via domestic nationality law, of exactly who may become such a European nevertheless indicates the contrary: the Union is 'between the *peoples* of Europe' and is thus not conceived as creating 'a European people' corresponding to its own 'European society'.

This conceptual obscurity presents two contrasting possibilities. First, Union citizenship may relate to a common but limited European society, which does not supersede but exists alongside its national counterparts. Secondly, Union citizenship may yet be associated with national societies. Thus, whilst 'Citizenship of the Union *in no way in itself* gives a national of another Member State the right to obtain . . .' any particular European citizenship '. . . or any of the rights, duties, privileges or advantages that are inherent in . . .'[5] that citizenship, it may nonetheless serve to 'lessen the disabilities of alienage'[6] throughout Europe. Union citizens residing

---

[5] The unilateral declarations of the Danish Government, as reported in the Presidency Conclusions to the Edinburgh European Council, Part B, Annex 3, Bull. EC 12–1992, I.42 (discussed by d'Oliveira, 1994: 134; his emphasis).

[6] *Paul* v. *Virginia* 75 US 168, 180 (1869).

in a member state other than their own may find themselves more privileged than 'non-Union aliens' in a manner which facilitates their contribution to that (alien) national society.

To confuse matters, however, Union citizenship contains elements providing support for both these scenarios. On the one hand the endowment of the Union citizen with the right to vote or stand for the European Parliament, regardless of the place of his or her own residence, seems to suggest that the Union citizen should be intimately connected with a European society. That this society is intended merely to supplement and not to supplant its traditional national bedfellows is confirmed by the declaration made at the Edinburgh Summit that Union Citizenship merely accords member state nationals 'additional rights' and does not 'in any way take the place of the national citizenship'.[7] On the other hand, the right of the Union citizen to vote and stand in municipal elections throughout the Union appears, through its lessening of the impact of alienage, to link this form of citizenship to national societies.

This is a novel situation: one concept or legal act giving rise to a schizophrenic citizen equipped with rights pertaining to two divergent forms of society. It is not, however, the most curious aspect of Union citizenship. After all, a tenuous analogy may be drawn between this supranational citizen/diluted alien and the federal/state citizen of orthodox constitutional government. However, the overwhelming confirmation of the unconventional nature of Union citizenship is the fact that while this citizen is 'attached' to two forms of society, it is master of neither.

A word of explanation is needed. A national of one member state resident in another now has the right to vote in municipal elections. He or she, however, may not take part in national democratic elections. In other words the Union citizen, as a 'diluted alien', is denied entry to the sovereign body politic which ultimately determines the course of the nation. Likewise, the Union citizen may exercise his or her right to vote for members of the European Parliament. The powers of this European Parliament, however, although augmented by the Treaty on European Union, remain heavily circumscribed.[8] In short, it is not now, nor is it intended to become the sovereign power within the Union. From this brief resumé the vast dichotomy between the traditional ideal of the

---

[7] Conclusions of the Presidency of the Edinburgh European Council, Part B, Annex 13, Bull. EC 12-1992, I.35.   [8] Arts. 137–144 EC.

citizen as governor and governed and the new concept of the Union citizen is apparent.

1.3 Underlying Uncertainties

The underlying cause of the conceptual obscurity of Union Citizenship is, however, easily pinpointed. Far from laying down a comprehensive and final identity for Europe, the Maastricht Treaty has instead ushered in a dynamic process of development which may or may not lead to European statehood. The Treaty on European Union, when read in terms of traditional constitutional thought, is itself an inherently schizophrenic document. On one hand its very commitment to the term citizenship, 'one of the deepest symbols of stateship' (Weiler, 1994a: 213), seems at once to betray an eagerness to create a 'superstate'. On the other, its opening dedication to the creation of 'an ever closer Union between the *peoples* of Europe', apparently continues to reinforce the supranationalist identity of the Community. Bluntly stated, the European Union remains an experiment in the creation of novel structures of government, with sovereignty shared between the traditional nation states and an increasingly independent supra-national authority.

Clearly, where there is general doubt as to the exact nature of a system of government, there can be no lucid formulation of the role of the citizen as a 'governor'. Such a situation, however, should not in itself be viewed as entirely negative. Whilst the split personality of the Union leads inevitably to indecision about whether its true power centre lies (or should lie) in the national capitals, in Strasbourg, or in Brussels, the Union citizen has at the very least acquired a political toehold in two of these places. Likewise, the dynamic element within Article 8 EC of Union citizenship ensures that if there is any evolution (conventional or otherwise) in the governmental composition of the Union, the concept of citizenship can adapt accordingly.

The equivocation of the Maastricht Treaty, however, gives rise to at least one cause for concern. According to one recent analysis the Treaty's ambiguity is merely a further manifestation of the fact that *fin de siècle* Europe is 'devoid of ideals' (Weiler, 1994a: 204). The potential for development within the structures of the Union is not due to any casual acceptance of the need to afford the Community sufficient institutional space to evolve in a possibly revolutionary manner. On the contrary, such ambivalence merely represents a tired institutional compromise between competing national and supranational interests in a Europe which has become 'an end in itself . . . [and] . . . no longer a means for a higher human end' (Weiler, 1994a: 214).

If that assertion is correct there is clearly a danger that the concept of Union citizenship will simply stagnate, increasingly pushed to the sidelines in the face of continuing friction between more traditional centres of power. That risk might, however, be alleviated if the concept of Union citizenship itself becomes a focal point for normative ideas of the role of the individual within the Union. Such a theoretical base could enable the evolution of a 'third force' within Europe, comprised of Europeans rather than European governments or institutions. The presentation of an ideal of citizenship, however, entails its own problems. If the Europe of the 1990s is itself somewhat lacking in idealism then logically it must also be intolerant of new ideals. Bearing this in mind, it is perhaps advisable to steer a more modest course and to refrain from the formulation of 'grand philosophical schemes'.

Consequently, a more pragmatic approach is proposed. As one author has suggested, the 'unique *sui generis* nature of the Community, its true world-historical significance' is constituted by its character 'as a cohesive legal unit which confers rights on individuals' (Curtin, 1993: 67). Clearly, the Union citizen is such an individual, receiving rights directly from the Union. It is, however, not the first entity to have played a similar part on the European stage. The forerunner to the Union citizen, the market citizen, was also distinguished as a bearer of rights *vis-à-vis* an international organization, the European Economic Community. In other words, a direct relationship between Europeans and Europe was in fact established by the Rome Treaties.

It would thus seem logical to preface any study of the potential of the concept of Union citizenship with an examination of the relationships already created between the institutions of Europe and Europeans. That line of research is similarly suggested by the fact that the rights of the market citizen, particularly that of free movement, have not merely been transferred to the Union citizen but continue to form the very core of that citizenship. The normative element within such an approach is provided by the dual question of whether the concept of market citizenship has given rise to any specific problems, and whether such difficulties should or could be ironed out through the medium of Union citizenship.

2. THE RELEVANCE OF THE IDEAL OF CITIZENSHIP

Before turning to the concept of market citizenship, however, it is helpful to consider in more detail the traditional concept of the citizen. Here a slight difficulty arises. Although 1978 saw an announcement that the concept of citizenship had finally gone out of fashion amongst political thinkers (Gunsteren, 1978) a recent article, confidently entitled 'The Return of the Citizen', has correctly stated that this assertion was in fact premature (Kymlicka and Norman, 1994). The past decade has instead witnessed a veritable avalanche of new work on the topic, with citizenship becoming 'the buzz word among thinkers on all points of the political spectrum' (Heater, 1990). That new literature has posed many and varied challenges to the orthodox understanding of citizenship, with authors questioning all its aspects, from the traditional linkage of citizenship to the nation state (Turner, 1993b) to its continued ability to secure political participation within the modern, techno-cratic state (Habermas, 1993). As a consequence, the 'modern' perception of citizenship is somewhat difficult to pin down. This notwithstanding, various common themes might be distinguished and the continuing relevance of the concept of citizenship in the modern world tentatively identified.

2.1 The Contested Ideal of Citizenship

As stated above, there is no single prevailing definition of the concept of citizenship. Two initial and recurring themes are, however, found in general 'citizenship' literature which account for this failing. The first of these is the supposedly inherent linkage between citizenship and particular communities (Turner, 1993c). The second is the normative character of citizenship. Citizenship is seen as entailing a vision. In essence, it concerns the manner in which people feel their particular community *should* be organized (Riesenberg, 1992).

Building upon these two strands of thought, those stressing the linkage of citizenship to community (though not necessarily to communitarianism) consequently emphasize the unique nature of each particular community's view of citizenship. The failure of such thinkers to identify one non-controversial definition of citizenship is thus simply revealed as follows: if citizenship primarily concerns relationships between each individual and his or her own community (and vice versa), and if communities are varied, then logically these relations cannot but differ from community to community, and from society to society (Turner, 1993c).

The second theme maintains that citizenship, the organizing force, gains vigour from its normative character. It is a powerful feature within political life precisely because it provides people with visions as to how the world in which they live might be ordered.

Of those who underline the normative nature of citizenship, one group, influenced by communitarian aspects of citizenship, would see this force as being cumulatively positive. 'The power of the citizenship ideal' lies in the fact that it is a means well suited to draw out the best in people . . . [I]t has survived so long and served in so many political environments because of its great inspirational challenge to individuals to make their neighbour's, their fellow citizen's life better and, by so doing, make their own nobler' (Riesenberg, 1992: xi).

A second group of writers, despite owing slightly more to individualism than to communitarianism, also highlights the normative nature of citizenship. They pragmatically suggest that individuals who are immediately concerned with their own interests will nevertheless take note of any existing concepts of citizenship and will seize upon them for their own ends. 'Ideas of citizenship . . . [thus become] . . . significant because of the part they play in the political rhetoric and the political calculations of governments, non-governmental agencies and political and social movements' (Hindess, 1993: 20).

The idealistic and the more pragmatic line of thought, however, have one thing in common. Just as different people have different ideas as to how the lives of their fellow citizens might be improved, so too different people use different ideas of citizenship to pursue different goals. In both cases the end result is clear: it is highly unlikely that one definitive vision of citizenship will emerge:

'Citizenship means many different things to different people' (Blackburn, 1993).

2.2 A Contested Definition of Citizenship

If the concept of citizenship is a 'contested truth' (Sommers, 1994: 64) any definition of citizenship can be viewed only as a general theory, around which discussion may revolve. Bearing this in mind, a return is made here to T. H. Marshall's path-breaking historical thesis of the development of citizenship (Marshall, 1950). This is not to suggest that it should be regarded as the finite formulation of the notion, but as a spring-board to identify the particular issues which surround citizenship.

Marshall traced the evolution of citizenship by observation, placing its origins in the successive development of civil rights in the eighteenth century, political rights in the nineteenth century, and industrial or social rights in the twentieth century. Taken together, these three families of rights amounted to a clear constitutive scheme, whereby the legitimacy of state power might be based upon the equal participation of all individual citizens. The development of civil rights liberated the populace from its feudal status. Armed with that legal confirmation of autonomy, individuals became free to contract with society at large. With political emancipation the populace emerged as the 'electorate', winning freedom to contract with the state and thus to determine the disposal of state power. Finally, social rights, in guaranteeing some degree of resource distribution, secured a measure of social equality and with this the *practical* ability of *all* individuals to contract both with society and with the state.

In summary, Marshall's thesis represented a scheme whereby successive groups were gradually 'included' into the integral areas of a national society until ultimately *all* could share in the exercise of power. Far from being a merely descriptive study of historical developments, however, Marshall's work also contained a strong normative message. In essence, the citizen was to be understood as being 'sovereign'. Accordingly, the sovereign citizen might issue demands, both to society and to the state: on one hand, a demand that the citizen be respected as an autonomous being; on the other, a demand to be included in the disposal of state power.

Dahrendorf's model of citizenship as a series of entitlements represents a modern and explicitly normative formulation of Marshall's thesis (Dahrendorf, 1992). This reformulation, however, lays a greater emphasis on the notion that citizenship is best understood as a 'status'. An initial distinction is drawn between entitlements and provisions. The citizen is afforded access to both provisions and entitlements; entitlements, however, are the citizen's by right, whereas provisions are merely a series of options, or qualified choices, with which that citizen is presented. In short, entitlements are the classic rights of citizenship, arranged in a series of concentric circles, with civil or civic rights forming the core, then political rights, and with social rights situated beyond these. Typically, provisions are options such as the qualified choice to enter the labour market or to trade, subject of course to personal ability or commercial availability.

Within this reformulation it is the notion of 'entitlement by right' which consequently creates the 'status' of citizenship; a status which is constitutive of the person, attaching to each and every individual regardless of his or her personal attributes or the prevailing labour or market conditions.

Returning to the question posed at the outset of this section, however, the pertinent query is now: what is the contemporary relevance of such notions of 'sovereignty' and 'status'? Briefly, it is contended that the guaranteed sovereignty and the secured status of the citizen, when taken together, remain the primary mechanism through which the 'allegiance' of the citizen is won.

As a slightly more detailed explanation, however, the modern citizen can be regarded as living under a constant and double threat. On one hand the citizen paradoxically remains a 'subject' against whom state authority might be exercised (Offe, 1987). On the other, that same citizen is uniformly imperilled by the vagaries of the market. Why then does this citizen tolerate such dangers, accepting without question restrictions placed on personal autonomy and the enduring threat of economic disadvantage?

Simply formulated, sovereignty and status act to neutralize such an intimidating situation. The sovereign citizen is to be understood as the 'creator' of state power who can dictate the exact limits to be placed on personal autonomy. Likewise, as the citizen is possessed of a status which is independent from the market, that same citizen might escape its less pleasing aspects.

In short, the contemporary relevance of the concept of citizenship lies in its function of ensuring that citizens 'accept' the norms imposed on them by the market and the state. Willingness to obey, or 'allegiance' to, the state and the market is thereby assured.

3. THE RELATION OF THE MARKET CITIZEN TO THE CITIZEN

The notion of the market citizen is not new. The specialized concept of the European market citizen is derived from older notions of the burgher, bourgeois, or economic citizen; this is a character well known in the national setting. According to one analysis, the person of this traditional economic or market citizen is distinguished from that of the citizen proper, but is *not* to be seen as distinct from it (Agh, 1994). Such a statement, however, immediately raises the question as to what the exact relationship between the citizen and the market citizen is.

From one point of view the term 'market citizen' is a misnomer. The linkage of the terms market and citizenship implies that the market citizen possesses much the same qualities in relation to the market as the citizen proper possesses with regard to the society in which he or she lives. Subject to the particular qualities ascribed to the citizen proper, however, that implication may need to be rejected. If the core of citizenship is to be seen as 'entitlement by right', the conjunction of the terms market and citizenship is misplaced because the market citizen is concerned with provisions rather than entitlements. Granted, the market citizen may possess certain legal 'rights', such as that to exercise the profession of his or her own choice. However, the ability to exercise such a right is fully dependent on both the personal characteristics of each market citizen and prevailing labour demands. In other words, market rights should not be understood as independent from, and thus constitutive of, the person.

Likewise, where 'sovereignty' is taken to be the defining characteristic of citizenship, the designation of the market actor as a market citizen would appear ill-judged. Whilst the term 'consumer demand' may be well known, it is equally apparent that consumers or market citizens are not sovereign. It is for the market to decide whether or not it will answer such demands. Simply stated, the market citizen cannot 'command' the market (Soltan, 1994).

If the 'market citizen' has neither status, and is not sovereign, why then do these two terms continue to be linked with one another? At a very general level it is often argued (Turner, 1994) that the development of citizenship proper was itself intimately connected with the evolution of the liberal market economy. This economy alone enabled the 'civil' citizen to realize his or her liberation from feudal economics, finding alternative sustenance in the market. Similarly, the wealth generated by this market ultimately furnished the economic basis upon which welfare rights might be founded.

Moving from the general to the specific, however, a more useful explanation of the connection between such opposing concepts concerns the supposedly 'associative' character of the market citizen (Preuß, 1994). In other words, the role of the market citizen is that which citizens proper are expected to undertake in the service of their community of residence. Just as the citizen may be transposed into the 'citizen in uniform' to maintain order within a society or to protect it from outside threat, so too the citizen is translated into the market citizen to meet the functional requirements of a community based upon a liberal market economy. In conclusion, the market citizen is the part which the citizen proper is 'expected' to play.

4. THE EUROPEAN MARKET CITIZEN

It transpires that, in common with notions of the burgher and bourgeois, the concept of the European market citizen entails a vital role which nationals of the member states have been expected to play: that of the legal and practical realization of the internal market. Ultimately, however, it seems that the highly productive character of the market citizen has also endowed Europe with a troublesome legacy. Having been so strongly instrumentalized with regard to the completion of the internal market, the market citizen had no choice but to become instrumentalist. In that self-interest alone drove the European market citizen in his or her dealings with Europe, a general allegiance to the Communities was not established. Arguably, therefore, the much vaunted legitimacy crisis with which Europe is confronted possesses a further facet: the lack of Europeans' allegiance to Europe; or the unwillingness of the individual European to 'accept' European norms which do not immediately appear to be in his or her self-interest.

4.1 The Role of the European Market Citizen

The degree to which the concept of the European market citizen has been instrumentalized, has been much obscured by the general legal euphoria which has surrounded the 'unique *sui generis* of the Community', or its endowment of individuals with rights. In celebrating such atypical behaviour on the part of a supranational organization commentators have generally failed to appreciate both the limited significance of those rights accorded to Europeans and the use which the Community itself could make of them.

The core rights afforded to the European market citizen were those of free movement of persons, freedom of establishment, free movement of services, and free movement of capital.[9] Initially those rights proved their worth, becoming the main plank upon which the Community strategy of negative integration might be based. That is, having failed to advance the cause of the internal market through positive negotiation amongst the member states the Community resorted to requiring those same member states to remove those of their laws which acted as a barrier to the internal market. Pivotal within this scheme was the Court of Justice's designation of the four freedoms as having direct effect within the member states. Economic entrepreneurs, mindful of the benefits which an integrated European market might bring to their businesses, were free to call upon their 'rights' as 'Europeans' to move labour, firms, products, and capital and to ensure that national barriers would fall. The Commission was ever willing to support such economic self-interest, championing the rights of market citizens against those of member states before the ECJ. With such a strategy, the legal integration of the European market was thus assured.

There remained, however, the matter of the practical realization of this internal market. While the activities of a minority group of large businesses trading across national frontiers had some demonstrative value, indicating that the internal market was open for business; the practical consolidation of that same market depended in no small part upon the willingness of large numbers of consumers themselves to engage in trade with those cross-border entrepreneurs. The person of the consumer thus became integral to Community strategies, and various aspects of the European market

---

[9] Arts. 48, 52, 58, and 67 EC.

citizen's character were accordingly translated into the secondary Community legislation designed to shape the newly opened internal market. The rights afforded to the consumer in secondary Community legislation indicated that this version of the European market citizen also be decidedly bullish. The European consumer was thus to be an aggressive consumer, being given by law 'access to the widest range of . . . [products] . . . in the Community so that he can best choose that which is best suited to his needs'.[10] On this basis, the most restrictive national provisions were to be superseded and consumers were to be aided in their forays into foreign market places. The practical realization of the internal market might thus be assured.

The key to this consumer version of the European market citizen is, however, provided by the emphasis placed on such terms as 'preference' and 'alternative'. The language of internal market directives encompasses a rhetoric of 'choice' and thus tangibly demonstrates that the European market citizen, like his or her national counterparts, is concerned not with entitlements but with provisions (Dahrendorf, 1992). The recent movement of the Community away from the aggressive consumer and towards the 'confident consumer' (Weatherill, 1995) has not modified this situation. Although the development of such instruments as the Unfair Contract Terms Directive has increased the protection for the European consumer actively engaged in the task of realizing the internal market,[11] this has not altered the true nature of the rights of market citizens. These remain provisions, the utilization of which is conditional upon the personal characteristics of individual Europeans and the prevailing conditions within the European internal market. In short, European consumers have the right to choose the product best suited to their needs only in so far as that product exists and they can afford it.

4.2 The Legacy of the European Market Citizen

The troublesome legacy of a European market citizen is easily pinpointed. The market citizen found in the national setting was a subsidiary role which citizens proper were expected to play. The

[10] Preamble to Third Non-Life Insurance Dir. (OJ 1992 L228/1), Consideration 19.
[11] Dir. 93/13 EEC, OJ 1993 L95/29.

attachment of such citizens to their national society had already been secured through the national institution of citizenship proper. Accordingly, such citizens could engage in market activities secure in the knowledge that while they might not command the outcomes of such activity, nor gain a guaranteed market status, their general status and sovereignty within the national setting were nevertheless affirmed. Consequently, they were ready to engage in economic activities in the service of the society in which they lived. These market citizens were therefore prepared to 'accept' possibly detrimental market outcomes and/or the potentially disadvant- ageous laws imposed by the state to regulate such outcomes.

The European market citizen, on the contrary, was not a subsidiary role but the major part which the nationals of member states were expected to play within Europe. As market citizenship cannot by itself create allegiance, the 'isolated' provisions accorded to that citizen were inevitably regarded merely as a series of choices, the effective manipulation of which could increase the welfare of each individual market citizen. The absence of an established European society, and of instruments creating allegiance to that society, determined that the market citizen be engaged in playing the European market, in the service not of Europe but of self- interest. Being instrumentalized, the market citizen had no choice but to become instrumentalist.

Naturally, such a situation is tenable where market outcomes appear to be in the individual interest. In such circumstances the laws designed to regulate the market will be accepted. What will happen, though, if European regulation no longer appears to be in the immediate self-interest of individual Europeans? Will they simply reject such laws? Similarly, the absence of allegiance to Europe was in the past largely compensated by the leading role of the member states in implementing and applying European legislation. Here, as national rather than European law was at issue, national allegiance might act to secure the acceptance of such 'European' norms by European nationals. The Treaty on European Union, however, with its proposed creation of a European Central Bank, with the power to make laws directly binding in the member states,[12] has raised the spectre of direct intervention by the Union

[12] Art. 4A and Title VI EC Treaty (as amended by the TEU). See also the Protocol on the Statute of the European System of Central Banks and of the European Central Bank.

into the lives of individual Europeans. What will be the basis of 'acceptance' of such norms if the intermediary allegiance owed the member states, is no longer available?

In conclusion, in so far as Europe has created direct relationships between European institutions and European nationals it has given rise only to a self-interested 'citizen' whose allegiance to Europe may not be simply taken for granted.

5. ALLEGIANCE AND THE UNION CITIZEN

In the light of that conclusion it seems that the most pressing concern to be addressed via the medium of Union citizenship is to establish some form of allegiance between Union citizens and the institutions of the Community. This functional requirement is increased by the surprising statement in the Maastricht Treaty that 'Citizens of the Union shall enjoy the rights conferred by this Treaty and shall be subject to the *duties* imposed thereby'.[13] Since the imposition of duties normally requires a high level of allegiance, the Union would be well advised to move away from 'self-interested constructions' as rapidly as possible.

Of course it may be argued that the new Union citizenship includes benefits which promote allegiance. These include the extension of the right of free movement to persons not seeking economic advantage or services; explicit confirmation that the Union is committed to fundamental civil rights; the communitarian aspects of Union policy, as exemplified by the Social Policy Agreement and the cross-border application of national social rights; and the (albeit heavily circumscribed) rights of political participation. All these may be considered as contributing to the strength of the concept of Union citizenship, and as increasing the Union's claim to allegiance from its citizens. However, it must be conceded that such mechanisms appear weak indeed compared with those of sovereignty and status evolved at national level. It therefore seems likely that the Union will be required to develop further allegiance-winning mechanisms.

How might Union citizenship be shaped to induce allegiance? This brings us briefly into the area of institutional design. Although

---

[13] Art. 8(2) EC, emphasis added.

there is no space here to engage in detailed suggestions, one point is emphasized. As suggested above, citizenship remains a 'contested truth'. Different people in divergent communities will have varying views as to the elements which should form its core. In this regard it should be noted that the European Union is a distinct Community, which may require a quite different form of citizenship from that developed at national level. In other words, the traditional model of the use of the notions of status and sovereignty to secure allegiance to a national society may not be transferable to the European context.

In conclusion, the search for a means of securing allegiance to the Union should be prepared to look beyond such historical mechanisms.

6. CONCLUSION

The European market citizen was individually motivated primarily by self-interest. This market citizen still forms the core of the Union citizen. A further facet of the European Union's legitimacy crisis may therefore be identified. In short, self-interested citizens ultimately owe no allegiance to the organization which created them. There is therefore a danger that individual Union citizens will at some time in the future simply withdraw their support for the European Union.

The concept of the Union citizen is nevertheless a dynamic notion, and accordingly there exists a mechanism through which the allegiance of Europeans may yet be won. The means by which these are to be achieved are not yet clear. Nevertheless, it is apparent that they must do more than reproduce those developed at national level.

In this vein, a final resort is made to the statement that '[c]itizenship has survived so long . . . because of its inspirational challenge' (Riesenberg, 1992: xi). Surely the inspiration most potently provided by the notion of Union citizenship is the idea that individuals can rise above the identity which is afforded them by their own, culturally restricted, national society.

Migrant workers and their families in the European Union: the pervasive market ideology of Community law

TAMARA K. HERVEY

Where Community law grants protections or entitlements to individual human beings[1] it appears, and claims, to do so universally and in accordance with the principle of equality. The ideas that legal rights are universal and that universal rights are to be applied impersonally, that is regardless of class, status, age, physical and mental ability, sexual orientation, race, or gender, are strands of the general concept of equal protection before the law, a guiding principle of the law of democratic states. It is not surprising, therefore, that the institutions of the Community lay claim to these ideas. In particular, the Court of Justice claims to be guided in its duty to ensure that 'the law is observed' (Article 164 EC) by principles common to the legal heritage of the member states.[2]

However, the legal language of universalism and equal application may form part of an ideological structure which serves to reinforce and perpetuate existing social and political arrangements, in particular the position of the dominant in those arrangements (Crenshaw, 1988: 1349–56; Fitzpatrick, 1987: 119, 121–2; Harris, 1994: 745–50). I contend that this general critical proposition may usefully be applied to the law of the European Community. Where Community law appears to entitle all individuals to certain benefits the effect of its provisions in practice may be to maintain structural inequality and thereby protect dominant interests. One mechanism by which this may be achieved appears to be reference to the concept of the 'market'.

---

[1] Natural persons, as opposed to legal persons, such as corporations, institutions, and companies.

[2] Case 11/70 *Internationale Handelsgesellschaft* [1970] ECR 1125 para. 4; Case 4/73 *Nold* [1974] ECR 503 para. 13; Case 44/79 *Hauer* [1979] ECR 3727 para. 15.

The following analysis concerns the Community law protections and entitlements concerning the free movement of individuals into and within the European Union.[3] These provisions are central to Community 'social law',[4] and focus on entitlements to free movement for the purpose of employment, without discrimination on grounds of nationality. They are also central to the Community's market enterprise: the creation, by the harmonization of laws, of a single European market within which the factors of production move freely, in accordance with free competition. Tension between the 'social' and the 'market' functions of these provisions is to be expected. This essay will show how that tension allows the institutions of the Community, while giving with one hand generous entitlements to social protections, to take away with the other hand by constructing the central concepts of the legal provisions which provide those social protections in a manner which perpetuates particularism and inequality.

Contrary to the rhetoric of the institutions of the European Union, the social protections concerning free movement of individuals contained in Community legal provisions are not universally applicable rights to or guarantees of equal treatment. Rather, the relevant provisions of Community law, as interpreted by the institutions, and particularly by the Court, are based upon presumptions which further marginalize members of groups already neglected by national legal systems, and who are excluded from protection at European Union level. The 'marginalized', 'peripheral', or 'minority' groups on which this chapter focuses are women and members of racial minorities.[5] I am aware that to use a discourse of community ('groups' of women and people of colour), is to run the risk of participating in the exclusion which this chapter aims to expose. The very choice of groups for the purposes of analysis gives an impression of uniformity which ignores the diverse

---

[3] It is beyond the scope of this chapter to extend analysis to other Community social policy measures affecting migrant workers and their families, such as labour regulation and consumer protection.

[4] It is not the purpose of this chapter to explore the competence of the Community or Union to legislate in the social sphere.

[5] The term 'racial minority' is, for the purposes of this chapter, interpreted from the position that the dominant racial group in the European Union is white Caucasian. Factors indicating membership of a racial minority are taken to include colour, religion, language, ethnography, history, and culture.

experiences of individuals. This is particularly the case for racial minorities because of the great differences between the histories, cultures, and religions of different minority groups.[6] I do not mean to adopt an 'essentialist' position (Harris, 1991) based on a unitary 'women's experience' or 'experience of people of colour', nor to imply that the experience of, for example, a Caribbean woman is reducible to the simple addition of racial and sexual disadvantage.[7] I have therefore tried, when discussing the people to whom Community law applies (as opposed to the legal norms themselves), to disaggregate, so far as is possible within the confines of a short essay, the categories of race and sex around which this essay focuses, by at least implicit reference to other relevant factors, such as nationality, class, and poverty. I have also tried to present differences as relational rather than inherent (Harris, 1991: 250, 252–3).

However, some categorization is necessary in order to formulate a critique which might lead to social change. Moreover, an 'outsider jurisprudence' (Harris, 1994: 744) of Community law, based on race and sex, might yield insights for others excluded by, for example, age, sexuality, ability, or poverty. To this end the present chapter explores the definition or 'construct' given by Community institutions to a number of interrelated concepts: 'migrant worker', 'family', and 'European'. Some facets of these concepts are already well developed in the jurisprudence of the Court of Justice. Others are emerging from secondary legislation, soft law, and activities under the 'third pillar' of the Maastricht Treaty. The central theme of this chapter is that the rhetoric of universalism and equality which surrounds these terms belies a particularized and unequal structural (social and political) reality; in particular, one which excludes women and members of racial minorities. The all-pervasive concept of the 'market' is one mechanism by which this marginalization may be achieved. The chapter aims merely to 'deconstruct' the terms listed above and, indirectly, the term 'market'. This critique is intended to help 'clear the way' (Harris, 1994: 749) for the more difficult task of reconstructing an inclusive European legal regime.

---

[6] Indeed, the very concept of 'race' itself is a contested one (Harris, 1994: 770–1).

[7] See also European Forum of Left Feminists and others, 'Confronting the Fortress: Black and Migrant Women in the European Community', Report to the European Women's Lobby, April 1993.

It is not my contention that the most effective means of protection for women and members of racial minorities is always by regulation at the level of the European Community or European Union. I do not intend to imply that the institutions of the European Union are competent, either under the Treaty of Rome or as a matter of political reality, to alleviate all the structural disadvantages experienced by women and members of racial minorities. Much of that restructuring is probably a task primarily for national legislatures. My point is that the Community's false claim of equality of treatment for all individuals in Community law has an adverse impact on women and members of racial minorities *in addition to* their disadvantaged position under national legal systems.

Of course, some attempts to improve the position of women or members of racial minorities have been promulgated at Community level. The Community provisions concerning equal pay and equal treatment for women in employment are well known.[8] As for racism, the Community institutions are unlikely to leave unheeded complaints that Europe is racially stratified, both politically and economically, and that racism and xenophobia should therefore be matters of Community concern. The European Union is unlikely to pursue an explicitly racist self-definition: at the very least at the level of rhetoric, Community institutions may be expected to respond to pressure to harmonize policies on a non-exclusive basis. Evidence of this is found in the European Parliament's Committees of Inquiry on Racism and Xenophobia[9] and the Joint Declaration against Racism and Xenophobia promulgated by the European Parliament, Council, and Commission.[10] However, none of these documents has been followed by 'hard law'[11] developments at the Community level

[8] Art. 119 EC; Dir. 75/117/EEC; Dir. 76/207/EEC; Dir. 79/7/EEC; Dir. 86/378/EC; Dir. 92/85/EEC; Commission Recommendation of 27 Nov 1991 on the Protection of Dignity of Women and Men at Work, OJ 1992 L49/3.

[9] European Parliament, (rapporteur, Mr Evrigenis) *Committee of Inquiry into the Rise of Fascism and Racism in Europe* (Dec. 1985); European Parliament (rapporteur, Mr G. Ford), *Report drawn up on behalf of the Committee of Inquiry into Racism and Xenophobia*, PE DOC AX-59-90-815-EN-C/91.

[10] *Declaration against Racism and Xenophobia* of 11 June 1986, OJ 1986 C158/1.

[11] In spite of continued efforts by the European Parliament to persuade the Commission to propose a directive on racism, most recently on 27 Oct. 1994, see *Europe* No. 6346, 28 Oct. 1994. The Commission itself has also indicated the need for action, in particular to press for a Treaty revision to include powers to act to combat racial discrimination: see the White Paper, 'European Social Policy: a way forward for the Union', COM(94) 333, 30, 40. It is possible, therefore, that amendments made at the 1996 IGC may provide a Treaty basis for future action.

(or even at the national level) (Cox, 1993: 59–60; Paul, 1991: 62–3; Szyszczak, 1992: 132, 135–7).[12] It is therefore stressed that one cannot simply assume that the rhetoric actually describes the 'structural reality of Europe' (Rex, 1992: 118). Rights in Community law are incorporated in terms 'whose neutrality is more apparent than real' (Meehan, 1993: 105).

1. MIGRANT WORKERS AND THEIR FAMILIES: THE RACIST IMPLICATIONS OF EC LAW

Community law offers a range of protections to 'migrant workers', in particular the free movement provisions in Articles 48 ff. EC. 'Migrant workers' in this sense are citizens of the European Union,[13] who may move freely to a member state other than that of which they hold nationality in order to work, or to look for work.[14] Migrant workers are entitled to reside in the host member state[15] and, with certain provisos, to remain there after they have ceased working.[16] 'Migrant workers' may not be discriminated against on grounds of their nationality.[17] They are entitled to enjoy the same 'social advantages' as nationals of the host member state.[18]

The rhetoric used to describe the position of migrant workers in Community law suggests universal protection by means of reference to the concepts of equality and 'fundamental rights' (to which all human beings are entitled regardless of status). Any tension between 'social' and 'market' aims of the legislation appears to be resolved according to a functional approach focused upon the humanity of the individuals to whom the legal provisions apply, for example:

'Whereas freedom of movement constitutes a *fundamental right* of workers and their families . . .'
'Whereas the right of freedom of movement, in order that it may be

---

[12] However, as Szyszczak suggests, soft law measures, such as the Joint Declaration, may have at least an indirect effect.
[13] Arts. 8 and 8A EC.
[14] Reg. 1612/68/EEC, Arts. 1–4; Dir. 68/360, Arts. 1–3.
[15] Dir. 68/360/EEC, Arts. 4–9.   [16] Reg. 1251/70/EEC, Art. 2.
[17] Art. 6 EC; Reg. 1612/68/EEC, Art. 7.
[18] Reg. 1612/68/EEC, Arts. 7 (2) and 9.

exercised . . . in freedom and dignity, requires that *equality of treatment* shall be ensured in fact and law . . .'[19]

'The migrant worker is not regarded by Community law—nor is he [sic] by the internal legal system—as a mere source of labour, but is viewed as a *human being*.'[20]

'. . . labour is not, in Community law, to be regarded as a commodity . . . [Community law] notably gives precedence to the fundamental rights of workers over satisfying the requirements of the economies of the Member states'[21] (emphases added).

However, closer consideration of provisions of Community law granting entitlements to migrant workers, particularly in the light of their application to members of racial minorities and women, reveals (as shown below) that universalist protection under Community law is more apparent than real.

The traditional position, evidenced in the jurisprudence of the Court of Justice, is that the term 'migrant worker' is to be given a generous, dynamic, Community definition (Craig and de Búrca, 1995: 662–73; Nielsen and Szyszczak, 1993: 55, 59–63; Pollard and Ross, 1994: 429–30; Steiner, 1994a: 209; Wyatt and Dashwood, 1993: 240–2). To qualify as a 'migrant worker' in the Community sense, an individual must undertake to perform services for and under the direction of an employer, for a period of time, in return for remuneration.[22] The work need not be undertaken full-time[23] and the remuneration need not meet the worker's subsistence requirements.[24]

1.1 The Distinction between third country nationals and European Union nationals

In spite of the broad Community definition of 'worker', the principal limitation of the free movement provisions is the scope of their application: they apply only to nationals of the member states of the European Union (EUNs). 'Migrant worker' thus denotes migrant EUN worker: a definition which excludes nationals of 'third

---

[19] Preamble to Reg. 1612/68/EEC.
[20] AG Trabucchi in Case 7/75 *Mr & Mrs F* v. *Belgian State* [1975] ECR 679, 696.
[21] AG Jacobs in Case 344/87 *Bettray* [1989] ECR 1621, 1637.
[22] Case 66/85 *Lawrie Blum* v. *Land Baden-Württemburg* [1986] ECR 2121, para. 17.
[23] Case 53/81 *Levin* v. *Staatssecretaris van Justitie* [1982] ECR 1035.
[24] Case 139/85 *Kempf* v. *Staatssecretaris van Justitie* [1986] ECR 1741.

countries' (TCNs). TCN migrant workers are those who have migrated to the European Union but have no Community rights to freedom of movement within its territory. Should a TCN wish to move to another member state the conditions of so doing, for example visa or work permit requirements, depend on national law. Thus, Community law implicitly creates two groups of migrant workers: 'mobile migrants' (EUNs, with full rights of free movement) and 'non-mobile migrants' (TCNs). The Community term 'migrant worker' refers only to the first group; the definition is no longer contested, although it has been suggested that Article 48 (1) EC could have been interpreted as granting freedom of movement (although not non-discrimination) to *all workers* within the Community (Böhning, 1973: 83; Plender, 1990: 605).

The concept of 'family' permeates the free movement provisions of Community law. Family members of EUNs who have exercised their right to free movement in order to work or to provide services are entitled to reside with the worker,[25] to be given residence permits by the member state in which they reside,[26] to move freely in the member state of residence,[27] and, if certain requirements are met, to remain in the host member state.[28] Some family members of EUN migrant workers have the right to work[29] or to exercise a profession[30] in the host member state. 'Social and tax advantages' to which an EUN migrant worker is entitled[31] include 'family benefits' in the broad sense of the term (Wyatt and Dashwood, 1993: 261).[32]

However, as with the term 'migrant worker', the multiplicity of provisions in secondary legislation granting entitlements to family members suggests a universality of protection which in reality is absent. The fullest entitlements are given to families of EUN migrant *workers*. The families of other EUNs who move, for example students,[33] are entitled to reside in the host member state only if the entire family is covered by health insurance and has sufficient

---

[25] Reg. 1612/68/EEC, Art. 10.   [26] Dir. 68/360/EEC, Art. 4 (3).
[27] Dir. 73/148/EEC, Art. 1.
[28] Dir. 1251/70/EEC, Arts. 1 and 3; Dir. 75/34/EEC, Arts. 1 and 3.
[29] Reg. 1612/68/EEC, Art. 11.
[30] Case 131/85 *Gül* [1986] ECR 1573.
[31] Reg. 1612/68/EEC, Art. 7.
[32] See e.g. Case 32/75 *Cristini* v. *SNCF* [1975] ECR 1085; Case 63/76 *Inzirillo* [1976] ECR 2057; Case 261/83 *Castelli* [1984] ECR 3199; Case 157/84 *Frascogna* [1985] ECR 1739.   [33] See Dir. 90/366/EEC, Art. 1.

resources not to become a burden on the host member state.[34] The families of TCN migrants are not included at all; their situation is at present still a matter for the national law of each member state.[35]

1.2 The Construction of 'European'

The above overview reveals that a central concept in the construction of provisions of Community law concerning migrant workers and their families is the distinction between EUN and TCN migrants, between mobile and non-mobile migrant, between 'European' and 'non-European'. To this end, the institutions of the European Union are in the process of creating a 'European' identity. 'European' in this context is defined not geographically (in fact the EU definition of 'European' excludes East and Central Europeans),[36] but ideologically, by reference to shared culture, heritage, and history (for example, the legacies of Greece, Rome, the Judeo-Christian tradition, the Enlightenment, liberalism, and Western democracy). The aim of this process is to foster a common idea of 'Europe' by blurring the diverse and complex cultural and historical identities of the various member states. One way of achieving commonality in the idea of 'European' is to stress the *otherness* or alien nature of those from outside, the non-Europeans (Brah, 1992: 23). 'European' is thereby constructed around an ideology of exclusion. The exclusion of TCNs does not appear to be founded solely on grounds of nationality: rather, the 'otherness' of non-Europeans becomes associated with characteristics such as race and ethnic origin, and especially, because of its visibility, colour. In spite of the imprecision of this definition—simply stated, there are many white non-Europeans and many Europeans of colour—its utility encourages acceptance of the concept of 'Europeanness'. The unifying idea of 'European' is conveniently translated into the exclusive idea of 'white European'; 'Europe' becomes defined as a

[34] Dir. 90/364/EEC, Art. 1.

[35] The position of family members of TCN migrants will eventually be covered by a common immigration policy of the European Union; see Art. K.1 (3) (b) TEU.

[36] Although this may not be the case in the future: the Europe Agreements (between the EU and Poland, Hungary, and the Czech, Slovak, Romanian, and Bulgarian Republics) contain provisions which enshrine the principle of non-discrimination on grounds of nationality for workers from the member states already established in a host state, according to national law (Ramsey, 1995: 167).

'White Man's Club' (Dummett, 1991: 169)—a definition which marginalizes in general on grounds of race and ethnic origin, and in particular on the ground of colour.

The Community/Union construct of 'European' informs the European Union's emergent immigration policy, which will cement the differentiation between 'European' and 'non-European' into a single common practice—'Fortress Europe' in terms of the movement of people, with freedom to move for those within the fortress and insurmountable barriers excluding those who are not.[37] The European Union's ideology of exclusion, focused around the construct of 'European', translates into a common immigration policy in which race determines entitlement to enter the European Union: a 'common market racism' (Sivanandan, 1988; Webber, 1991: 16). The 'negative list' of countries whose nationals will require a visa in order to cross the European Union's external border contained in the Commission's draft regulation on a common visa policy[38] was justifiably dubbed the 'black list' by the media, due to the over-representation on the list of countries in Africa, the Caribbean, the Indian subcontinent, and the Middle East. The Commission's communication on immigration and asylum policies[39] includes such phrases as 'action on migration pressure' (implicitly assuming that migration is a problem) and 'action on controlling migration flows' (implying the imperative of keeping aliens out). Terms such as 'pressure' and 'control' reveal that the institutions of the European Union see a common immigration policy as an answer to a problem, the problem being how to exclude 'non-Europeans' (defined according to a racially discriminatory construct of 'European') from the single European market.

It is implicit in the proposals for a common European immigration policy that enjoyment of the social and economic gains promised from the single European market is only for those *within* the market. Indeed, the sub-text of those proposals is that the market cannot bear a 'flood' (exclusionary language again) of economic migrants. In times of economic recession and high

---

[37] See e.g. the Commission's Communication on Immigration and Asylum Policies, COM(94) 23, 11.

[38] Communication from the Commission to the Council and the European Parliament on Immigration and Asylum Policies, COM(93) 684.

[39] COM(94) 23.

unemployment the benefits of a unified European Union can only be enjoyed if exclusionary policies are adopted to keep 'non-Europeans' out (Gregory, 1993: 62). Policies which ensure the effective functioning of the market are presented as justifing the policy of exclusion.

The internal impact of promoting a common European identity is to alienate more members of racial minorities within the European Union. 'European' is by implication white European; the claims of members of other cultures resident in the European Union are marginalized or silenced. For example, the texts concerning the promotion of culture at European level contain no definition of culture, but stress commonality in European cultural heritage and values.[40] Members of 'visible minorities', that is those who are identifiable by their colour as 'others', find themselves excluded from this European identity even if they are in fact EUNs (Forbes and Mead, 1992: 4–5, 73). EUNs who are members of a racial minority are likely to experience discrimination as a consequence of their exclusion from the dominant ideology of 'European'. For example, they are likely to be disadvantaged by association with stereotyped 'problem' (i.e., TCN) groups: 'the equation of black with crime, and crime with illegal immigration' (Webber, 1991: 13). It is noteworthy that at the European level the same forums (the Trevi group and the Ad Hoc Group on Immigration) discuss immigration issues as discuss drug trafficking and terrorism (Rex, 1992: 116). The visibility of people of colour is likely to lead to greater harassment, arising from the differential rights to freedom of movement of TCNs and EUNs, for example by immigration officials or the police. The Community view of an integrated white Europe tends to see all members of racial minorities as TCNs (Paul, 1991: 56–7). Moreover, due to structural race discrimination at national level, particularly in employment and education, EUNs of colour are likely to experience difficulty in acquiring the transferable 'Euro-skills' necessary to become migrant workers and to exercise free movement rights (Szyszczak, 1992: 127).

TCN members of racial minorities are also excluded by the

---

[40] See e.g. Conclusions of the Council and the Ministers of Culture meeting within the Council of 12 Nov. 1992 on guidelines for Community cultural action, OJ 1992 C336/1; Communication from the Commission on New Prospects for Community Cultural Action, COM(92) 149.

ideology of white Europe. Perhaps more significant, however, is that unfavourable treatment of TCNs in Community legal provisions concerning free movement *itself* has a disparate racial impact. Statistics on the race and ethnic origin of EUNs and TCNs do not appear to be available from the Community institutions. Statistics on citizenship of residents in the European Union[41] suggest that of the approximately ten million TCNs resident in the European Union, around 70 per cent are members of racial minorities.[42] This is a sufficiently high proportion to suggest that detrimental treatment of TCNs will have a disproportionate impact on grounds of race, that is, it will be indirectly racially discriminatory (Forbes and Mead, 1992: 74). The Community construct of 'migrant worker' as EUN mobile migrant perpetuates this discrimination.

The status of TCNs already resident in the European Union ranges from guestworkers through refugees awaiting asylum to illegal immigrants, and their families. Many, though not all TCNs, for example those who work in the service sector and as unskilled workers, and in the unofficial economy, form part of a cheap and immobile labour force, which is indispensable to and forms the basis of western Europe's post-industrial economy (Webber, 1991: 11–12; Rex, 1992: 117; Paul, 1991: 53–6). However, the position of these TCNs, both economically and legally, is insecure: they are the first group to be affected in times of recession, and they are relatively rightless in terms of protection under both national[43] and Community law as compared with EUNs. For example, the families of TCN ('non-mobile') migrants do not benefit at all from Community law provisions protecting families of migrant workers. It is inherent in a guestworker system that workers are treated only as factors of production in the labour market, and not as human beings. Protection of family life, and entitlements of residence for family members, are excluded in that situation (Morokvasic, 1991: 73; JCWI report, 1994). This is the case even though the member states of the European Union consider that the family is a basic institution of society and that the right to family life is a 'fundamental right'.[44]

---

[41] EUROSTAT: Population and social conditions—Monthly No. 7/94; See also *Agence Europe*, 29 Oct. 1994, 15.

[42] See above for working definition of 'racial and ethnic minority'.

[43] Workers in the unofficial economy, for example TCN women who provide domestic labour, do not enjoy even basic employment protection under national law.

[44] Art. 8, European Convention on Human Rights and Fundamental Freedoms.

The status of these TCNs may therefore be defined as that of an 'underclass' in an emergent 'politically stratified system of groups' in the European Union (Paul, 1991: 56; Morokvasic, 1991: 75; Rex, 1992: 117–18).

1.3 Racism and the role of the 'market'

Integration of the single European market dictates that mobility be granted to workers to create a level playing field of competition in order that, at least in theory, labour may move where conditions are best or, more relevant in the 1990s, where jobs are available. To encourage and facilitate free movement of workers, members of their families are also entitled to move. On the other hand, however, the 'market' has an interest in keeping some workers relatively immobile, rightless, and without protection, as a cheap factor of production (Morokvasic, 1991: 75). By defining 'migrant worker' so as to exclude all TCNs, Community law maintains the benefits of this paradoxical position. Whereas the tension between 'social' and 'market' functions of free movement provisions is, broadly speaking, resolved in favour of social protection for *EUN* migrant workers, the fine rhetoric concerning the humanity of workers in Community law does not appear to apply to *TCN* migrant workers. To reach this position the Community institutions exploit the market function of Community law, and in particular its scope. For example, in *Germany* v. *Commission*[45] the Court held that part of a Commission decision concerning cultural integration of TCNs and their families was *ultra vires* and therefore invalid. Migration policy, the Court explained, falls within the scope of Community law only as regards the impact of TCN migrant workers on the Community employment market.[46] The Commission was not competent in relation to social entitlements for TCN migrants. As explained above, the Community construction of 'migrant worker', with its detrimental treatment of TCNs, has a disparate impact on members of racial minorities. The Community legal order, based on the market, appears to be 'innocent' (Fitzpatrick, 1987) as concerns race, because of the universalism of law and the ostensible even-handedness of the market. However, just as national law, because of limitations upon

---

[45] Cases 281, 283–5 & 287/85 *Germany, France, The Netherlands, Denmark, and United Kingdom* v. *Commission* [1987] ECR 3203.   [46] Ibid. para. 23.

its scope and competence to intervene, may be compatible with racism (Fitzpatrick, 1987: 121–31), so may the definition of the scope of Community law reveal compatibility with racism to be inherent in the Community legal order.

Community law, despite its 'general principle' of non-discrimination on the ground of nationality (Article 6 EC), does not prevent detrimental treatment of TCN (as compared with EUN) migrant workers. For example, the exclusion of families of TCN migrants from the Community protections for family members of migrant workers is consistent with Community law. It has been suggested that this exclusion is directly discriminatory on the ground of race, or even intrinsically racist, and in breach of the 'fundamental right' to family life (Szyszczak, 1992: 126–9; Bhabha and Shutter, 1994: 212–27; JCWI report, 1994).[47] Another example may be found in the 'reverse discrimination' case-law, in which the Court has consistently held that Community law may not be invoked unless the worker has exercised his or her Community right to freedom of movement;[48] no TCN migrant has the option of exercising such a right. The detrimental treatment of TCN migrants is justified by the assertion that, unless there is a *Community* migrant worker, there is no integrative market interest mandating the interference of Community law. However, it might equally be argued that unfavourable treatment in employment of TCN migrants (and of nationals of the host member state) on the ground of race could act as a disincentive to intra-EC migration. An EUN migrant worker is entitled only to the level of protection available to other workers in the host member state. Where there are no effective race discrimination laws mobility within the EC might be prevented or hindered, either because potential migrant workers choose not to move to a state where there is a low level of protection or because migrant labour is being exploited (Szyszczak, 1992: 134). The 'market' justification for the narrow application of Article 6 EC, while giving an appearance of even-handedness, conceals an avoidance of race

---

[47] EC Migrants Forum Information and Proposals to the Ad Hoc Immigration Group, 1994; SCORENews, 1994, published by the Standing Committee on Racial Equality in Europe.

[48] See e.g. Case 175/78 *R* v. *Saunders* [1979] ECR 1129; Cases 35 & 36/82 *Morson & Jhanjhan* v. *Netherlands* [1982] ECR 3723; Case 298/84 *Iorio* [1986] ECR 247; Case C370/90 *R* v. *Immigration Appeal Tribunal and Surinder Singh*, ex p. *Secretary of State for the Home Department* [1992] 3 CMLR 358.

issues and perpetuates the protection of majority EUN migrant workers and of employers' interests in keeping a pool of guest-workers whose rights to move elsewhere in the single European market in order to work are curtailed.

2. MIGRANT WORKERS AND THEIR FAMILIES: THE GENDERED IMPLICATIONS OF EC LAW

The Community constructs of 'migrant worker' and 'family' in the context of social protections, by relying on a particular market ideology, preserve a position of dominance for majority interests and maintain structural inequality on the ground of race. The same may be said of the Community constructs of 'migrant worker' and 'family' in respect of structural inequality on the ground of sex (Ackers, 1994).

2.1 The construction of 'worker'

To qualify as a 'migrant worker' in the Community sense an EUN must undertake work constituting an 'effective and genuine economic activity', not one which is 'marginal and ancillary'.[49] Although the Court has defined 'work' in this sense generously, for example including part-time work and work for pay lower than subsistence levels, the construct is based on a dichotomy of 'public' and 'private' work, where only work carried out in the public domain qualifies as genuine work. That construction marginalizes the activities of many women, such as care for dependents and unpaid work in private households, as being outside 'true' market activity (Schweiwe, 1994: 243; Lacey, 1987: 413). Although Community law formally requires equality of opportunity in employment for women,[50] the ideology of women's difference, and domesticity, has not been rejected in Community policy, nor in European society. The rhetoric of the legislative framework therefore cannot be translated into practices which challenge institutionalized and structural discrimination.

---

[49] Case 53/81 *Levin* [1982] ECR 1035; Case 139/85 *Kempf* [1986] ECR 1741; Cases 389 & 390/87 *Echternach* [1989] ECR 723; Case 196/87 *Steymann* [1988] ECR 6159; Case 344/87 *Bettray* [1989] ECR 1621.   [50] *Supra* n. 8.

(Glasner, 1992: 81; Pillinger, 1992: 171). Moreover, the gendered division of (public) work and (private) domestic family life is carried over into the construction of the Community provisions concerning families of migrant workers. Community competence to regulate free movement of workers is based on the market justification of free competition in the single European market: 'factors of production' are entitled to move. However, the concept of the market here is used to exclude a 'factor of production' in the European economy: the part played by those (predominantly women) who carry out domestic activities and care for the dependents of workers. Workers and employers alike benefit from those activities, since they enable work to be structured around constant and permanent availability of employees, for example with no need for child-care provision or parental leave. Dominant interests in the market are promoted at the expense of the marginalized group by the construction of 'migrant worker'.

2.2 The construction of 'family'

The gendered construction of 'migrant worker', with its implicit public/private distinction, dovetails with the Community construction of 'family'. The Court's interpretation of the relevant provisions of secondary legislation reveals certain presumptions which inform the construct of 'family' and operate to exclude those who do not fit the presumptive model. The Court's approach to the scope *ratione personae* of the provisions is static and conservative in character and focuses narrowly on the formal legal position in member states. For example, in *Reed*[51] the Court rejected a definition of the term 'spouse' in Regulation 1612/68/EEC which would include couples cohabiting in stable relationships without legal marriage. Rejection of a dynamic interpretation, reflecting social diversity in the member states, has the result of excluding all but those families which conform to the dominant norm (Emmert, 1993: 379; O'Higgins, 1990: 1643). The Court's reasoning is based on the formal legal position in the member states rather than the 'social presence of millions of alternative forms of families in all member states' (Emmert, 1993: 373–4), and thus perpetuates formal structures to the detriment of those excluded by their difference from the

---

[51] Case 59/85 *Netherlands* v. *Reed* [1986] ECR 1296.

perceived norm reflected in those structures. This construct of 'family' excludes in particular on the ground of sex.

The *Diatta* case[52] concerned an EUN husband separated, but not formally divorced, from his TCN wife. The Court held that the woman could benefit from the protections of Community law,[53] but only until the marriage was formally annulled. The effect of the ruling, in the context of German family law, was to give the EUN husband control over expulsion of his wife: on divorce she would cease to be a member of the family for the purposes of Community law. The construct of 'family' implicit in the *Diatta* decision is indirectly discriminatory on the ground of sex. Women are less likely than men to be in the position of 'migrant worker' (Hecq and Plasman, 1991; Jackson, 1990; Schweie, 1994: 249) and thereby to acquire their own residence rights, given that the Court's construct of 'worker' reflects a model of work and family which excludes the work undertaken by many women from the status of 'work'. The disadvantaged position of women in the labour market has the result that women are more vulnerable than men after divorce to exclusion from the member state of residence of the family. TCN women, whose residence rights in the European Union arise only from their legal relationship with an EUN husband, suffer a double jeopardy. Even if they have been able to find work they may still be excluded from the European Union if their marriage breaks down.

Moreover, the Community's formal construct of 'family' is based upon a traditional model which excludes 'atypical' families, for example single parent families. These families are predominantly headed by women;[54] where that woman is not a worker, let alone a Community 'migrant worker', then the family is unable to benefit from the provisions of Community law. If the woman is a worker some form of child-care is necessary and will generally be carried out by another woman, for example a grandparent, aunt, or an unrelated close associate (Glasner, 1992: 84). That unpaid woman carer will only fall within the Community definition of 'family' if she is a dependent ascendant. The Community construct of family reflects a norm which is not experienced by all families, and has a restrictive impact on women, since it is their experience which it least reflects.

[52] Case 267/83 *Diatta* v. *Land Berlin* [1985] ECR 567.
[53] In this case, an entitlement to residence.
[54] EC Commission Communication on Family Policies, COM(89) 363, 7.

2.3 Women and the 'Market'

The Court expressly assumes that the function of provisions concerning family members is to encourage and facilitate the free movement of workers or self-employed persons[55] (Weiler, 1992: 88–9), and, that the rights of family members derive from those of the workers.[56] This has gender implications; as Langan and Ostner point out: 'men are commodified, made ready to sell their labour power on the market, by the work done by women in the family. Women on the other hand are decommodified by their position in the family' (Langan and Ostner, 1991: 131). Community law takes into account the commodification of (male) workers by further commodifying migrant workers with the entitlement of their families to move and reside with them. Since migrant workers are mostly men, the gendered construct of 'family' and the stereotype of the passive, dependent migrant woman are perpetuated. Market considerations, the integration of the single European market, justify the facilitation of men's mobility, but the market justifications have not resulted in structural policies such as child-care facilities, protection of atypical employees and flexible careers, which could increase women's mobility as workers (Ackers, 1994: 393–4; Schweie, 1994: 251).

Even when women do acquire 'worker' status it tends to be as low-paid, low-skill workers, who are less likely to be mobile and to benefit from free movement in the single market (Pillinger, 1992: 57–8; Springe, 1993: 111). TCN migrant women workers are likely to be grouped in work at the periphery of recognized, official economic activity, in the grey economy areas of domestic service, petty trade, seasonal work in agro-industry, or garment manufacturing, assembly work carried out at home (Morokvasic, 1991: 75). 'Migrant workers' in the Community sense, those who are mobile, unencumbered by dependents, with transportable skills, and able

[55] See e.g. Case 40/76 *Kermaschek* [1976] ECR 1669, para. 7; Case 63/76 *Inzirillo* [1976] ECR 2057, para. 17; Case 65/81 *Reina* v. *Landeskreditbank Baden-Württemberg* [1982] ECR 33, para. 12; *Diatta supra* n. 52, para. 16; Case 157/84 *Frascogna* [1985] ECR 1739, paras. 15–17; Case 59/85 *Netherlands* v. *Reed* [1986] ECR 1283, para. 28; Case 131/85 *Gül* [1986] ECR 1573, para 14; Case 249/86 *Commission* v. *Germany* [1989] ECR 1263, para 11; Case C-370/90 *R* v. *Surinder Singh* [1992] 3 CMLR 358.

[56] *Kermaschek supra* n. 55, para. 7; *Frascogna supra* n. 55, paras. 15–17.

therefore to benefit from the labour opportunities in the single European market, are predominantly male (Hecq and Plasman, 1991; Jackson, 1990; Schweiwe, 1994: 249). Women have historically been excluded from positions of dominance on the labour market, partly due to expectations of women as carers and partly through lack of education or acquisition of skills necessary to attain prestigious employment. The Community construction of provisions entitling migrant workers and their families to move freely in the internal market perpetuates structural inequalities in that market.

3. CONCLUSION

The orthodoxy is that the single European market is a level playing field in which all may compete to gain benefits from the free play of competition. Those benefits are eventually to be felt by all through the process of continual improvement of the European economy (Treaty of Rome, Preamble; Article 2). It is assumed that market forces are a beneficial mechanism for economic and social arrangements, whereby the optimum allocation of resources is achieved, and that increased integration through the operation of the market is always desirable. Thus, the idea of the market pervades all substantive areas of Community law including the subject of this essay, Community social law concerning the free movement of persons. The construction of those legal provisions is informed by market interests and justifications: provisions entitling migrant workers and their families to move freely in the European Union are to be understood functionally, in terms of their purpose in the market enterprise.

The metaphor of a level playing field of competition is, however, a false metaphor when it is applied to the labour market. Structural inequalities in the labour market, arising particularly from differential educational qualifications, training and skills, and different expectations and opportunities, result in unequal starting points for the competitors. Individuals enter the labour market from more or less dominant political, economical, or social position and are thus better or worse equipped to compete 'fairly' in the market. This is the real 'two-speed Europe': it can be seen if one compares the experience of the dominant group—mobile migrant workers in full employment—with that of the marginalized group, many of whom are TCNs, members of racial minorities, women, holding guest worker status, and in low paid, low skill employment or unemployed. The position of members of groups which are marginalized at national level is exacerbated by additional discrimination through the operation of market forces at Community level. As far as labour is concerned one cannot (and should not) assume that the 'market' provides a neutral mechanism for the allocation of resources: the market reflects the political and legal constraints within which it functions. The European labour market is permeated by structural and historical discrimination on grounds of race and sex. The institutions of the European Union claim to grant social protections universally and equally, irrespective of race and sex. In many circumstances those social protections appear to be viewed not as constraining the market, but rather constructed in the context of market interests and considerations. The market does not take account of, much less tackle, structural or historical inequalities; in fact, market justifications for policies simply perpetuate existing political or social dominance.

Moreover, as this Chapter has shown, European institutions do not merely promulgate a 'neutral' *idea* of market forces but proceed by reference to a predetermined functional market *ideology*. The function of the Community market ideology seems to be to determine *precisely which* interests are to be promoted in the name of the market. It is this market ideology, not simple free competition, which informs, for example, the (directly or indirectly) racially discriminatory construct of 'European', which in turn defines 'migrant worker' and 'family' in the context of Community law. 'European' in this context promotes the interests of those already within the Community labour market but excludes on the ground of race. The scope of the (potential) European labour market in this context is not defined neutrally, for example by reference to a global labour market, but according to a protectionist distinction between 'real' European workers (EUNs) and other workers. Similarly, the Community's market ideology constructs 'work' so as to exclude voluntary domestic or caring work, work which commodifies 'real' market actors, thereby protecting their interests, but excludes on the ground of sex. The pervasive market ideology of Community law does not only promote dominant interests, it appears to translate the rhetoric of universal protection of Community social provision into particularism and exclusion, *inter alia* on grounds of sex and race. In the light of this observation, the outcome of the interplay between the 'social' and 'market' functions of Community social legislation, such as that enabling the free movement of workers, appears to depend upon the context in which that interplay takes place. The Community provisions are constructed according to their universalist 'social' function only where to do so actually serves a latent 'market' ideology. In other words, in this context the distinction between 'social' and 'market' function appears to be a misleading dichotomy because all matters are ultimately resolved by reference to market ideology.

W(h)ither Social Policy?

ELAINE A. WHITEFORD

Despite repeated political affirmations in the past that member states attach the same significance to the development of the EC social dimension as they do to its economic activities, the results of Community activity in the social sphere have been disappointing. The member states were presented with the opportunity to remedy this state of affairs by the Intergovernmental Conferences launched in December 1990 which had the objective of preparing amendments to the Treaty of Rome. As a consequence of the resulting Treaty on European Union (TEU), alongside the existing social chapter of the Treaty (Articles 117–22 EC) which applies (currently) to all fifteen member states, a Protocol on Social Policy ('the Protocol') was signed to which was appended the Agreement on Social Policy ('the Agreement'). The Agreement provides the Community with more extensive powers to adopt legislation in the social sphere, although any texts adopted will not apply in the United Kingdom.[1] Additionally, and alternatively, machinery is put in place which appears to serve the objective of granting collective agreements concluded at European level with binding status (excluding the UK) under Community law. The social partners are given the opportunity to freeze the conventional legislative process for the purposes of reaching agreement themselves. In the event that such agreement is reached they may require that the Council enshrine the agreement in a decision, with decision-making either by unanimity or qualified majority. This is a significant advance on Article 118B EC which merely provides for relations between the social partners 'based on agreement'.

The position advanced in this essay is that it is extremely unlikely that either of these procedures will result in the adoption of a significant body of EC social law. Rather, it will be demonstrated

---

[1] Barnard, 1992; Bercusson, 1993, 1994; Bercusson and van Dijk, 1995; Fitzpatrick, 1992; Rhodes, 1993; Schuster, 1992; Seché, 1993; Shaw, 1994; Szyszczak, 1994, 1995; Watson, 1993; Weiss, 1992; Whiteford 1993a, 1993b.

that to the extent that any measures seem likely to emerge in the
social field, they will take the form of soft law (Wellens and
Borchardt, 1989). The first of the following sections will focus on the
legislative path leading to the adoption of measures by the reduced
Council. While the objective of that section will be to predict the
likelihood of substantial legislative measures emerging from
the process, the analysis will also demonstrate the reasons why the
results of the social dimension to date have been so disappointing.
Additionally, an attempt will be made to unearth the hidden
agendas of the individual member states when debating subjects in
Council. The second section of the paper will examine the procedure
for allowing the social partners to reach agreement at European
level. Again the object will be to assess the chances of this procedure
producing the kinds of agreement envisaged by the drafters. On the
basis of the conclusions of those two sections, a recommendation will
be made as to the path which the Commission should follow in the
future to maximize the social dimension of the internal market.

1. THE MEMBER STATES

The impression has always been given by both academics and
politicians that the blame for the inadequate results obtained in
relation to the social dimension can be laid squarely at the door of
the UK government which, as a consequence of its scepticism in this
field, often appeared prepared to veto all proposals. It would seem
reasonable to expect that, freed from the ideological shackles worn
by the recent governments of that state, the other member states
would be able to reach agreement on a more impressive body of
social regulations. Indeed, initial developments seemed to bear out
these expectations. After the Intergovernmental Conferences had
been concluded, but prior to the signing of the TEU on 7 February
1992, the then Dutch Prime Minister, Ruud Lubbers sent a letter to
each of the signatories of the Agreement on Social Policy in which he
proposed that the member states meet to water down the text of the
Agreement with the objective of securing UK adherence and further
progress as twelve.[2] This initiative foundered when only the
Portuguese demonstrated any willingness to proceed along this

---

[2] See *Agence Europe* No. 5632, 18 Dec. 1991, 6.

path.[3] It is therefore possible to interpret this chain of events as evidence of political commitment finally to ensure that the activities carried out to develop the social dimension were the equal of those pursued in the economic field.

In this respect considerable scope for legislative activity is created by the provisions of the Agreement. In terms of the traditional legislative process (*in casu*, for the adoption of Directives) Article 2 of the Agreement considerably expands the number of subjects over which the 'Community' is granted legislative competence. Thus, 'Community' action can be taken as regards (i) the working environment and health and safety, (ii) working conditions, (iii) equality between women and men with regard to labour market opportunities and treatment at work, and (iv) the integration of persons excluded from the labour market.[4] Decision-making on these subjects can be by qualified majority vote. Article 2(3) mandates the adoption of Directives dealing with social security and social protection of workers, worker protection on termination of employment contracts, rights of representation and collective defence, employment conditions for legally resident third country nationals, and financial contributions for employment creation outwith the framework of the European Social Fund. Although any decisions taken on these subjects require unanimity these do represent the first provisions granting the Community specific competence over these matters. Nevertheless, pay, the right of association, the right to strike, and the right to impose lock-outs are subjects over which the Community still has no competence.[5] Although Community legislative competence is expanded by the TEU

[t]he extension is largely confined to issues that are essentially regulatory in character, preventing producers from using certain work practices and conditions to enhance their competitiveness. Such practices are those that tend to be used more often by the relatively lower technology, more labor-intensive producers, more heavily concentrated in the poorer countries and regions of the Community (Lange, 1993: 12).

Thus it is possible that, rather than being utilized to improve the levels of worker protection throughout the EC, the Agreement will in

---

[3] *Staatscourant* no. 249 1991, 25 Dec. 1991, 1.
[4] Art. 2(1).   [5] Art. 2(6).

fact have an asymmetrical impact on the member states, imposing the most burdensome obligations on the poorest member states.

In the pre-Maastricht period all member states could be reasonably certain that the British would block all or most proposals in the social field. Consequently, high-sounding political declarations of commitment to the social dimension and of raising the living and working conditions of Community citizens could be made with impunity, safe in the knowledge that they would not have to be translated into hard political deeds. Therefore, as Lange has observed, the political rhetoric of the pre-Maastricht period is singularly unreliable and even misleading, and is no basis upon which to predict the future shape of EC social policy (Lange, 1992: 235). Nevertheless, it is suggested that the past conduct of the member states, as revealed by the texts agreed in Council and the voting patterns, can usefully serve as a base for such a prediction. In fact the debates carried out in Council and the texts which finally emerged suggest that the member states have already been pursuing a course deliberately designed to have such asymmetrical impact.

The most recent pre-Maastricht initiative effectively to launch the social dimension was the Community Charter of the Fundamental Social Rights of Workers (Bercusson, 1990a; Watson, 1991). This solemn declaration, which was agreed by eleven of the twelve member states (the UK excepted) in December 1989, did not contain any autonomous machinery for its implementation. Consequently it was to be implemented through the normal legislative machinery of the Community the results of which would be binding on all twelve member states, despite the UK's refusal to sign the Charter. However, the results obtained in implementing it have hardly matched the expectations created on its launch since the interminable negotiations produced weak texts[6] and reveal deep

---

[6] The texts are weak in the sense—elaborated below—that they require only the least regulated states to increase the level of protection accorded to employees, with the majority of member states being able to maintain their *status quo*.

Compare the Commission's proposals in COM(90) 563 and OJ 1991 C24/3 with the resulting Dir. 91/533 on the employer's obligation to inform employees of the conditions applicable to the contract or employment relationship, OJ 1991 L288/32. The memorandum stated that the directive 'specifically concerns those workers who have neither a written contract of employment nor a letter of appointment'. However, the directive as adopted covers 'every paid employee having a contract of

divisions between the various member states.[7] Thus, prior to the entry into force of the TEU, the Directive on the protection of pregnant women at work pitted the Italians, who wanted more far-reaching measures, against the other member states who were much more conservative, with the British admittedly the least enthusiastic. As for the draft directive on the organization of working time,[8] the British challenged the necessity for such a proposal, with the French and the Germans at daggers drawn concerning the reference period for the calculation of hours worked, each staunchly defending their national position. The Spanish expressed particular reluctance as regards the recommendation on sufficient means in social protection systems,[9] deeming that the Community should first create a solidarity fund to aid the poorer member states, an example which vividly illustrates the kind of horse-trading which regularly takes place in Council. Equally, the southern member states have in general been unenthusiastic as regards the draft directive on the posting of workers abroad[10] for fear of the consequences of this proposal for their competitive positions.[11] This small selection of examples demonstrates that although UK opposition can virtually be taken as read, the other member states are much more cautious in reality than their rhetoric would suggest. They too seek to defend their current national positions.

employment or employment relationship defined by the law in force in a Member State and/or governed by the law in force in a Member State'. In other words, if the employee is able to prove under national law that he has an employment relationship, he is also covered by this directive. An examination of the proposals presented pursuant to the Commission's Action Programme reveals that the proposals have without exception been so watered down that they simply fail to meet the objectives set on their launch. On this subject, and for further examples, see Whiteford, 1993a.

[7] Much of the information for this section has been obtained from reports of Council meetings made to the Dutch Parliament. Where this is the case the document number is prefaced by the parliamentary year and the abbreviation TK (*Tweede Kamer*), the second chamber of the Dutch Parliament.

[8] OJ 1990 C254/4. Eventually adopted as Dir. 93/104, OJ 1993 L307/18. The British opposition to this Directive remained unweakened and has in fact led to a challenge of the Directive's legal basis. See Case C-84/94 *UK* v. *Council*, OJ 1994 C120/13.

[9] Recommendation 92/441, OJ 1992 L245/46.

[10] OJ 1991 C225/6. It appears that the other member states have been strongly divided as to the content of this proposal and its legal basis has been particularly thorny. TK 1994–5, 21 501–18 nr 40, 2. See the reports of the meeting of the Social Affairs Council of 27 Mar. 1995 in *Agence Europe* No. 6448, March 25 1995, 9–10 and No. 6449, 27–8 Mar. 1995, 6–7.

[11] TK 1992–3, 21 240 nr 17, 12; reaffirmed at TK 1992–3, 21 501–18 nr 20, 12.

One of the most high-profile areas of Commission action to implement the Charter concerned the position of atypical workers.[12] Admittedly, one of the three proposals did reach the statute book in the form of Directive 91/383, although in a greatly watered down form.[13] However, the remaining two proposals containing the more important substantive rights have divided the member states deeply. The original draft directive on certain employment relationships with regard to competition[14] based on Article 100A EC received the support of few (if any) member states, the legal base chosen being rejected by many[15] and the linkage of social policy with competition being rejected by others.[16] In practice both objections mean that the only alternative is a proposal based on a Treaty Article requiring unanimity, either Article 100 or Article 235 EC. The parallel directive on certain working conditions based on Article 100 EC has scarcely been discussed, and was in fact rejected in its entirety by the European Parliament because of the choice of legal basis.[17] In an attempt to resolve the impasse the recent Belgian Presidency relaunched an old German compromise document on atypical work. Although no text of this proposal has been published it is reported to have taken the form of a framework directive and to have been based on Article 100 EC. The proposal apparently envisaged that all atypical employees would be granted the same rights to a minimum wage, annual holidays, and statutory social security accrual, and would be included in the workforce for the purposes of calculating representativity thresholds. The Dutch at least are on record as objecting to the extension of social security rights to this group. Although it was British demands for derogations which finally resulted in the death of this particular initiative, it appears that objections were voiced from several quarters. When stalemate was

[12] 'In the eyes of the Commission, this proposal is of great importance', Communication from the Commission concerning its Action Programme relating to the Implementation of the Community Charter of Basic Social Rights for Workers, COM(89) 568, 15.

[13] Dir. 91/383, OJ 1991 L206/19. Cf. the original draft published at OJ 1990 C224/8 and the Commission's explanatory memorandum, COM(90) 228.

[14] OJ 1990 C224/6.

[15] They consider that the Directive concerns the 'rights and interests of employed persons' which is excepted from Art. 100A by Art. 100A(2). For a vigorous rejection of this 'narrow' approach by the member states see Bercusson, 1990b.

[16] TK 1990–1991, 21 501–18, nr. 5.

[17] OJ 1990 C324/96.

finally reached on this initiative, another German initiative, also based on Article 100 EC, promptly replaced it. This, however, further reduced the number of individuals who would benefit. References to social security have also apparently been removed from this draft, thereby stripping it of much of its practical significance.[18] Although British opposition has finally convinced the remaining member states that if progress is to be made the mechanism of the Agreement will have to be used, it should be noted that the weakening of the text was not solely due to British objections. Moreover, it is far from certain that the legislative path available under the Agreement will lead to the adoption of a text. It is also worth noting that after the entry into force of the TEU in the context of this specific proposal, the Dutch counselled against too speedy resort to the mechanism of the Social Policy Agreement, where it was uncertain, as here, that this procedure would have significantly greater chances of success. Consequently, it remains at best uncertain what value any resulting legislative provision will provide for employees in the majority of member states.

In short, while the UK objections to Community action in the social field appear to have been consistent and predictable, the positions taken by other member states diverge significantly from their public affirmations of support for the social dimension.[19] Particularly when qualified majority voting was possible, blame for the weak texts cannot be laid solely at the door of the British. The observation that 'Rather than moving in the direction of common objectives which would signify social progress, the national ministers (and their technical experts) generally conducted the negotiations by reference to their existing national legislation, concerned to stay as close as possible to the situation in their own country and above all, not to weaken their own competitive position' (Hutsebaut, 1993: 28) seems to be borne out by experience. The kinds of opposition voiced by the various national politicians seem in fact to indicate that economic considerations related to their

[18] All these details can be found in TK 1993–4 21 501–18 nr 10 and TK 1993–4 21 501–18 nr 20.
[19] See also the comment of the Luxembourg President of the Council that 'the inability of the Council to decide was not always imputable to the single "non-continental" Member State he had [previously] cited' (referring to the UK), *Agence Europe* No. 5492, 16 May 1991, 10.

competitive positions dominated the debate. None of the member states seems willing to agree standards and, by implication, costs which raise protection in their jurisdiction. The conclusion seems inevitable and unsurprising: political reality differs significantly from the political rhetoric and, despite political declarations to the contrary, actions in this field are influenced by economic rather than purely social considerations.

If this is true, it is also the case that this approach has a long pedigree at EC level, since the EC has traditionally viewed its social dimension in economic terms. In the 1956 ILO Report into *Social Aspects of European Economic Co-operation* the experts in question concluded that

[i]nternational differences in the general level of worker's remuneration, far from being an obstacle to freer international trade, are, so long as differences in productivity persist, indispensable, though not in themselves sufficient, to ensure the allocation of manpower and capital in each country to those industries in which it has the greatest advantages or the smallest disadvantages, so as to ensure maximum output and incomes in all participating countries.[20]

As a consequence the drafters of the Treaty of Rome granted the EC no competence to harmonize social costs as this was not seen to be necessary for the creation of the single market. It is stressed that the EC's abstention from social affairs is premised on the market ensuring that appropriate costs are set in each national market. While market factors differ, different social costs are viewed as a natural consequence and as presenting no threat to the operation of the single market. On this view, social dumping occurs not where social costs differ between member states but where one member state artificially depresses its social costs as an instrument of improving competitiveness.

Although this still remains the orthodoxy, the debates and texts discussed above create the impression that the member states actually consider that differences in social costs *are* an extremely important determinant of their competitive position. As was demonstrated, they invariably defend their existing national positions staunchly, the majority preferring to increase the regulatory burden on the least regulated rather than to improve

---

[20] Studies and Reports, ILO New Series No. 46, Geneva, 1956, 111.

the level of legal protection enjoyed by their own citizens.[21] In fact it is possible to characterize the current political 'enthusiasm' for the development of the social dimension as an attempt by the more highly regulated economies to 'raise their rivals' costs' (Vaubel, 1995; Lange, 1993). This argument suggests that among the high-cost majority member states, lower social costs elsewhere are seen as a threat to the higher standards pertaining in the majority. Therefore votes can be won at home by introducing common minimum standards higher than those prevailing in the low cost economies and effectively raising rivals' costs. This can most easily be engineered where only a qualified majority of the votes are needed to pass a proposal. This allows the high-cost member states to group together to impose the standards applicable in the lowest 'high-cost' economy on the low-cost economies of the minority,[22] a strategy which, as observed above, can be seen to have become significantly easier as a consequence of the Agreement on Social Policy.

These economic and political considerations may explain both the attitudes in Council mentioned above and the generally low level of legal protection contained in the texts finally agreed. However, it also suggests that, stripped of the predictable objections of the UK, agreement in the 'reduced' Council (in which talk is no longer cheap) will remain difficult and the resulting texts will remain weak. In fact, if the UK opt-out is explained in terms of raising rivals' costs, it may of itself make agreement in the reduced Council significantly more difficult. Ironically, the absence of the UK from the negotiating table may prove as effective a barrier to reaching agreement at EC level as did its ideological opposition in the past.

In sum, it seems that the removal of UK objections will not make agreement on social policy measures in the Council easier. Rather, it will force the other member states to reassess their position on EC social policy as the 'threat' of expensive social legislation becomes more real following the extension of the possibilities for taking

---

[21] Indeed, a perusal of recent reports concerning developments at the national level seems to indicate that national policies of deregulation, lowering the legal protection afforded to workers, are being followed, albeit with varying degrees of intensity. See e.g. EIRR 252 (1995), 2–11.

[22] Vaubel and Lange have designed tables illustrating which member state is pivotal for which proposal (Vaubel, 1995; Lange, 1993).

decisions by qualified majority. This extension may encourage the majority to attempt to raise the costs of the minority in an attempt to retain majority competitiveness, a thesis which seems to be supported by the Council discussions outlined above. Whether political agreement will in fact ever be reached remains an open question, but it seems certain that any texts which are adopted by the Council pursuant to the procedures put in place by the Agreement will be weak, designed not to improve the protection of workers throughout the Community but instead to impose costs on particular low-cost producers. In this respect, and contrary to what might be expected, the Agreement on Social Policy seems likely, if anything, to achieve social dumping in reverse, whereby the high-cost economies impose certain costs on their low-cost competitors, to the detriment of the latter.

2. THE SOCIAL PARTNERS

The increased role accorded to the social partners by the TEU is significant and has already been the subject of extensive academic analysis (Bercusson, 1993, 1994; Fitzpatrick, 1992). Instead of the Commission merely being obliged to promote social dialogue with the objective of stimulating relations based on agreement, the social partners now have the right to be consulted on the contents of any proposals made in the social sphere. This is a significant alteration in their position, the informal and essentially undemocratic process of lobbying by both parties being replaced by institutionalized procedures for consultation. In short, the social partners are accorded a formal role in the legislative process in the social field.

Under the previous arrangements (ETUI 1992, 1993a, 1993b, 1994) any dialogue between the social partners could lead to 'relations based on agreement', whose precise legal status was extremely unclear. This procedure was initially established at the instigation of the Commission President Delors in an attempt to un-block some of the social dossiers from the paralysis then afflicting the Council. In fact, pursuant to this so-called 'Val Duchesse process' a number of 'joint opinions' were concluded, although they had no influence whatsoever on the conduct of the actors at national level (Christensen, 1993). The TEU addresses this problem, providing that the social dialogue can lead to 'contractual relations, including agreements', which appears to envisage legally binding arrange-ments.[23] Furthermore, depending on the subject matter of the measures in question, these agreements may be implemented either by means of a Council decision or 'in accordance with the procedures and practices specific to management and labour and the Member States'.[24] This clearly marks the intention of the drafters that agreements should enjoy binding legal status. As such, the Agreement represents a significant advance in the position of the social partners.

However, it is suggested that a number of circumstances make it extremely unlikely that many such European level collective agreements will be concluded (Szyszczak, 1995: 24–5).[25] Obviously, the operation of the system is premised on the good faith of both parties. The text of the Agreement was the result of negotiations between the social partners at European level.[26] However, it has been suggested (Bercusson, 1993; Fitzpatrick, 1992) that the acquiescence of employers was only obtained because they feared that failure to reach agreement would result in a more far-reaching text over which they could exercise little influence. This hardly bodes favourably for the future of the bargaining process put in place by the arrangement. So the first problem is the extent to which it seems reasonable to expect that agreement will be reached between employers and employees at the intersectoral European level. In this respect the results of the current Val Duchesse process seem far from encouraging. Although eight Joint Opinions were adopted in the six years following the beginning of the process in 1985, by 1988 the ETUC was already complaining about UNICE's apparent lack of committment to the process (Hutsebaut, 1993: 58). The situation in the pre-Charter period is succinctly described as follows:

---

[23] Art. 4(1) of the Agreement on Social Policy.

[24] Art. 4(2) ibid.

[25] Also Communication concerning the application of the Agreement on Social Policy presented by the Commission to the Council and to the European Parliament, COM(93) 600.

[26] At the request of Ms. Papendreou, then Commissioner of Social Affairs, the Steering Committee on the Social Dialogue (bringing together officials from ETUC, UNICE, and CEEP and chaired by the Commission) set up an *ad hoc* group to examine the role of the social partners in the new institutional setting of a revised treaty (Christensen, 1993: 45) (see also ETUI, 1992: 65).

Even though the partners stated their political will to continue the dialogue it was different rationales which dictated the political willingness. ETUC wanted legislation, especially focusing on the nascent discussion of the Social Charter and subsequently on the Social Action Programme (SAP). A refusal to discuss a subject within the framework of the dialogue was perceived to put at risk the possibility of legislation.

The attitude of the employers was that a joint opinion was second best to doing nothing, but that not to participate in the dialogue was perceived to invite legislation, which was considered even worse (Hutsebaut, 1993: 44).

A recent example seems to confirm the distance which separates the partners in approaching negotiations. In the post-Maastricht period the social partners were given the opportunity to reach agreement on the subject of Works Councils. Negotiations on this subject had been ongoing in Council for more than twenty years and it had become abundantly clear that the major obstacle to reaching agreement on a text was British opposition. So on the entry into force of the TEU, the Commission already had a text which was, by and large, acceptable to the eleven and which, in the event that negotiations between the social partners failed, could be submitted to the reduced Council for adoption.[27] In this case the Commission text appears largely to have reflected the wishes of the employee representatives. As a consequence, the parties can be seen to have commenced the bargaining process from different situations, in that bargaining was largely 'in the shadow' of a text acceptable to the employee representatives but not to the employer representatives. Indeed the President of UNICE suggested as much, observing that it was extremely difficult to negotiate with one partner who knows that if the negotiations fail the other partner has more to lose.[28] In fact, the 'bargaining in the shadow of the law' (Bercusson, 1993) put in place by the TEU is best summarized thus: 'the Protocol shifts a good deal of agenda setting initiative to the collective bargaining partners, [and therefore] the effect of the new rules depends substantially on an intricate game between European unions and employers' associations played in the context of expectations about

---

[27] The proposal was adopted as Council Dir. 94/45/EC of 22 Sep. 1994 on the establishment of a European Works Council or a procedure in Community-scale undertakings and Community-scale groups of undertakings for the purposes of informing and consulting employees, OJ 1994 L254/64.

[28] *Agence Europe*, No 6202, 31 Mar. 1994, 16.

the likely behaviour of the Commission and, ultimately, and therefore crucially, the Council' (Lange, 1993: 13).

It seems inevitable that one party will always have an interest in the failure of the negotiations. The preceding section concluded that it was extremely unlikely that the Council would agree texts which would significantly improve the protection afforded to workers in the majority of member states. Accordingly it seems that, in contrast to the situation for works councils, employee representatives have most to gain from negotiation, and that employers run little risk if negotiations fail and therefore need make few concessions to employee demands. As Rhodes observes: 'Concerned at the loss of its ally should the eleven take the Social Agreement path, the employers now have a means of replacing the United Kingdom veto with their own' (Rhodes, 1993: 300–301).

In intersectoral negotiations, agreement seems doubly unlikely because of the variety of interests which must be represented. This was demonstrated in the contributions recently made to the Commission's White Paper *European Social Policy—A Way Forward for the Union*,[29] which includes a summary of the parties' (governments', NGOs', the social partners') positions on a catalogue of social issues. For these purposes, dissonance between the social partners can be observed on 'the balance proposed between legislation and collective bargaining', with the unions including a wide range of issues in their list of legislative demands. The employers, on the other hand, were considerably more reticent, going so far indeed as to indicate a number of issues which they wished explicitly to be excluded from legislative activity.[30] Equally, no agreement can be discerned as to the level at which norms should be set:

EU-level collective agreements are supported by the unions, especially in industry branches and for trans-national companies but employers' organisations generally reject the need for these and say it should be left to national level collective bargaining ... There is, however, a general agreement that EU action in [relation to labour law and policies on working conditions] should be in the form of framework agreements, achieved in close consultation with the social partners and other relevant groups and respecting their autonomy. There is a call for binding minimum standards (unions, NGOs, several governments, local authorities) in the field of labour law, with a convergence towards higher levels. Employers' organisations are

[29] COM(94) 333.

generally less supportive of this view and would also in this field prefer a 'natural rhythm' of convergence, in line with financial realities.'[31]

This suggests that agreement will in fact prove extremely difficult and that it is therefore unlikely that the machinery put in place by the TEU will ever result in any significant number of intersectoral agreements.

Whether intersectoral agreements have ever been a realistic prospect remains a moot point. Agreements at sectoral level seem to offer a much greater chance of success since the groups concerned are more heterogeneous (ETUI, 1993a). Nevertheless: 'it seems both naïve and ahistorical to ignore the substantial dissonance of interest within classes, and the possible confluence of interest across classes, that occurs within and across nations in an environment of intense economic competitiveness and rapid economic change.' (Lange, 1992: 238)

In other words, it is precisely at the sectoral level that the interests of politicians representing high-cost economies in raising their rivals' costs through Council legislation are likely to be shared by unions and employers (ETUI 1992, 1993a, 1993b, 1994). It is therefore possible that, in contrast to the division in intersectoral negotiations which seems set to be between employers and employees, the fissure in sectoral negotiations will, as in the Council, be between high- and low-cost countries.

In conclusion, it seems likely that no substantial body of legislation will ever be agreed between the social partners at the EU level; the interests being represented seem too diverse to allow agreements to be reached. Additionally, as was concluded above, it is unlikely that the Council will agree to legislative measures to increase employee protection. Consequently, incentives for the social partners to carry out serious negotiations are likely to be uneven: employees have every incentive to argue for regulation; employers precisely the opposite.

3. WHITHER SOCIAL POLICY?

Over the last decade the role played by the Commission in relation to social affairs has been transformed. Led by its President, Jacques

---

[30] Ibid. 3.   [31] Ibid. 14.

Delors, it shrugged off the paralysis which afflicted it in the early 1980s and became the motor driving the (re-)launch of the social dimension. This determination can be seen in its success (encouraged by the Economic and Social Committee and the European Parliament)[32] in effectively setting the agenda for the Charter initiative and keeping it on course. Equally, its swift response to the Charter mandate to draw up an Action Programme for the implementation of Charter rights (drawn up even before the formal adoption of the Charter text) allowed the momentum behind this initiative to be maintained and maximum results to be squeezed from the Council.[33]

The policy in the social field which has traditionally been pursued by the Commission is best described as laying down minimum standards applicable in all member states. In this the Commission could be seen as trying to ensure that a basic floor of rights was put in place at Community level (Mückenberger and Deakin, 1989). Indeed, the Commission recently reaffirmed its support for this position: 'The establishment of a framework of basic minimum standards, which the Commission started some years ago, provides a bulwark against using low social standards as an instrument of unfair competition and protection against reducing social standards to gain competitiveness.'[34] Nevertheless, an examination of recent initiatives discloses a blurring of the traditional Commission line. In the past the Commission seemed committed to the Community law norm being the minimum level of protection pertaining in the Community. However, both the Directive on Working Time and that on the protection of young people at work[35] contain a breathtaking number of provisions from which derogation is permitted.[36] This development, while undoubtedly a response to political demands of member states in Council, represents a departure from the traditional Community approach to legislation

---

[32] See the Opinion of the Economic and Social Committee on basic Community social rights, OJ 1989 C126/4 and Resolution of the European Parliament on the Community Charter of Fundamental Social Rights, OJ 1989 C323/44.

[33] This is of course not to say that the results of the Charter are particularly impressive. Rather it recognizes that the Commission probably obtained the results which were politically feasible.   [34] COM(94) 333, 5.

[35] Dir. 94/33, OJ 1994 L216/12.

[36] Art. 17 of the Working Time Directive, *supra* n. 9. Art. 5(3), 7(3), 8(5), 10(4), and 17(1)(b) of the Directive on the protection of young persons at work, ibid.

in this field, and hollows out the (meagre) norms agreed at supranational level.

More concrete evidence of a change of attitude in the Commission can be distilled from other recent documents. In the recent White Paper on *Growth, Competitiveness and Employment*[37] it deduces from the contributions of the member states the policies which should be pursued for the future. This White Paper was prompted by one consideration: unemployment. It identifies as the cause of the structural unemployment currently crippling Europe the poor functioning of the labour market, particularly lack of flexibility *vis-à-vis* the organization of working time, wages, and mobility.[38] Compulsory social security deductions are also cited as a barrier to employment creation, and branded as a disincentive for seeking work. More generally, the Commission concludes that the social security systems of the member states have had negative effects on employment, particularly because the rules primarily protect those in employment, at the expense of others. The proposed solution is the fundamental reform of the employment market to encourage more flexible organization of employment and division of working time, lower wage costs, better qualifications, and a more active employment policy.[39] The sub-text is clearly the dismantling of the frameworks built up in the past for the legal protection for workers.[40] Although it observes that the member states seem to be in agreement on these issues, the Commission concludes in the White Paper on Social Policy that there is no consensus amongst member states about the shape which EC Social Policy should take in future.

In certain respects this conclusion is unsurprising. As outlined in the preceding sections, the position in the Council is complex. Despite the high-sounding political rhetoric, there is in fact little political will to act in the social sphere, beyond measures (apparently) aimed at raising the costs of the lower-cost member states, which has become considerably easier as a consequence of the Agreement on Social Policy. This is the reality which the Commission must bear in mind when making proposals in the social

[37] Bull. EC Supp. 6/93.
[38] This makes it clear that the flexibility sought is for the employer rather than for the employee.
[39] In this respect the Commission is aligning itself with national developments.
[40] See G. More below.

sphere, a reality which discourages overly ambitious legislative proposals. Equally, however, recent pronouncements indicate that the Commission has moved significantly closer to the position defended by the majority of the member states in Council and is consequently now much more chary of improving worker protection for fear of negative economic consequences. In other words, it is unlikely that the Commission will come forward with legislative proposals involving a high level of employee protection. This position appears to be based on a political conviction within the Commission itself, but can also be seen as a pragmatic response to the political currents within the Council.

Accordingly, and moving on to the second section of this essay, the social partners need not expect that their negotiations will take place 'in the shadow of the law' providing a high level of protection. Consequently, collective agreements on matters of substance seem to be a largely theoretical possibility. In short, it is unlikely that a significant body of binding measures (of whatever form) will emerge from the machinery put in place by the TEU.

Assuming that it wishes to maximize the political rhetoric which continues to surround the social dimension, what ought the Commission to do? Far-reaching legislative texts seem likely only to antagonize factions within the Council and will remove much of the urgency of negotiations for one of the social partners. On the other hand, doing nothing can hardly be an attractive option for the Commission, if its professions of commitment to the social dimension are to be believed. Accordingly, it is submitted that the best course is one which the Commission has already begun to follow: the path towards soft-law, non-binding measures.[41] Such measures are politically non-threatening in that they do not require any action to realize the agreed objectives. On the other hand, they do provide the actors in the field with guidelines against which the conduct of governments, employers, and employees can be measured. As such, these measures can be seen to have at least moral or persuasive force and some of them will not be without legal effect, since 'national courts are bound to take recommendations into consideration in order to decide disputes submitted to them, in

---

[41] For a recent example see the Commission's Action Programme in response to the White Paper on Social Policy, a document singularly bereft of proposals for binding measures, COM(95) 134.

particular where they cast light on the interpretation of national measures adopted to implement them or where they are designed to supplement binding Community provisions'.[42]

The fact that agreement to such soft measures does not require translation into binding national provisions means that political agreement should be more easily reached. Additionally, this will be free of the shadow of the agreement having been reached with the objective of raising rivals costs. The path to soft law can thus be seen to free the debate on social policy from the economic straightjacket within which it has been constrained for so long, allowing 'principled' decisions to be taken. In this respect soft law can be viewed as the most effective method of obtaining political support for the maintenance of social standards at a time when nationally they have come under sustained attack. Indeed it is not inconceivable that such international standards will act as a buffer against the worst excesses of the deregulatory zeal curently gripping Europe. The somewhat ironic conclusion must therefore be that, precisely at the moment in time when the mechanisms have finally been put in place to allow a significant body of social legislation to be adopted at Community level, events have conspired to ensure that soft law is not only the most likely but also the most promising way forward for EC social policy.

[42] Case C-322/88 *Grimaldi* v. *Fonds des Maladies Professionnelles* [1989] ECR 4407, para. 18.

The Acquired Rights Directive: Frustrating or Facilitating Labour Market Flexibility?

GILLIAN MORE

The purpose of this essay is to explore the apparent contradictions between the aim of employment protection pursued by Directive 77/187 on the approximation of the laws of the Member States relating to the safeguarding of employees' rights in the event of transfers of undertakings, businesses, or parts of businesses (hereinafter, the 'Acquired Rights Directive')[1] and the aims of the governments of the member states of the European Union in pursuing labour market flexibility. A consideration of this contradiction has been prompted by the lobbying of some member states to change the wording (and hence application) of the Acquired Rights Directive in the course of the revision of the Directive proposed by the Commission.[2] The agenda behind such lobbying is clear: certain member states—the United Kingdom and Germany in particular—seek to reverse the effect of judgments of the Court of Justice which have held that the Acquired Rights Directive can apply to protect employees transferred by virtue of the contracting out of services.[3] The attempt to rewrite the Directive appears to be motivated by a belief that the Court's interpretation of the Directive considerably restricts the utility of contracting out as a flexible form of business organization.[4] The debate around the Directive therefore puts in clear focus the tension between guaranteeing employment protection on one hand and promoting flexibility of business operation on the other. Moreover, the debate feeds into one of the

---

[1] OJ 1977 L61/26. [2] COM(94) 300.

[3] Case C-209/91 *Rask* v. *ISS Kantineservice A/S* [1992] ECR I-5755; Case C-392/92 *Schmidt* v. *Spar- und Leihkasse der früheren Ämter Bordesholm, Kiel und Cronshagen* [1994] ECR I-1311.

[4] See e.g. 'Britain close to victory on contracting-out of services' *Financial Times* 31 May 1994.

wider debates evident in the Commission's 1993 White Paper on Growth, Competitiveness and Employment,[5] namely: to what extent is employment market regulation in the European Union compatible with the maintainance of global competitiveness and the achievement of economic growth.[6]

This essay examines first the background of the Directive, and then considers how it has been interpreted by the Court of Justice. There follows a brief consideration of criticisms of the Court's decisions in relation to the application of the Acquired Rights Directive to contracting out. These criticisms are developed further in the context of a discussion of the meaning of labour market flexibility and, in particular, of the nature of contracting out as a flexible employment form. What the essay then seeks to establish, on policy grounds, is that the detrimental implications of contracting out for the employment relationship are such that a minimum level of protection for employees must be provided. This, it is argued, has been provided by the Court's interpretation of the Acquired Rights Directive.

1. THE ACQUIRED RIGHTS DIRECTIVE

The Acquired Rights Directive originated in the 1974 Community Social Action Programme, which was intended to give the European Community a 'human face' (Shanks, 1977: 3–6). The programme was meant to ameliorate the 'unacceptable by-products of growth': the geographical unevenness of growth, the exclusion of certain groups from the benefits of growth, and especially the deleterious effects on the workforce of the restructuring of capital within the common market.[7] Michael Shanks, Director-General for social affairs in the European Commission during the period in which the Social Action Programme was drawn up, summed up his view of the programme thus: 'Above all, what the social action programme of 1974–1976 sought to do was to humanise the process of industrial change, on the basis that if this were not done the process of

---

[5] EC Commission, *Growth, Competitiveness, Employment: the Challenges and Ways Forward into the 21st Century* Bull. EC, Supp. 6/93.

[6] A wider discussion of this debate is provided by E. Whiteford's essay, above.

[7] Bull. EC, Supp. 2/74, 13.

economic growth could itself be stopped by a backlash of social and political resistance. All of this to my mind was, and remains, politically valid, even though its base in the Treaty of Rome was and remains tenuous' (Shanks, 1978: 5).

On the basis of the Programme the Commission proposed two directives which would affect the labour law of the member states: first, it proposed a directive on procedures for collective dismissals, 'in order to reduce job insecurity, which is today a potent and evident cause of industrial unrest and suspicion'; secondly, and with no additional rationale, it proposed a 'directive on the protection of the rights of workers in mergers'.[8] The latter was the Acquired Rights Directive in embryonic form.

The Acquired Rights Directive was unanimously adopted by the Council of Ministers in 1977 in accordance with Article 100 EEC. The legal basis demonstrated that the agreement to the Directive was motivated also by the desire to eliminate distortions of competition.[9] In a common market it was considered unfair for businesses in certain member states to be subject to much lower costs in terms of reducing their workforce than in others (Hepple, 1977: 490).

The protection given by the Directive can be summarized as three basic requirements. First, it requires that employees' representatives be informed and consulted about the implications of a proposed transfer for employees [Art. 6(1)].[10] Secondly, it requires, where there is a 'transfer of undertaking' within the meaning of Article 1(1) of the Directive, that employees continue to be employed on the same terms and conditions as before [Art. 3(1)].[11] Thirdly, Article 4(1) of the Directive provides that the transfer in itself shall not be a ground for dismissal, although dismissal will be permitted if the employer can prove that the dismissals take place for 'economic, technical, or organisational reasons entailing changes in the

---

[8] Ibid. 19. The first proposal became Council Dir. 75/129 EEC of 17 Feb. 1975 on the approximation of the laws of the member states relating to collective redundancies (OJ 1975 L48/29), as amended by Council Dir. 92/56 EEC of 24 June 1992 (OJ 1992 L245/3).

[9] See the Preambles to Dir. 77/187 and 75/129; also the Social Action Programme itself, Bull. EC, Supp. 2/74, 13.

[10] See Case C-382/92 *Commission* v. *UK* [1994] ECR I-2435.

[11] Art. 3(2) requires the transferee to observe the terms and conditions of any collective agreement with the transferor.

workforce'. In the United Kingdom the implementation of the Directive significantly increased protection for employees in relation to business transfers: the Directive changed the position at common law, where previously a change in employer had meant the termination of one contract of employment and the (possible) commencement of another.[12] Moreover, in United Kingdom labour law the acquisition of many employment protection rights is contingent upon the completion of two years of service.[13] The implementation of the Directive secured this vitally important continuity of service on a transfer.

2. THE INTERPRETATION OF THE DIRECTIVE BY THE COURT OF JUSTICE

The Court of Justice's interpretation of the Acquired Rights Directive has consistently been in keeping with its aim of employment protection and its origins in the Social Action Programme, holding that the Directive is applicable to the protection of the rights of employees in an ever-wider range of situations (de Groot, 1993: 344). The Court considers its application in terms of whether 'there is a change in the legal or natural person who is responsible for carrying on the business and who by virtue of that fact incurs the obligation of an employer *vis-à-vis* the employees of the undertaking'.[14]

It has held that there can be a 'legal transfer' within the meaning of the Directive regardless of whether transfer of ownership of the undertaking has been effected and regardless of whether there is a contractual relationship between transferor and transferee. The Court has stated that the Directive protects employees in situations such as the transfer of a lease of a business,[15] the surrender of a lease of a business to the original owner,[16] and the transfer of a local authority subsidy from one charitable foundation to another.[17]

---

[12] The Directive was implemented into UK law by the Transfer of Undertakings (Protection of Employment) Regulations 1981, SI 1981/1794, now amended by s. 33 Trade Union Reform and Employment Rights Act 1993.

[13] Parts IV, V, and VI Employment Protection (Consolidation) Act 1978.

[14] Case 287/86 *Ny Molle Kro* [1987] ECR 5465, para. 12 of judgment.

[15] Case 324/86 *Daddy's Dance Hall* [1988] ECR 739.

[16] *Ny Molle Kro, supra* n. 14.

[17] Case C-29/91 *Sophie Redmond Stichting* v. *Bartol* [1992] ECR I-3189.

Moreover, the Directive can apply when only a part of the undertaking has been transferred: the decisive criterion, the Court has held, is the link between the employee and the part of the undertaking transferred.[18]

In view of this broad interpretation, it was doctrinally no surprise when in *Rask* the Court of Justice held that the contracting out of canteen services by a Danish branch of the electronic giant, Philips, could constitute a 'legal transfer' within the meaning of the Directive.[19] There had clearly been 'a change in the legal or natural person who incurs the obligation of an employer *vis-à-vis* the employees of the undertaking'. The fact that there had been a transfer of an ancillary activity only—the provision of canteen services—did not prevent the Directive from applying, provided there was a link between the employees and the ancillary activity transferred. Neither did the fact that the transfer of this ancillary activity took the form of an agreement to provide services in return for a fee exclude the transfer from the scope of the Directive.

The question of whether there is a 'legal transfer' within the meaning of the Directive is a question of law within the jurisdiction of the Court of Justice. Whether the Directive will actually apply to protect employees transferred by virtue of a particular contract is dependent on a second issue—a question of fact to be adjudicated by national courts. For the Directive to apply, an 'undertaking'—an identifiable economic unit—must have been transferred: '. . . the decisive criterion for establishing whether there has been a transfer [of undertaking] within the meaning of the Directive is whether the business retains its identity, as would be indicated, in particular, by the fact that its operation was actually continued or resumed'.[20]

To assist national courts in the determination of this issue, the Court of Justice laid down detailed guidelines:

. . . it is necessary to consider all the factual circumstances characterising the transaction in question, including the type of undertaking or business concerned, whether the business's tangible assets, such as buildings and moveable property, are transferred, the value of its intangible assets at the time of transfer, whether or not the majority of its employees are taken over by the new employer, whether or not its customers are transferred and the degree of similarity between the activities carried on before and after the

---

[18] Case 186/83 *Botzen v. Rotterdamsche Droogdok Maatschappij* [1985] ECR 519.
[19] *Supra* n. 3.   [20] Ibid. para. 19.

transfer and the period, if any, for which those activities are suspended. It should be noted, however, that all those circumstances are merely single factors in the overall assessment which must be made and cannot therefore be considered in isolation.[21]

The opinion of Advocate-General van Gerven in *Rask* indicated how these guidelines could apply to contracting out in practice. He argued that on that facts of *Rask* an 'undertaking' had been transferred: ISS had entered into a contract to take over the staff permanently employed by Philips; ISS used the same premises and facilities as had been used when the canteen services were provided in-house; the 'customers' of the canteen were the same before and after the transfer; the activity carried on was identical before and after the transfer; and the agreement expressly forbade ISS to undertake any rationalization within the first six months of the contract.

The Court of Justice's judgment in *Rask* provoked a flood of litigation in the United Kingdom. Individuals and trade unions who had been adversely affected by the government's policies in relation to the compulsory competitive tendering of services by the National Health Service and by local authorities, or by the transfer of the provision of services from the public sector to the private or 'quasi-private' sector (Freedland, 1994; Harden, 1992) sought to rely on the Acquired Rights Directive to protect the erosion of their terms and conditions of employment (More, 1993; Napier, 1993). Whilst much of the litigation was successful[22] national courts had obvious difficulties in applying the guidelines given by the Court of Justice as to whether an actual 'undertaking' had been transferred. In particular, courts were unclear as to whether a transfer involving a 'bare contract for service', which did not involve the transfer of any assets, could constitute a transfer of an 'undertaking' for the purposes of the Directive.[23] The Court of Justice, however, held that this type of contract *could* constitute a transfer of an 'undertaking' in the case of *Schmidt*, decided in April 1994.[24]

---

[21] Ibid. para. 20.

[22] Although thousands of compensation claims against the UK for its failure adequately to implement the Acquired Rights Directive (confirmed in Case C-382/92 *Commission* v. *UK* [1994] ECR I-2435) are awaiting the outcome of the preliminary ruling of the Court of Justice in Cases C-46 & 48/93, *Factortame* (No. 3) and *Brasserie du Pêcheur*.

[23] E.g. *Dines* v. *Initial Health Care Services and Pall Mall Services Group* [1993] IRLR 521.   [24] *Supra* n. 3.

Schmidt involved the transfer of a cleaner, Frau Schmidt, when the
branch of the bank where she was employed contracted out its office
cleaning to a firm already responsible for cleaning other branches.
The significance of the decision lay in the increased guidance given
by the Court on the question of whether an 'undertaking' had been
transferred. The Governments of both the United Kingdom and the
Federal Republic of Germany submitted arguments that there could
be no transfer of an 'undertaking' since there had been no transfer of
tangible assets: this was merely a contract for service which did not
constitute an 'undertaking' within the scope of the Directive.[25]
However, the Court of Justice adhered firmly to the guidelines it had
established in earlier cases, reiterating that the transaction must be
assessed as a whole in order to determine whether an undertaking
had been transferred. The absence of the transfer of physical assets
alone was not decisive. The Court then broke precedent and decided
for itself whether there had been a transfer of an 'undertaking',
justifying this move on the ground that all the relevant information
was contained in the order for reference. It stated:

According to the case law, the retention of . . . identity is indicated *inter alia*
by the actual continuation or resumption by the new employer of the same
or similar activities. Thus in this case . . . the similarity in the cleaning work
performed before and after the transfer, which is reflected, moreover, in the
offer to re-engage the employee in question, is typical of an operation which
comes within the scope of the Directive and which gives the employee whose
activity has been transferred the protection afforded to him [sic] by that
directive.[26]

The argument that the Directive could not apply to transfers
without assets was effectively quashed. Moreover, the decision
suggests that the continuation of the same activity and the re-
engagement of the same workers is sufficient to constitute a transfer
of an economic unit.

The judgment met with strong reaction in both the United
Kingdom and Germany (the reactions of other member states are
not available). The judgment strongly influenced the outcome of an
important test case on the application of the Directive in the United
Kingdom: in *Dines* v. *Initial Health Care Services* the English Court of
Appeal held that there had been a transfer of an economic unit when
a contract passed from one private contractor to another as a result

---

[25] Ibid. para. 16 of judgment.   [26] Ibid. para. 17 of judgment.

of the second round of competitive tendering for a contract to clean a hospital.[27] Trade unionists were jubilant as this decision significantly strengthened their ability to protect their members in both the queue of backlogged cases and the inevitable stream of cases to follow. Indeed, in order to avoid the risk of litigation, many contractors were content to recognize the application of the legislation: the agreement between the public sector union, UNISON, and the multinational service business, ISS, was a clear illustration of this trend (McMullen, 1994: 239).

The United Kingdom Government, on the other hand, was clearly unhappy. Commenting on the outcome of the *Dines* case, the Business Services Association, a public sector contractors' lobby group, described it as 'a devastating blow to the government's policies of market testing and compulsory competitive tendering'.[28]

The Government reinvigorated its campaign to revise the wording of the Acquired Rights Directive. Newspaper reports indicate that its position was backed by the German Government, which was also indignant at the impact of the *Schmidt* judgment on contracting out.[29] Certainly, the *Schmidt* judgment has met with criticism in German academic literature (Bauer, 1994; Waas, 1994). In particular, commentators have criticized the Court of Justice's concept of an 'undertaking': the Court's assertion that an activity— without any accompanying requirement of business goodwill or know-how—is sufficient to constitute an 'undertaking' has not been accepted by German labour lawyers (Waas, 1994: 529–30). The Court is criticized, moreover, for giving inordinate weight to the protection of the employee and, correspondingly, for failing to balance this against the enterprise's right of operational autonomy. The root of the criticism appears to be that the Court's decision increases the transaction costs for the negotiation of such contracts for service, which ultimately restricts the utility of contracting out (Waas, 1994: 531).

3. THE QUEST FOR FLEXIBILITY IN EMPLOYMENT

The suggestion that the Court of Justice has unduly restricted the operational autonomy of businesses by requiring onerous standards

---

[27] [1994] IRLR 336. [28] *Financial Times* 20 May 1994, 8.
[29] *Supra* n. 4.

of employment protection feeds into a wider debate over the cost of labour market regulation in the European Union. The Commission's 1993 White Paper on Growth, Competitiveness and Employment identified the 'inflexibility of the labour market' as responsible for high labour costs (hence presumably for poor competitiveness) and for a large part of the Union's structural unemployment.[30] The link between poor labour market flexibility and unemployment—and hence poor economic performance—is also emphasized in the OECD's 1994 Jobs Study (OECD 1994a: 69). Both the Commission's White Paper[31] and the OECD Jobs Study acknowledge that improved labour market flexibility involves the promotion of a number of policies, namely: enhancing labour mobility, encouraging the use of 'new' employment forms (such as part-time working), adopting active labour market policies, *and* relaxing employment protection provisions (OECD 1994b: 63).

Despite the importance of the quest for flexibility in employment in both reports, it is significant that the meaning of flexibility is barely addressed in either. In human resource management (HRM) literature, however, the concept of flexibility has been thoroughly discussed. Atkinson, one of the foremost analysts in this field, has noted that a number of assumptions underlie the use of the term 'flexibility': first, it is generally assumed that 'flexibility' means labour flexibility; the increased flexibility of other factors of production (such as capital, managerial expertise or technological ability) is not addressed. Secondly, 'labour flexibility' tends to be viewed from the employer's standpoint, and the employees' distinct needs for flexibility (for example in relation to working-time arrangements) are overlooked (Atkinson, 1990: 51–2). Atkinson shows, moreover, that distinct types of flexibility are sought by employers: first, numerical flexibility (the changes in the *volume* of labour deployed from time to time); secondly, functional flexibility (the changes in *tasks* required of an employee); and thirdly, financial flexibility (the desire to ensure that pay and other employment costs reflect the supply and demand in the external labour market) (Atkinson, 1984).

All three types of flexibility are facilitated through the use of a 'peripheral' workforce of part-time, temporary, and sub-contracted

---

[30] Supra n. 5, 16–17, 123.   [31] Ibid.

workers. Moreover, the use of 'externalization' or 'distancing'—
when 'contracts of employment are displaced by commercial
contracts'—allows employers access to an even more 'peripheral'
and flexible workforce (Atkinson, 1984: 58). 'Externalization' is the
process whereby employers decide to distance '. . . activities in
which they possess no competitive advantage, which absorb a
disproportionate amount of managerial effort, and which they can
procure more cheaply by buying in rather then conducting within
the organisation' (Atkinson, 1990: 58).

Externalization using short commercial contracts allows the
number of workers to be adapted to meet demand; it permits
the selection of staff whose skills are particularly in demand at a
certain time; and it ensures that wage rates are at the level of the
external market rate. One of the principal forms of externalization
being used by firms is of course contracting out: in North American
terminology, 'outsourcing'.[32]

This view of labour flexibility highlights the fact that decisions of
the Court of Justice on the application of the Acquired Rights
Directive to contracting out have required certain standards of
employment protection for what is in fact an employment
form designed to facilitate a high degree of labour flexibility.
Given the current economic environment and the promotion of
flexibility as an unqualified good (Atkinson, 1990: 52), the Court's
decisions appear at first sight to fly in the face of such trends. Indeed
it appears possible to advance the argument that the Court's
promotion of the aims of a Directive which originated in the very
different circumstances of the 1970s is simply not compatible with
today's economic environment. The remainder of this essay seeks to
establish, however, that the nature of contracting out and its
implications for the employment relationship require that the
interests of employees be safeguarded. The Court of Justice's
interpretation of the Acquired Rights Directive has done this: giving
precedence to the Directive's overriding aim of employment
protection has enabled the Court to adapt the Directive to
the changing economic environment through the process of
interpretation.

---

[32] Externalization can also include franchising, self-employment, home-working,
and networking.

4. THE NATURE OF CONTRACTING OUT AND ITS IMPLICATIONS FOR THE EMPLOYMENT RELATIONSHIP

The use of contracting out as a form of business organization has significantly increased in Europe in recent years (Brewster *et al.*, 1994: 171). Whilst in HRM literature it is disputed whether the increase is a result of a specific strategy to achieve flexibility or whether it is, in fact, a result of a sectoral shift to the service sector of the economy (Pollert, 1990: 75; Brewster *et al.*, 1994: 188), there is no doubt that contracting out has gained in popularity as a means of creating leaner, more efficient, and more cost-effective businesses. Firms and organizations, which previously strove to achieve a fully integrated vertical process of production, are now 'dis-integrating' and contracting out the provisions of certain parts of their operations to other businesses (Collins, 1990: 353). A striking example is that of the Eastman Kodak conglomerate, which in October 1989 transferred the whole of its data-processing operation to IBM (PLC, 1993: 17).

In the United Kingdom the phenomenon of public sector contracting out possesses a political dimension of its own: whilst clearly designed both to improve the efficiency and to cut the costs of providing public services, contracting out also promotes the ideology of dismantling the 'public sector' and of improving consumer accountability (Painter, 1994; Pollert, 1990: 75). The result of the exercise (as also with contracting out in the private sector) has been the creation of a network of contractual relationships between procurers and providers of services, each established as individual 'corporate' entities (Freedland, 1994: 90).

The advent of this 'hybrid' business organization, based on a complex web of contractual relations between small units rather than on a single corporate identity, is the starting point for Teubner's critique of the concept of flexibility. The business organization based on multiple contractual relations, he recounts, is justified by economists as being much more flexible than the monolithic corporate giant, particularly in its responsiveness to changes in market conditions.[33] However, Teubner subjects economic rationality to a legal critique. In particular, he argues that

---

[33] As demonstrated by Atkinson's analysis of flexibility.

business has adopted this organizational structure as a way of avoiding legal regulation. For lawyers, he writes, 'Flexibility is a euphemism for evasion' (Teubner, 1993: 215).

Teubner points to the ways in which the new contractual form can avoid legal regulation: if the performance of a particular task is delegated to a sub-contractor, then only the sub-contractor can be held subject to contractual or tortious liability for any defects in the performance of the task; there are none of the legal duties imposed on large corporations by national company laws; there is no corporate liability; and there is no equivalent of 'lifting the corporate veil' in respect of complex systems of contractual agreements (Teubner, 1993: 215–20).

Moreover, the contractual organization of business is also an efficient mechanism for avoiding liabilities in employment law (Teubner, 1993: 216–17). The core enterprise may make a decision affecting employment in all of its satellite suppliers, but only the suppliers bear responsibility towards their employees. For example, if a firm does not renew its contract for the provision of a service by a smaller firm, the larger firm is not responsible for the dismissal, re-deployment, or redundancy costs of the employees deployed in the provision of that service.

Collins' arguments reinforce those of Teubner. Collins argues convincingly that the vertical disintegration of production brings with it significant savings in labour costs (Collins, 1990). First, a business can cut down the 'quasi-fixed costs associated with employment such as hiring and training' (Collins, 1990: 360). Secondly, wage rates paid by the external contractor may be lower than those paid in the internal market of a business, due to 'non-union rates, regional differences and labour market segmentation' (Collins, 1990: 360). Thirdly, the business can impose stricter conditions for the performance of the contract in view of the fact that it is not subject to 'the co-operative give and take typical of long-term contracts of employment which predominate inside organisations' (Collins, 1990: 360). Fourthly—and this is where Collins' argument clearly links with Teubner's—by contracting out a firm can reduce or avoid the costs of compliance with employment protection laws. In addition, Collins makes the point that contracts for the provision of a service are often of short duration, so that employees are often on temporary, fixed-term contracts of employment (Collins, 1990: 360). This means, as in the United Kingdom for example, that employees are less likely to achieve the two years' continuous service required to qualify for a whole host of employment protection rights, such as protection from unfair dismissal and the right to statutory redundancy pay.[34] The employment flexibility of contracting-out appears, therefore, to have two distinct aspects: first, the core enterprise shifts any obligations towards employees onto the contractor and can adjust production without concern for employee-related costs; secondly, the contractor uses short-term, 'flexible' contracts of employment, which of themselves bear fewer employment protection rights.

Teubner denounces the economic argument that evasion of legal regulation can be justified in terms of reducing transaction costs: he argues that law should act as a 'filtering mechanism', preventing illegitimate cost savings (Teubner, 1993: 223). In particular, he reasons that cost savings achieved by means of shifting risks onto third parties must be regarded as illegitimate (ibid. 222). In relation to employment law, we should not consider it legitimate for a business to reduce its operational costs merely by shifting the risks of market unpredictability (in particular, the risk of unavailability of work) onto its employees (Collins, 1990: 377–9).

Teubner's and Collins' analyses shed a new light on the conclusion of the HRM specialists that contracting out is a highly flexible form of business organization. The attraction of contracting out is, clearly, its potential for reducing costs of operation. However, a significant contribution to this reduction of costs is achieved by means of avoiding employment-related costs for those workers undertaking the work of the contracts. The burden of employment protection may be shifted to the contractor, but the contractor in turn may evade this through the use of short-term contracts. Overall, the use of contracting out leads to the undermining of employees' job security, it weakens unionization (Foster, 1993), and moreover, it seriously decreases the provision of long-term benefits such as training and pensions. Experience in the United Kingdom in relation to the contracting out of public services has demonstrated this (Escott and Whitfield, 1995).

The conclusion to be drawn is that, to a large extent, the flexibility of contracting out and the guarantee of employment protection are diametrically opposed. If workers have to be protected, the

[34] Employment Protection (Consolidation) Act 1978.

flexibility/cost benefits of contracting out are reduced. This is the basis on which the Court of Justice's judgments in relation to the application of the Acquired Rights Directive have been criticized. Nonetheless, the foregoing discussion also underlines the considerable costs which are transferred to employees by the use of contracting out. The question thus becomes one of policy: how far is it legitimate to promote flexibility whilst demolishing employment protection? Indeed, is there an argument that the pursuit of labour market flexibility must necessarily include a 'minimum floor' of protective rights (Deakin & Wilkinson, 1994)?

5. JUSTIFYING THE APPLICATION OF THE DIRECTIVE TO CONTRACTING OUT

Whilst advocating greater labour marker flexibility, the Commission's influential 1993 White Paper on *Growth, Competitiveness and Employment* acknowledged that the wholesale pursuit of flexibility without countervailing actions could in fact produce new inflexibilities. First, it acknowledged that flexibility policies have 'often led to the growth of two-tier labour markets—those with secure permanent jobs and those with insecure temporary jobs'.[35] This in itself is seen as creating barriers to labour mobility. Secondly, the White Paper acknowledged that the pressure to increase labour market flexibility 'reduced, rather than increased the incentives for individuals to invest in much needed training and re-training'.[36] This again affects labour mobility but, more importantly, it affects long-term competitiveness. Both these negative phenomena alluded to by the Commission are, it is submitted, direct by-products of the untrammelled use of contracting out as a form of business organization.

The White Paper implies that the achievement of flexibility must therefore carry with it safeguards for workers. This proposition is most explicit in the context of the promotion of part-time working: the Commission clearly advocates reinforcing the employment benefits of part-time workers as a way of facilitating the promotion of part-time work.[37] This approach is mirrored in the advice of the 1994 OECD Jobs Study (OECD 1994a: 98–100).

---

[35] Supra n. 5, 129. [36] Ibid. [37] Ibid. 126–31.

The proposition that employees' needs should be taken into account in order to facilitate labour market flexibility is considered in detail by Atkinson. With particular relevance for contracting out, he discerned two principal needs of employees. First, in order to enhance mobility between employers there should be transferable and compatible benefits for employees (Atkinson, 1990: 64). Secondly, he recommended 'A shifting of the focus from the workplace to individual workers through pressing for *priority rehiring and retained rights*. Such arrangements would encourage trade union membership among the most disadvantaged workers, would significantly reduce the pernicious effects of employment insecurity, would prohibit 'churning', and would greatly improve the quality of life for peripheral workers' (emphasis added) (ibid. 1990: 65).

Whilst Atkinson's first recommendation is not (as yet) regulated by EC law,[38] there is no doubt that his second recommendation has been largely met by the Court of Justice's interpretation of the Acquired Rights Directive. The decisions in *Rask* and *Schmidt* mean that the peripheral workforce *do* now have rights in relation to rehiring and retaining the terms and conditions of their service. The decisions implicitly recognize that employees may be prejudiced through contracting out: therefore, by guaranteeing certain transfer rights, the Court has alleviated the pernicious effects of the current drive towards labour market flexibility.

It is, moreover, not possible to argue that the Directive is unbalanced in its protection of employees at the expense of flexibility. The application of the Directive provides only a minimum standard of protection. The Court has on a number of occasions underlined that the Directive is aimed only at partial harmonization.[39] The Directive provides for the protection of rights and conditions of service merely upon transfer. The long-term protection of such rights is still a matter for national law.[40] The

---

[38] The Commission has, however, proposed reactivating its proposal for a Directive for mobile occupational pensions within the European Union: EC Commission, 'European Social Policy—A Way Forward for the Union', COM(94) 333, 28.

[39] Case C-209/91 *Rask, supra* n. 3, para. 31; Case C-392/92 *Schmidt, supra* n. 3, para. 19; Case C-382/92 *Commission* v. *UK, supra* n. 10, para. 28.

[40] Art. 3(2) stipulates in relation to collective agreements that member states may limit the term for observing such terms and conditions, provided that it is not less than one year. No protection period for individual terms and conditions is stipulated.

Directive also permits member state legislation to provide that the burden of liability for obligations to employees be shared by both transferor and transferee.[41]

Furthermore, the Directive expressly limits its application: Art. 4(1) states that dismissals for 'economic, technical or organizational reasons entailing changes in the workforce' are not to be regarded as dismissals in connection with a transfer, and are therefore not automatically unfair. If a firm can demonstrate that it has substantially reorganized the provision of a service, and that employees have been dismissed because they do not fit into the reorganized operation, then it is possible to avoid the impact of the Directive.[42] Union legal officers indicate that this is the direction which litigation is taking within the United Kingdom. This derogation in the Directive brings the discussion back to the point made by Teubner: that flexibility is in essence evasion of legal regulation.

The final aspect of flexibility given by the Directive is that of avoiding altogether the scope of its application. Whilst a strict interpretation of the *Schmidt* decision suggests that the Directive will apply to most contracting out transactions, some commentators still believe that the Court has left scope for arguing that the Directive does not apply (Buggy, 1994). It appears likely that, at least in the private sector, lawyers will be kept busy drafting contracts in such a way as to avoid the impact of the Directive.

6. CONCLUSION: IS THE TRANSFER OF UNDERTAKINGS DIRECTIVE COMPATIBLE WITH THE AIM OF EMPLOYMENT FLEXIBILITY?

This essay has attempted to address the question of whether the application of the Acquired Rights Directive to contracting out is an unwarranted restriction on labour market flexibility. It has been

[41] The proposed revision of Art. 3(1) of the Directive would require joint liability of the transferor and transferee for contractual obligations for the first year after transfer: COM(94) 300, 13.

[42] E.g. *Porter and Nanayakkara* v. *Queen's Medical Centre (Nottingham University Hospital)* [1993] IRLR 486. Also, it would appear that firms with a degree of internal flexibility, where employees perform a number of functions, may be able to evade transferring an 'undertaking' if some of those employees are moved out to perform one function only.

clearly shown that contracting out is a flexible employment form, but that a large measure of its flexibility derives from the possibilities it offers to entrepreneurs to avoid legal regulation, in particular to avoid the requirement of employment protection law. The costs for employees affected by contracting out are therefore particularly high. On this basis, therefore, the argument is advanced that some protection is required of employees affected by contracting out. The pursuit of labour market flexibility must, as the Commission recognized in its 1993 White Paper, be balanced to include safeguards for employees.

The Court of Justice decisions in *Rask* and *Schmidt* have resulted in the introduction of certain safeguards for workers affected by contracting out. The Court's teleological interpretation of the Acquired Rights Directive has allowed it to be adapted to meet the needs of employment protection, albeit in a changed economic environment. The application of the Directive is, moreover, not as rigid as some critics have suggested: a derogation in the Directive allows dismissals to be made on economic grounds; the Directive merely protects rights upon transfer; actions taken after a transfer are subject only to national law. There is, it is argued, scope to *improve* the protection given to employees by the Directive (Hepple, 1990; Loughney, 1995).

To date, the fate of the proposed revision to the Directive is undecided. Trade unions are lobbying hard to oppose amendments which would prejudice the application of the Directive to contracting out. The irony of the position of the United Kingdom Government is also particularly evident: having protested so loudly against the use of qualified majority voting to enact any socially orientated legislation, the amendments to the Directive have to be approved by unanimous voting by virtue of Article 100 EC. Unanimity can only be achieved if there is a consensus that flexibility requires less employment protection. In the author's opinion, it is not clear that this consensus exists.

GATT and Community Law: rethinking the 'regulatory gap'*

JOANNE SCOTT

This chapter resurrects a familiar theme in Community law—the existence of a 'regulatory gap' and the relationship between 'negative' (market) and 'positive' (policy) integration—and seeks to introduce a new dimension into that debate. The paper is predicated on four fundamental propositions.

First, it is premised on an expectation that the post-Uruguay Round General Agreement on Tariffs and Trade (GATT 1994)[1] will be considerably more effective than its predecessor (GATT 1947) in providing a framework for the regulation of international trade relations. In large measure this will be due to the changes introduced by the *Understanding on Rules and Procedures Governing the Settlement of Disputes* which abolishes the veto power of the contracting parties at various stages in the dispute resolution process. It is argued that the significance of these changes lies not only in their capacity to reinforce the application of GATT as public international law but also as Community law, since they tend to promote acceptance by the Court of Justice of the direct effect of the GATT, or at least of parts of it.

Secondly, the paper is predicated on the supposition that political power or sovereignty is determined not only by the legal framework within which it is exercised but also by the economic context in which it is to operate. In particular, it is argued that the *de facto* sovereignty or regulatory capacity of political actors is constrained in a scenario of 'negative' integration, given the increased choices and mobility which this generates for economic actors, and the 'competition between rules' implicit within it.

* I would like to thank Marise Cremona, Wade Mansell, Philippe Sands, Julia Sohrab, and the other contributors to this volume for their helpful comments and suggestions. The usual disclaimers apply.
[1] The scope of GATT 1994 is defined in Annex 1A of the WTO Agreement.

Thirdly, this essay assumes that regulatory endeavours in the environmental sphere often operate to impose additional burdens on economic actors, or are perceived as being capable of so doing. Where these costs cannot be offset by constraining 'negative' integration (for example by restricting market access) the *de facto* capacity or willingness of political actors to pursue such measures will be undermined by the revolution of a treadmill of competitive deregulation.

Finally, the paper seeks to demonstrate the manner in which GATT renders illegal efforts to offset these additional costs which are often associated with environmental regulation. Efforts by a state or group of states to export its own (or in certain circumstances even internationally accepted) environmental ethics or standards to its trading partners, in the interests of achieving a level playing field, are (at least in so far as these concern process regulation) liable to infringe the normative order constructed by GATT.

In the light of this the paper argues that, while few would doubt the need for an effective, predictable, and transparent framework for the regulation of international trade, the model currently constituted by GATT is deeply flawed. Focusing upon the movement of goods and environmental protection, it argues that the implications of a strengthened GATT for the dynamics of single market integration are profound and, not least from an environmental perspective, profoundly negative. The traditional marginalization of GATT within Community law has led to a dangerous complacency concerning its substantive provisions, the implications of which may only now become apparent. Many of the benefits which might be expected to flow from the Community's internal market project may well emerge as illusory in the light of the pervasiveness of the fierce and uncompromising economic logic of GATT and its capacity to prise open the regulatory gap. Where the political remains a lowly servant of the economic, the prospects of inventing '. . . a structural and ethical normative basis for the Community legal order' (I. Ward, 1994b: 329) begin to appear hopelessly and depressingly remote.

1. GATT AND COMMUNITY LAW

Although the capacity of GATT to bind the Community institutions has been recognized by the Court of Justice since 1972,[2] its role in shaping the Community legal order in general, and the premises underlying its external trade law in particular, have been less profound than might have been anticipated. Its limited impact during the years 1972 to 1994 is directly attributable to difficulties surrounding its application both as a part of Community law and as a body of public international law.

As an international treaty binding upon the Community, GATT in principle enjoys primacy over conflicting Community legislation. Yet in practice it is not clear how this primacy is to be secured. In the *International Fruit* case the Court of Justice identified two conditions to be satisfied before a provision of international law might be employed, via Article 177, to challenge the validity of an act of a Community institution. While the first, that the Community be bound by that provision of international law, was clearly satisfied in respect of GATT, the second, that the international law be 'capable of conferring rights on citizens of the community which they can invoke before the courts', was not. (For a forceful critique of the Court's decision to deny the direct effect of GATT, see Petersmann, 1983). Hence by denying the direct effect of GATT, and by asserting that direct effect is a precondition for the operation of Article 177 (though interestingly not in respect of Article 177 in so far as it concerns the interpretation of Community law), the Court restricted the procedural means whereby the GATT might be introduced before it, as a superior norm in the light of which the validity of Community legislation should be considered.

In the absence of direct effect, GATT has proved ineffectual as part of Community law, and its primacy largely illusory. Contrary to earlier speculation (see Schermers, 1975) the Court of Justice has admitted a small number of direct challenges by private parties premised upon the GATT.[3] However, neither this fact nor the dispute settlement mechanisms indigenous to the GATT itself have proved sufficient to compensate for its lack of direct effect. In respect

---

[2] Joined Cases 2-4/72 *International Fruit Company NV* v. *Producktschap voor Groenten en Fruit* [1972] ECR 1219.

[3] See e.g. Case C-69/89 *Nakajima All Precision Co. Ltd.* v. *Council* [1991] ECR I-2069; Case C-105/90 *Goldstar Co. Ltd.* v. *Council*; *Matsushita* v. *Council* [1992] ECR I-677; Case C-188/88 *NMB (Deutschland) GmbH, NMP Italia Srl and NMB (UK) Ltd.* v. *Commission* [1992] ECR I-1689; Case 70/87 *Fediol* v. *Commission* [1989] ECR 1781.

of Article 173 EC, the impediments faced by a would-be challenger are well known (Hartley, 1994). It is only by virtue of the Court's effective relaxation of the standing criteria in Article 173 in respect of quasi-judicial decisions that even a small, and substantively narrowly focused, number of applications have been held admissible (see Greaves, 1986). Even here, in respect of the Community's anti-dumping law, the Court of Justice has demonstrated a marked reluctance to interfere with the Council's exercise of discretion in situations which necessitate an appraisal of complex economic facts, preferring in the *Nakajima* case to construe the margin of 'reason-ableness' permitted by the GATT anti-dumping code in such a way as to legitimate the highly contentious reasoning of the Council (Hindley, 1988). At any rate such anti-dumping cases concerned Community legislation which was intended to implement specific GATT obligations. Where, on the other hand, Community law neither implements nor expressly refers to specific provisions of GATT, the Court has recently asserted that this precludes 'the Court from taking provisions of GATT into consideration to assess the lawfulness of a regulation in an action brought by a Member State under the first paragraph of Article 173 of the Treaty'.[4] Hence, in an unexpected and dramatic step, the Court has acted further to limit the role of GATT within the Community legal order and to limit its usefulness in direct actions before the Court of Justice.

Turning to the limitations inherent in the GATT itself as an instrument of international law, it quickly becomes apparent that it is predicated upon a system of dispute resolution which is so bizarre as to dismay all but the most seasoned and sceptical public international lawyers. Robert Hudec (in Schott, 1990: 181) observes in the context of the Uruguay Round negotiations that:

There was also general agreement about the core problem: like every other part of the GATT's decision-making process, GATT dispute settlement procedures are run by consensus. No decision is adopted unless everyone, including the defendant country, agrees. The defendant must consent to the creation of a panel, its members, and its terms of reference. If the panel rules against the defendant, the defendant must also consent to adoption of that ruling by the GATT Council. And finally, the defendant must consent to any retaliation that is proposed in response to its noncompliance. In short, the defendant has the power to block the dispute process at any point.

---

[4] Case C-280/93 *Federal Republic of Germany* v. *Council (Bananas)* [1994] ECR I-4873, para. 109.

It is clear that at international level the effective enforcement of GATT has proved to be as much a question of political expediency as of legal necessity. Needless to say, the European Community, like the United States, has proved more than willing to exercise its 'blocking' power in such a way as to delay or thwart Council adoption of panel rulings.

Hence from 1972 to 1994 the Community's legal commitment to GATT has proved more rhetorical than real. For reasons which are readily explicable in terms of political realism and Community autonomy, though clothed in the language of legal necessity, the Court of Justice has facilitated the Community's capacity to talk the required language of trade liberalization, while engaging in forms of protectionism which are at once more covert and more responsive to the Community's needs. Yet by 1995, following the conclusion of the new World Trade Organization (WTO) Agreement, it appeared increasingly likely that the politics of the Community's earlier approach to GATT might be undermined and that there might emerge an almost irresistible case for the recognition of the justiciability of GATT norms.

The WTO Agreement[5] includes, in Annex 2, an Understanding on the Rules and Procedures Governing the Settlement of Disputes (the Understanding) which elaborates and modifies the principles for the management of disputes applied under Articles XXII and XXIII of GATT 1947.[6] If, as Hudec points out, it has been the consensus requirement and the inherent right of any individual GATT member to 'block' decision-making which has impeded the effectiveness of GATT dispute resolution, then few would deny that this Understanding strikes at the very heart of the problem. Article IV of the WTO Agreement establishes a General Council, the duties of which include dispute resolution. This body, comprised of representatives of GATT members, will in the circumstances specified in the Understanding convene as a Dispute Settlement Body (DSB). It is to this Body that requests for the establishment of a panel should be brought, and following such a request a panel will

---

[5] Art. 2 of the WTO Agreement provides that its annexes are to constitute an integral part of the agreement.

[6] It is beyond the scope of this Chapter to present a comprehensive outline and evaluation of post-Uruguay dispute resolution, premised as it is upon a complex blend of consultation, conciliation, arbitration, and retaliation. For a full analysis see Petersmann, 1994 and Lowenfeld, 1994.

be established unless the DSB decides by consensus *not* to do so. Similarly, the DSB will automatically adopt panel reports (except where one of the parties to the dispute notifies it of its decision to appeal) unless there is a *negative* consensus among members. Where, notwithstanding the best efforts of the DSB, a party fails within a reasonable time to implement rulings adequately, and where consultations regarding appropriate compensation fail, a party to the dispute may request authorization to suspend concessions or other obligations under the relevant GATT rules. Again, such authorization will be granted by the DSB unless it decides by consensus *not* to do so. It remains open to the party against whom sanctions are to be applied in certain circumstances to have the matter referred to arbitration although the application of the sanctions will not be suspended during the course of the arbitration.

One further aspect of the Understanding which merits special attention is Article 17 which introduces the possibility of appellate review of panel reports by a standing Appellate body to be established by the DSB. It is open to parties to appeal against a panel decision on a matter relating to an issue of law or legal interpretation. In this event the panel report will not be considered by the DSB until this appeal is completed, a process which in general is to last no more than sixty days. The appellate report will be accepted by the DSB and unconditionally by the parties to the dispute unless the former decides by consensus *not* to do so.

The significance for Community Law of this Understanding should not be underestimated. The Court of Justice, in assessing the scope of GATT within the Community legal system, has emphasized the need to look to its spirit, general scheme, and terms.[7] In so doing it has consistently cited three features of GATT as militating against its direct effect and as tending necessarily to limit its role in direct actions before it. GATT is, in the view of the Court, 'characterized by the great flexibility of its provisions, in particular those conferring the possibility of derogation, the measures to be taken when confronted with exceptional difficulties and the settlement of conflicts between contracting parties'.[8] As such, 'to a large degree the elaborated dispute settlement procedure of the GATT also constitutes one of the obstacles to its direct effect' (Maresceau, 1986: 122).

---

[7] Case 280/93 *Germany* v. *Council, supra* n. 4, para. 105.   [8] Ibid.

Yet the Court cannot fail to observe that the Understanding on the Settlement of Disputes marks a 'significant legalization' and a 'quasi-judicialization' of GATT dispute settlement procedures (Petersmann, 1994: 1215) and a shift from 'conciliation and consensus' (Maresceau, 1986: 122) to formal, binding, and independent adjudication. While panel members are to be selected with a view to ensuring their independence, the Appellate Body is to comprise persons of recognized authority, with demonstrated relevant expertise, and who are not affiliated with any government. The latter will not participate in the consideration of any disputes that would create a direct or indirect conflict of interests, for example one to which their state of origin is party. The Understanding precludes the possibility of unilateral suspension of concessions, favouring instead collectively controlled suspension, and '[t]he explicit right of third WTO members and of the DSB to challenge bilaterally agreed dispute settlements and arbitration awards . . . underlines the multilateral public law nature of the WTO Agrement *vis-à-vis* bilaterally agreed departures from WTO rules' (Petersmann, 1994: 1215). All of this is, of course, a far cry from the language of contingency and 'self-regulation' which led the Court to cite the dispute settlement mechanisms of the GATT as a factor contributing to its inherent flexibility and hence as a barrier to its justiciability. That this new unified system of dispute settlement is also to apply to consultations and the settlement of disputes arising under the Uruguay Round Agreement on Safeguards raises yet further doubts as to the legitimacy of the Court's reasoning in the era of the WTO.[9]

It might then be anticipated that the coming years will see an expansion of the Court's jurisdiction to examine the compatibility of

---

[9] The third factor cited by the Court, relating to the possibility of derogation was unconvincing even prior to the WTO Agreement. The Court accepted in Case C-192/89 *Sevince* [1990] ECR I-3461 that 'the mere existence of powers to derogate will not always prevent direct effect' (Cheyne, 1994: 591). The Court will, in all probability, be faced with similar questions regarding the direct effect and justiciability of the other agreements annexed to the WTO Agreement. That the General Agreement on Trade in Services and the Agreement on the Application of Trade Related Aspects of Intellectual Property Rights including trade in Counterfeit Goods are mixed agreements raises further complications in this respect: see Opinion 1/94 [1994] ECR I-5267. It is important to observe that Decision 94/800 (OJ 1994 L336/1) contains a statement in the Preamble to the effect that the GATT/WTO Agreements are not directly effective.

Community legislation in the light of GATT. At the very least, the Community will find its hands tied in the formulation of its external trade law due to the more effective application of the new GATT, as international law, which is implied by the new rules and procedures governing the settlement of disputes. The implications of this, in terms of the Community's internal regulatory capacity, notably in the environmental sphere, are next considered.

2. THE 'REGULATORY GAP' REVISITED

In 1986 the Netherlands Scientific Council published a report which recorded a fundamental disjuncture between 'negative' and 'positive' integration in the Community (Netherlands Scientific Council, 1986). This report offered sustenance to those who sought to argue that inherent in the Community project was a deregulatory bias leading to the emergence of a pervasive 'regulatory gap' (see, for example, Bourgoignie & Trubek, 1987; McGee & Weatherill, 1990). This well known argument was essentially premised upon the Community's greater success in undermining the regulatory competence of the member states in the interests of market integration than in substituting comprehensive Community-wide norms for divisive national standards. The Community institutions, it implied, had proved more adept at national deconstruction than Community reconstruction, exhibiting a structural preference for deregulation rather than re-regulation.

More recently the continuing validity of this argument has been subjected to renewed scrutiny, with one author concluding that fears of 'regulatory meltdown' (Charny, 1991: 423) have proved exaggerated as the scope and effectiveness of Community inter-vention have increased (Dehousse, 1992).[10] There is a growing perception that the Community is today striking a more appropriate balance between negative and positive integration and that the Community project need not necessarily operate in support of the neo-liberal political and economic discourses dominant in the 1980s. This partial closure of the regulatory gap can be attributed to a wide range of factors, not least the expansion of Community

---

[10] Dehousse nonetheless concludes that Community endeavours in the sphere of social regulation have in general been less effective than those in the United States.

legislative competence, increasing recourse to qualified majority voting in Council, changing conceptions of the relationship between national and Community law, and a rejection of classical notions of preemption in a Community setting (Weatherill, 1994).

However, the purpose of this Chapter is to consider whether it might be premature and misleading to celebrate the end of the regulatory gap, and to locate this scepticism in the context of an invigorated and more authoritative GATT. It will be argued that inherent in this instrument is a capacity to prise open the gap by undermining the structural power of the Community and by denying its potential as an agent of regulatory intervention. It will seek to highlight the significance of international law as a factor 'that shape[s] the nature and dynamics of regulation and that condition[s] and limit[s] the reception and adoption of new regulatory ideas' (Dyson, 1992: 3–4). Whereas in general the external trade law of the Community and the dynamics of single market integration are conceived as separate and distinct areas of study (except perhaps in respect of Article 115 EC) with the latter at least discussed in isolation from the former, this Chapter will seek to demonstrate the central role of Community trade policy, as mediated through GATT, in shaping the process of single market integration and in defining the parameters of, and the relationship between, negative and positive integration. In view of the breadth and complexity of modern GATT law these arguments will be exemplified with reference to a specific and core area, namely the movement of non-agricultural goods with emphasis on the contentious issue of environmental protection.

I have argued elsewhere that a regulatory gap emerges when international economic liberalization precedes corresponding political or policy integration and that inherent in the former is a diminution of both *de jure* and *de fact* political sovereignty (J. Scott, 1995). Whereas the loss of *de jure* sovereignty is directly attributable to positive normative prohibitions associated with negative integration, the latter has its origins in increasing economic mobility and the resulting inter-jurisdictional 'competition between rules'. Hence while governments might retain an apparent legal capacity to regulate a given sphere of activity, where the costs implicit in such regulation impinge negatively upon economic actors operating within their jurisdiction, the threat of industrial or capital relocation may render such intervention economically inconceivable. Trapped

within a culture of regulatory 'divide and rule', political ideals tend
to be sacrificed on the altar of transnational competition while the
resulting political vacuum can only be filled by co-ordinating
economic and political integration. While the Community project
represents just such an experiment in the synchronization of market
and policy integration, GATT, at least in respect of movement of
goods, is unequivocally biased in favour of the former. As shown in
the following section, its norms are essentially prohibitory in nature
and the capacity of its members to restrict market integration in
favour of defined policy objectives is limited. Its potential to
relaunch the Community onto a treadmill of competitive deregulation should therefore not be underestimated. The following section
exemplifies this in respect of regulatory endeavours in the
environmental sphere.

3. TURNING THE TREADMILL: GATT *V.* THE ENVIRONMENT

Regulation in the environmental sphere can be usefully, albeit a
little crudely, divided into two broad categories, namely product
and process regulation. The former refers to measures which seek to
define the composition or substance of a given product, relating
to its inherent characteristics or qualities, while the latter prescribes
the manner in which a product is created, the impact of the
production process on the physical environment, or the natural
resource implications of the manner or quantity in which the specific
commodity is produced or exploited. Both types of regulation can
occur at either national or supranational (regional) level, or
alternatively by way of international environmental agreements,
and both *may* raise issues of competitiveness in that 'industries
operating in countries with strict environmental regulations will
incur higher costs and consequently be less competitive than those
operating in countries with more lax regulation' (Thomas &
Tereposky, 1993: 34).

The relative significance of environmental factors in determining
a firm's competitiveness is a matter of continuing debate. For every
empirical study which claims that environmental regulation has
only a minimal impact upon productivity, trade, or capital location,
or even that there is a positive relationship between more stringent
levels of regulation and competitiveness, there is another which

seeks to highlight its centrality, notably in respect of industrial location.[11] Even the Court of Justice, perhaps inadvertently, has contributed to this debate in the course of addressing the question of the appropriate legal basis for Community environmental legislation. In distinguishing between Article 100A EEC and Article 130S EEC the Court has acknowledged the capacity of environmental measures to affect substantially the competitiveness of undertakings and the role of harmonization in eliminating such distortions of competition. In one such case the Advocate General introduced Commission data which purported to establish the substantial costs inherent in efforts to reduce pollution from titanium dioxide waste.[12]

While it is beyond the scope of this Chapter to evaluate the methodological premises of such studies, two observations concerning those which seek to refute the existence of any link between environmental measures and economic competitiveness are pertinent. The first was highlighted by Stewart (1993: 2084–5) who pointed out that these studies are almost always predicated upon data recorded during the 'first phase' of environmental regulation and hence that they do not 'deal with the potential effects of the more ambitious second phase of requirements in which the USA and its principal international competitors are now engaged. The indirect costs of US-style regulation and liability rules are probably substantially greater in the second phase of environmental requirements than the first. ... Accordingly, the studies understate the adverse effects of current US environmental law and regulation on competitiveness.'

Related to this is the fact that such studies are based on the whole on an assessment of existing rather than proposed legislation. By ignoring regulatory standards which might have been introduced but for concerns about competitiveness they fail to strike at heart of the matter. In other words they cannot know to what extent the current regulatory framework is itself shaped by the existence of a 'regulatory gap'.

Secondly, and of crucial importance, is the availability of substantial evidence which suggests that firms and governments

[11] See Stewart, 1993 for a useful overview of the literature.
[12] Case C-300/89 *Commission* v. *Council (Titanium Dioxide)* [1991] ECR I-2867, para. 7.

perceive a negative relationship between regulation and competitiveness. Ludwig Kramer observes simply that '. . . it is commonplace
that environmental measures cost money . . . [and that] hardly any
measure which intends to protect the environment is without some
economic consequences and thus, one way or another [affects] the
competitiveness of economic agents' (1993: 29, 32).

Yet '[i]n politics appearance and belief become reality' (Stewart,
1993: 2085), and corporate and governmental decisions are as likely
to be premised on the former as the latter. Concerns about the
competitiveness of the Community's proposed tax on carbon dioxide
and energy are expressed within the proposal itself[13] while similar
concerns have led to a 'dilution' of the Community's 1989 proposal
concerning civil liability for damage caused by waste,[14] a proposal
which even in this form has yet to be adopted.

If then the debate is less about the capacity of environmental
regulation to affect, and to be seen to affect, the relative competitiveness of firms and more about the degree and manner in which it does
so, two crucial questions arise. First, to what extent does the central
GATT principle of non-discrimination between imported and
domestic goods imply that goods produced outside the jurisdiction
of the importing state can be required to satisfy the same process
and product standards as those produced inside? Secondly, if GATT
has been read in such a way as to limit the 'extra-jurisdictional'
applicability of domestic standards, then in what circumstances,
and through recourse to which instruments, might the importing
state justifiably restrict the flow of goods into its territory or at least
seek to redress the competitive balance between domestic and
imported goods?

In addressing the first question it is necessary to examine GATT
Article III, which in prohibiting discrimination between 'like'
domestic and imported products outlaws the levying of differential
taxes or charges and the differential application of internal laws,
regulations, or other national requirements. It requires simply that
national regulations impose an equal burden on like products,

[13] See the Preamble and Article 1 of the *Proposal for a Council Directive Introducing a
Tax on Carbon Dioxide Emissions and Energy* COM(92) 226. So great are the concerns
about competitiveness that the proposal provides that the tax arrangements
envisaged by it should not be introduced until such a time as the other OECD states
have introduced a similar tax or measures having an equivalent financial impact.
[14] *Amended proposal for a Council Directive on Civil Liability for Damage Caused by Waste*,
OJ 1991 C192/6.

regardless of the origin of the goods in question, and hence legitimates the enforcement of, for example, national product or compositional requirements *vis-à-vis* imported goods. Imported products can thus be required to satisfy domestic product regulations aimed at environmental objectives in so far as they relate to final character or composition. However, where imported and domestic goods share the same essential physical characteristics and are thus indistinguishable in terms of quality, GATT members are prohibited from discriminating between them in respect of the manner in which they were manufactured or produced. Hence for the purposes of Article III 'like' is defined exclusively in terms of *product standards* and, where goods are alike, discrimination premised upon the *production process* is unlawful. In effect Article III renders domestic product regulation effective in relation to imported goods, while denying the 'extra-territoriality' of process regulation.

That the same essential distinction between product and process regulation is inherent in GATT's explicit environmental exceptions to be found in Articles XX(b) and XX(g) is evident from infamous (unadopted) GATT panel decision relating to American tuna fish imports from Mexico.[15] This case examined the legitimacy of a US decision to ban the importation of yellowfin tuna from Mexico on the ground that the Mexican fleet employed fishing methods which resulted in a dolphin-kill ratio which was significantly higher than that accepted by US domestic legislation, in the form of the Marine Mammal Protection Act. In rejecting the legitimacy of the United State's measures which constituted a quantitative restriction within the meaning of Article XI, the GATT panel not only questioned their 'necessity' within the meaning of Article XX(b) and doubted whether they were aimed 'primarily' (within the meaning of Article of XX(g)) at conservation, but also, vitally, held that the 'extra-jurisdictional' applicability of these standards rendered them incompatible with GATT. It emphasized that members may not restrict imports with a view to protecting life or health or conserving natural resources outside of their jurisdiction,[16] and that to suggest otherwise would imply that:

---

[15] *United States—Restrictions on Imports of Tuna*, Report of the Panel (1992) 4 *World Trade Materials* 20–51. See H. Ward, 1994 for a discussion of this report.

[16] It has been suggested that as a result of this reasoning existing Community measures such as the Leghold Trap Regulation (Council Reg. (EEC) No. 3254/91 OJ 1991 L308/1) and the Seal Pup Directive (Council Dir. 83/129/EEC OJ 1983 L91/30) are 'probably illegal under the GATT' (Cheyne, 1994: 595).

. . . each contracting party could unilaterally determine the life or health [or conservation] protection policies from which other contracting parties could not deviate without jeopardising their rights under the General Agreement. The General Agreement would then no longer constitute a multilateral framework for trade among all contracting parties but would provide legal security only in respect of trade between a limited number of contracting parties with identical internal regulations.[17]

This panel report highlights a number of interesting and important issues and questions. Not only does it exemplify the significance of the new procedures relating to Council adoption of panel reports but it also goes straight to the heart of the competitiveness conundrum. Here, in so far as it is premised upon a distinction between internal and external effects, it surely misses the point. The United States has already banned the use of large-scale drift-net fishing while the Community plans to do so by the end of 1997. Were the Community to seek similarly to prohibit the importation of fish products harvested in this way few would accept that the Community was motivated exclusively, or even primarily, by an altruistic concern for 'foreign' fish! Rather, any such external prohibition would stem from a recognition that internal policy in this respect would be economically unsustainable if its own fleets were required to compete on such unequal terms. External measures would operate indirectly to bolster internal measures, although the link between the two would be economic rather than material.

This panel report begs more than one important question, not least that relating to the problem of 'drifting pollution' which arises when production processes in one jurisdiction create a perceptible, although indirect, environmental impact in the jurisdiction of the importing state, for example in respect of migrating fish or bird stocks, deforestation, the use of chlorofluorocarbons (CFCs), or carbon dioxide emissions. In such circumstances might Articles XX(b) or XX(g) legitimately be invoked?

Although this question remained unanswered in the first panel report, in a second more recent report the panel, taking a more nuanced approach to the jurisdictional issues, appears to suggest

[17] *Supra* n. 15, 64. It is interesting to observe that such concerns have not yet undermined the determination of states to apply their anti-trust norms in such an extra-territorial manner. In the Community context see Case 89/85 etc. *Ahlstrom* et al. v. *Commission* [1988] ECR 5193.

that they might.[18] In this later report the panel insists that it is not the location of the resource to be conserved or the living thing to be protected which is crucial, but rather the purpose and the effect of the measure itself. In so far as the trade measure is such as to implement policies directly within the jurisdiction of the state introducing the measure, and to render effective domestic environmental policies, it might fall within the parameters of the Article XX exceptions. However, to the extent that it would be capable of achieving such ends only if the exporting (or intermediary) state were to change its policies or practices within its own jurisdiction these exceptions cannot apply.

The conclusions of this second panel are welcome in that they acknowledge the reality of physical interdependence between states. However, they still fail to recognize the significance of what have been called 'psychic' or emotional 'spillovers', which reflect the 'existence' or spiritual value of environmental goods even for those who do not directly use them, and even for those who reside in a different jurisdiction (Wils, 1994: 89).[19] Moreover these findings are equally premised upon a conception of sovereignty which, as shown by the above arguments relating to regulatory divide and rule and diminishing *de facto* authority and control, is unduly narrow. The practices of the exporting state may not in any physical sense undermine the capacity of the importing state to implement its domestic policies but, as a result of competitiveness concerns, it may render these policies politically and economically unworkable.

If global 'negative' integration is to continue largely unhindered by unilateral state or supra-state regulation, at least in respect of process regulation, then a question remains as to the role of international positive integration measures, in the form of international environmental agreements. For those sensitive to the

[18] *General Agreement on Tariffs and Trade: Dispute Settlement Panel Report of United States Restrictions on Imports of Tuna* (1994) 22 *Intl. Legal Materials* 839.

[19] The current protests in the UK regarding the conditions in which veal calves are reared in certain member states exemplify the nature of this concept. Notwithstanding that the threat to the environment occurs outside the territory of the state in which the protesters reside, they feel justified in pressing for the introduction of trade restrictions (export bans) by the UK Government. In so far as any such ban were predicated upon concern over farming methods in countries other than the UK, and in so far as this trade measure is not necessary to render effective environmental protection policies within the UK, it would, according to the logic of GATT, be unlawful. The Court of Justice scrupulously avoided addressing similar questions in Case C-169/89 *Gourmetterie van den Burg* [1990] ECR I-2143.

tensions between multilateralism in trade and environmental protection, and to the threat which each potentially poses to the other, the solution must, it is frequently argued, lie not in the curtailment of negative integration through unilateral measures susceptible to abuse but rather in the promotion of corresponding positive or policy integration. Leaving aside the difficult issue of state voluntarism in international law, this begs the crucial question as to the relationship between GATT and international conventions which seek to harmonize standards and to legitimate Trade Related Environmental Measures (TREMs) where these standards are not respected. The issue is more than merely hypothetical, as demonstrated by agreements such as the Convention on International Trade in Endangered Species of Wild Fauna and Flora (CITES) and the Montreal Protocol to the Vienna Convention for the Protection of the Ozone Layer. The former allows parties to prohibit the importation and exportation of endangered and threatened species; the latter requires the phasing out of the production and use of CFCs and other ozone-depleting chemicals, permitting the progressive banning of controlled substances from non-parties, as well as of products containing, or those made with but not containing, controlled substances. There is little doubt that both contain provisions which are inconsistent with GATT (Schoenbaum, 1992: 717–20).

Article 30 of the Vienna Convention on the Law of Treaties addresses the question of incompatible agreements. For states which are parties to both treaties, it determines that the earlier treaty will apply only in so far as it is compatible with the later. For a state which is party to both treaties and another which is party only to one, it requires that their rights and obligations be determined by that to which they are both party. Hence in circumstances where trading partners are both party to a later environmental agreement, this agreement will prevail over inconsistent GATT norms. However, where only one is a party the other can legitimately expect its rights under GATT to be respected, unless a waiver is granted under GATT Article XXV(5). Few would disagree with Schoenbaum (1992: 720) when he observes that:

. . . this is an unsatisfactory state of affairs. Unlike the unilateral USA tuna embargo, multilateral international agreements such as CITES and the Montreal Convention should be upheld in their entirety. There should be no doubt as to their validity under the GATT. . . . What is needed is an explicit statement—perhaps by amendment to Article XX—by the GATT contracting parties validating trade restrictions relating to . . . the enforcement of international environmental agreements.

If the situation was unsatisfactory when Schoenbaum wrote, it is clearly more so today. Pursuant to the conclusion of the Uruguay Round and the entry into force of the WTO Agreement, global trade relations are now governed by GATT 1994, as defined in a general interpretative note to Annex 1A of this Agreement, and the unilateral trade agreements also annexed thereto. Article 11(4) of the WTO Agreement asserts that GATT 1994 is 'legally distinct' from GATT 1947. GATT is now the later agreement and as such will take precedence over inconsistent earlier agreements, including CITES and the Montreal Protocol to the Vienna Convention, even as between states which are party to each. This applies notwithstanding the commitment in the WTO Preamble to 'sustainable development', the protection and preservation of the environment, and the activities of the GATT Group on Environmental Measures and International Trade.[20] Negative integration measures now take precedence over the results of earlier positive integration and in so far as the trade-related environment aspects of international conventions conflict with GATT their effectiveness is undermined.[21]

Such a position exemplifies the intransigence of GATT in respect of national efforts to offset the additional costs often associated with environmental regulation through recourse to TREMs. By focusing on process regulation and quantitative restrictions it has unfortunately side-stepped crucial questions relating to the legitimacy of additional forms of intervention, not least tariffs, subsidies, border tax adjustments, and countervailing duties. A number of acute studies have been undertaken which analyse their usefulness and legitimacy in a trade-related environmental context (see Düerkop, 1994; Charnovitz, 1993). Notwithstanding the ingenuity and creativity of these authors in seeking to identify 'GATT-consistent'

---

[20] For details of the role and activities of this group since its first meeting in October 1993, see O'Connor & van de Ven, 1995.

[21] It has been correctly observed that 'the GATT has never ruled that a trade measure taken pursuant to an environmental treaty is GATT-illegal' and that 'it seems unlikely that the GATT Council would take that suicidal plunge. But the GATT has been unable to do anything . . . to assure environmentalists that such an outcome would not happen' (Charnovitz, 1994:28). Lawyers, like environmentalists, are well advised to remain sceptical of such conclusions premised upon political hope rather than legal reason.

means of protecting the environment while confronting the competitiveness issue, each concludes that although trade liberalization and environmental protection are not essentially incompatible objectives, the tension between the two can only be substantially relieved through a reassessment of GATT rules in the light of environmental concerns.

4. CONCLUSION

This Chapter has sought to highlight a dilemma at once profound and pressing. On one hand, few would endorse the hypocrisy of a Community which, while rhetorically committed to GATT, fails to construct the legal mechanisms required to ensure its respect by its own executive and legislative organs. That it fails to do so at a time when weaker and poorer nations are obliged to pursue rapid trade liberalization in the name of structural adjustment implies a moral agnosticism unbefitting the Community. On the other hand, it has been the thesis of this Chapter that the fundamental premises of GATT, as they currently stand, are themselves deeply flawed in that they fail to reconcile the tension between trade liberalization and other societal interests, not least the protection and preservation of the environment. The deregulatory impetus inherent in the current GATT privileges free trade 'over all', depicting it as an end in itself rather than as a means of achieving goals recognized by the international community. The *de facto* capacity of the Community (and of the United States) to be selective in compliance with GATT operates merely to disguise the nature of the tensions to which it gives rise, and to undermine the apparent urgency of the need to reappraise the origins of the regulatory gap, together with efforts at international level to achieve a more sustainable balance between 'negative' and 'positive' integration. If, as has been argued, the politics of the Community's earlier approach to GATT may have been undermined by the WTO Agreement, and if the Community's commitment to sustainable development and an improvement in the quality of life of the citizens of the Union is not to disintegrate in the face of a merciless quest for competitive supremacy, the urgency of these tasks must now be acknowledged. Failure to do so poses a threat not only to the environment but ultimately also to the credibility of notions of free international trade.

Regulating the free movement of goods: institutions and institutional change*

KENNETH A. ARMSTRONG

In the past attempts to theorize the development of the European Union have been grounded in the work of political scientists. In particular, international relations theory has produced the most enduring methodological and theoretical tools in the form of the concepts of (neo)functionalism (e.g. Haas, 1958; Tranholm-Mikkelson, 1991), intergovernmentalism (Moravcsik, 1991, 1993), and interdependency (Keohane and Nye, 1977; Keohane and Hoffman, 1990). A central controversy for each of these approaches concerns the role of political institutions in shaping the development of the European Union. My task in Section 1 is to establish why paying attention to the activities of political institutions is a potentially fruitful methodological approach to an analysis of the governance of the European Union. In Section 2, the issues raised in Section 1 will be illustrated through a discussion of the regulation of the free movement of goods.

1. THE ROLE OF INSTITUTIONS AND INSTITUTIONAL ACTORS IN DECISION-MAKING PROCESSES

March and Olsen, through their work on 'new institutionalism' (1984, 1989), have sought to reorientate the attention of political scientists towards the impact of institutions on political life. Their

* The author would like to thank the many people who have commented on earlier drafts of this chapter, in particular the participants at the November 1994 Workshop hosted by the Europa Institute, Edinburgh, and Simon Bulmer. I owe a particular debt to Simon as the work here has its inspiration from a project conducted with him on *The Rule-Making Process in the Single Market* (a project under the auspices of the Economic and Social Research Council's *Single Market Initiative*–Award no: W113251014). An earlier version of the paper was presented at the 1994 Law and Society Conference, Phoenix, Arizona.

work is a reaction against what they see as a growing tendency to conceive of institutions as mere arenas in which policy inputs are simply aggregated. In particular, they are concerned with a conception of political life which views policy outcomes as the aggregate consequences of the rational choices of individuals acting upon preferences developed exogenously to the political system. Hence their concern is to provide an account of the manner in which political institutions and political systems shape the form and content of policy outcomes.

This reorientation of attention is particularly appropriate in the case of the governance of the European Union (Bulmer, 1994). With the demise of neofunctionalism as a 'whole theory' and the ascendency of intergovernmental accounts of European integration, the role of political institutions in shaping patterns of integration has become marginalized (Wincott, 1995a). In Moravcsik's (1993) 'liberal intergovernmentalism', political institutions are reduced to arenas in which domestic societal and economic interests are aggregated (through the transmission belt of the governments of the member states).

My aim in this Chapter is to provide an institutionalist 'account'[1] of the governance of the European Union. The central contention is that institutions *matter*. Through an exploration of the central claims of institutionalist writers I seek to provide an account of how and why institutions matter and why this orientation of inquiry may provide a useful foundation for a discussion of the governance of the European Union. In the process I hope to clarify some ambiguities of institutionalist writings.

1.1 Institutions and Institutional Actors

Institutional theory has tended to be bedevilled by a failure to clarify the relationship between institutions and institutional actors. Clearly, it would make little sense to argue the case for an institutionalist approach to European integration without clarifying the central terminology.

---

[1] I use the term 'account' because the approach adopted is more a methodology than a theory. There is no claim to a grand overarching theory of Union governance. Rather, the aim is a more modest contribution to an understanding of the political and legal dynamics of integration.

Institutionalist writers are making two related moves. The first is an attempt to bring political institutions such as courts, legislatures, and bureaucracies back into the discussion of why policy outcomes are what they are. I suggest that this strand of institutionalism is concerned with an identification of 'institutional actors'; who gets to participate in the policy-making process, through which channels, and with what intensity?

If the proper identification of institutional actors were all that institutionalism had to offer it would indeed be a limited reorientation. The central concern of institutional writers, however, is in an understanding of the role of institutions in shaping the decision-making process. In this sense 'institutions' can be defined as the rules, norms, beliefs, rhetorics, ideologies, and procedures which shape the interaction between institutional actors and which orientate institutional actors to their allotted functions.[2] Thus, institutions shape the procedural and substantive dimensions of decision-making.

Two different strands of institutional thought can be identified. In one sense institutions can be viewed as the 'rules of the game' of any system. This has given rise to a form of 'rational choice institutionalism' which, as Thelen and Steinmo (1992: 7) note, views a system's game rules as creating not merely constraints on behaviour but also a context for strategic action. A good example of this is the tax system in which the taxation rules both constrain action and permit strategic action in the form of tax avoidance or creative compliance (see Levi, 1988). What is significant is that this form of institutionalism does not depart from approaches which view macro-consequences as the result of the aggregation of rational micro-behaviour (March and Olsen, 1984; 735).[3]

However, institutionalism also exists in another variant: 'historical institutionalism'. While not denying that conclusions may be drawn as to the rationality of action, it does deny that action must

---

[2] This definition is inspired by Hall's definition of institutions as '. . . the formal rules, compliance procedures and standard operating procedures that structure the relationship between individuals in various units of the polity and economy' (1986: 19).

[3] Although Thelen and Steinmo consider 'rational choice institutionalism' to fall within the same rubric as other forms of institutionalism, it is suggested that there are significant incompatibilities with the entire institutionalist approach.

necessarily be rationally defined. As Thelen and Steinmo contend (1992: 9):

> ... historical institutionalism would not have trouble with the rational choice idea that political actors are acting strategically to achieve their ends. But clearly, it is not very useful simply to leave it at that. We need a historically based analysis to tell us what they are trying to maximise and why they emphasize certain goals over others. ... By shaping not just actors' strategies (as in rational choice) but their goals as well, and by mediating their relations of cooperation and conflict, institutions structure political situations and leave their own imprint on political outcomes.

It is in the style of historical institutionalism that this chapter will endeavour to explore the regulation of the free movement of goods.

1.2 Historical Institutionalism and 'Rational' Policy-Making

Rational-choice approaches to decision-making view decisions as the outcomes of choices made by individuals on the basis of their preferences. The methodological individualism which underpins such an approach simply takes preferences as given, with rationality as the presupposed corollary to the discernible existence of strategic action.[4]

Historical institutionalist approaches seek to problematize the issues of preference-dependent outcomes and rationality. They endeavour to indicate the manner in which outcomes are shaped by institutional actors and institutions. Thus while the 'procedural' dimension of institutions has already been mentioned, it is also necessary to consider their substantive dimension. That is to say that institutions shape policy outcomes in terms of their content by orientating institutional actors towards some choices rather than others. In the case of regulatory policy-making, institutions mediate between the means and ends of regulation. In particular, it is suggested that norms of appropriateness are endogenously created through processes of 'learning by doing' which structure how regulators relate to the regulatory means at their disposal and the possible goals which they might pursue.

An important aspect to this substantive institutional component relates to the history of decision-making in a given area. The

---

[4] This notion of rationality as 'presupposed' is drawn from Lukes' discussion of rationality (Lukes, 1991).

suggestion is that the history of decision-making in a given policy area creates a *path-dependency*. Thus action at any given time is framed by the legacy of past problems and past solutions. This point is important in that it provides a viewpoint from which to reflect upon the idea of a 'rational regulator'.

A rational regulator will choose the optimal regulatory outcome from the range of all possible solutions to any given problem, with full attention being paid to the consequences of each possible course of action. In this sense regulating is 'rational' in that the process starts with a problem and—on the basis of perfect information and unlimited resources—makes its way towards a unique solution.[5]

Historical institutionalism seeks to identify the ways in which solutions to problems are often not unique but 'routineized'; similar problems tend to be solved by the same solutions. Further, limitations on resources and attention spans curtail the search for optimal solutions.[6] In a more radical form, however, instead of solutions being viewed as the unique answer to a specific problem, solutions can often be said to be in search of problems:

Alternatives are not automatically provided to a decision-maker; they have to be found. Search for alternatives occurs in an organized context in which problems are not only looking for solutions, but solutions are looking for problems. Information about the consequences of alternatives is generated and communicated through organized institutions, so expectations depend on the structure of linkages within the system, as well as the ways in which biases and counter biases cumulate (March and Olsen, 1984: 740).

Through research into the history and evolution of different governance regimes we can identify: the extent to which solutions to problems are routineized; the role of organizational linkages in shaping decision-makers' reconciliation of problems and solutions; and the manner in which solutions are in search of problems. These ideas inform the approach to the regulation of the free movement of goods discussed in Section 2.

The empirically based approach of historical institutionalism is in

---

[5] On rational policy-making paradigms see Lindblom, 1968; Diver, 1981.

[6] As Weinberger notes (1993: 178): '. . . the practice of teleological deliberation is reduced by different advice e.g. by pre-established decisions which are incorporated into the analysis as a whole, by fixed intentions which form the basic framework of a life-plan and are only put into question under special circumstances; in most cases it is not the entire field of possibilities which is scrutinised and subjected to a relative evaluation, but only a subset which encompasses a satisfying possibility.'

sharp contrast to the *a priori* assumptions of methodological individualism. It problematizes the notion of 'rationality' and reduces it to a formal concept which has meaning only in a formal world in which problems and solutions are epiphenomenal to the task of decision-making. Thus, while it may be contended that a historical institutional approach discloses but provides no means of critiquing the 'policy failure' of decision-makers, it nonetheless provides a means of explaining why decisions were made in the way they were. If decision-making is concerned more with the search for 'satisfactory' than for 'optimal' outcomes (March and Simon, 1958: 140–1) it is less than clear what kind of critique theories which assume that human or organizational behaviour is otherwise can hope to provide.

1.3 Institutional Change

A potentially serious challenge to an institutionalist methodology concerns the issue of institutional change. The idea that institutional actors and institutions play a profound role in shaping the form and content of policy outcomes runs the risk of dissolving into a form of determinism in which policy outcomes are determined by institutions and institutional actors rather than mediated. Further, this determinism would tend to give an account of institutions and institutional actors as being 'static'.

The view adopted here is that the relationship between institutions and institutional actors is dynamic. New institutional actors may emerge (for example the Committee of the Regions) or existing institutional actors may develop new powers (for example the empowerment of the European Parliament under Article 189B EC Treaty, the 'co-decision' procedure). Both these examples could be said to support the liberal intergovernmentalist claim that high profile treaty revisions are the most significant form of institutional change. On this argument the central role of member states in the negotiating process would be highlighted to the detriment of institutional actors. To be sure, treaty revisions do constitute a highly significant form of institutional change. Nonetheless to view institutional change as wholly referable to the demands of the member states would be erroneous. Rather, institutional actors are capable of shaping their own institutional contexts. A good example of this is the use of Articles 85 and 86 EC by the Commission (sanctioned by the Court of Justice) to develop a system of European Community merger control prior to the adoption of a specific instrument of merger regulation.[7] Another example is the use of Articles 100 and 235 EC to create an environmental policy competence. In short, norms of appropriateness are created which guide existing institutional practice. Existing means can be attached to new goals.

Institutional actors may also create new means by which to attain existing goals. This is of particular relevance to the regulation of the free movement of goods. An example is the use of European technical standards and mutual recognition to achieve free movement. These issues will be considered in Section 2.

It is worth responding to a serious criticism that by ascribing some autonomy to institutional actors (their ability to shape the means and ends of their regulatory function) I have only succeeded in bringing institutional actors—as rational decision-makers—into the picture. In this sense policy innovation could simply be seen as the rational choice of autonomous institutional actors. It would be paradoxical to provide an account of the role of institutions and institutional actors in the policy process which did not also provide an account of their contribution to policy innovation in a manner consistent with institutionalism.

One can contend that policy innovation is, to use Weir's terminology (1992), 'bounded innovation'. This notion works in a number of different ways. For example, the range of possible policy positions is itself highly dependent upon the history and flow of ideas and opportunities. Thus policy change may be highly dependent upon the flow of ideas from other institutional actors (emphasizing organizational linkages); from professions (one might highlight the dominance of lawyers and economists within bureaucracies); from interest groups (raising the issue of the 'openness' or 'closure' of the decision-making process to interest-group lobbying); or from 'epistemic communities'[8] (consider the role played by the management consultants W. S. Atkins in providing the 'expert' knowledge

---

[7] See Case 6/72 *Europemballage Corporation and Continental Can Co. Inc.* v. *Commission* [1973] ECR 215 and Joined Cases 142/84 & 156/84 *British American Tobacco Co. Ltd. & R.J. Reynolds Industries* v. *Commission* [1987] ECR 4487.

[8] Haas defines an 'epistemic community' as '. . . a network of professionals with recognized expertise and competence in a particular domain and an authoritative

which formed the basis of the *Cost of Non-Europe* studies, in turn used by the Commission to justify the need for the completion of the internal market).

A different example of 'bounded innovation' can be drawn from Majone's insight that 'The ability of policy makers to innovate often depends more on their skill in utilizing existing models than on inventing novel solutions' (1991: 79).

In this way, regulatory 'imitation'[9] may be more prevalent that innovation. Majone highlights cross-national regulatory imitation, but one might also refer to regulatory imitation across policy areas. While the freedom to provide services is not discussed in this Chapter it is evident that the Court of Justice has adopted an approach to the regulation of services which parallels that of the freedom to provide goods (see Weatherill & Beaumont, 1993: 516–17).

Finally, one can highlight the path-dependency of policy innovation by drawing on the idea of 'learning by doing'. Those engaged in the task of regulating adapt their strategies according to their perception of the success or failure of past action. The emphasis, however, should be placed on the issue of 'perception' rather than concerns with 'success' or 'failure', because the construction of experience is the focus. In this way it can be argued that policy innovation is more likely to be effected by incremental refinements than radical changes. Existing policy approaches tend to persist, with new strategies being additional to, rather than displacements of, past approaches.

---

claim to policy-relevant knowledge within that domain or issue-area' (1992: 3). The use of 'experts' as knowledge-providers is clearly salient in relation to the development of policies in given areas. Their use may be informally attached to the decision-making process or more formally institutionalized in the form of expert committees. As Haas notes: '. . . by pointing out which alternatives are not viable on the basis of their causal understanding of the problems to be addressed, the community members can limit the range of alternatives under consideration. While the actual choice of policies remains the domain of the decision makers, it can also be influenced by community members. As Herbert Simon points out, almost all organizations engage in some form of 'satisficing' or procedural rationality in consideration of policy alternatives. If rationality is bounded, epistemic communities may be responsible for circumscribing the boundaries and delimiting the options' (Haas, 1992: 16) (footnote omitted).

[9] Regulatory styles are described as 'imitated' to highlight the fact that these styles must nonetheless be adapted to a 'particular political, institutional and economic context' (Majone, 1991: 80).

1.4 Summary

It is suggested that analysis of the relationship between institutional actors and institutions can reveal much about the dynamics of European integration. In Section 1 I gave a detailed sketch of the issues which an institutionalist approach would tackle. Not all the issues raised can be illustrated in Section 2 where the evolution of the governance of the free movement of goods will be discussed. Nonetheless, it is hoped that the discussion can be used by others to frame future research strategies.

2. REGULATING THE FREE MOVEMENT OF GOODS

The free movement of goods within the European Community has for long been a central policy goal. The regulatory means for the attainment of that goal were established in the EC Treaty in Articles 30–6 (the prohibition of national barriers to trade) and in Articles 100, 100A-B (the creation of harmonized rules, conformity to which allows access to the market). Whereas the first of these strategies places the national courts and the Court of Justice in the role of decision-maker, the second strategy brings into focus the role of the Commission in its function as the initiator of the legislative process.[10]

In this section I shall explore the way in which institutional actors have constructed their roles in the regulation of the free movement of goods. What rules or norms have been institutionalized to guide the means and ends of regulation? To what extent are solutions 'routineized' responses to policy problems? In what way are solutions in search of problems? And what role is played by organizational linkages in shaping how regulators undertake their tasks?

The application of the rules in Articles 30–6 EC by the Court of Justice will be considered. This will be followed by a discussion of the Commission's initiation of the legislative process to create harmonized Community rules.

---

[10] The roles of the European Parliament and the Council of Ministers in the legislative process are not considered here; my aim is to discuss the institutional rules and norms which surround the decision of the Commission to initiate rule-making.

2.1 The Court of Justice and the free movement of goods

In Moravcsik's 'liberal intergovernmentalist' account the contribution of the Court of Justice to the dynamics of integration is
presented as an 'anomaly' (1993: 513). As will be indicated, this
anomaly is explicable in terms of the relative autonomy of the Court
and its ability to shape the institutional context in which it and other
actors must operate. Through the restriction of national 'exit'[11]
(Weiler, 1991), the Court has succeeded in allocating to itself and to
the Commission the task of reconciling the demands of integration
with the pursuit of legitimate regulatory objectives (Dehousse,
1992). However, there is some evidence of a re-allocation of this task
back to the institutions of the member states. This is the subject of
the first analysis.

The Court, in its development of the 'state of origin' principle (to
use Reich's terminology: Reich, 1994), has also contributed to the
manner in which the Commission exercises its right of legislative
initiative. Thus, the concept of 'mutual recognition' has emerged
both as a new regulatory strategy and as a regulatory principle to
guide the scope of Community legislation. This is discussed below.

2.1.1. Reconciling Regulation and Integration: The Role of the Court of Justice

The *Dassonville–Cassis* Regime

Article 30 EC prohibits member states from maintaining restrictions having equivalent effect to quantitative restrictions. The most
obvious form of restriction is one which discriminates directly
against goods emanating from another member state, for example
by imposing conditions which imported products alone must satisfy.
Accordingly, the Court has found little difficulty in determining that
such restrictions fall foul of Article 30. While Article 36 EC provides
a mechanism by which national measures which are caught by
Article 30 may nonetheless be considered legal, the Court has
routinely given a restricted interpretation to the scope of Article 36
(Shaw, 1993: 293–5).

The more vexed issue concerns 'indistinctly applicable' measures.

---

[11] By 'exit' I refer to the competence of the member states to exercise their
traditional regulatory functions.

That is those national measures which, while applying to domestic
and imported products alike, still have the effect of restricting intra-
Community trade. These measures form the focus of this section.

In its important *Dassonville* decision[12] the Court extended the
ambit of Article 30 to measures which 'directly or indirectly,
actually or potentially' hindered trade between member states. Thus
a low level of connection between a measure and its impact upon
trade was all that needed to be shown for a measure to fall foul of
Article 30. This created a form of *per se* illegality[13] of national
measures. This approach to Article 30 was significant in the early
period of the Community in bringing as wide a range of measures as
possible within the scope of Community regulatory control.
Through the restriction of national regulatory competence, the
Court simultaneously asserted its own authority to review national
regulatory measures while legitimating the Commission's role in the
harmonization of national laws. While there has been some
softening of the *Dassonville* doctrine as the case law of the Court has
evolved, its mechanistic citation by the Court (Reich, 1994: 465)
nonetheless provides an indication of the unwillingness of the Court
to retreat from the institutionalization of Community control in
relation to the free movement of goods.[14]

The difficulty with the Court's approach, however, concerned the
danger of 'regulatory gaps' emerging. It is one thing to seek to
transfer regulatory competence to the Community level because of a
fear of protectionist national measures, but this must be predicated

[12] Case 8/74 *Procureur du Roi* v. *Dassonville* [1974] ECR 837.
[13] This terminology is used to highlight the parallels with EC competition policy;
in its early development the Commission tended to treat activities as falling foul of EC
competition rules without an in-depth economic analysis of activities, but relying on
the existence of a scheme of exemptions to permit activities (subject to conditions in
many cases). The important point is the wide casting of the regulatory net.
[14] It is worth pointing out that through the late 1960s and early 1970s the Court
also developed the doctrine of the 'pre-emption' of national laws where the
Community had adopted common rules for the organization of a market or had
exhaustively regulated an area. As Waelbrock notes, in this period the Court
appeared to take a 'conceptualist federalist' approach meaning that the Court
appeared to have adopted an approach by which it would apply this doctrine
mechanistically without a case-by-case weighing of the effects of the national measure
on trade within the Community (Waelbrock, 1982). Once again, this can be viewed
as the institutionalization of the appropriateness of Community control. However, as
Weatherill has indicated, the introduction of Article 100A(4) EC and the use of New
Approach directives tend to undermine the notion of pre-emption (Weatherill, 1994).

on the ability of the institutional actors of the Community to adopt new measures which both protect legitimate regulatory objectives and ensure the free movement of goods. With the decisional deadlock of the Council of Ministers in the 1970s it became clear that regulatory gaps might well emerge.

The Court could not have been blind to the events within the Council. Hence in its judgment in *Cassis de Dijon*[15] the Court created a regulatory space in which national restrictions, while rendered 'suspect' and subject to scrutiny by the Court, might nonetheless be declared compatible with the Treaty. Indistinctly applicable measures (that is to say national measures which do not *ex facie* discriminate against importers) which actually or potentially hindered trade could be justified in so far as was *necessary* for the pursuit of national 'mandatory requirements' (listed as 'the effectiveness of fiscal supervision, the protection of public health, the fairness of commercial transaction and the defence of the consumer' but extended in other cases to include the protection of the environment[16] and the protection of national or regional culture[17]). Mandatory requirements would survive scrutiny provided they were proportionate.

Thus the Court opened up a regulatory space for legitimate national measures. However, it was a space to be controlled by the Court (Alter and Meunier-Aitsahalia, 1994: 540). In short, the *Cassis* 'solution' served to ensure the centrality of the Court of Justice in the integration of the Community market in goods. In this manner the Court was not so much finding a unique solution to the facts of the case as defining a solution capable of adaptation to indistinctly applicable measures generally. The *Cassis* 'solution' can be seen to be composed of three elements:

a) the finding that an indistinctly applicable measure actually or potentially hinders trade,

b) the categorization of the measure as fulfilling legitimate mandatory requirements (i.e. the measure pursues a legitimate regulatory objective), and

---

[15] Case 120/78 *Rewe-Zentrale AG* v. *Bundesmonopolverwaltung für Branntwein* [1979] ECR 649.

[16] See e.g. Case 302/86 *Commission* v. *Denmark* [1988] ECR 4607.

[17] See e.g. Cases 60, 61/84 *Cinéthèque* v. *Fédération Nationale des Cinémas Français* [1985] ECR 2605; Case C-145/88 *Torfaen BC* v. *B & Q plc.* [1989] ECR 3851.

c) the application of a proportionality test by which the chosen regulatory strategy is tested.

While logically there are three elements, the case law since *Cassis* has indicated that there are really two main issues: the effect of a measure on interstate trade and the ability of a member state to justify the imposition of mandatory requirements. However, the legacy of the *Dassonville* doctrine has been the subordination of the 'impact on trade' question to the issue of the national justification of measures. In this way the incantation of the *Dassonville* test has been more by way of a claim to *jurisdiction* than the application of substantive criteria with which to judge the effects of a measure upon trade.

The empowerment of the Court of Justice (and to an extent the national courts) at the expense of national legislators has been achieved through three mechanisms. First, the *Dassonville–Cassis* approach has created an institutional structure through which traders may bring actions in their national courts to require national regulators to justify the imposition of measures which may have an impact on the ability of traders to engage in economic activity. Utilizing the organizational linkage provided by the Article 177 reference procedure, cases have appeared before the Court of Justice. In turn, the Court has given sufficient guidance to the national courts on the 'justification' issue to constrain the actions of the national courts.

On a related point, the Court has invoked the (invisible, rational) Community consumer to wage war against the national regulator. That is to say, in giving its preliminary rulings to national courts, the Court of Justice has identified a clear preference for national measures which impose information requirements (for example, in the form of the labelling of products) over requirements which mandate the adaptation of products. The narrative employed by the Court is one in which the 'paternalistic' nation state is brought to its 'rational' senses by intelligent consumers capable of distinguishing margarine from butter[18] through the simple act of reading product-packaging.

---

[18] A good example is Case 261/81 *Walter Rau Lebensmittelwerke* v. *de Smedt PvBA* [1982] ECR 3961 where the Court stated that a Belgian law prohibiting the marketing of margarine in anything other than cube-shaped containers was a disproportionate measure compared with a simple labelling requirement.

Thirdly, the Court has placed national regulators in competition with one another. In *Cassis* the Court not only established the 'mandatory requirements' test, it also established that 'in principle' goods lawfully marketed in one member state should be permitted access to another (the argument being based on the functional equivalence of national measures). This 'state of origin' principle (or 'mutual recognition') provides an important institutional tool through which to defuse the justificatory force of a member state's claim to impose different requirements. Not only must the regulator in the importing member state justify national measures, it must also justify any difference between its regulatory goals and those of the exporting member state. One might conclude that in fact the 'state of origin' principle served as a presumption against the legality of national measures.

In summary, the *Dassonville–Cassis* regime, as evolved by the Court through its process of adjudication, institutionalized Community control over the free movement of goods. The question of the impact of a measure on patterns of trade became subordinated to a concern with the ability of national regulators to justify national measures. As suggested above, this was a far from simple task.

From *Cassis* to *Keck*

In Section 1 the importance of path-dependency to a historical institutional analysis of policy-making was noted. With this in mind, it can be argued that the *Dassonville–Cassis* approach contained its own potential undoing. The governance regime stabilized[19] with its regulatory environment in so far as the measures litigated were 'product-specific', such as rules relating to the nature and composition of products, the packaging and presentation of products, or rules governing the advertizing and sales promotion of specific products. To a large extent the fact that measures related directly to products and the right of traders to engage in economic activity (Chalmers, 1994) was sufficient to deal with the trade issue. As for the justification of measures, the Court adopted a highly sceptical position.

---

[19] That is not to say that the approach of the Court of Justice was always clear or consistent. It is merely suggested that the governance regime could operate according to the rules and norms which had been institutionalized without the need for institutional reform.

However, this 'solution' was forced to confront itself in a number of cases beginning in the early 1980s. One can explain why this 'solution' became problematic in terms of the history of integration. As Wils cogently notes (1993: 485), as time has gone by the easy trade barriers have been exposed and removed, leaving the Court with the difficult cases where national measures have a speculative effect on trade and pursue highly valued regulatory goals. Importantly, the twin issues of the effect on trade and the legitimacy of national controls have become central precisely because the stage of integration has been reached where the need to reconcile integration with regulation has become more difficult and more political.

In consequence, while the Court has ritualistically recited the *Dassonville–Cassis* approach, trade and regulatory issues have moved more to the fore. An example is the *Blesgen* case.[20] Drawing on a line of cases in which the Court concluded that indistinctly applicable price controls did not fall within the ambit of Article 30[21] the Advocate General concluded that unless an indistinctly applicable measure created a 'specific restriction on patterns of trade' it would not fall within Article 30. In this sense, there is a move away from an all-encompassing jurisdiction under Article 30 and an attempt to locate its scope on actual and demonstrable restrictions on imports (hence a limitation on the *Dassonville* test of 'potential' impacts upon trade).

A classic example of increased attention towards the regulatory objectives of national measures is the Court's *Cinéthèque* judgment[22] concerning a French law prohibiting the sale or hire of video films within the first year of a film's release. The Court does not depart from its incantation of the *Dassonville–Cassis* formula in that it

---

[20] Case 75/81 *Blesgen* v. *Belgium* [1982] ECR 1211. Here, the Court concluded that a Belgian law preventing *inter alia* the sale of alcoholic spirits for consumption on premises open to the public did not fall within Art. 30. What is interesting is that the Advocate General relied on statistics provided by the Commission which indicated that the Belgian law did not have a negative impact on the import of spirits. Further, the Advocate General made clear that the social goal of the prevention of alcoholism would be sufficient to justify the measure.

[21] See e.g. Case 13/77 *GB-INNO-BM* v. *Vereniging van de Kleinhandelaars in Tabak* [1977] ECR 2115.

[22] Cases 60-61/84 *Cinéthèque, supra* n. 17.

repeats that any disparities in regulatory systems between member states is liable to create trade barriers. However, the socio-cultural objective of preserving the role of the cinema in French cultural life is deemed sufficient to justify the measure. The difficulty here, however, is that far from the *Community* consumer being the 'invisible' recipient of the benefits of the operation of the 'invisible hand' of the market, the *French* consumer is actually rendered more visible. In this sense the Court has to move from promoting the given preferences of Community consumers to determining the appropriateness of the cultural preferences of 'real' French consumers. The task of reconciling integration with regulation consequently becomes a more obviously political task.

The increased difficulty of reconciling integration with regulation became apparent in the Sunday trading cases.[23] Traders sought in a series of cases to challenge national laws prohibiting or limiting trading on Sundays. While such measures were indistinctly applicable, unlike previous cases they were not product-specific. This raises the problem of the determination of the effect of such measures on trade (for example, trade in what products and between what states?) Further, Sunday trading laws reflect national cultural and religious considerations. Thus, these cases concerned measures which involved speculative effects on trade and valued regulatory objectives. Should the *Dassonville–Cassis* formula be applied in these cases?

The approach of the Court in the early cases such as *Torfaen* was to repeat the *Dassonville–Cassis* formula but to leave national courts to decide the issue of whether the regulatory objective justified restrictions on trade. From an institutional perspective, it is interesting that the Court of Justice should adopt such an inactivist position. Of course, this position is explicable in terms of the political nature of judging national cultural traditions. The consequence of national courts determining the proportionality of national measures was, however, inconsistency. This inconsistency threatened the integrity of judicial regulation of the free movement of goods. Thus in the later *Stoke-on-Trent* case the Court of Justice decided the proportionality issue itself.

In summary, the *Dassonville–Cassis* 'solution' collided with cases

---

[23] See *Torfaen supra* n. 17; Case C-169/91 *Council of the City of Stoke-on-Trent* v. *B&Q plc* [1992] ECR I-6635.

where there was only a speculative impact on trade in combination
with valued national regulatory objectives.

Keck

In the judgment in *Keck*[24] the Court indicated an important
institutional shift. The Court stated that

> contrary to what has previously been decided, the application to products
> from other Member States of national provisions restricting or prohibiting
> certain *selling arrangements* is not such as to hinder directly or indirectly,
> actually or potentially, trade between Member States within the meaning of
> the *Dassonville* judgment . . . provided that those rules apply to all affected
> traders operating within the national territory and provided they affect in
> the same manner, in law and in fact, the marketing of domestic products
> and of those from other Member States. (Emphasis added.)

Thus, through the adoption of the legal category of 'selling
arrangements', the Court has removed a sphere of national
measures from the ambit of Article 30, but on condition that a
measure does not actually distort patterns of trade (the difference
between this and the *Blesgen* judgment rests with the abandonment
of the ritualized recitation of the *Dassonville–Cassis* formula).

Much has been written in the wake of the *Keck* decision and no
attempt is made here to repeat those comments (see Chalmers, 1994;
Gormley, 1994; Moore, 1994; Reich, 1994). Rather, the significance
of *Keck* will be constructed in institutional terms.

For institutional actors, *Keck* is a clear attempt by the Court to
redefine the boundaries of its jurisdiction. It has done so by creating
a category of cases which might be termed legal *per se* (in contrast
with the tendency of its previous approach to treat national
measures as illegal *per se*). In this sense there is a limited (and
categorically bound) renunciation of jurisdiction. As the Court
pointed out, strain had been placed on the Court's limited resources
by the tendency of traders to invoke Article 30 as a means of
challenging an array of national measures. One appreciates the
Court's wish to limit the ability of traders to do this, in order to
reduce pressure on the Court's case-load.[25]

---

[24] Cases C-267 & 268/91, *Keck and Mithouard* [1993] ECR I-6097.
[25] One might argue, however, that the ambivalence of the term 'selling
arrangements' will produce its own litigation.

The significance of *Keck* is not so much its resolution of the particular facts of the case as in its treatment of the three mechanisms (noted above) which combined to support the Court's jurisdiction under the *Dassonville–Cassis* approach. First, there is an obvious retreat from the empowerment of traders to impugn national measures. Secondly, as Reich notes (1994: 484), the role of the Community consumer does not even appear to enter into the Court's analysis. Finally, far from national regulatory authority being rendered suspect, there is a tacit approval of the legitimacy of national control (drawing Reich to the conclusion of a possible connection between the timing of *Keck* and the emergence of subsidiarity). These factors together suggest a redefinition of the boundaries of national and Community control within the boundaries (whatever they may be) of the category of measures called 'selling arrangements'.

In one sense *Keck* is not all that revolutionary. As Reich argues, it is an evolution in the Court's approach covering a limited range of measures. It does not dismantle the *Dassonville–Cassis* approach to product-specific measures. However, *Keck* is revolutionary at the symbolic level. By referring to the Court's previous ritualized application of the *Dassonville–Cassis* formula I want to suggest that the formula provided an important symbol of Community control and Court jurisdiction over the free movement of goods. That symbol was ritually reinforced even in cases, like *Cinéthèque*, in which the measure did not fall foul of Article 30. In *Keck* it is not so much that, as Gormley puts it (1994: 67): 'reasoning was renounced on the altar of expediency', but more that a powerful symbol of Community control was sacrificed.

2.1.2 Conclusion

The contribution of the Court of Justice to the regulation of the free movement of goods has been highly significant. In effect it has, through the process of regulating, institutionalized the appropriateness of Community control, at least where the measures impugned are product-specific. It has sought to place itself at the centre of that system of control and has harnessed rules, norms, organizational linkages, categories, and symbols through which to achieve that end. However, it would appear that the Court is in the process of relinquishing its own centrality from that system of control. Its judgment in *Keck* is only one (and perhaps even a less significant) example of a process of redefinition of the boundaries of national and Community control.

2.2 Regulating the free movement of goods: the role of the Commission

This final section concerns the role of the Commission in the regulation of the free movement of goods. Among the institutional actors of the EC, it is the Commission which has the right to initiate the Community's legislative process. What determines how that task is understood? When is it appropriate to use legislation as a solution to policy problems within the area of the free movement of goods?

Institutionally, Article 100A EC (and previously Article 100 EEC) provides the legal basis for the adoption of harmonization measures in the area of goods. Following a discussion of the evolution of the harmonization regime for goods prior to the Single European Act (SEA), the impact of the SEA as a source of institutional change is examined. Alternatives to rule-making are then highlighted. This section concludes with a discussion of the impact of subsidiarity.

2.2.1 Initiating Rule-Making: The Role of the Commission

The regulatory character of the Community has been one of its dominant characteristics (Majone, 1991; Dehousse, 1992). That is to say that the solution of rule-making to the problem of trade barriers was the principal regulatory tool established by the EEC Treaty. The power to initiate rule-making—vested by the Treaty of Rome in the Commission alone—also performed an important symbolic function in terms of the institutionalization of the Commission as *the* policy-initiator. Moreover, as Majone has noted (1991), rule-making at Community level utilizes less of the limited resources of the Community than the costs of implementation which are borne directly by the member states.

The use of rule-making to attain the goal of the free movement of goods can be problem-specific. Events within the regulatory environment (whether the adoption of national measures which inhibit free movement or litigation which exposes the need to reconcile the demands of integration with a desirable regulatory objective) may trigger the rule-making process. An example is the adoption of the Community's packaging directive as a response to the German Töpfer ordonance requiring manufacturers to reclaim waste packaging.

However, Community rule-making may have a more proactive and programmatic dimension. Examples are the 1968 *General Programme*[26] and more obviously the Commission's 1985 White Paper on the Internal Market[27] which contains an extensive list of legislative proposals necessary for the attainment of the Internal Market. A programmatic approach may also be taken at the level of particular product groups. A classic example is motor vehicle regulation in which the Commission sought to establish a complete body of rules, conformity to which would permit motor vehicles access to the Community market. Through the exhaustive regulation (the concept of 'total harmonization') of particular types of motor vehicles (the concept of 'vertical harmonization') the free movement of motor vehicles was to be ensured. The 'programmatizing' of proposals can be significant in treating proposals as part of a 'package deal' covered by a similar logic or justification. Hence the adoption of one measure in the package increases the likelihood of the adoption of the others.

During the early period of the Community's development the Commission adopted a routineized response to rule-making which, in combination with the control held over the legislative process by the Council of Ministers, resulted in the much noted 'Eurosclerosis' of the 1970s.[28] There was a need for institutional change. Three particular forms of change ensued.

The first source of change provides a good example of the institutionalists' call for analysis of organizational linkages and the way in which solutions attach themselves to problems. As noted above, the Court of Justice in *Cassis* established that goods placed on the market in one jurisdiction should in principle have access to the

[26] EC Commission, 'General Programme for the elimination of technical barriers to intra-Community trade arising from disparities among national laws', COM(68) 138 3 Mar. 1968.

[27] EC Commission, 'Completing the Internal Market', COM(85) 310.

[28] Thus, while the Commission routinely adopted new proposals for legislation, the Council of Ministers (through the device of the Luxembourg compromise) had amended its voting procedures to ensure unanimity where important national interests were claimed. While these standard operating procedures ensured Council control over the decision-making process, they created the familiar legislative log-jam of the 1970s.

jurisdiction of other member states (mutual recognition). As Alter and Meunier-Aitsahalia have noted (1994) the concept of mutual recognition was seized upon by the Commission to redefine the roles of political and institutional actors.[29] On one hand it sent an important signal to member states as to their potential inability to exercise their national regulatory competence to inhibit the import of goods. On the other hand, *Cassis* produced a change to the institutional context for the initiation of rule-making by requiring a higher level of justification for the adoption of Community rules. In short, where trade barriers arise from disparities between national regulations Community rule-making should only be initiated where mutual recognition cannot successfully remove the barrier.

The second form of institutional change arose with the Commission's adoption of the 'New Approach'[30] to harmonization in which groups of products would be the subject of harmonization directives (a move from vertical to horizontal harmonization) and 'priority areas' (mechanical engineering, building materials, and electrical appliances) would be targeted. Only the essential health and safety requirements would be harmonized, with the technical details to be subject to work by the private European Standards Committees. The centrality of European regulation is maintained but its form is altered to achieve a more effective delivery of harmonization directives. The ends of regulation thus remained the same, but the means to achieve these ends were altered. In the process, the use of European technical standards served to empower a new set of institutional actors in the form of the European Standards Committees.

What is significant about these two related sources of change is the lack of any formal change to the Treaties establishing the Community. This highlights the importance of institutionalized (and inductively created) rules and norms to guide the rule-making task. However, it also raises an important question as to the impact

[29] The Commission also 'appropriated' the concept of mutual recognition and produced an 'interpretative communication' on the 'meaning' of *Cassis* ((OJ 1980 C256). This emphasizes that the use of information by institutional actors can be highly significant in shaping the preferences and expectations of political actors e.g. the centrality of the Cecchini report in committing member states to the Internal Market programme.

[30] EC Commission, 'Technical harmonization and standards: a new approach', COM(85) 19.

of formal treaty change. Does such change automatically result in institutional change? This can be explored in terms of the third potential source of change arising from the Single European Act.

The Single European Act changed the legal basis for the adoption of harmonization legislation for the Internal Market by the introduction of Article 100A, which introduced qualified majority voting (QMV) and the co-operation procedure (involving the Parliament more directly in the legislative process). The introduction of QMV deprived individual member states of the power to veto legislation, emphasizing a transfer of power to the Community. As the *quid pro quo* for this loss of control, the member states sought to institutionalize—through formal Treaty change—their competence to take national measures on grounds of major need (as identified in Article 36) or for the protection of the environment or working environment, even where the Community has adopted a harmonization directive. Article 100A(4) was consequently added to permit member states to request permission from the Commission for the continued application of national measures where a harmonization directive had been agreed on the basis of QMV.

How did Article 100A(4) 'fit' with prevailing institutional rules and norms? Plainly, it did not correspond to the institutionalized Community competence in the area of the free movement of goods nor the basic idea of the prevention of unilateral departure from collectively agreed rules. Yet this was precisely what the member states sought to achieve in Article 100A(4). The key question, therefore, was how the Commission would interpret the scope of this rule. What norm of appropriateness would guide its operation?

The answer appears to be that the Commission has subverted Article 100A(4) by its unwillingness to give the benefit of this provision to member states. In many ways this is consistent with the Court of Justice's reluctance to define Article 36 expansively. Thus the norm of the appropriateness of Community regulation through harmonization extends to exclude the unilateral defection from bargains agreed by the member states except when the most clear and pressing reasons are given. Indeed, only in one case has the Commission permitted a member state to continue to apply national measures after the adoption of a harmonization directive. In March 1991 the Council adopted Directive 91/173/EEC regulating the use of pentachlorophenol (PCP). In August 1991 Germany notified to the Commission its decision to continue to apply its own laws prohibiting the use of PCPs. By a decision of 2 December 1992[31] the Commission confirmed the application of the German law. However, the French government successfully argued that the Commission's decision was inadequately reasoned and ought to be annulled.[32] The potential for litigation may make the Commission in future even more wary of exercising its discretion under Article 100A(4).

Thus, while the formal Treaty change sought to alter the relationship between national and Community regulation, the Commission's relative autonomy has subverted any radical change. Article 100A(4) may, however, have an unexpectedly greater role within the context of Council bargaining. The threat of unilateral defection from a bargain could alter the bargaining positions of other member states. Thus, the impact of Article 100A(4) may actually be at its most potent prior to the adoption of a measure. It is important to see even the most intergovernmental arenas as institutionally bounded.

2.2.2 *Alternatives to Rule-Making*

It was noted at the start of this Chapter that the Treaty originally provided two means to achieve of the free movement of goods: the prohibition of trade barriers (Articles 30–6) and the harmonization of legislation (Articles 100–100B). The emergence of mutual recognition as a judicial strategy and as a norm guiding the 'appropriateness' of Community harmonization have also been discussed. With the 1992 legislative programme near completion, and in anticipation of Article 100B of the Treaty on European Union (requiring an inventory of remaining trade barriers to be drawn up), in 1990 the Commission began a process of seeking information from the member states regarding remaining barriers to trade. Once identified, the Commission originally considered that national measures could then be made subject to Council decisions (a form of individualized rule-making) requiring member states to treat the provisions of one member state as equivalent to those in another: compulsory mutual recognition.

However, in its communication on the result of the inventory of

---

[31] OJ 1992 C334/8.
[32] Case C-41/93 *France* v. *Commission* [1994] ECR I-1829.

measures drawn up under Article 100B[33] the Commission concluded that there was no need for specific measures for the recognition of equivalence, primarily because the problem areas appear only to involve 'bilateral relations between a few member states and concern a particular product in isolation'. The conclusion which the Commission seems to have drawn is that any Community action in the form of harmonization or of a Council decision on the equivalence would be a disproportionate response to the problem.

Accordingly, the Commission has decided that where mutual recognition has not taken place and the measures concerned are not clearly prohibited under Community law, then a 'pragmatic method' for swiftly resolving disputes is required. Thus any measure taken by member states to fulfil mandatory requirements or on the grounds noted in Article 36 is to be notified to the Commission to enable some form of *ex ante* action to be taken to resolve disputes. The Commission thereby seeks to expand its institutional roles of legislative proposer and litigator to include that of mediator. To be sure, the Commission has always possessed an important mediating function. Nonetheless, it is significant that whereas disputes concerning individual products tended to be routinely treated through adjudication, the Commission wishes to assume that role by resolving disputes at a political level. One might tentatively suggest that, if the problem of the 1970s was that attempted over-regulation by the Commission resulted in a judicial rescue in the form of *Cassis*, the problem of judicial over-regulation has given rise to a Commission rescue in the form of mediation. Hence, the importance which an institutional perspective attaches to organizational linkages can be seen to be of relevance.

2.2.3 *The Impact of Subsidiarity*

Having argued that rules and norms have been created to structure the exercise of Community competence, it will be clear that the normative context which has developed has institutionalized the role of the Community in the regulation of the free movement of goods at the expense of the member states. But has the introduction of the subsidiarity principle in Article 3B of the Treaty on European Union amounted to an enforced change in the rules and norms of

[33] EC Commission, 'Management of the mutual recognition of national rules after 1992', OJ 1993 C353/4.

appropriateness? Has the inductive development of the institutional arrangements for the regulation of the free movement of goods been swept away by this express external change to the formal treaty?

It should be noted at the outset that the concept of 'exclusive competence', which in theory conditions the operation of the subsidiarity principle, is judicially manufactured. It has no foundation in the original Treaty, and indeed the member states have conspicuously sought not to institutionalize and delineate areas of shared or exclusive competence precisely because this would be to create the sort of federal constitutional structure that some member states do not wish to see. Thus the very inclusion of the words 'exclusive competence' serves to highlight the importance of the Court as an institutional actor in framing the terms of negotiation by member states.

That the Community has exclusive competence in the area of the free movement of goods should have ensured that this area remained immune from the changes created by the subsidiarity debate. This has not proved to be the case precisely because the Commission, in seeking to minimize attempts at a radical re-allocation of competence to the member states, has turned the subsidiarity principle into a technical principle about rule-making, centred around the principles of proportionality and transparency.[34] Since these principles cut across areas of both shared and exclusive competence they have had an impact upon the Commission's approach to rule-making in the area of goods.

At its 1992 Edinburgh Summit the European Council requested the Commission to prepare a report on the adaptation of Community legislation to the subsidiarity principle.[35] This report[36] framed the basis of the Commission's approach to the adaptation of both existing and proposed legislation. Legislation and legislative proposals are to be considered in terms of their need to be 'recast', 'simplified', or 'withdrawn':

---

[34] Given the fundamental divergence of views as to what subsidiarity really means in terms of the allocation of competence within a divided governance structure, it is hardly surprising that the Commission was able to shift attention away from the issue of the allocation of competence to concerns of the exercise of regulatory competence.

[35] For a fuller discussion of the impact of subsidiarity and of the legislative review see the contribution by Maher to this collection.

[36] EC Commission, 'Report to the European Council On the Adaptation of Community Legislation to the Subsidiarity Principle', COM(93) 545.

a) the *recasting* of Community legislation: in essence this involves a codification of existing rules to aid transparency (the area of pharmaceutical products has been targeted).

b) the *simplification* of Community legislation: in response to the criticism that Community directives have become over-detailed, the Commission is to consider greater use of 'horizontal harmonization' (that is, directives which do not cover single products but product 'families' such as foodstuffs) and 'New Approach' directives.

c) the repeal of existing legislation or *withdrawal* of proposals: the repeal of legislation concerning goods will be largely a result of the processes of recasting and simplification rather than a result of a radical re-appraisal of Community regulation. The Commission's 1994 Report on subsidiarity[37] does not evince any intention to withdraw proposals in the area of goods.

Two comments can be made on the impact of subsidiarity on the free movement of goods. First, it is striking that the Commission—the institutional actor with the most to fear from subsidiarity—has, through its construction of subsidiarity as a technical tool, sought to prevent a drastic reappraisal of Community competence. Admittedly, this Chapter has focused on an area in which the competence of the Community has become institutionalized and it is therefore not surprising that subsidiarity has not had a more radical impact. Secondly, however, and connected with the first comment, the technical approach to subsidiarity has encouraged a review of the Commission's approach to the regulation of goods. This review has been conducted using existing institutional categories developed through the process of regulating the area, namely the potential for mutual recognition, the use of horizontal harmonization, and increased use of New Approach directives. This calls to mind Majone's observation (noted above) that policy innovation is more a matter of using existing tools than the development of 'novel solutions' (Majone, 1991: 79).

In summary, the adoption of the subsidiarity principle has created an opportunity to reappraise the use of existing institutional means to attain the existing institutional goal of free movement. The Commission is currently attempting to ensure that these existing

---

[37] EC Commission, 'Report to the European Council on the Application of the Subsidiarity Principle', COM(94) 533.

means are used more effectively. It can therefore be suggested that the 'solutions' evolved to tackle problems of free movement have become the adaptable elements within a relatively stable institutional system. As Weinberger suggests (1993: 178): 'We live in a system of action that is built up successively during the course of our lives and comprises a reservoir of preformed—but adaptable—elements.'

3. CONCLUSION

Institutions matter. At a procedural level institutions identify the participants in the policy-making process and structure the relationships between them. Organizational linkages provide an important means to transfer information and to structure decision-making. Through the evolving formal and informal rules, norms, and operating procedures institutions also determine the amount of time (and other resources) to be devoted to decision-making. At the very least, institutions establish the 'rules of the game' of the policy-making process.

However, as the study of the free movement of goods identifies, institutions possess a substantive dimension. Whereas approaches to the policy process which start from the premise of the centrality of 'choice' tend to focus on the uniqueness and rationality of policy solutions, a historical institutionalist perspective problematizes the issues of choice and rationality. Policy solutions are viewed as routineized responses which are satisfactory rather than optimal. Solutions survive through incremental rather than radical changes. Solutions are transferred through organizational linkages. The tools of regulation may be imitations of strategies tested in other jurisdictions or other policy domains. Further, the availability of regulatory tools owes much to the historical path-dependency of regulation in a given area. Finally, the relationship between regulatory means and ends can be seen to be structured through the collective and historical experience of 'learning by doing' and the institutionalization of norms of appropriateness.

It is suggested that a historical institutional approach to the governance of the European Union provides a framework for policy analysis which goes beyond theories derived from international relations scholarship, and which makes possible future research strategies grounded in comparative policy analysis.

Changing Patterns of European Community Utilities Law and Policy: An Institutional Hypothesis*

COLIN SCOTT

This essay examines the dynamic characteristics of European Community law and policy in relation to the public utilities sectors.[1] The utilities sectors were for a long period substantially neglected by the Community institutions. The 1980s saw greater interest, as the Commission developed a liberalizing agenda in relation first to telecommunications, then to energy and postal services. By the mid-1990s, however, it was arguable that Community utilities law and policy was entering a new phase in which concerns about integration of utilities markets through liberalization were being balanced by more co-ordinative and co-operative concerns, notably in respect of the protection and development of public service obligations and the co-ordination of trans-European networks. This essay argues that although questions of policy and the activities of policy actors have had an important role in shaping outcomes, more attention should be paid to the way in which institutions shape the conditions under which policy is made. The term 'institutions' is used in the essay to refer not simply to organizations (though these are the most concrete form of institution) but also to political, social, and legal cultures,

* I am grateful to participants at the Workshop held in November 1994 at the Europa Institute, Edinburgh for comments on an earlier draft of this essay, particularly Peter Cullen, Imelda Maher, and Kenneth Armstrong, and also to Damian Chalmers and Tony Prosser. Responsibility for errors and infelicities remains mine.

[1] This Chapter chiefly addresses the energy, telecommunications, and postal sectors. Transport is the subject matter of its own title in the Treaty and, being a diverse sector, raises complex issues beyond the scope of this Chapter; See generally Greaves, 1991; McGowan, 1994. The main concerns of policy with water at Community level are environmental, which again fall outside the scope of this chapter. An institutional approach to the development of Community water law is offered by Richardson, 1995.

and constitutional rules. The hypothesis is that institutions, in this broad sense, have played a significant role in shaping change in utilities law and policy, and that a simple policy explanation is incomplete.

The organization and operation of public utilities, telecommunications, energy, postal services, water, and transport provide a significant obstacle to the European Community's objective of securing economic integration. Historically most of the member states have organized the provision of utility services in protected public monopolies along national lines. Notwithstanding the apparent authority within the EC Treaty to pursue competition and internal market policies in respect of the utilities sectors, the Commission has in fact for many years neglected these areas (McGowan, 1993a: 71). In the 1980s the climate changed significantly and Community policy towards the utility sectors grew in importance, with policies of liberalization (or regulatory reform: Argyris, 1993: 31) being very much at the centre of Community policy and dominating the development of legal instruments of integration. The central position of utilities liberalization in Community policy today is demonstrated by the keynote address of the President of the Commission to the Davos World Economic Forum in January 1995, in which he identified as the first of four key issues facing the European Union '[c]ompleting the Single European Market in key areas like energy and telecommunications . . .'[2]

Notwithstanding the continuing pre-eminence of liberalization in Community utilities policy, there have always been other more co-ordinative or co-operative aspects of policy, for example promoting research and development in telecommunications (Flynn, below) and ensuring security of energy supply. It is arguable that co-ordinative policies such as those concerned with public service obligations and co-ordination of networks are now receiving a renewed emphasis, balancing the commitment to liberalization. Arising from these major shifts in emphasis of Community policy are two related questions which this essay seeks to address. First: why, when attention focused on the utilities in the

---

[2] 'Speech by Mr Jaques Santer to the Davos World Economic Forum', *Rapid* 31 January 1995.

1980s, did it predominately take the form of policies directed towards liberalization? Secondly: given the policy path of the Community towards liberalization of the utilities sectors, how can the new emphasis on more co-ordinative and co-operative measures discernible in the mid-1990s be explained?

As for the first question the dominant explanation is that when attention did turn to the utilities sectors, policy concerns at the time required liberalization: liberalization of the utilities sectors is perceived as vital to the competitiveness of the European economy. Other instruments of integration, such as harmonizing legislation, would not create the conditions for economic success. Although such an explanation commands wide support, its basis exclusively in policy analysis is not wholly satisfactory. It suggests that policy prescriptions provide good explanatory tools for understanding what has happened in public policy. The theory of public choice, and other theories which focus on the role played by the interests of both citizens and firms, as well as politicians and bureaucrats, in shaping public policy have effectively brought such assumptions into question (Wilson, 1980a). In turn the naïve assumptions of public choice theory, that individuals are rational and (implicitly) omniscient utility maximisers, and that these traits explain policy outcomes, have also been questioned (Kelman, 1988).

One step beyond public choice theory are the neo-institutional theories which see the imperfections in knowledge and inability to execute policies as major explanatory factors in the development of institutions which are designed to curb the ability of policy actors to divert their activitities away from the public interest, whether in the private (Williamson, 1988; 1993) or the public sector (Macey, 1992; McCubbins, *et al.* 1989). Beyond this we find a theory of institutions which sees institutions (Koelble, 1995; Powell and di Maggio, 1991; Thelen and Steinmo, 1992) or systems (Clune, 1992; Luhmann, 1986; Teubner, 1987a; 1991) not as the *products* of problems with knowledge and rationality, but rather as evolutionary phenomena which are themselves major factors in shaping policy outcomes. One of the attractions of these approaches is that they permit consideration of law not simply as a neutral implementing device but rather as an institution or system with the capacity to shape emerging policy outcomes. Although it is apparent that there are similarities between institutional and systems approaches, no attempt will be made here to locate the discussion within the latter paradigm. Rather, this

essay seeks to develop a hypothesis concerning change in the policy
outcomes in relation to European Community utilities which takes
such institutional effects seriously (following Bulmer, 1994b).

Within the historical institutional approach we find no agreed
definition of what is an institution (cf. Armstrong, above). However,
in order for attention to institutional factors to be helpful, the
conception of institutions must extend beyond formal organizations
to include informal rules and procedures, and possibly also the
social and organizational norms (Bulmer, 1994b: 353; Thelen and
Steinmo, 1992: 2). This broad definition of institutions pays
attention not just to the formal holding of power within a policy-
making framework but also to the informal exercise of influence both
by policy actors and by those who have established and developed
the procedures through which institutions operate. Jepperson
suggests that there are three primary carriers of institutions:
organizations, regimes, and culture. A regime consists of explicitly
codified rules and sanctions, but with no systematic central
enforcement, for example a constitutional system. Culture consists
of rules, procedures, and goals which are not institutionalized in a
formal organization responsible for developing, monitoring or
sanctioning in relation to them. An institution may be simultaneously
both a regime and a culture (for example citizenship), but
maintaining the distinction helps to identify shifts over time in the
form or degree of institutionalization (Jepperson, 1991: 150–1).

For Hall (1986: 19) the major effects of institutions in policy-
making are first to establish the degree of power held by particular
policy actors, and secondly to influence how such actors define their
own interests and therefore seek to exert pressure. We might add to
this a third effect: defining the options for the way in which
such power as is held is exercised (Thelen and Steinmo, 1992:
2–3). Complexity is established by exploring the relationships
between institutions over time and the way that they deploy those
opportunities and instruments which are available to them in
shaping policy outcomes. Institutions both facilitate and constrain
activity, providing 'the rules of the game' (Hancher and Moran,
1989a; Jepperson, 1991: 146). Institutions do not *determine* policy
outcomes but do substantially shape the opportunities, possibilities,
and instruments within which policy outcomes occur. In any
particular policy context, therefore, it is possible to develop a
hypothesis that where policy outcomes proceed down one path

rather than others which might, in policy terms, have been available, the adoption of that particular path is the result of the interplay of institutional rather than policy variables. Put into the concrete terms of this essay, the policy outcomes in the Community utilities sector are not determined purely by considerations of policy. This essay demonstrates that the legislative process, which provides the main institutional focus of the essay, plays a central role in the allocation of power between policy actors and the shape and nature of legal instruments, and therefore in shaping policy outcomes. Consideration of the implementation of legislation at member state level falls outside the scope of the essay, but would further support the general hypothesis.

1. UTILITIES WITHIN NATIONAL INSTITUTIONAL FRAMEWORKS

In policy terms the key characteristics of the utilities sectors in the member states are economic. Historically the high sunk costs associated with the network utility services have resulted in the characterization of such services as natural monopoly, where one supplier can supply more efficiently and cheaply than two (Foreman-Peck and Millward, 1994: ch. 1). A further characteristic is the tendency to regard services as being subject to 'joint production' and vertically integrated organization 'which render controversial or questionable the allocation of costs to any particular activity' (Foreman-Peck and Millward, 1994: 341; McGowan, 1993b: 180). The consequence of these characteristics has been close regulation of private enterprise (the dominant model in the United States) or regulation through public ownership (the dominant model in most of the EU member states) and a high degree of integration in monopolistic units. These economic characteristics are not necessarily static, and in particular may be subject to technological or other changes. Technological change has been an important factor in re-evaluating the economic aspects of provision of telecommunications services, whereas it has had little role to play in the provision of water. The key issues to be addressed by legislators and regulators are the following: access to networks; pricing of (residual) monopoly services; development of networks; and social and distributional consequences of pricing. These matters are widely perceived as requiring co-ordination at some level (Helm,

1993: 6) although views on the intensity and character of such intervention differ.

The group of services defined as utilities is not, however, determined simply by reference to shared economic characteristics. There are also shared cultural assumptions which add a further dynamic element. These cultural assumptions are to a large degree bound up with broader ideas about what are the appropriate 'economic borders of the state' (Helm, 1989), a question to which answers will differ across time and location. A key cultural assumption has been that a utility provider, given certain protections by the state, must also bear certain obligations, which in the common law countries have derived from the doctrine of common callings (Craig, 1991). The central obligation is the provision of universal service. It must be noted that the definition of a utility has not always carried the expectation that every citizen would be able to afford the service. When Theodore Vail, chairman of AT&T, coined the term 'universal service' in 1904 he was apparently referring to the right of a company to service the entire region without competition, rather than the right of everyone in the region to receive affordable service (Mueller, 1993). Thus the importance of the notion of the right to service among the cultural assumptions concerning utility provision is comparatively recent. We may conclude from this example that the cultural assumptions concerning utility services are subject to change with changing social and economic expectations. Policies of liberalization in the European Community have provided significant challenges to cultural assumptions in many member states.

In organizational terms there has been an historical preference in the most EU member states for publicly owned monopoly as the dominant form of organization for utility provision. However, a wide range of forms of public ownership are hidden behind this characterization, including public corporations (national and regional), municipal corporations, state holdings of otherwise private companies, and operation through government department.[3] Furthermore, the public ownership tendency has been challenged in the last fifteen years. This change has occurred for a number of reasons, partly because of the strain that public

---

[3] In respect of modes of energy operation in the member states see McGowan, 1993a: 79–80; for telecommunications see Noam, 1992. More generally, see Mayer, 1989.

ownership has imposed on public sector finances and partly for
ideological reasons (McGowan, 1993a: 70). Re-evaluation of
organizational form has resulted both in policies of privatization
and, in some cases, liberalization of markets. To some degree the
new interest of the Community institutions, and particularly
the Commission, in the utilities sectors builds on existing trends of
liberalization in the member states. However, a key problem for the
Commission is that member states have differing cultural
assumptions, economic characteristics, and organizational forms in
their utilities sectors (McGowan, 1993a: 71).

2. AN INSTITUTIONAL APPROACH TO THE COMMUNITY INSTITUTIONS

Within the European Community the central position of the
Commission as policy initiater and guardian of the Treaties is not
contested (Usher, 1994: 146–8). Though relatively powerful, the
Commission is constrained in its activities by its own institutional
position in relation to the other main institutions (Peters, 1994: 13).
Peters describes a three-level game in which member states are
attempting to get as much out of the Community for the lowest
possible cost (in terms of both finance and sovereignty), the
Community institutions are seeking to enhance their power relative
to the other institutions, and within the Commission the various
Directorates General are seeking to enhance their power at the
expense of the others (Peters, 1992: 106–7). However, these games
are being played in conditions where the objectives of the players are
determined by their institutional position, and the available
strategies open to them are shaped by institutional conditions. The
institutional conditions are shaped by the complex relationship
between the culture and world view of each player and the
substantive and procedural contents of the EC Treaty which give to
the players their location in terms of role and powers. For example
the Commission has tended to use its pre-eminent role in the policy-
making process to extend its competences and thus continually
develop its institutional power. Majone notes that 'any satisfactory
explanation of the remarkable growth of Community regulation
must take into account both the desire of the Commission to increase
its influence—a reasonable behavioural assumption—and the

possibility of escaping budgetary constraints by resorting to regulatory policy-making' (Majone, 1991: 96).[4] Thus for the Commission there is a strong institutional bias towards regulation as a dominant mode of policy-making.

The Commission itself is not a monlithic entity (Cram, 1994). Rather it is an organization of sometimes competing Directorates General all of which 'have an incentive to capture potentially significant policy initiatives and shape them in manner compatible with the assigned tasks of the organization' (Peters, 1994: 14).

Responsibility for the utilities is divided between Directorates General (DGs) with cross-sectoral responsibility, notably those responsible for competition (DG IV) and industrial and internal market policy (DGs III, XV), and those with sectoral responsibility (notably telecommunications (DG XIII), energy (DG XVII), and Transport (DG VII). It is the cross-sectoral DGs which have embraced policies of liberalization bringing them into tension with the DGs with sectoral responsibilities. The 'logic of liberalization', espoused most particularly by DG IV, comprises a number of different arguments which, taken together, have forged major changes in the political culture of the member states and the Community to varying degrees over the past twenty years (Helm, 1989). There is, first, a concern that markets allocate resources better than the decisions of bureaucrats, but linked to this is the powerful financial incentive for the member states that removal of utility monopolies from their purview reduces the financial risks for the state. For the Community this concern is mirrored by an objective of minimizing the distortions of the market which are created by state monopolies run along national lines and by the provision of state aids (as defined in Articles 92–4 EC). For the Commission there is also a concern to support rationalization of industry through the market, in a way which may generate competing European companies and networks within a 'single European market' rather than in protected national markets.

In Community utilities sectors policy the preference for liberalization has occurred because the institutional location of DGs III and IV has resulted in them favouring liberalization and having the capacity to ensure that their views, rather than those of the sectoral

---

[4] See also Mazey and Richardson, 1994: 180. But cf. Peters' (1992: 94) refutation of the argument that the Commission has only fragile budgetary resources.

DGs, prevail in the policy-making process. The Commission has had the institutional capacity to develop some aspects of this policy with a degree of autonomy from the other institutions. In areas of policy where the Commission has been substantially dependent upon other institutions the development of policy has been much less certain. While the Court of Justice has tended to support the development of the institutional capacity of the Commission, notably in relation to competition policy, some member states have tended to challenge it and the Parliament is emerging as a more substantial force in shaping policy. Furthermore, implementation of Community measures in the member states has been a particular problem in the utilities sectors (Flynn, below). Thus we might expect that the Commission will continue to seek to use those instruments which give it the greatest institutional autonomy.

2.1 Deployment of Policy Making Tools

The European Community faces major policy issues in relation to the utilities sectors, notably how to achieve economic integration in sectors dominated by nationally organized monopolies. The Commission, dominated by the DGs III and IV, has come to define this question in terms of removal of barriers to entry and, in the cases of energy and telecommunications, giving third parties rights to use networks. The development of policy has sought to address both the special and exclusive rights granted to utilities undertakings by member state governments and the behaviour of the undertakings themselves in exploiting dominant position in markets. A key technique developed by the Commission, in a classic example of institutional innovation, is the preparation of policy documents (notably green papers) addressed to the utilities sectors, in which policies of liberalization are presented as both necessary and inevitable. The widespread use of green papers is supposed to facilitate consultation, and on this basis it was agreed at the Edinburgh European Council that their use would be developed (Westlake, 1994: 241–2). In telecommunications the key initiating document for the Commission's policy of liberalization was the Green Paper published in 1987[5] and in energy the adoption of a

---

[5] EC Commission, 'Towards a Dynamic Economic: Green Paper on the Development of the Common Market for Telecommunications Services and Equipment', COM(87) 290.

202 *Colin Scott*

Working Paper in 1988.[6] The postal services sector has also been the subject of recent policy documents.[7] From these policy documents have flowed more detailed legislative programmes, which have acted to mediate between the EC Treaty and the recognition of the special characteristics of the utilities sectors. In some cases policies of liberalization have required the deployment of re-regulatory instruments, particularly in order to ensure rights of access to networks for new entrants to markets. Such re-regulation, however, seeks generally to provide the conditions for liberalization in the face of obstacles created by both firms and governments in the member states (Knieps, 1990; Majone, 1990a). By far the most successful area of policy for the Commission has been telecommunications, where the urgent tone of these policy documents is perhaps most convincing. Policies of liberalization in energy and postal sectors have been much more difficult for the Commission to proceed with.

Following considerable policy development in telecommunications from 1987, further urgency has been given to liberalization by the ingenious linking of this policy to broader questions of employment and economic growth in the 1993 White Paper on Growth, Competitiveness, and Employment (Cockbourne, 1995: 122).[8] The report of the High-Level [Bangemann] Group on the Information Society,[9] established under the White Paper, emphasized the development of new infrastructure through market mechanisms, particularly through liberalization of communications. The proposal in the Report that telecommunications and other infrastructures (such as those used by cable television and other utilities companies) be liberalized has subsequently been adopted by the Commission and the Council and will now require

[6] EC Commission, 'The Internal Energy Market', COM(88) 238.
[7] EC Commission, 'Green Paper on the Development of a Community Market for Postal Services', COM(91) 476; EC Commission, 'Guidelines for the Development of Community Postal Services', COM(93) 247; see also Chung, 1994.
[8] EC Commission, *Growth, Competitiveness, Employment: the Challenges and Ways Forward into the 21st Century* Bull.EC, Supp. 6/93.
[9] 'The Bangemann Report' available electronically through DG XIII's World Wide Web server (http://www.echo.lu/eudocs/en/com-asc.html); see EC Commission, 'Europe's Way to the Information Society. An Action Plan', COM(94) 347, July 1994.

legislation.[10] One commentator concludes that the Commission has failed to institutionalize its general success in telecommunications policy, noting the absence of a European telecommunications network operator and a European regulatory authority (Fuchs, 1994: 42). The Bangemann Group recommended the development of a Community telecommunications regulatory authority, possibly to emerge from an existing organisation such as the ONP Committee, which comprises representatives of national regulatory authorities (Sauter, 1994a). This proposal remains contentious.

The Working Paper on the Internal Energy Market, adopted in 1988, indicated an approach which emphasized liberalization rather than co-ordination of the market.[11] Though the Commission was accepting of the special characteristics of the sector (such as technical complexity, non-storability of electricity, etc.) it took the view that there was considerable room for structural change, especially the separation of different operations in the industry such as generation and distribution and transmission (Argyris, 1993: 31–3; Hancher, 1992: 6; McGowan, 1993a: 82). The most controversial and difficult aspect of Community policy in the energy sector has been the proposal that third party access to energy networks should be an established principle of Community law (Argyris, 1993: 38–43). The Green Paper on European Union Energy Policy published in January 1995, although indicating that completion of the internal energy market will continue to be the main element of policy, calls also for better co-ordination in areas such as environmental protection and security of supply.[12]

In relation to postal services a 1991 Green Paper sought to balance proposals for liberalization against the development of guarantees for the maintenance of universal service.[13] The Commission's 1993 *Guidelines for the Development of Community Postal Services*[14] revealed that there was still considerable disagreement between the Community and the member states over basic questions

---

[10] See EC Commission, 'Green Paper on the Liberalisation of Telecommunications Infrastructure and Cable Television Networks', Part I COM(94) 440, October 1994; Part II COM(94) 682, January 1995. It is evident that there is considerable tension between DG XIII and DG IV over the speed of liberalization: 'Liberalization Storm Blows in at G7 Summit' *Electronic Times* 2 Mar. 1995.

[11] EC Commission, 'The Internal Energy Market', COM(88) 238.

[12] EC Commission, 'Green Paper on European Union Energy Policy' COM(94) 659, January 1995, ch. III.   [13] COM(91) 476.

[14] COM(93) 247.

such as the definition of universal service and the link between universal service and reserved services (Chung, 1994). This policy impasse creates the possibility, which has been substantially avoided in other sectors, that liberalization will occur through the application of general Community principles on competition law, state aids, etc., rather than through the development of legislation within a sectoral policy framework (Chung, 1994; Hancher, 1994a).[15] The Council's request for the publication by the Commission of proposals for liberalization by July 1994 had not been met by January 1995. The Commission has apparently considered using Article 90(3) as the basis for legislation to clarify the application of the Treaty competition principles to the sector.[16] Application of the Treaty rules more generally to the postal sector seems to anticipate liberalization of express delivery services, delivery of publications, direct mail and cross-border mail (Chung, 1994).

2.2 Competition and Internal Market Jurisdictions

With regard to the implementation of policy, the use of the competition jurisdiction is in many ways more attractive to the Commission than the internal market jurisdiction. Legislation implementing internal market policy requires a qualified majority vote in the Council of Ministers (Article 100A EC) and is also now subject to a veto by the Parliament under the co-decision procedure (Article 189B) (Bradley, 1994: 194–6). To date the Parliament has used this power only once, to reject the Directive on Open Network Provision in Voice Telephony, with the consequence that the legislation was lost and the Commission had to start again.[17] However, it has been much more common for internal market legislation to be delayed and significantly modified by the Council

[15] Case C-320/91 *Procureur du Roi* v. *Corbeau* [1993] ECR I-2533.

[16] Hancher (1994b: 122) suggests that a 'two-pronged attack' may be the most appropriate, following telecommunications, using Article 90(3) as the basis for a measure requiring member states to abolish exclusive rights and provide for unbundling, while an Article 100A directive would be used for general aspects of harmonization.

[17] The rejection of the Directive was part of a continuing dispute concerning comitology, but the Parliament was also concerned that the Council adopted the Directive without the Parliament's amendments: see Sauter, 1994b.

of Ministers. The most notable example of such delay in the utilities sectors has occurred in the energy sector, where the continuing debate over third party access to energy networks has prevented the adoption of the directives to complete the internal energy market.[18] In relation to telecommunications, the passage of internal market legislation to develop principles of Open Network Provision was reasonably successful until the rejection of the Voice Telephony Directive. In postal services the Commission has not yet brought forward legislation, fearing that there is not yet sufficient consensus among the member states and the Parliament. These institutional factors make implementation of policy through internal market legislation hazardous for the Commision and encourage it to develop policy through application of competition law, where it has greater autonomy of action, wherever this is possible and justifiable. This in turn tends to consolidate the institutional power of DG IV.

In its competition jurisdiction the Commission has powers of rule making, investigation, and enforcement, subject only to review by the Court of First Instance and/or the European Court of Justice. These powers consequently form a key part of the Commission's available resources (Usher, 1994: 159–61). These powers are governed partly by the EC Treaty directly, and partly by Regulations issued under the Treaty, in particular Regulation 17 of 1962 (Goyder 1993: 33–8). Although for many years the Court of Justice has played a leading role in the development of competition policy, renewed confidence in the Commission in the 1980s and 1990s, fostered in part by the Court, together with a clear liberal policy approach developed by Commissioners Sutherland and Brittan at DG IV between 1984 and 1992, has led to a new emphasis on the Commission's role in formulating and executing policy (McGowan and Wilks, 1994: 10–14). With this change in institutional emphasis there has been a shift away from a juridical to a more political concept of competition law (Gerber, 1994a). During this period, in which the Commission generally has emphasized the completion of the single market, a structural approach to the application of the competition rules has been

---

[18] Amended Proposals for a European Parliament and Council Directives Concerning Common Rules For the Internal Market in Electricity and Gas, COM(93) 643.

evident, leading to an emphasis on policies of liberalization in the
utilities sectors.

The Commission has substantially succeeded in developing
interpretations of the relevant principles which favour its strategic
objectives. Article 222 EC states that the Treaty shall in no way
'prejudice the rules in Member States governing the system of
property ownership'. That is, member states are free to continue
with nationalized industries. However member states must
'progressively adjust any state monopolies of a commercial
character so as to ensure that when the transitional period has
ended no discrimination regarding the conditions under which
goods are procured and marketed exists between nationals or
Member States' (Article 37). Article 90 provides the chief
instrument of mediation between the public enterprises and the
Treaty provisions. The basic principle of Article 90(1) is that all
the rules of the Treaty are to apply to public enterprises (enterprises
to which member states have granted special or exclusive rights).
This principle is directed at the member states, prohibiting them
from maintaining, in respect of public enterprises, legislation which
is contrary to the Treaty principles. Thus Article 90(1) suggests that
not only the competition rules but also internal market and other
principles are to be applied to public enterprises. The objective of
this provision is regarded not as preventing state intervention but as
preventing member states from avoiding their Treaty obligations
through the use of public enterprises to achieve strategic objectives
(Marenco, 1983: 509–10).

Article 90(2) expresses a similar principle in respect of undertakings entrusted with 'services of a general economic interest', but
provides that the competition rules and other Treaty principles are
only to apply to such undertakings to the extent that they do not
interfere with the performance of these services.[19] Article 90(2) was
drafted as a compromise beween the founding member states to
protect against national sensitivities (Marenco, 1983: 516–17;
Schindler, 1970: 67). Article 90(2) may provide a firm with a defence
to competition proceedings, but only when it is clear that there is a

---

[19] Many questions of interpretation arise in relation to Article 90(2). For example,
does 'entrusted' require that there is primary or secondary legislation which has
imposed duties on the undertaking? Does the term services apply also to goods
(Deringer, 1965; Marenco, 1991)?

conflict between the particular task assigned to it and the application of Treaty competition rules (Goyder, 1993: 452–9). It has been left to the Commission and the Court of Justice to define the parameters of this exception. In the *Telespeed* case the Court held that the pre-privatization British Telecom abused its dominant position in refusing to permit forwarding of messages by private messaging services from originators to recipients each of whom was in another country. No defence was available under Article 90(2) as BT's decision was based upon its own commercial strategy decisions rather than the pursuit of any public task since the Court held that BT was not obliged to adopt ITU rules of 1973 which prohibited message-forwarding agencies.[20]

The Court of Justice recently had to consider the compatibility of the Belgian postal monopoly with Articles 90, 85, and 86 EC.[21] The Court held that under Article 90(2) a postal monopoly was justified to ensure collection and delivery of mails, with universal service at a uniform price. Permitting competition would permit cream skimming, thereby undermining the economic basis of universal service. However this monopoly was only justified in so far as it was necessary to allow the Belgian postal service to carry out its duties and, applying the test of proportionality, this did not mean that competition could be completely excluded. Where particular services could be separated from the basic service, for example because there was some form of added value, such as greater speed, then permitting these would not threaten the economic basis of the basic service. The Court, perhaps seeking not to be too involved, held that it was for the national court to determine this issue, applying the proportionality principle, under which measures can be justified only if they are necessary. In the energy sector, Advocate General Darmon has sought to provide a rigorous definition of those public service obligations in the electricity sector which might provide grounds for exemption. These obligations include the duty to ensure, on demand, continuous supply to all types of consumers, on the basis of uniform tariffs and without discrimination, throughout the area of the concession.[22] Assuming that all these elements are present, and that the same reasoning would be applied

---

[20] Case 41/83 *Italy* v. *Commission* [1985] ECR 873 (Kohnstamm, 1990).
[21] Case C-320/91 *Corbeau supra* n. 15.
[22] Case C393/92 *Almelo* v. *Ijsselmij* [1994] ECR I-1477.

to other sectors, then this is an emergent juridical definition of public service obligations in the utilities sectors, and also a definition which may prevent exemptions being justified where the criteria are only partially satisfied. Given this developing jurisprudence it is now possible for the Commission to argue that if it fails systematically to develop policies of liberalization, then there is the risk that the Court will do the job in a less systematic way through the application of Article 90.

The development of the Article 90(2) jurisprudence may partly explain the new emphasis of the Commission on regulating the compliance of member states with competition requirements, particularly in monopolized sectors. This is seen as a key substantive turn of the 1980s and 1990s (Gerber, 1994a: 137–8). A number of techniques have been used by the Commission to develop and implement competition policy in the utilities sectors. First there was pre-clearance of agreements, under both Article 85(3) EC and the Merger Control Regulation[23] (for example in the case of the BT–MCI strategic alliance[24]). Pre-clearance can be used to shape mergers, alliances, and agreements in accordance with Comunity policy. Uniquely in telecommunications the Commision has published guidance on how the competition rules were to be applied in that sector.[25] The application of the competition rules may also be achieved through enforcement proceedings against undertakings or member states, such as those presently being pursued in respect of import and export monopolies,[26] but such proceedings are more time-consuming and costly than the other alternatives.

Finally, Article 90(3) provides a procedure whereby the Commision may issue directives and decisions to member states to clarify the application of Article 90 generally (Usher, 1994: 153–6). Considered in the abstract, before its use by the Commission, Article

---

[23] Council Reg. (EEC) 4064/89 OJ 1989 L395/1, corrigendum at OJ 1990 L257/13.
[24] Commission Decision of 13 Sep. 1993, OJ 1993 C259/3 (Merger Control Regulation); Commission Decision of 30 Mar. 1994, OJ 1994 C93/3 (Art. 85(3)).
[25] EC Commission, 'Guidelines on the application of EEC Competition Rules in the telecommunications sector', OJ 1991 C233/2.
[26] Actions have been commenced against Spain, France, Italy, The Netherlands, and Ireland, Cases C-156–159/94. The actions are of particular interest as they are brought by the Commission under Article 169 of the Treaty, and consequently will require the Court to come to a determinative ruling on the application of Article 90(2) to the energy sector.

90(3) was conceived of by commentators as a curious procedural device. It was thought that it might be used to address non-compliance with the Treaty by a single member state, offering a simpler enforcement mechanism than proceedings under Article 169 (Deringer, 1965: 132; Schindler, 1970: 71). However, the Commission has used Article 90(3) as the basis for three directives applying to all member states, one general in nature[27] and two in the telecommunications field.[28] The use of Article 90(3) in the tele-communications directives 'allowed the Commission to avoid the need for formal Council approval, when the necessary political consensus was lacking' (Ravaioli and Sandler, 1994: 5). Each directive issued in this way was challenged by one or more member states. At issue in each case for the member states was not necessarily the terms of the particular directive but rather the principle that the Commission could legislate in general terms using Article 90(3). In each instance the Court of Justice upheld the Commission's view that under Article 90(3) it was entitled in its supervisory capacity to make rules in the form of directives to clarify the obligations of the member states, though the telecommunica-tions Directives were in some respects imperfect (see further Flynn, below).[29]

Notwithstanding the Commission's success in defending its Article 90(3) jurisdiction in the Court, it is now extremely cautious about the use of Article 90(3) as the basis for legislation (cf. Goyder, 1993: 459). This is largely for political rather than legal reasons. The caution is demonstrated in two ways. First it is apparently Commission practice to consult informally both the Council and the European Parliament over the terms of directives issued in this way (Ravaioli and Sandler, 1994: 5 at fn. 39). Secondly legislation to lift exclusive service provisions in the energy markets of the member states, which could have been proposed under Article 90(3), is

---

[27] Commission Directive 80/723/EEC on the Transparency of Financial Relations between Member States and Public Undertakings, OJ 1980 L195/35.
[28] Commission Directive 88/301/EEC on Competition in the Markets in Telecommunications Equipment, OJ 1988 L131/73; Commission Directive 90/388/EEC on Competition in the Market for Telecommunications Services, OJ 1990 L192/10.
[29] Joined Cases 188–190/80 *France, Italy, and UK* v. *Commission* [1982] ECR 2545; Case 202/88 *France* v. *Commission* [1991] ECR I-2223; Joined Cases C-271/90 etc. *Spain, Belgium, and Italy* v. *Commission* [1992] ECR I-5833.

instead being pursued in the two energy directives under Article 100A which requires Council legislation. Nevertheless the Commission has used Article 90(3) to expand the Services Directive into new areas. Accordingly, satellite services were liberalized by a Commission Directive agreed in October 1994,[30] and in December 1994 the Commission approved a directive aimed at lifting the restrictions on the use of cable television infrastructure for multi-media (though not at this stage voice telephony) services.[31] The Commission has reserved its position on whether it will attempt to use Article 90(3) as the basis for legislation liberalizing tele-communications infrastructure.

3. CHANGING INSTITUTIONAL PATTERNS

3.1 The Lurch Away from Liberalization

Although Community utilities policy since the 1980s has been dominated by a 'logic of liberalization' there are now signs of renewed emphasis on policies which seek to pursue the goal of integration through more co-operative or co-ordinative means (Henry, 1993). Most notable is the new emphasis on policies seeking to ensure the maintenance of universal service, and the new policies in relation to trans-European networks. This more co-ordinative emphasis is explicable partly in economic terms (a concern to maintain the value of networks through ensuring maximum possible access) and partly in institutional terms. Institutional factors include the increased relative strength of the European Parliament, achieved through both Treaty changes and other techniques, each of which has contributed to a widening of the 'policy space' between the Council of Ministers and the Commission (Judge et al., 1994: 30). The Parliament is more cautious about liberalization than the Commission. Related to this is renewed institutional confidence in the sectoral DGs and new activity by pressure groups opposed to some aspects of liberalization. The EC policy-making process is regarded as being extremely open to lobbying efforts (Mazey and Richardson, 1994; Richardson, 1995: 141) and, provided that they

---

[30] Commission Dir. 94/46/EC on Satellite Services, OJ 1994 L268/15.
[31] Agence Europe, 22 Dec. 1994.

are able to penetrate into the inner policy circle, we might expect the organization and activity of new lobby groups in the Community to have considerable impact in challenging the historically more dominant lobby groups of large users, particularly multinational firms, who have favoured the 'logic of liberalization'.

Accompanying this wider involvement in the policy process has been a gradual cultural change under which utilities law and policy is increasingly seen as a political rather than a technical area, and therefore an area in which political debate is possible (Judge *et al.*, 1994). For example Prosser has argued that there are latent public service principles, such as universal service and non-discrimination within UK utilities law, and that these public service principles, rather than economic arguments, should shape the development of EC utilities policy (Prosser, 1994: 16). One possible instrument through which the social aspects of utility provision may be emphasized is the proposed European Public Service Charter, first mooted by the Commision in 1993, which seeks to provide a framework within which minimum service standards may be set. This approach has been welcomed by the utilities providers as it goes some way to constraining policies of liberalization which threaten their interests. Though the Commission has shown some muted enthusiasm for such a Charter, it has fallen to the interest group which represents public enterprises in the member states, the European Centre for Enterprises with Public Participation (CEEP) to develop its principles, which it has done through a series of meetings (Riccardi, 1994). The CEEP is seeking to provide a counter-balance to those interests groups, such as the International Telecommunications Users Group (INTUG), which have supported the logic of liberalization. The CEEP's plan is to present to the Commission a virtually complete policy for adoption, although it is not certain that the new Commission will support such a policy instrument. A critical factor which may lead to success for the CEEP is that it has the support of the Parliament.

3.2 Universal Service

In the energy, telecommunications, and postal sectors there are fears that policies of liberalization will remove protections for smaller and remote consumers hitherto provided through state monopoly. In the energy and telecommunications sectors the costs of network provision have, in varying degrees, been cross-subsidized for smaller and remoter users by larger and urban users. Transparency requirements in costing and pricing of networks, perceived as essential to the liberalization of services, threaten such arrangements unless either new principles are simultaneously introduced to maintain and finance universal service obligations or it can be assured that provision will be made through the market.

The amended draft directives to complete the internal energy market provide that the Member States 'may, in accordance with Community law, impose public service obligations on undertakings operating in the [electricity/gas] sector as regards the security, regularity, quality and price of supplies' (Art. 3(2) of each draft directive).[32] It is for member states to determine the content of such obligations (Art. 4 of the draft electricity directive). It increasingly appears that the Community will legislate to require member states to ensure that Universal Service Obligations are maintained in the utilities sectors. The Green Paper on a European Energy Policy, published in January 1995, recognizes for the first time that, although regulation must be kept to a minimum, it has 'essential and legitimate' elements concerned with 'the protection of public service missions; the security of supply; environmental protection; energy efficiency'.[33]

In telecommunications the Commission is using the development of universal service principles as a means to achieve the widest possible support for policies of liberalization. Setting standards above current minima in the member states gives positive incentives to those concerned with the social effects of liberalization, such as the Parliament, to approve the measures. For those member states which will need to make greatest progress in developing technology, accounting, and regulatory structures, the incentive to do so will come in the form of the promise of funding for development of infrastructure from the Community's Structural Funds. In November 1993 the Commission adopted a Communication on universal service in telecommunications, which sets out minimum standards to include the right to have a telephone connected, to have clear standards on installation times and repairs, to have clear dispute resolution mechanisms, and progressively

---

[32] COM(93) 643, recitals, 13.   [33] COM(94) 659, January 1995.

to gain access to new services.[34] The Draft Directive on the Application of Open Network Provision to Voice Telephony will advance these principles and, if it meets a happier conclusion than the earlier draft directive discussed above, will be the first legislative provision for universal service in the telecommunications sector.[35] The possible methods for financing the universal service obligation (USO) are canvassed in the second part of the Green Paper on Telecommunications Infrastructure. One possible model is the development of a system of access deficit contributions (ADCs) which consist of payments from interconnecting telecommunications operators (TOs) to the dominant operator, to reflect the dominant operator's losses associated with providing affordable access to the network for all customers. This approach has been pioneered in the UK, but the UK Office of Telecommunications has recently indicated that it may abandon the ADC regime.[36] The alternative, favoured by the Commission, is to create a universal service fund into which all operators must pay and to use this fund to subsidize those operators who offer or are required to provide universal service.[37]

3.3 Trans-European Networks

Article 129B provides for the creation of Trans-European Networks (TENs). Specific reference is made to the development of trans-European networks in energy, telecommunications, and transport as a policy objective, representing a considerable *coup* for the sectoral Directorates General which are concerned to institutionalize this area of policy in the face of policies of liberalization. It provides recognition that trade policy alone cannot bring all the benefits promised by the internal market.[38] The TENs

---

[34] Approved by Council Res. of 7 Feb. 1994 on Universal Service in the Telecommunications Sector, OJ 1994 C48/1.

[35] COM(94) 689.

[36] Office of Telecommunications, *A Framework for Effective Competition*, December 1994.

[37] EC Commission, 'Green Paper on the Liberalisation of Telecommunications Infrastructure and Cable Television Networks', Part II, COM(94) 682, January 1995, 85–6.

[38] EC Commission, 'Towards Trans-European Networks For a Community Action Programme' COM(90) 585 (Hancher, 1991: 264). *White Paper on Growth, Competitiveness, Employment*, COM(93) 700, 28–33.

policy pulls in the opposite direction from liberalization, having
characteristics of 'co-operation, co-ordination and standardization'
(McGowan, 1993b: 179). The TENs programme, first proposed in
1989, exploits the network metaphor to draw together various
strands of infrastructure policy (McGowan, 1993b: 183–4). The
political appeal of the TENs programme is precisely that it provides
a counter-trend to liberalization, and is thus strongly supported by
the powerful interests involved in managing the utilities providers in
the Union (McGowan, 1993b: 184). Commission estimates suggest
that transport and energy will require investment in the order of
ECU 250bn, and telecommunications ECU 150bn between 1993
and 2000 in order to achieve the objectives of the TENs policy.[39]
These investment decisions are subject to the co-decision procedure
under Art 189B EC. In support of investment on this scale the
Commission proposes to create new EU financial instruments,
Union Bonds, and Convertibles guaranteed by the European
Investment Bank, although most of the investment is to be provided
by the private sector. Nevertheless, financing of the policy is likely to
remain a key problem.

4. CONCLUSION

Commentary on the development of EC utilities policy has been
dominated by a policy-orientated view in which change is perceived
simply as a response to policy concerns. This essay has sought to
provide a modest corrective to this literature by suggesting that
institutions matter also. It is unlikely that the Commission pursued
policies of liberalization in the utilities sectors much before the
1980s, not just because this was not on the policy agenda but also
because the institutional pattern did not favour it. The emphasis on
liberalization in the 1980s has occurred because the institutional
dynamic of the Community has simultaneously retained for
the Commission a central place in policy-making and given
pre-eminence to the instruments developed for the exercise of
competition policy and completion of the internal market. Utilities
policy may be seen as a product of that broader dynamic.

However, it should be noted that the liberalizing agenda has not

---

[39] COM(93) 700, 34.

met with uniform success. While liberalization of telecommunications has moved at a remarkable pace, liberalizing measures in the energy sector have been stalled, and the Commission has not been able to bring forward proposals in postal services. However, this policy failure on the part of the Commission provides only a partial explanation for a change in emphasis in policy. Institutional changes, notably in the Treaty on European Union, have significantly changed the institutional balance within the Community. The combination of substantive changes, such as the institutionalization of the trans-European networks policy, and procedural changes, notably the enhanced powers given to the Parliament in the co-decision procedure, have been important in shaping a changed emphasis in utilities policy which is spawning more co-ordinative and co-operative approaches to integration of Community utilities markets. Directorates General within the Commission and pressure groups are taking advantage of these institutional changes to strengthen their positions.

The prospects for utilities law over the next few years are for a more balance agenda of liberalization and co-ordination. As state co-ordination is the norm in the utilities sectors of all member states (including even the privatized UK utilities sectors) it would seem that greater emphasis on co-ordination at EC level has the potential to reduce tensions between the member states and the Community institutions. New legal instruments are likely to balance integration through liberalization with integration through protection and development of public service obligations, and both industrial and competition policy are likely to emphasize a balance between liberalization of and support for European industry in the utilities sectors. This is a profound cultural change, the explanation of which lies not only in matters of policy but also in the dynamic aspects of institutions.

Telecommunications and EU Integration

LEO FLYNN

Telecommunications policy has had mixed fortunes at the Community level over the last two decades. It played a part in several information technology-related initiatives attempted by the European Commission in the 1970s, which, for the most part, failed. Collaborative technology research programmes undertaken during the 1970s such as PREST, CREST, and COST, while ambitious in conception, received minimal backing from national governments (Sandholtz, 1992: 7).[1] The Commission's record in the 1980s and 1990s has been more successful in this field; in his study of the EC ISDN research strategy Fuchs claims that the 1980s 'have been a decade of complete success for the Commission (in relation to telecommunications issues)'. He explains that the Commission has established itself as 'a determined and influential actor in the field, procurement policies are being opened up and the national manufacturers have been going along with the Commission's broad policy aims. A wave of mergers and of concentration in the industry is also under way, thus fulfilling the hopes of the Commission to create pan-European corporations' (Fuchs, 1992: 85).

Fuchs is only one of a number of writers who have 'discovered' the leading role of the Commission in the development of an EC telecommunications strategy (Schneider *et al.*, 1994; Sandholtz, 1992). However, these accounts are seriously incomplete. While the significance of the Commission's telecommunications activities is great, an account of EC telecommunications strategy which rests solely on the relative leadership capabilities of the Commission and the member states is inadequate to capture the complexities of policy-making in the EC context. This paper seeks to develop an

---

[1] PREST—Politique de Recherche Scientifique et Technologique; COST—Co-opération Scientifique et Technologique; CREST—Comité de la Recherche Scientifique et Technologique.

account of the Commission's status as an actor in policy formulation within the telecommunications sector which will fill some of those gaps. It will first consider the Commission's response to policy log-jams at national level and its use of litigation in the Court of Justice as a means of carving out influence for itself. The paper will then provide some analysis of the Court of Justice as an policy player in its own right, and finally examine the Commission's ability to retain political primacy in the face of opposition from players at national level.

1. INSTITUTIONAL ACTORS AND EUROPEAN INTEGRATION

Political science accounts of policy development and implementa-tion in the European Community/European Union over three decades have been constructed around several distinct models, which include amongst others proto-federation (Hallstein, 1969), international regime (Hoffmann, 1982), and concordance system (Puchala, 1972). These conceptualizations each stressed different aspects of the relationships between the member states and the EC; however, they all tended to focus on the activities of national governments as actors engaged in bargaining and negotiation, albeit with varying degrees of autonomy depending on the model employed. Each government's loss (or lack) of autonomy is fed into the power and resources attributed to the Community in the relevant model. The Community is rarely conceptualized as an autonomous actor in its own right and its role is that of an ambient factor, an environmental constraint on the interplay of the member states. An institutional actor is one empowered by its founders to act in a specified field by means of the transfer of resources such as legal authority, money, and personnel. This process enables the actor to do more than merely articulate the aggregated interests of others: it can develop and pursue its own interests and may begin to assert itself autonomously. Some recent literature shows a greater willing-ness to ascribe an active role to the Community; more particularly there is an increasing recognition of extent of the European Commission's autonomy as a corporate actor engaged in policy formulation (Andersen and Eliassen, 1993; Bieber, 1988). It is attributed with a capacity to identify policy gaps or failures at the level of the member states, to construct coalitions between actors at national and European levels, and to mobilize these in order to develop new policy solutions.

These accounts are, in their own terms, a challenge to the insufficiently sophisticated works which have indicated the main directions of EC policy analysis and theorizing. However, from the perspective of an EC lawyer with interests in the ongoing internal market project and the institutional dynamics of EC law, this description of the Commission's newly discovered status as an institutional actor is itself insufficiently complex.[2] There is a silence, and sometimes a misunderstanding, about the Commission's need to support its leadership role by reference to legal norms, and a consequent failure to appreciate the role of the Court of Justice of the European Communities in the interaction of institutional actors. Without replicating studies of the Court which have tended to portray it in a quasi-heroic mode (Weiler, 1994b), it is important to understand that the Court does more than merely indicating to the Commission a path to follow and conferring its imprimatur on the resultant policy. The Court can take a very active role as an institutional actor in its own right, establishing and legitimating quite specific regulatory mechanisms. The other gap in these accounts is that relatively little attention is given to the activities of the member states in implementing policy. Thus the increasing volume and frequency of EC legislation are taken to evidence a stronger leadership role for the Commission (Schneider *et al.*, 1994: 486), without inquiring into the concrete effect which this 'success' has had in reshaping the expectations and transactions of firms, unions, and individuals, and the feedback which this can have on subsequent rounds of policy formation.

The following sections outline some of the key features of the development of telecommunications law and policy at EC level. There can be no doubt about the comprehensive and cohesive nature of the legal and policy instruments in this key sector which have emerged in a little over a decade. The Commission's efforts in this evolution will be the chief concern of this essay; this first requires an analysis of the conditions which gave rise to its ability to

---

[2] For example Schneider and Werle (1989) conceive of the Commission as an actor with significant competences and resources but limited in its actions by member states' veto powers; this overlooks its powers of independent initiative under Art. 90 EC which are so important in this area.

carve out a platform from which to exert a leading role. The second
issue examined is the way in which the Court has boosted the
Commission's status from that of a broker between member states,
albeit with its own preferences, to a decision-maker with a certain
degree of autonomy. This is followed by a study of the Court's use of
its own judicial power as an instrument of policy formulation.
Finally, the paper attempts to evaluate the success of some parts of
the liberalizing reforms advanced by the Commission and to
establish the effects of interaction between the Commission and
actors, other than governments, at national level.

2. THE COMMISSION AND AN EVOLVING EUROPEAN
TELECOMMUNICATIONS POLICY

The Commission laid the ground for an EC dimension in telecommunications by fostering the 'need' for an industrial policy
at a Community level (Peterson, 1991; Tsoukalis, 1993: 49),
complemented by the related development of an EC Science and
Technology Policy from the mid 1970s onward (Stubbs and Saviotti,
1994). More concerted EC activity in the telecommunications sector
can be traced back to the 1985 White Paper on the Single Market.[3]
However, the 1985 White Paper was notably silent on the question
of telecommunications and it was left to the 1987 Telecommunications Green Paper[4] to indicate the principles which the Commission
proposed to follow. The 1987 Green Paper, described as 'an
admirable document, which provided the road map for European
telecommunications' (Cullen and Blondeel, 1994: 11), presaged a
transformation of the legal and regulatory principles governing the
sector at a Union level. The new regulatory framework which has
emerged under the Commission's guidance has been based on three
principles: liberalization, harmonization, and competition (Taylor,
1994: 323). Access to national markets which were formerly the
exclusive privilege of state-sponsored telecommunications operators
(TOs) would be liberalized, allowing TOs from other member states
or from the private sector to provide services or supply goods in

---

[3] COM(85) 310.
[4] *Green Paper on the Development of the Common Market for Telecommunications Services and Equipment*, COM(87) 290.

these formerly reserved sectors. Market entry would be eased by harmonizing standards throughout the EC, removing the obligation on new entrants to comply with regulatory controls which were unique to national markets, unless these served some objective end such as the technical integrity of the telecommunications network. Both harmonization and liberalization would increase the numbers of undertakings in these markets, leading to greater competition which was to be safeguarded by the application of rules based on principles within existing EC competition law. The Green Paper has been succeeded by a series of policy documents on specific aspects of the telecommunications market, and by a small avalanche of directives, decisions, resolutions, and guidelines relating to telecommunications equipment and services. By the end of 1994 a significant body of legislation had been established within the context of a well developed policy framework.

In contrast to the political science accounts of policy formulation lawyers have been more consistently aware of the Commission's capacity to mobilize support for the policies which it has developed. However, their understanding of how it does so has tended to be unsophisticated. In a paper given in 1988 on EC telecommunications law and policy Amory notes the extensive activity of the Commission directed at liberalization of the telecommunications markets, and observes that 'this raises the question *why is the Commission so active in this area?*' (Amory, 1990: 751; emphasis in the original). The question is important because several provisions of the EC Treaty are potentially relevant here. While the competition rules in Articles 85 and 86, the non-discrimination provisions in Articles 30, 48, 52, and 59, and Articles 90 and 92 on state intervention in the markets could all be seen to have a bearing on the sector, the Commission only began to consider the potential barriers to trade and distortions of competition created by regulated industries of this type in the 1980s. The telecommunications industry was an early target of that attention. There were few earlier attempts to enforce these rules in relation to telecommunications, and Amory attributes this to a low level of dissatisfaction with the organization of the sector until the late 1970s when the advent of new technologies and the possibility of new services led to a desire for more liberal market access to allow private operators to provide novel services which the publicly owned companies had found difficult to adopt. This is a technology-driven account, in which the

Commission, recognizing the uneven introduction of more liberal market rules which would result from a purely private invocation of EC law and realizing that this would contribute to an ever-widening technology gap between the EC and Japan and the USA, intervened with the 1987 Green Paper and subsequent implementation measures (Amory, 1990: 752). The inadequacy of this analysis is that it does not fully acknowledge the interaction between national and EC actors, nor does it refer to the interplay of positions adopted by EC level actors.

A better understanding of the Commission's role in the evolution of EC telecommunications policy requires consideration of how telecommunication services and products are provided at national level. Telecommunication services in almost all member states have traditionally been provided within a framework characterized by what might be termed 'a classical approach', associated with a strong state monopoly with exclusive rights accompanied by a confusion between regulatory and operating functions (Poullet, 1990: 391). Until 1985 telecommunication services in most member states were organized as a regulated industry and provided under a monopoly or exclusive privilege granted by national legislation to one TO which was directly related to the state. These monopolies generally also covered the installation of telecommunications networks and the provision of telecommunications equipment, and procurement policies were managed so that domestic manufacturers provided a preponderance of these goods. As a result of these favourable local conditions a small member state such as Belgium could become a major exporter of telecommunications equipment, notwithstanding a small domestic market which preclude long production runs. In some member states the service provider was a legally autonomous corporation, in others a division of a state ministry, but in all the member states TOs were ultimately financed by the state and subject to state supervision in policy formulation. TOs assumed responsibility for fulfilling public service duties in exchange for these *de facto* or *de jure* exclusive rights to provide telecommunications services. In addition, the TOs often carried out regulatory tasks such as establishing and enforcing standards for equipment used to provide the service. TOs were employed by the member states as a tool of economic management, frequently concerned with employment levels and industrial policy. As a result, many telecommunications service providers did not operate purely on the basis of commercial considerations. The cost of service provision did not necessarily relate to the price charged; tariff structures, capital expenditure, and operating costs were often justified on political grounds, and their income was treated as a contribution to national exchequer receipts (Hall, 1993: chs. 8 and 9).

In the EC the vertical linkages between the market for telecommunications equipment provision and those for tele-communications networks and service provision (and ultimately other information technology markets) have been crucial in the development of the Commission's role as policy formulator. Those links made it extremely difficult for reform of these markets to be initiated at national level but they also provided an opportunity for the Commission to assert its leadership in this field. The tele-communications equipment industry has been under increasing competitive pressure to restructure over the past two decades. The increasing amount of value added to components and the attempts of component and computer manufacturers such as IBM, Nixdorf, and others to integrate forward into the telecommunications equipment market have led to rationalization of plants and a reduction of the labour force in the industry. The significant costs of research and development in this field provide another major problem; however, because the downstream market for tele-communications networks and services has generally been organized as a monopoly, the national TOs' technology policies have been utilized to diminish the pressure on the equipment industry. TOs have tended to subsidize domestic manufacturers, for example by buying prototypes developed to domestic specifications. Tele-communications service-users ultimately provided a captive source of subsidy for equipment manufacturers while the TOs themselves appeared increasingly inefficient. Domestic political opposition to direct restructuring of the telecommunications equipment market was rooted in technology and employment policy concerns. These barriers moved attention to the restructuring of the linked market of telecommunications services, an option which was viable only where all the member states increased the efficiency of their TOs' service provision. If some countries retained the inefficient *status quo* they might nonetheless benefit from the reforms introduced by others which reduced advantages available to their own manufacturers. This Prisoner's Dilemma allowed the Commission to advance a solution which gave it a leadership role and avoided the potential free-rider problems associated with uncoordinated reforms. The Commission was able to take up this role by pointing to the economies of scale in production and distribution available in an EC market[5] and by identifying the barriers created by national service monopolies and nationally oriented procurement policies (Muller, 1990: 314–15).

3. ARTICLE 90 EC: INTERACTION OF THE COURT OF JUSTICE AND THE COMMISSION

The Commission's advancement of telecommunications reform proposals marks it as an actor able to assert itself autonomously. However, in the absence of a unique competence to convert these proposals into a binding legislative form, the Commission remains largely dependent on its founders, the member states. In other words, the Commission has developed a degree of autonomy, to the point where it articulates and pursues its own preferences in the process of policy formation, but it still cannot, for the most part, execute these without establishing a consensus with the member states. Although the increased use of qualified majority voting procedures in relation to the internal market programme has augmented the Commission's status as a policy broker between member states with differing agendas on particular subjects, this does not put it beyond the reach (or the interests) of the member states. Such autonomy is dependent on the possibility of the Commission defying the intentions of the member states, and the Commission's drive for such freedom was at the centre of several cases which came before the Court of Justice in the early stages of the telecommunications reform process.

Key elements of the reforms envisaged in the 1987 Green Paper emerged when the Commission adopted Directives on equipment[6] and on services,[7] under Article 90(3) EC, which permits the

---

[5] For example the Commission observed in the 1987 Green Paper that none of the member states represented more than 6% of the world market: COM(87) 290, 72.

[6] Dir. 88/301/EEC on competition in the market for telecommunications terminal equipment, OJ 1988 L131/73.

[7] Dir. 90/388/EEC on competition in the market for telecommunications services, OJ 1990 L192/10.

Commission to adopt decisions or Directives to ensure the implementation of Article 90 EC. These two directives were both challenged by several member states on the ground that the Article 90 EC was an inappropriate legal basis for the measures adopted. The Equipment Directive was challenged by France, joined with Italy, Belgium, Germany, and Greece,[8] while the Services Directive was challenged by Spain, Belgium, and Italy, with France intervening.[9] Germany initially considered joining the challenge to the Services Directive but refrained from doing because its own domestic policy on telecommunications and liberalization had shifted in the period between the two court actions. While the UK did not participate in either challenge because it supported the substance of the measures adopted, UK spokespeople did make statements which questioned the Commission's use of Article 90 EC as an avenue for intervention into the member states' economies (Woolcock *et al.*, 1991: 96). The opponents to the use of Article 90 EC also claimed to support the substance of the measures but argued that a Council directive under Article 100A EC was the appropriate legal basis for such a measure on the ground that it was a piece of harmonizing legislation. As Amory noted (although this was presented as a debate about legal basis): 'it might be an interesting legal debate but it is primarily a policy debate which has been started by those who want to postpone services liberalization and limit its scope' (Amory, 1990: 752).

The Commission's decision to employ Article 90 EC in this way was without direct precedent and it was said at the time that it required 'an important decision by the Court of Justice, with the outcome far from certain' (Lake, 1990: 297).

The Court of Justice largely upheld the Commission in both cases. It endorsed the use of Article 90 EC as a means of specifying the obligations of member states under Article 90(1) EC, and thereby validated the Commission's policy-making powers (Emiliou, 1993; van der Woude, 1992). The Commission obtained an important endorsement of its policy-formulating powers through the judgment in this case. The decision of the Court in the *Equipment* case meant that the outcome of the challenge in the *Services* case was easy to

---

[8] Case C-202/88 *France* v. *Commission* [1991] ECR I-1223.
[9] Joined Cases C-271/90, C-281/90, and C-289/90 *Spain* v. *Commission* [1992] ECR I-5833.

predict, but the member states involved persisted in their challenge. It should be noted that the Services Directive had been drafted by the Commission a year before its adoption and that this delay was intended to allow the Council to adopt the Open Network Provision (ONP) Framework Directive (Anonymous, 1990: 64). In addition, the original draft was modified to deal with objections by member states, several of whom later commenced the Article 173 EC action. When faced with member states' objections to the legal basis of the Services Directive, the Commission took the view that while the ONP Framework Directive created a new policy which was subject to consultation under Article 100A EC with the member states, the directives adopted under Article 90(3) EC enforced existing Treaty rules which had not been implemented and so came under its supervisory powers. In contrast, Montagnon suggests that the crucial difference between these proposals was that ONP policy had to be enforced by the member states and required active participation in drafting the rules (Montagnon, 1990: 57–8). The limits on the Commission's Article 90 EC legislative powers necessitate a co-operative attitude to the national governments in order to develop its telecommunications policies, in addition to the prudent reasons for doing so.

McGowan and Seabright point to the Court's pro-Commission interpretation of Article 90 EC as an instance of the way in which 'the legal framework of regulation can take on a momentum of its own' (1995: 245). In the context of telecommunications, the decisions of the Court in the two cases can be seen as strengthening the ability of the Commission to force the restructuring of this sector throughout the EC. For example, in the 1987 Green Paper the Commission had proposed that all services bar basic voice telephony be liberalized. Voice telephony was left as a reserved service on the basis of Article 90(2) EC in order to secure the universal provision of a telecommunications network. It was said to be the only service which could legitimately be subject to a monopoly and was to be exempted from liberalization 'in order to ensure the financial viability of the network providers, given their infrastructural duties.'[10] As telephony accounts for some 90 per cent of the EC telecommunications market, giving 85–90 per cent of the tele-communication service providers' revenues, this was an important

---

[10] Recital 18, Dir. 90/388/EEC.

concession. However, by 1992 the Commission had extended the proposed scope of liberalization under the Open Network Provision Directive to voice telephony. This was made possible by the increased leverage enjoyed by the Commission in other sectors such as mobile and digital communications, services, and equipment following the Court's vindication of its stance. The result is the 1993 Council Resolution[11] which requires that basic voice telephony be liberalized in the Member States by 1998 with exceptions for small and less developed countries whose markets need not be opened until 2003. Although the Commission's agenda on liberalization has been put into legislative form this has not necessarily meant any immediate conversion, even on the part of those member states which have supported these developments. However, in so far as liberalization is still opposed, this is because of failure to implement new policies, rather than opposition to their adoption. The judgments in the *Equipment* and *Services* cases therefore mark a transition in the Commission's status within the telecommunications field. From the role of policy broker or entrepreneur, proposing solutions to problems which demand European co-ordination and which are not politically feasible at a domestic level, it moves to that of an actor capable of asserting itself autonomously and overreaching the objections of other players, including the member states.

4. REGULATION AND ENFORCEMENT: THE COURT OF JUSTICE AS POLICY-MAKER

The Court of Justice decisions concerning the adequacy of the legal basis of the Directives adopted under Article 90 EC mark an unsuccessful litigation strategy on the part of those member states opposed to the Commission's reform proposals. Their net result was a major recasting of regulatory competences in the telecommunications field, affording the Commission a higher standing. In some ways this appears to be typical of the Court's interventions—an independent body with a *communautaire* attitude which tends to give its blessing to the Commission as the voice of the Community

---

[11] Council Resolution of 22 July 1993 on the review of the situation in the telecommunications sector and the need for further development in that market, OJ 1993 C213/1.

interest. This representation of the Court's strategies gives it a power which is vital but exercised in the background; it sets the stage but then steps out. This view of the Court might be summarized as 'passive activist' as though the Court could choose the game to be played and mark out the boundaries within which play will occur, but deliberately eschewed direct participation, preferring the role of referee. More detailed consideration of the development of EC telecommunications law and policy indicates that this image underestimates the willingness of the Court in this context to move, beyond designating where regulatory competence exists, into specifying the details of how regulatory structures are to be constructed.

The 1988 Equipment Directive has been implemented by all the member states and the basis for a fully competitive terminal equipment market has, at least as far as the legal and regulatory principles for the telecommunications sector are concerned, been established throughout the Union (Cullen and Blondeel, 1994: 15). In so far as the United Kingdom's experience indicates the effect of such liberalization, the separation of service provision from the supply and installation of equipment has resulted in lower prices and greater consumer choice.[12] While the Commission obviously retains its usual monitoring and enforcement role in respect of the Equipment Directive and associated legislation, the Court of Justice has also been called on to consider their effect in national law in the context of preliminary references under Article 177 EC. On 27 October 1993 it made four rulings on references from the Belgian and French courts on the issue of separating regulatory and operational activities. In *Procureur du Roi* v. *Lagauche and Evrard*[13] the Court of Justice examined a Belgian law prohibiting the sale or hire of radio transmitters and receivers which had not been previously approved by the Belgian TO, RTT, as complying with the technical requirements laid down by the Minister. The Court held that the creation of an authorizing role within the context of a regulatory system of the type existing in Belgium did not contravene Articles 30, 37, or 90(1) in conjunction with Article 86 of the Treaty, so that

---

[12] A divorce between supply of equipment and services was achieved in the UK prior to the 1988 Directive by the Telecommunications Act 1981; its effects have been assessed by Vickers and Yarrow, 1988: 231.

[13] Joined Cases C-46/90 and C-93/91 [1993] ECR I-5267.

the national system did not contravene EC law in the period prior to 1 July 1989, the implementation date of the Equipment Directive. The Court did not rule expressly that it was legitimate for the RTT to grant type-approval, but this was implicit in the way in which it distinguished this situation from *RTT* v. *SA GB-Inno-BM*[14] where the Court had held that Articles 3(f), 90, and 86 of the Treaty preclude a member state from granting to its TO the power to set standards and verify compliance by economic operators with whom it was competing. However, in so far as the issue came within Directive 88/301 on telecommunications terminal equipment, Article 6 of the Directive precluded national rules making it a punishable offence to offer for sale or hire apparatus no specimen of which has been approved by a public undertaking offering goods and/or services in the field of telecommunications.

Article 6 of Directive 88/301 was further considered in *Decoster*[15] and *Taillandier-Neny*,[16] decided on the same day as *Lagauche*. The Court held that in the absence of assurance of the independence of the body which issues type approval and formalizes technical specifications, Article 6 did not allow French rules prohibiting the import, sale, or distribution of terminal equipment without prior approval to indicate compliance with essential requirements relating to the protection of users and the proper functioning of the network. The independence of the approving body must be established in relation to every operator offering goods and/or services in the telecommunications sector. The exercise of both regulatory and operational functions by different departments of the same Ministry did not ensure adequate independence. However, the Court also held in *Rouffeteau and Badia*[17] that Directive 88/301 does not preclude national rules which prohibit traders from importing terminal equipment which has not been approved for release for consumption, possessing it with a view to sale, selling, distributing, or advertising it, even if the importer, holder, or vendor has clearly stated that such equipment is intended solely for re-export, where there is no certainty that it will actually be re-exported and the equipment is not suitable for connection to the public network.

---

[14] Case C-18/88 [1991] ECR I-5941.
[15] Case C-69/91 [1993] ECR I-5335.
[16] Case C-92/91 [1993] ECR I-5383.
[17] Case C-314/93 [1994] ECR I-3257.

The decisions of the Court of Justice in these cases have a significance which extends beyond telecommunications equipment, because *Lagauche and Evrard* and *Decoster* delineate which regulatory structures will pass muster under Article 90 EC. The case law of the Court establishes the parameters within which debates on how other utilities should be regulated in the EC will be conducted by redefining the previous understandings of the member states and the Commission. When the head of the French telecommunications regulatory agency set out the key aspects of the agency's activities in 1988 he emphasized that the functional separation of operations and regulation within the Ministry was 'in harmony with the recommendation of the European Community's Green Paper', and came 'within the context of a truly European policy on tele-communications, both within the EEC and the rest of Western Europe' (Chamoux, 1990: 416–17). This confidence has been overturned by the active approach to regulatory policy development taken by the Court of Justice.

5. IMPLEMENTING EC TELECOMMUNICATIONS POLICY: THE COMMISSION AND NATIONAL TOS

The Commission's development as a leading policy actor in the telecommunications field does not allow it to advance its own agenda without reference to the preference of other actors, whether at EC level (such as the other EC institutions and the member states) or at national level. The latter group includes the national TOs and they move our attention to a different level of the policy game, one which cannot be overlooked in evaluating the success of the reforms advanced by the Commission or in considering how it can retain its primacy in this sector. These issues will be examined in the context of the implementation of the Equipment and the Services Directives.

5.1 Equipment Directive 88/301/EEC

Notwithstanding the adoption of the Equipment Directive into national law in all member states, many have been unenthusiastic about its objectives. Several retained a requirement that the first telephone purchased or rented by an end-user be obtained from the member state's TO (Naftel, 1993: 110), a classic 'tying' practice designed to restrict competitors' access to the market. The 1988 Directive is essentially directed at negative integration by removing formal barriers to market entry based on nationally conferred exclusive rights. Mutual recognition of conformity with national terminal equipment standards is necessary to promote positive integration of this sector and this is now governed by Council Directives 91/263/EEC and 93/97/EEC.[18] The regulatory mechanisms employed in this area rely on the publication of mandatory standards, Common Technical Regulations (CTRs). When such standards have been developed for a wide range of terminal equipment it will be possible to develop a single European telecommunications equipment market, but not before. ETSI, the European Telecommunications Standards Institute, is central to the production of the CTR mandatory standards, but it has not been successful in meeting deadlines and target dates. As of November 1994 less than fifteen CTRs had been adopted, and this is at least in part due to the opposition of national regulatory authorities to proposed measures which will jeopardize the position of their national TOs. Directive 91/263 also required that member states adopt measures to ensure mutual recognition of telecommunications equipment conformity by November 1992, but the Commission noted in June 1994 that four of the member states had failed to do so, and that Germany had inadequately transposed the Directive.[19] All in all, the member states' approach to the telecommunications equipment sector has been less than fully co-operative. While an integrated, competitive market for telecommunications equipment is emerging, this is occuring more slowly than the (relatively) well established body of secondary legislation in this field might indicate.

---

[18] Council Dir. 91/263/EEC on the approximation of the laws of the member states concerning telecommunications terminal equipment including the mutual recognition of their conformity, OJ 1991 L128/1; Council Dir. 93/97/EEC supplementing Council Dir. 91/263/EEC in respect of satellite earth station equipment, OJ 1993 L290/1.

[19] OJ 1994 C154/19. In addition, the Commission commenced an Article 169 EC action against Greece in September 1994, Case C-260/94, for failure to adopt and notify the measures necessary for the transposition of Dir. 91/263/EEC.

5.2 Services Directive 90/388/EEC

The 1992 Leased Lines ONP Directive[20] clarifies the Services
Directive and imposes conditions of non-discrimination upon the
dominant telecommunications firms, a crucial issue when the
interconnection of leased lines with other networks is considered.
This deals with a tactic formerly commonly employed by national
TOs and regulatory authorities to exclude new market entrants,
because they can no longer prohibit certain types of interconnections
as undesirable by means of introducing specific technical restrictions. Traditionally member states and their TOs have used
technical restrictions, such as prohibitions on carrying third-party
traffic, on the use of leased lines which are inter-connected with the
public telecommunications network in order to exclude potential
competitors. In view of the high demand for sophisticated and cross-
border telecommunications services, the elimination of such restrictions was thought to be necessary for rapid development of the
market for telecommunications services, particularly in market
sectors such as that for data transmission services where annual
growth of 15 to 20 per cent has been forecast for the next few years.

Member state TOs have expressed a view that in those areas
where EC legislation has been passed to harmonize conditions and
liberalize access to markets, a 'light-handed' approach to regulation
should be adopted. For example, Manuel Avendaño, Steering
Committee Chairman of European Public Telecommunications
Network Operators' Association (ETNO) has argued that interconnection agreements should be left to market participants, subject
to dispute mechanisms set up at a national level (Avendaño, 1994:
7).[21] If this approach were accepted ONP regulation would be
confined to *ex ante* application of the EC competition rules on a case-
by-case basis to deal with bottlenecks. In addition, there would be
no general attempt to deal with access to the market other than with
problems arising from bottlenecks (Avendaño, 1994: 6). This
proposal represents a hostility, not to regulation as such but to

---

[20] Council Dir. 92/44/EEC on the application of open network provision to leased
lines, OJ 1992 L165/27.
[21] The difficulties which this approach would create can be seen in *Telecom
Corporation of New Zealand Ltd.* v. *Clear Communications Ltd.*, Privy Council, 19 Oct.
1994.

regulation at a level other than at that of the individual member states. At present, under Article 12 of the ONP Leased Lines Directive, a two-stage conciliation procedure is to be established to deal with interconnection disputes. The first stage takes place at national level with the national regulatory authority for tele-communications, and the member states have drawn up a wide variety of procedures to deal with this stage. The second stage of the procedure occurs at EC level and was put into practice in July 1994 when Espirit Telecom complained to the Commission of the failure of Telefónica, the Spanish telecommunications provider, and DGTel, the Spanish national regulatory authority, to provide it with a leased line in Spain within a reasonable timescale, and of the lack of transparency in the national procedures involved. The complaint was resolved by a meeting of a Working Group on 26 July 1994 convened by the Chairman of the ONP Committee. It should be noted that although Nick White, chairman of INTUG Europe, the international telecommunication service users group, felt that this was an instance of ONP 'living up to expectations' (White, 1994: 7), DGTel participated only on an informal basis.

The relative paucity of competition in the EC telecommunication services markets makes it difficult to assess the success of the Services and ONP Directives. The attempts by Telsystem, an independent Italian supplier of telecommunications services, to interconnect with the public telecommunications network system illustrate this problem. The Italian market is dominated by Telecom Italia which is the world's sixth largest network, and the twenty-fifth largest company in Europe by market capitalization (Cane, 1995). Telsystem sought for eighteen months to lease lines from Telecom Italia who refused access on the ground that it was complying with existing Italian rules on the sector. Although the Services Directive should have been in force for almost four years, it had not been incorporated into national law at that point. The Italian antitrust authorities did hold in January 1995 that Telecom Italia had abused its dominant position and wrongly disregarded EC liberalizing rules (Hill, 1995). However, instances such as the Telsystem/Telecom Italia dispute demonstrate that national TOs have few incentives to abandon a system of regulation which guarantees their exclusive rights, or with which they are simply familiar, if the member states fail to implement EC norms. A similar process can be seen in Germany where Deutsche Telekom currently holds a national monopoly on telephone voice services. While there is no obligation to introduce full competition to this sector until 1998, the German authorities have made it clear that there will be no licensing of competitors prior to that time even though it is technically possible and is likely to generate significant savings to consumers, particularly international services users (Lindemann, 1995b). Liberalization is proceeding slowly and reluctantly (Lindemann, 1995a). The implementation of liberalizing and harmonizing measures in respect of equipment and services by the member states and their TOs is, for the most part, a painfully slow process and belies the impression of relatively rapid progress in this sector created by the pace and the extent of legislative activity.

6. CONCLUSION

The Commission has played a key role in transforming the structure of Europe's telecommunications industry. It has done this by attacking the service and operating monopolies which have classically been a hallmark of this sector and by ending national procurement policies in respect of telecommunications equipment. The extent of this shift can be judged by the manner in which the Commission brought forward the end of the monopoly in voice telecommunications services, despite the fact that this continued to exist in most member states and that very few states had indicated any desire to change this dispensation. In the process the Commission has acquired and consolidated a new range of power and influence, underpinned by the Court of Justice, and exercised in dialogue with national and EC actors. The contents of these policies are of less concern here than the manner in which this development has occurred. As observed elsewhere, the Commission is not 'one' consistent actor; different groups within it support diverging strategies (Fuchs, 1992: 81; Scott, 1994). It is not possible to understand the evolution of the present EC telecommunications policy without taking the central role of the Commission into account. However, as demonstrated here, irrespective of whichever telecommunications policy is favoured, the Commission cannot be treated as the only non-government player at Community level, nor can its own relations with actors in national policy formulation be ignored save at the risk of distorting our understanding of how the EC operates.

Legislative Review by the EC Commission: Revision without Radicalism*

IMELDA MAHER

There is a review of legislation currently under way in the Community under the auspices of the Commission. This Chapter examines why there is such a review and how it is being conducted. The Commission is primarily responsible for reviewing existing legislation under both the Sutherland Report and the principle of subsidiarity. The former has led to a process of consolidation to make EC legislation more transparent, with the objective of improving the effectiveness of the Internal Market programme. The latter is a slow and potentially fraught process of repeal and replacement through the retroactive application of a politically vague and legally unsustainable principle. The techniques of codification, clarification, simplification, and repeal used by the Commission are shaped by institutional factors, notably the change in culture brought about by the inclusion of the subsidiarity principle in the Treaty on European Union. This essay focuses on the impact of the review on existing institutional structures and its effect on the *acquis communautaire*.[1] In its broadest sense, this denotes the full body of Community rules, principles, and policies, which is marked out for special protection in Article B TEU. The chapter examines the appropriateness, from a legal perspective, of the tools used in the review. It argues that the greater transparency which will result from review may push the question of democratic accountability higher up the political agenda. At the same time, the

* Thanks to Gráinne de Búrca, Linda Luckhaus, Colin Scott, and Daniel Wincott for comments on an earlier draft of this essay. A version of this paper was presented at the European Communities Studies Association (ECSA) Conference, Charleston SC, May 1995. Thanks to the British Academy, to ESCA and to Warwick University for funding my attendance at the conference.
[1] An examination of the impact of the review on individual policy sectors falls beyond the remit of this Chapter.

acquis communautaire will undeniably be affected by the review of legislation under the subsidiarity principle.

1. WHY LEGISLATIVE REVIEW?

Power has never been definitively allocated between the member states and the Community. Instead, power has been shared in the light of mutually beneficial objectives (Steiner, 1994b: 57). Within this system of incomplete competences, the Commission has acted opportunistically to expand its powers and those of the Community: it has exerted gradual bureaucratic pressure on the Council, often through the use of soft law initiatives which act as precursors of legally binding policy initiatives (Cram, 1993: 143). The vacuum created by the absence of a policy-driven government at the centre of the Community has also been exploited by the Commission to develop the competences of the Community (Richardson, 1995: 142). At the same time, the Community remains dependent on member states to ensure that its regulation is rendered effective: thus co-operation with the member states is important for enforcement. As long as enforcement of Community law remained lax, member states were willing to sign up for EC legislative initiatives (Snyder, 1993: 52). However, with the introduction of qualified majority voting under the Single European Act and improved enforcement of EC law, partly through the development of the jurisprudence of the Court in relation to direct effect and remedies, the states became more sensitive to the measures coming before the Council and more conscious of the potential impact of regulation at Community level.

Mutual recognition acted as a smoke-screen for the copious deregulation needed at national level for completion of the common market and its replacement by EC measures (McGee & Weatherill, 1990: 582). This deregulation at national level, combined with what appeared to be ever-expanding competences of the Community, prompted the introduction of the principle of subsidiarity into the Treaty on European Union (Peterson, 1994: 55). A product of political compromise, the principle is given legal expression in Article 3B of the Treaty where the issue of creeping Community competence is directly addressed through the principle of attribution, which asserts that the Community can only exercise those powers attributed to it by the member states. The second paragraph contains the subsidiarity principle itself and requires EC action to be taken only where the objectives cannot be adequately achieved at national level and can be better achieved by EC action. However, these two tests only apply when the EC acts outside its exclusive competence. The third paragraph repeats the proportionality principle as developed by the Court of Justice.[2]

The principle of subsidiarity is concerned with the level at which power is to be exercised within the Community. This necessarily precludes the subnational level from discussion and also appears to limit the application of the principle to the procedural and somewhat technical question of how it is to be applied within the existing decision-making processes of the EC. This does not point to a possible legislative review, yet such a review was the outcome of the political events surrounding the ratification of the Maastricht Treaty. It was the vagueness of the principle which gave rise to the flurry of clarification following the first Danish referendum which rejected the Maastricht Treaty. Subsidiarity would not have received so much attention but for that referendum and the ability of the British Eurosceptics to prevent a speedy ratification of the Treaty in the UK (Peterson, 1994: 119). In the light of public concern about democratic accountability within the EC, the principle of subsidiarity was held up as the device through which accountability would be improved. Clarification of how the principle would achieve this was attempted in an atmosphere of political compromise and panic at the Edinburgh Summit, where rather than addressing the shortcomings of the legislative process itself the focus was turned to the outcomes of that process resulting in the Commission's Edinburgh List, indicating existing proposals which it would remove from the legislative agenda.[3] This list was supplemented by the Brussels Report where the Commission indicated how existing legislation would be reviewed in the light of the subsidiarity principle.[4] This part of the subsidiarity review is seen by the Commission as simply the next stage in a deregulation

---

[2] See Ward above.

[3] Annex II of the Presidency Conclusions to the Edinburgh European Council, Bull. EC 12–1992, 16.

[4] EC Commission, Report to the European Council on the Adaptation of Existing Legislation to the Subsidiarity Principle, COM(93) 545 (the 'Brussels Report').

process, the first step of which was the harmonization programme
which reduced the volume of national legislation.

An earlier and largely unrelated development was the Sutherland
Report.[5] This committee of experts was set up to examine how the
full benefits of the Internal Market could be secured in practice after
1992 (Wainwright, 1994: 102). It emphasized the importance of
transparency and in that regard recommended that legislation
should be consolidated. The Commission welcomed the recommendations and has set about implementing them while also
developing a further, distinct initiative.[6] In September 1994 it
set up a group of independent experts to examine the impact
of Community and national legislation on employment and
competitiveness. The Commission published their report in June.[7]
It recommends simplification of Community and national
(including local) law. It also recognises that simplification may lead
to deregulation at Community and national level. It makes a
number of recommendations to alleviate the problem of transposing
directives into national law, including the use of regulations. Such a
move would be in contrast to the trend towards framework
directives in the light of the subsidiarity principle.

2. LEGISLATIVE REVIEW

Rather than tackle the critical issue of how and at what levels power
is exercised in the Community, the member states side-stepped the
question of improving accountability by seeking to resolve
the democratic deficit through greater transparency and legislative
review rather than through institutional reform (Lodge, 1994: 344).
The review is proceeding under three different initiatives, most

---

[5] 'The Internal Market After 1992: Meeting the Challenge', Report to the EEC
Commission by the High Level Group on the Operation of the Internal Market.
[6] See e.g. EC Commission, Communication from the Commission to the Council
and the European Parliament, 'The Operation of the Community's Internal Market
after 1992—Follow-up to the Sutherland Report, SEC(92) 2277; Communication
from the Commission, Follow-up to the Sutherland Report—Legislative
Consolidation to Enhance the Transparency of Community Law in the Area of the
Internal Market, COM(93) 361.   [7] COM(95) 288.

importantly under the principle of subsidiarity. The Commission is required to produce an annual report on the application of the principle and in the first of these reports it analyses how the review is being conducted.[8]

The review has led to the withdrawal of a large number of existing proposals. This process dates from the Edinburgh List.[9] A total of nine proposals were withdrawn by the Commission by the end of 1993 after it had considered the recommendation of the Parliament that most of the proposals be retained.[10] In addition, 150 technically obsolete or outdated proposals were withdrawn in that year.[11] All new proposals now have to be justified in the light of Article 3B, and it therefore follows that proposals which do not comply with the principle will not be put forward. Instead, the review may lead to their modification, as happened in 1994, for example when a proposed directive relating to zoo animals was to be replaced with a non-binding recommendation.[12]

The burden of ensuring that proposals comply with the principle falls on the Commission.[13] The practical consequence of this burden is the production of an explanatory memorandum with each proposal examined in the light of subsidiarity. Each memo answers a list of questions including, in situations of shared competence, what is the most effective solution and the added value of EC action. Each proposal also includes a recital addressing subsidiarity.[14] This process ensures that the principle is adhered to and the removal or modification of proposals which breach it. As a result there has been a reduction in the number of proposals emanating from the

[8] COM(94) 533, (the '1994 Report').
[9] See Annex II of the Presidency Conclusions to the Edinburgh European Council, Bull. EC 12–1992, 16.
[10] See Resolution on the Possible Withdrawal or Amendment of Certain Commission Legislative Proposals (Edinburgh List), OJ 1993 C268/166 and the Brussels Report, *supra* n. 4.   [11] The Brussels Report, *supra* n. 4, 5.
[12] The 1994 Report, *supra* n. 8, 15–16.
[13] The Brussels Report, *supra* n. 4.
[14] See e.g. Proposal for a Council Directive on harmonization of the Main Provisions Concerning Export Credit Insurance for Transactions with Medium- and Long-term Cover: 'whereas, pursuant to the third paragraph of Article 3b of the treaty, harmonisation is necessary to ensure that export policy is based on uniform principles and that competition between Community undertakings is not distorted', OJ 1994 C272/2.

Commission from almost 190 in 1990 to just over forty in the first ten months in 1994.[15]

The final part of this process is the review of existing legislation. The Commission proceeds cautiously. Only legislation arising out of shared competence is reviewed under both the second and third paragraphs of Article 3B, that is it will be reviewed to see if it meets the need-for-action test and the proportionality test. Review is limited to legislation over two years old, and to binding measures which affect firms and individuals—areas where major changes are being considered will not be reviewed. The Commission indicated in its report on the adaptation of existing legislation to the subsidiarity principle that the success of the review is conditional on: greater delegation of implementing powers to it; giving more weight to mutual confidence especially in relation to matters involving health; and removing the mutual lack of confidence between national administrations which is particularly apparent with the development of mutual recognition, this last point echoing the opinion of the Sutherland Report.[16]

Review of existing legislation falls under three headings: rules and regulations to be recast, simplified, and repealed. Recasting applies to mature legislation where the fundamental principles can be identified along with the core rules, and secondary measures can be replaced with a single implementing procedure. For example in its 1994 legislative programme the Commission proposed amending current directives concerning rights of residence with a view to recasting them.[17] Simplification allows for the removal of excessive detail from legislation through proposing more general measures, for example proposals have been put forward to simplify directives on foodstuffs and mineral water, and a framework directive is also proposed in the 1994 report. Finally, some measures have been repealed although repeal without replacement seems very unlikely. Instead, repeal will only occur where measures are being recast or simplified, e.g. the Commission is proposing to replace the thirteen regulations on export refunds in the CAP with a single

---

[15] The 1994 Report, *supra* n. 8, 4. Of course, post-1992 the number of proposals would have reduced anyway.

[16] The Brussels Report, *supra* n. 4.

[17] COM(93) 588. Work was continuing on it when the 1994 Report, *supra* n. 8, was presented by the Commission.

regulation. Thus legislative review is a process of regulatory reform rather than deregulation.

In the 1994 Report the Commission also indicated that it is seeking alternative solutions to Community legislation or action through decentralized implementation by member state authorities. This is a statement of long established practice and also echoes the view that subsidiarity should result in decisions being taken closer to the people. The report mentions co-operation with national authorities in relation to the enforcement of Articles 85 and 86 EC, especially where the Commission is dealing with matters which predominantly affect one member state. If this example is typical, then the Commission is looking to national authories to build on existing responsibilities rather than to take on wholly new responsibilities.

The most obvious impact of the review in the light of the subsidiarity principle is that, in addition to the withdrawal of existing proposals, the number of new proposals emanating from the Commission has greatly reduced. However, in the post-Internal Market phase a reduction of new proposals would anyway have been likely. The reduction should lead to greater co-ordination between DGs, who will have to compete with each other to get their proposals onto the new streamlined, and public, legislative agenda. Such developments are to be welcomed, the Commission having been criticized in the past as a composite bureaucracy with poor internal policy co-ordination (Richardson, 1995: 143).

There is very little repeal of legislation, amendment of existing legislation being preferred. Some measures are being replaced with either non-binding or less detailed measures and there is greater reliance on mutual recognition. This creates the need for improved co-ordination and mutual confidence between national authorities. If the Community is to apply 'a lighter touch', then national authorities will have to be more responsive to their Community responsibilities. This issue was highlighted by the Sutherland Report, which pointed to the lack of trust and understanding between national administrations responsible for ensuring mutual recognition of each others' standards. Steps are being taken to overcome this problem.[18] The *quid pro quo* of more framework

[18] See e.g. Council Resolution on the Development of Administrative Cooperation in the Implementation and Enforcement of Community Legislation in the Internal Market, OJ 1994 C179/1; Council Resolution on Coordination with Regard to Information Exchange Between Administrations, OJ 1994 C181/1.

directives and less centralized EC legislation is therefore an
increased commitment from member states to enforce the law. Thus
the Commission refers to the principle of mutual confidence in the
Brussels Report and there is a declaration by member states in
the Treaty to apply EC law with the same rigour and effectiveness as
national law.[19] The review is ongoing and in the medium term will
lead to greater transparency of existing legislation, thanks to the
process of clarification and modification, while the overall volume of
existing legislation will be slightly reduced.

A related but separate aspect of the legislative review is that of
consolidation under the Sutherland Report. Legislative consolidation is the combination of an initial legal text and all amendments
into a single authoritative text, with the repeal of all the earlier
texts.[20] It is published in the L series of the Official Journal and at
the moment follows standard decision-making procedures.[21] No
amendment of the law is involved. Since 1990 a number of proposals
for consolidation have been suggested by the Commission but have
been delayed at Council level. The Council uses the consolidation
proposal as an opportunity to reopen debate on the substance of the
measures, or suggests postponement because there are other
amendments of the legislation forthcoming. The Commission would
like to see the task of consolidation delegated to itself as it is purely a
procedural task, involving no policy considerations.[22] The
Commission's view is that if the Council will not delegate, then
suitable works practices need to be devised. This is a view echoed by
the Parliament, which has called for an interinstitutional agreement
on the method of codification.[23] Until there is such an agreement or
delegation then delays in codification are likely to continue.[24] Such

---

[19] The Brussels Report, *supra* n. 4; Declaration no. 19 TEU.
[20] See the Conclusions of the Presidency of the Edinburgh European Council, Bull.
EC 12–1992, 20.
[21] The example provided by the Presidency is Council Regulation on the Common
Organisation of the Market in Fishery Products, OJ 1991 L354/1.
[22] See Commission Communication, Follow-Up to the Sutherland Report:
Legislative Consolidation to Enhance the Transparency of Community Law in the
Area of the Internal Market, COM(93) 361.
[23] See Resolution of the European Parliament on the 1994 Legislative Programme,
OJ 1994 C60/26, para. 10. The Parliament approved the inter-institutional
agreement on codification on 18 Jan. 1995, see OJ 1995 C43/4.
[24] The Commission proposed the codification of 12 directives and 3 regulations in
its 1994 Legislative Programme, see COM(93) 588.

reforms apart, the Commission has also highlighted the lack of resources in relation to preparing texts in all the EC languages. A possible short-term solution is greater use of declaratory codification where material is consolidated informally to make it accessible on the INFO92 database.[25]

The committee of experts set up to suggest simplification of both national and Community laws to ensure a positive impact on employment and competitiveness can be seen as a way around the problems surrounding consolidation under Sutherland. If substantive review is unavoidable then the Commission may be able to ensure it occurs for the best possible reasons, that is on grounds of competitiveness and employment. Therefore substantive changes will have to justified in the light of these two principles as well as of subsidiarity.

3. OVERALL EFFECTS: THE *ACQUIS COMMUNAUTAIRE* AND THE INSTITUTIONAL BALANCE

Both consolidation of the body of EC regulation under Sutherland and streamlining of the legislative programme are to be welcomed. The former because it will improve transparency and the latter because it may improve co-ordination between the DGs of the Commission. However, the review of existing legislation raises two fundamental issues: the impact of the review on the *acquis communautaire* and the review as a wholly inadequate and inappropriate response to the lack of democratic accountability in the EC legislative process.

The scope of the principle in relation to the review of legislation is broader than is suggested by a literal reading of Article 3B. The second paragraph contains the subsidiarity principle itself and requires EC action to be taken only where the objectives cannot be adequately achieved at national level and can be better achieved by EC action. However, these two tests only apply when the EC is acting outside its exclusive competence. This implies that review in light of the principle should only occur where there is shared

---

[25] See the Conclusions of the Presidency of the Edinburgh European Council, Bull. EC 12–1992, 20, where emphasis is also placed on improving the Celex database and using electronic mail.

competence. This is the only provision of the EC Treaty which expressly refers to 'exclusive competence' and as no attempt has been made to define this term by the Council or Commission it has been the subject of much academic debate (cf. Toth, 1992; Emiliou, 1992). The boundaries of competence remain vague and the scope of review under the principle is therefore unclear. In its 1994 report on the application of the subsidiarity principle the Commission raises the problem of differentiating between exclusive and other competences, especially in the area of completion of the internal market. In this area the implementation of the four freedoms is within the exclusive competence of the EC, but accompanying measures designed to facilitate the operation of the internal market are not.[26] It skirts the issue by failing to offer any substantive comment, indicating instead that it has issued staff guidelines on preparation of legal instruments. It also notes that it will have to be increasingly strict in the criteria which it applies, without giving any indication of what those criteria might be, while ironically also emphasizing the need for transparency.

The Commission is also reviewing legislation in the light of subsidiarity even though the principle did not exist when the legislation was passed. The extension of the principle to previously existing legislation arose out of the European Council meeting in Lisbon, which requested the Commission to investigate how such a review could be conducted. This led to the Brussels Report, in which the Commission indicated that existing legislation could be reviewed in the light of the principle, subject to some limitations, notably that only legislation more than two years old would be reviewed.

This review could be justified as a pragmatic move by the Commission in a new political climate which is concerned about the level and amount of Community regulation. However, the principle is now being applied retroactively (Toth, 1994: 46) and that body of Community law which does not fall within the ill-defined 'exclusive competence' of the Commission is being surveyed in the light of subsidiarity. If the principle is applied retroactively to Community measures only, and binding legal measures are replaced with non-binding measures, then ultimately the scope of Community law will be gradually diminished.

The Treaty on European Union states that it builds on the

---

[26] The 1994 Report, *supra* n. 8, 3.

existing *acquis communautaire*, but if existing legislation can be revised in the light of subsidiarity then the existing body of law is being not merely adapted but changed. Change is not problematic *per se*, but it is important that it be effected on the correct basis. The principle is expressly stated not to affect the *acquis communautaire*, nor to be concerned with the allocation of power.[27] A revision of existing legislation which predates the principle inevitably counters the stated absence of effect on the *acquis communautaire*, and merely obfuscates the legal meaning and consequences of the principle. This obfuscation undermines one of the other rationales of the principle and of all current legislative reviews, which is to improve the transparency of the legislative process. If transparency is an objective of the review then that objective is undermined by the failure of the institutions to acknowledge that review via the principle of subsidiarity *is* capable of affecting the *acquis communautaire*, even in those cases where the primary aim of the review is to clarify and simplify legislation.

Legislative review under the principle of subsidiarity is further compounded by its impact on the interrelationships of the main EC institutions. As with the declared preservation of the *acquis communautaire*, the principle is not meant to have any effect on the institutions.

The review process under subsidiarity can be seen as a rationalization of the existing body of law. The incentive for this review came from the European Council. The Council skilfully ensured that the Commission became the focus for public concern about the accountability of the legislative process of the EC (Lodge, 1994: 345). By focusing on transparency and by using the principle of subsidiarity, in itself a legally obscure device, the issue of rendering the policy-making process more open to the elected representatives of the people in the European Parliament was side-tracked. Instead it became the responsibility of the Commission to make the system more transparent using legislative review to simplify and consolidate. Such review will make the scope of EC legislation more apparent but will do nothing to reform the existing legislative procedures, except in so far as the reduced volume of proposals will allow more time for prior consultation and improve policy

---

[27] Interinstitutional Agreement on Implementing the Principle of Subsidiarity, Bull. EC 10–1992, 119.

co-ordination within the Commission. Even after the review is complete, the Council will still remain the most powerful and the most hidden of the institutions.

The review remains primarily within the purview of the Commission, which has proceeded cautiously in relation to the review of existing legislation while pushing for greater assumption of powers in the technical exercise of consolidation. The responsibility for the application of subsidiarity remains shared between the institutions, a point which the Commission continues to make where it feels its position being undermined by the Council. Thus it has consistently reiterated that the *acquis communautaire* remains unaffected, a point accepted by the Council.[28] Yet in the Brussels Report the Commission felt it necessary to remind the Council that it must accept that the Commission may act at international level and not introduce internal legislation which would duplicate international agreements.[29] This implies a concern on the part of the Commission about challenges to its ability to act internationally, a concern borne out by its defeat in the *France* v. *Commission*[30] decision, where the Court held that the Commission could not negotiate an agreement on competition enforcement with the USA.

At the Edinburgh Summit the Commission indicated that, in keeping with the general reduction in the number of legislative proposals, it would no longer accept informal suggestions from the Council that it should introduce proposals for directives. This reflects the Commission concern, expressed in its earlier Commun-ication, that it is perceived as meddling.[31] By refusing suggestions for legislation from Council it is refusing to be co-opted to implement unpopular regulatory measures. In the same spirit, it indicated that it would refuse Council amendments which run counter to proportionality or unnecessarily compound legislation. In its 1994 Report it underlined this view by criticizing member states which adopt positions in Council inconsistent with Article 3B.[32]

Although the principle of subsidiarity was not meant to affect the institutional balance, there was recognition that some agreement

---

[28] Interinstitutional Agreement on Implementing the Principle of Subsidiarity, Bull. EC 10–1992, 119.   [29] The Brussels Report, *supra* n. 4.
[30] Case C-327/91 [1994] ECR I-3641.
[31] Commission Communication on the Principle of Subsidiarity presented to the Council and the Parliament, Bull. EC 10-1992, 119.
[32] The 1994 Report, *supra* n. 8, 2.

between the institutions was necessary as to how the principle was to be applied in decision-making. The Agreement on Procedures for Implementing Subsidiarity was issued together with a Declaration on Democracy, Transparency, and Subsidiarity, and reaffirms the institutions' respect for the democratic principles of the member states and their commitment to transparency.[33] The limitations of the principle are clearly stated, that is: it is only concerned with *how* power is exercised by the EC and not with the question of *what* powers are conferred. All three institutions accept responsibility for application of the principle. The Agreement asserts that the *acquis communautaire* is unaffected, as is the balance of power between the institutions. Where there is a dispute between the institutions as to the Agreement, the presidents of the institutions will convene a conference to overcome any difficulties. This lends weight to the view that the Agreement is not legally binding and hence not subject to judicial review (Monar, 1994).

The review process marginalizes the Parliament. Both Council and Parliament must be told by the Commission why a proposal is being withdrawn although the opinion of the Parliament is not binding. Its relatively weak position can be seen in a comparison of the 1993 and 1994 legislative programmes. In the works programme for 1993/4 the Commission indicated that there would be a strict but positive application of the principle of subsidiarity. Thus it would focus on action which was essential for the objectives laid down by the programme.[34] These undertakings are given substance in the legislative programmes. As already mentioned, in the 1993 programme the Commission simply reproduced the Edinburgh List.[35] A similar number of measures were proposed for consolidation in 1994.[36] Obviously, because subsidiarity was now in operation, there were no proposals to be withdrawn, as all proposals would be subject to the principle and would not be put forward unless the Commission believed that the principle had been

---

[33] Interinstitutional Declaration on Democracy, Transparency and Subsidiarity, Bull. EC 10–1993, 188; Interinstitutional Agreement Between the European Parliament, the Council and the Commission on Procedures for Implementing the Principle of Subsidiarity, Bull. 10–1993, 119.

[34] SEC(93) 58; Bull. EC Supp. 1/93, 16.

[35] Commission's Legislative Programme for 1993, COM(93) 45.

[36] Commission's Legislative Programme for 1994, *supra* n. 17.

complied with: this is certainly the implication to be drawn from the Brussels Report.

There are some noticeable differences between the 1993 and 1994 programmes. In the former the Commission is careful to indicate the number of measures proposed and to be removed. It also gives a clear and categorical commitment to subsidiarity, promising to examine each proposal closely to see if it would be best carried out at EC level. It also states that each proposal is examined in the light of the costs and benefits for national public authorities and for interested parties. A full list is provided of measures both pending and proposed. Such caution seems to reflect the political climate in which the programme would be published: it was the first programme to be published even though such programmes have been in existence since 1988. In 1994 reference to subsidiarity is limited to an indication that all proposals are examined in strict compliance with that principle, as defined in the interinstitutional agreement. No appendix of pending proposals is provided and those proposals carried forward and included in the programme are not highlighted, thus a careful comparison of the two programmes is needed to discover which proposals are new and which are carried forward.[37] The 1993 programme was greeted warmly by the Parliament.[38] The 1994 programme was less well received, suggesting weaknesses in the procedures agreed and perhaps reflecting the concern of Parliament that it was again being sidelined by the Council and Commission.[39] Parliament criticized the Commission: for failing to provide a timetable for submission of proposals; for the delay in publication of the programme; and for failing to indicate the Treaty provisions on which proposals would be based. More importantly, Parliament had not been informed about the postponement, dropping, or transformation of a number of proposals, despite the commitment given by the Commission in its report.[40]

For its part, the Council had agreed in the interinstitutional Agreement to respond to the proposed legislative programme before its final adoption. In essence, it agreed to respond directly to the

---

[37] This defect was remedied by the 1994 Report, *supra* n. 8.
[38] Parliament Declaration on the 1993 Legislative Programme, Bull. EC Supp 1/93, 68.
[39] Resolution of the European Parliament on the 1994 Legislative Programme, OJ 1994 C60/26.   [40] Brussels Report, *supra* n. 4, 4.

views of Parliament on the programme. This could have resulted in real dialogue between Council and Parliament about the future direction of the EC and the content of its legislative programme (Monar, 1994: 710). However, the Council's response was disappointing.[41] Short and general in nature, it placed more importance on subsidiarity than either the Commission or Parliament. The final joint declaration does go some way to meet Parliament's criticisms, with deadlines included for some measures. The institutions also agreed to draw up a joint calendar for common positions and second reading and to ensure reciprocal information on the progress of work concerning priorities of common interest.[42] These proposals for action obviously represent a compromise between Council and Parliament, especially as there is a footnote in the declaration indicating that the Parliament expects the sharing of information to include the participation of its representatives at Council meetings. The Council, despite its lack of such experience, is intended to liaise with the Parliament, as borne out by the response of the Council to the 1994 legislative programme (Curtin, 1993: 43). Its relationship with the Parliament could become more fruitful over time, but only if there is a genuine will on the part of the Council to acknowledge Parliament's credibility as a key institution in the legislative process. This process shows that the good intentions of the interinstitutional Agreement have not been realized and that there are continuing internal problems in the relationship between the institutions. These problems are based on inability or unwillingness to see the Parliament as a credible democratic and accountable institution (Lodge, 1994: 360). Review under the subsidiarity principle and the Sutherland Report appears technical and bureaucratic. It has no major substantive objectives other than an overall reduction in the number of policy initiatives emanating from the Commission and a clarification of existing legislation. How can clarification be achieved by the retroactive application of a politically complex and legally obscure principle? It is an impossible task and if the Commission succeeds in achieving some measure of revision which simplifies and consolidates, then that is to be welcomed.

[41] Council Declaration on the 1994 Legislative Programme, OJ 1994 C60/25.
[42] Joint Declaration of the European Parliament and the Commission on the 1994 Legislative Programme, OJ 1994 C60/1.

The key issue identified in the political aftermath of Maastricht is that of accountability mechanisms within the Community. Legislative review which consolidates, simplifies, and reduces the overall number of proposals amounts neither to a deregulatory programme nor to a system of improved accountability. It may, however, as a result of the greater transparency which it produces, further highlight the shortcomings in the system. This could force the accountability issue onto the political agenda in such a way as to prevent it being subsumed by vague political principles like subsidiarity.

4. CONCLUSIONS

The main impact of the subsidiarity principle has been to introduce a cultural change in the Community. There is a greater onus on the Community to justify its actions to the member states on whom it relies for the implementation and enforcement of its rules. Legislation is being 'tidied up', but the process is slow, complex, and despite much mention of transparency, also relatively opaque. The absence of agreement between the institutions as to the scope and function (particularly of the review) seems to render the task more difficult. This is best illustrated by the problems surrounding legislative consolidation and the sharp criticism by the Parliament of the Commission's proposed 1994 Legislative Programme.

The review has been shaped by its institutional context, especially the Community culture in which it was undertaken.[43] That culture has changed, a phenomenon which has itself been institutionalized by the inclusion of the principle of subsidiarity in the Treaty on European Union. 'Culture' here is a shorthand expression for a variety of influences on regulation (Hancher and Moran, 1989b: 3). Expectations about the purpose of regulation, about who are legitimate participants, and about relationships between those participants are formed by cultural references such as time, location, the nature of the economic sector being regulated, and the legal culture within which regulation occurs. The exercise of public power over private economic power rests on legal authority which is made legitimate by appeal to the public will (Hancher and Moran, 1989a:

---

[43] See Armstrong above.

272). Thus the range and form of regulation are deeply influenced by the prevailing conception of the scope and purpose of law. The proper role for law rests in turn on notions of the appropriate allocation of sovereign authority among those who are deemed legitimate participants. If this view of the relationship between culture and regulation is accepted then the central importance of democratic accountability and allocation of competences within the EC can be seen. Yet the legislative review addresses neither of these issues and thus fails to address the most fundamental issue currently facing the Community. It fails to do so because of the unwillingness of member states, in the guise of the Council, to address the problem (Lodge, 1994: 345). Instead it shifted the debate about the lack of accountability to focus on the Commission, diverting attention from the positions of the powerful Council and the relatively impotent and unsaturated Parliament.

The tensions between the institutions point to more fundamental problems, which arise out of the subsidiarity principle itself. As long as the principle remains substantively vague there is scope for disagreement as to its aims and objectives. In particular, the legitimacy of decision-making processes will continue to be questioned as long as the myriad procedures remain to obfuscate and apparently to remove decision-making ever further from democratic accountability (Curtin, 1993: 38). A hierarchy of norms is needed to provide the substantive criteria under which deregulation can occur, if deregulation is really the intention behind the principle of subsidiarity—an issue which remains unclear and, given the nature of the principle, is likely to remain so. Review intended to promote simplification and consolidation is welcome, but the laudable objective has been hijacked by the inappropriate retroactive application of the subsidiarity principle to a pre-existing body of law. Change will come about, but at the expense of the *acquis communautaire* and as a result of the continuing failure of the EC institutions to face up to fundamental and irrepressible concerns about democratic accountability.

A European Litigation Strategy: the Case of the Equal Opportunities Commission*

CATHERINE BARNARD

[Interest group litigation] is ... a form of political expression. Groups which find themselves unable to achieve their objectives through the ballot frequently turn to the courts ... and under the conditions of modern government, litigation may well be the sole practicable avenue open to a minority to petition for the redress of grievances.—Justice Brennan in *NAACP* v. *Button*.[1]

Interest groups have long played an important role in policy-making at national level. A growing number of diverse interest groups have an important input into policy-making in the European Union. Interests are represented through Brussels-based Euro-groups[2] or national associations lobbying independently on particular issues. While Eurolobbying is dominated by commercial interests[3] interest groups concerned with social matters have also begun to make their presence felt as the EC has moved to develop its own social policy.

Establishing equality of treatment between men and women in the workplace has formed one of the pillars of European social

* My thanks to Catherine Hoskyns and Jenny Steele for comments on earlier versions of this paper. I am also grateful to those in the Equal Opportunities Commission, in particular Lorraine Fletcher, who have given assistance and to the European University Institute in Florence for its support during the research which forms the background to this paper.

[1] (1963) 371 US 415, 429–30.

[2] Euro-groups are federations officially recognized by the Commission, such as the Union of Industrial and Employers' Confederations of Europe, UNICE, and the European Trade Union Confederation, ETUC.

[3] For example, industrial and commercial employers' interests account for almost 50% of the Euro-groups, 25% are connected with agriculture, 20% with the service sector and just 5% represent trade union, consumer and environmental interests (Mazey and Richardson, 1993a: 7).

policy,[4] prompted in part by the inclusion of Article 119 on equal pay for equal work in the Treaty of Rome. Article 119 and the subsequent Directives, notably Directive 75/117/EEC on equal pay,[5] Directive 76/207/EEC on equal treatment,[6] and Directive 79/7/EEC on social security,[7] have been invested with considerable significance by a series of judgments of the Court of Justice. A prime mover in this litigation before the Court has been the British Equal Opportunities Commission (EOC) and its sister organization in Northern Ireland (EOC (NI)). Between them, the two organizations have funded fifteen references to the Court of Justice, including highly significant cases such as *Marshall (No. 1)*[8] and *(No. 2)*,[9] *Johnston*,[10] *Barber*,[11] and *Enderby*.[12] This figure represents about one third of all references heard by the Court on matters relating to equal pay and equal treatment at work.[13]

The use of the Court as a weapon in a litigation armoury has received relatively little attention from either litigators or commentators. This contrasts markedly with the United States where the courts, particularly the Supreme Court, have long been an important forum for interest groups. It may be that the Court of Justice is only gradually developing a policy-making function such as that by the United States Supreme Court, or it may be that, as presently constituted, it is not a friendly environment for interest group representation (Harlow and Rawlings, 1992: 279). However, the EOC has pioneered the use of a European litigation strategy in order to take full advantage of the supremacy and direct effect of EC law. This strategy has involved references to the Court of Justice, raising points of EC law in the national courts, and to a limited extent lobbying the other institutions of the European Union. This essay considers the EOC's objects as a litigator and its litigation

[4] See e.g. the Social Action Programme, EC Bull. 10–1972; the Social Charter Action Programme, COM(89) 568; and the Commission White Paper on the Future of Social Policy, COM(94) 333.　　　　　　　　　　　　[5] OJ 1975 L45/19.
[6] OJ 1976 L39/40.　　　　　　　　　　　　　　　　[7] OJ 1979 L6/24.
[8] Case 152/84 *Marshall* v. *Southampton Area Health Authority* [1986] ECR 723.
[9] Case C-271/91 *Marshall* v. *Southampton AHA* [1993] ECR I-4367.
[10] Case 222/84 *Johnston* v. *RUC* [1986] ECR 1651.
[11] Case C-262/88 *Barber* v. *Guardian Royal Exchange* [1990] ECR I-1889.
[12] Case C-127/92 *Enderby* v. *Frenchay AHA* [1993] ECR I-5535. The EOC hopes to fund a reference in the case of *Rudling* concerning the meaning of 'disparate impact'.
[13] This excludes references made in relation to Dir. 79/7/EEC concerning equal treatment in social security.

strategy, in order to assess whether its courage, investment, and persistence have been rewarded.

1. THE POWERS AND FUNCTIONS OF THE EOC

The EOC, modelled on the American Equal Employment Opportunities Commission, was created by the Sex Discrimination Act (SDA) 1975 as a quasi-autonomous non-governmental organization, or quango (Barker, 1982; Coote, 1978: 734). While it is constitutionally separate from central government it is funded by an annual grant-in-aid, originally paid by the Home Office and now by the Department for Education and Employment.[14] The grant for 1993/4 was £5,794,000 (£5,282,000 for 1992/3). The minister responsible can also appoint the Commissioners who head the EOC. The EOC's semi-official status[15] distinguishes it from other interest groups. However, in common with other non-statutory groups, it tries 'to influence the policy of public bodies in (its) chosen direction' (Finer, 1966: 3) and it fights to make its views heard and to exert pressure, sometimes in the face of government resistance. Consequently it has been described as a statutory pressure group (Harlow and Rawlings, 1992: 285).

The EOC is under a duty:

(a) to work towards the elimination of discrimination,
(b) to promote equality of opportunity between men and women generally, and
(c) to keep under review the working of the SDA 1975 and the Equal Pay Act 1970 and, when they are so required by the Secretary of State or otherwise think necessary, to draw up and submit proposals for amending them.[16]

[14] The EOC was under the Sex Equality branch of the Department of Employment. Although the EOC probably had more contact with the Department of Employment, it was concerned to be seen as an agency interested only in employment and women. The Commission for Racial Equality remains under the auspices of the Home Office.

[15] According to one commentator 'The designation of official is the sign manifest that the bearer is authorised by social understanding to exercise against all groups and individuals certain powers which they may not exercise against him' (Latham, 1965: 35). [16] S. 53(1) SDA 1975.

To help fulfil these objectives the EOC has a wide variety of powers in respect of research, education, and publicity.[17] Perhaps most importantly, however, the EOC is permitted by s. 75 to grant 'assistance'[18] to complainants under both the Equal Pay Act 1970 and the Sex Discrimination Act 1975, either because the case raises a question of principle or because it is unreasonable to expect the applicant to deal with the case unaided due to the complexity of the issues involved, the applicant's position in respect of the respondent, or by reason of any other special consideration.[19] This last heading includes clarification of the law. Its legal budget for 1993/4 was £306,571,[20] about 5 per cent of its total budget, compared to £657,016 (about 12 per cent of its total budget) in 1992/3. This reduction in expenditure can be attributed partly to a change in accounting methods and partly to a large increase in funding in 1992 to support one significant case.[21] Nevertheless, the trend in legal expenditure is firmly downwards.

In order to perform its broader strategic role the EOC also has the power to conduct formal investigations[22] into an organization where it suspects that the discrimination is so widespread, covert, or

[17] Ss. 54 and 56A SDA 1975 respectively. It can also issue codes of practice, review discriminatory statutory provisions particularly in the field of health and safety at work, and more generally keep the anti-discrimination legislation under review (ss. 55 and 53(1)(c) SDA 1975 respectively).

[18] This can include offering advice, trying to procure a settlement, arranging for advice to be given by a solicitor, or arranging legal representation (s. 75(2)). Moreover, s. 75(3) provides that the expenses incurred by the EOC in providing financial assistance constitute a first charge for the benefit of the EOC on any costs or expenses obtained by the applicant. In 1993, s. 75 assistance was requested in 302 cases and granted in 195 cases, including to the 78 applicants in Case C-408/92 *Smith* v. *Advel Systems* [1994] ECR I-4435.

[19] When in 1992 the EOC was faced by a 47% increase in the number of complaints it received about sex discrimination in the workplace, it laid down criteria, other than the merits of a particular case, against which prospective applications for financial assistance under s. 75 SDA 1975 were assessed. Priority was to be given to assisting cases in the area of equal pay, part-time work, selection (including promotion and recruitment), pregnancy, and sexual harassment (EOC, 1993: 30).

[20] This figure does not include staff salaries. If the EOC wins a case, any money which is recovered in costs in the following financial year must be returned to the government. The EOC must therefore budget as if it is going to lose every case it brings.

[21] The Alison Halford litigation, concerning sex discrimination at a senior level in the police force.

[22] s. 57 (1). See generally Appleby and Ellis, 1984: 236.

institutionalized that providing assistance in an individual case would not be sufficient to reveal the full scope of the discrimination. Nevertheless, hostile public reaction,[23] fear of judicial review,[24] and a cumbersome procedure (largely due to judicial demands) have meant that formal investigations are no longer considered the primary means of law enforcement. Consequently, faced by increasing demands for financial assistance from individuals, the EOC decided to allocate more resources to individual cases in the hope of achieving more visible 'success'.

By 1979 it was becoming clear that the initial impact of the British Sex Discrimination legislation had begun to wane[25] and the British government seemed disinterested in actively pursuing equal opportunities policies.[26] The potential offered by EC law as a vehicle for challenging discriminatory national legislation and practice was highlighted by the test-case strategy in the three *Defrenne* cases[27]

---

[23] E.g. Ian Gilmour MP accused the EOC of playing 'policewoman, prosecutor, judge, jury and even probation and after-care officer for those caught in this particular brand of sexual delinquency': HC debates, vol 889, col 534. Unfavourable media and academic comment was not confined to formal investigations: see e.g. 'The EOC ought to be quietly or perhaps ceremoniously dismantled', Leeds Evening Post 26 Nov. 1976; 'MPs demand equal rights waste enquiry', *Sunday Telegraph*, 19 Sep. 1976; 'The EOC seems determined to keep the enemies of liberation supplied with material', *Sheffield Morning Telegraph*, 19 Sep. 1976. See also Byrne and Lovenduski, 1978; Appleby and Ellis, 1984; Meehan, 1983; Sacks, 1986.

[24] The EOC's sister organization, the Commission for Racial Equality (CRE), also has powers to conduct formal investigations. Its investigation procedures were regularly challenged in respect of breaches of natural justice. In *Science Research Council v. Nasse* [1979] 1 QB 144, 170, Lord Denning described the formal investigation powers as 'inquisitorial . . . of a kind never before known to the law . . . you might think that we were back in the days of the inquisition'. See also *R v. CRE, ex parte London Borough of Hillingdon* [1982] 3 WLR 159; *R v. CRE, ex parte Amari Plastics* [1982] 2 All ER 499; *R v. CRE, In re Prestige Group plc* [1984] IRLR 166. See further Sachs and Maxwell, 1984: 334.

[25] Progress towards equality in measurable respects, e.g. in terms of earnings, had come to a halt. Women's average gross hourly earnings reached a peak of 75.5% of those of men in 1977 and declined steadily as a proportion in subsequent years. In 1978 the figure fell to 73.9% and in 1979 it stood at 73% (Department of Employment, 1979).

[26] The EOC found that government departments were not co-operative in developing equal opportunities policies, nor did the TUC or CBI recognize their responsibilities under the new Act (EOC, 1979: 4). Government policies, including proposals to change the immigration rules, often ran contrary to the principle of non-discrimination (EOC, 1980: 1–2).

[27] Case 80/70 *Defrenne* v. *Belgium (No. 1)* [1971] ECR 445; Case 43/75 *Defrenne* v. *Sabena (No. 2)* [1976] ECR 455; Case 149/77 *Defrenne* v. *Sabena (No. 3)* [1978] ECR 1365.

pioneered by the Belgian lawyer Eliane Vogel-Polsky, who had been responsible for drafting the Equal Pay Directive 75/117/EEC (Harlow, 1992: 348). Until then the EOC had scarcely considered the EC rules on sex equality. This was partly due to the fact that the Sex Discrimination Act 1975, content of which was heavily influenced by Title VII of the American Civil Rights Act 1964, had been drawn up with little reference to the contemporaneous drafting of the Equal Pay and Equal Treatment Directives.

2. THE EOC AS LITIGATOR

In the United States interest groups have used litigation as a weapon in their campaigning armoury since the turn of the century.[28] The National Association for Advancement of Colored People (NAACP), the largest and most effective civil rights organization in the USA, began its litigation strategy in 1909. Limited success, coupled with its failure to win support from Congress, led the NAACP to make litigation fundamental to its programme during the 1930s.[29] In this respect the EOC differs markedly from such interest groups since it was the clear intention of both the drafters of the English legislation and Parliament that the primary role of the EOC was to act and to be seen as acting as a strategic law enforcement agency.

Whatever the reason for turning to the courts, any litigation begins with the assumption that judicial interpretation will favour worthy claimants and that administrative bodies will automatically implement court rulings. Interest groups tend to seek out test cases—cases judged to be significant in legal or factual terms—which are deliberately designed to procure change (Galanter, 1986:

---

[28] E.g. the National Consumers League (NCL) organized a Committee on Legislation and Legal Defense of Labour Laws in 1908. Its tactics were to provide distinguished outside counsel, including Louis Brandeis and Felix Frankfurter, as well as preparing sociological material. The first NCL victory was *Muller* v. *Oregon* 208 US 412 (1908).

[29] A separate organization, the NAACP Legal Defense and Educational Fund, was incorporated for this purpose (Vose, 1955). The NAACP shepherded through the courts the major cases leading up to the landmark decision in *Brown* v. *Board of Education* 347 US 483 (1964). See also Olsen, 1993: 132.

32–3) by eliciting a favourable interpretation of legislative provisions in order to establish precedents from which a class of claimants will subsequently benefit. Bringing a series of test cases may form part of a litigation strategy.

First and foremost, a successful case enables plaintiffs to secure a declaration of their rights and/or other forms of remedy. A favourable precedent may also procure social change in the longer term. Even when test cases are lost, there is still the hope that the proceedings will persuade the legislature of the error of its ways and that statutory reform will follow.

Successful litigation is also believed to have beneficial consequences for the interest group itself. It is thought to give legitimacy to the goals and aspirations of the organization as well as to increase its respectability. Litigation is also considered to be an important method of consciousness raising, making victims aware of their rights and also alerting violators of their duties. Publicity generated by a case is a valuable means of communicating this information in an accessible form to those most affected.

Nevertheless, some commentators have cast doubt on the validity of these assumptions. Scheingold (1974) questions whether courts are the guardians of fundamental rights and liberties. He doubts whether litigation can secure a declaration of rights from the court, whether such a declaration is sufficient to assure the realization of those rights, and whether that realization can amount to meaningful social change. Rosenberg (1991: 2–3) is also critical of the view of 'the dynamic court', i.e. that courts are powerful, vigorous, and potent proponents of change. He develops the model of the 'Constrained Court', representing courts as weak, ineffective, and powerless. In the context of women's rights in America he argues that precedent-setting decisions have produced little benefit because courts lack the tools necessary for any institution to implement change. He concludes: 'Without the presence of non-court actors offering incentives, or imposing costs, without a market mechanism for change, and without willing actors, court-ordered change in women's rights has changed little' (Rosenberg, 1991: 227).

Despite these concerns, interest groups continue to invest considerable effort into developing a litigation strategy. As a result a considerable body of literature has developed identifying factors necessary to improve the organization's chances of success. For example O'Connor, drawing on a generation of research, identifies a list of key factors (1980: 17).[30] She notes that interest group longevity is critical if an organization wishes to use litigation to establish favourable precedent; regular salaried staff allow interest group litigants to keep abreast of potential test cases and monitor ongoing cases; a network of affiliates enables the central office to learn of favourable cases; issue focus and control over a case allow an organization to concentrate all its efforts in one area; moreover, as its lawyers bring a series of cases, their competence increases. Repeated intervention at Supreme Court level also allows the Court to become familiar with the interest group's expertise. Well financed litigation is critical since the costs are high, especially if the group has been involved from trial level. The use of technical, non-legal, or statistical data and the generation of well timed publicity in the media and in law journals is also considered important. Finally, in order to secure further progress towards a change of rules, litigation should whenever possible also be linked to other forms of political action, such as lobbying, media contact, and grass roots organization.

Compared to the precarious financial position experienced by most interest groups the EOC enjoys a privileged position. A guaranteed income, albeit less than the EOC would hope for, enables it to employ a full-time, capable, and dedicated legal staff who are able to work together as a team at the EOC's headquarters in Manchester.[31] They can monitor recent legal developments and apply these in later cases. This provides the continuity necessary to bring a large number of cases to the court. The EOC has also benefitted greatly from the advice and support of leading academic lawyers and practitioners.[32]

Its stable structure and financing have enabled it to become, in Galanter's terminology (1974: 95), a 'repeat player' litigant. Since the stakes are lower for the EOC than for an individual 'one-shot'

[30] For criticisms of her views, see Harlow and Rawlings, 1992: 299–305.
[31] In Manchester there are 6 qualified lawyers and 6 support staff. EOC (NI) has been able to support every litigated case of discrimination in the Province. Complex cases used to be dealt with in-house, with the remaining cases being sent to outside solicitors. The EOC provided the solicitors with information packs and advised on the choice of counsel. However, more recently EOC assistance to pay for a solicitor became the exception rather than the rule (EOC, 1993: 30).
[32] E.g. Anthony Lester QC has taken an active interest in the legal work of the EOC since he returned to practice from the Home Office in 1976 where he was responsible for drafting the Sex Discrimination Bill.

litigant it is able to adopt strategies calculated to maximize gains over a long series of cases. It is also in the fortunate position of being able to play the long game, lobbying the British government and the European Commission for eventual changes in legislation. In addition, the EOC has the resources and, to some extent, the contacts to ensure that rules which are favourable to women are in fact enforced at field level. A network of actively co-operative women's groups would assist the EOC further in this objective.[33] The EOC is therefore able to lend the advantages it acquires as a repeat player to the legally impoverished one-shot litigant. Their priorities, however, may be different and tension may develop between the two. Individual involvement and control is effectively supplanted for the good of the whole organization.

The EOC can be classified as both an outcome-oriented constitutional litigant,[34] bringing test cases before the Court of Justice in the hope of securing a favourable judicial decision, and as a publicity-oriented litigant, litigating to create publicity both for itself and the issues it supports. A favourable decision raises the EOC's own profile as a respected, effective organization and provides it with a platform on which to campaign for changes in domestic law (Harlow, 1986: 122). For example the decision of the Court in *Barber*,[35] that a contracted out occupational pension scheme could constitute pay within the meaning of Article 119, provided the EOC with grounds to fight for the early introduction of flexible retirement or equal pension ages in both state and occupational schemes. Similarly, the recent decision of the Court in *Enderby*,[36] that separate collective bargaining was not sufficient objective justification for the

---

[33] With certain exceptions, such as the Pay Equity Campaign, Hoskyns (1985: 36) is critical of the women's movement in the UK for failing to network. This contrasts with the NAACP which relies heavily on its vast network of supporters. It also enjoys easy access to the black press and has secured the full co-operation of the black churches. Interviews with the members of the EOC suggest that while the EOC is able to identify the issues needing to be tested before the courts, with the exception of pensions where the EOC is inundated with requests, it does not have an effective grass-roots network to help it find appropriate cases.

[34] The National Consumers' League (NCL) is a further example of an outcome-oriented litigant. Its major goal was to improve working conditions through the enactment or enforcement of protective legislation. The NCL moved into litigation to protect legislation for which it had successfully lobbied in the past. Sorauf (1976: 94) terms these litigants 'constitutional': the ultimate guiding consideration in litigation is the long-range precedent, not the immediate remedy or organizational publicity that is the goal.   [35] *Supra* n. 11.   [36] *Supra* n. 12.

difference in pay between two jobs, has made its easier for the EOC
and others to challenge indirect discrimination in pay systems
(EOC, 1994: 26).

In the EC it seems that the EOC is considered a 'respectable'
organization,[37] due to its statutory status and the experience it has
gained in the field of gender discrimination during the last twenty
years. Although the EOC is not the only equality agency in the EC it
was one of the first and most important organizations in this field
and the only one to fund regular references to the Court of Justice.[38]
This gives weight both to the cases it supports and to its submissions
before the Court.[39] It also benefits from not having to fight against
an effective, organized opposition.

In conclusion, examination of O'Connor's list of factors necessary
for success suggests that the EOC has the odds stacked very much in
its favour. Nevertheless, it is rare for any litigation strategy to come
as neatly packaged as the North American literature would suggest.
More often, interest group litigation is conducted according to a
tight budget and strategy is influenced by the cases brought to the
group's attention. Factors such as the personal preferences of
the present staff and external pressures, such as the need to be seen
to be effective, can influence a strategy as much as any planning.
This needs to be considered when examining the EOC's litigation
strategy.

[37] On the importance of 'respectability', see Harlow and Rawlings, 1992: 307.

[38] When the Commission established the Advisory Committee on Equal
Opportunities, all member states established some form of 'agency' to address equal
opportunities issues, whether as part of a government department in France, or quasi-
autonomously, as the Employment Equality Agency (EEA) in the Republic of
Ireland. It has been suggested that the Emancipatieraad in the Netherlands and the
Irish EEA have been more challenging and pro-active than the EOC (Letter from
Catherine Hoskyns, 22 May 1995).

[39] The presence of only one major organization in the field has been noted as
critical to the NAACP (LDF)'s victories in several areas (Westin, 1975: 104–128).
The Women's Rights Project of the American Civil Liberties Union (ACLU(WRP)),
by contrast, was unable to control the flow of cases to the court in the same way, given
the plethora of women's and public interest groups that were established in the 1970s
(Rosenberg, 1991: 224). In the Netherlands a women's group has also brought test
cases such as Case 30/85 *Teuling-Worms* [1987] ECR 2497 in respect of equal
treatment in social security (Atkins and Luckhaus 1987: 117) and in Germany a
single lawyer, Dr Klaus Bertelsmann, was responsible for finding and litigating Case
79/83 *Harz* [1984] ECR 1921, Case 184/83 *Hofmann* v. *Barmer Ersatzkasse* [1984] ECR
3047, Case C-33/89 *Kowalska* [1990] ECR I-2591, and Case C-184/89 *Nimz* [1991]
ECR I-297.

3. THE EOC'S LITIGATION STRATEGY

The EOC's litigation strategy has developed over the last fifteen years. At first it aimed to make Article 177 references to the Court of Justice because it thought, in the light of the ruling in *Defrenne (No. 2)*, that the Court was keen to achieve equality in the workplace, and that the litigant would enjoy the benefits of the Court's creative and teleological approach to decision-making. Cases such as *Macarthy's v. Smith*[40] and *Barber v. Guardian Royal Exchange*[41] tended to support this view. The Article 177 reference procedure also allowed the EOC to rely on the benefits of the Court's policy-oriented approach while using the medium of the national court to implement its decisions. This extended national habits of obedience to domestic judicial authority to include compliance with decisions of the Court of Justice.

From interviews[42] it is clear that the EOC never had a clear litigation strategy which was planned in its first year and then followed.[43] Suitable cases, such as *Macarthy's v. Smith*[44] and *Jenkins v. Kingsgate*[45], emerged on *ad hoc* basis; lawyers recognized their potential and they were then pursued. This situation is not unique to the EOC. Prosser notes that in the case of the Child Poverty Action Group, a non-statutory British pressure group: '. . . justifications for the different types of activity were often retrospective rather than representing a clear initial aim . . . it would be a mistake to suppose that there was a clear set of aims for the test cases . . . indeed the

---

[40] Case 129/79 [1980] ECR 1275. The Court required equal pay for men and women even where the woman and her male comparator worked successively.

[41] *Supra* n. 11. The Court was prepared to recognize that contracted out occupational pensions were pay within the meaning of Art. 119 and that the ages at which they were paid had to be equalized with respect to benefits payable after 17 May 1990, despite provisions to the contrary in Dir. 86/378/EEC (OJ 1986 L225/40).

[42] Jennifer Corcoran, first legal officer at the EOC (interview in Manchester, 26 April 1990), Lorraine Fletcher, pension caseworker (interviews in Manchester 1 May, 11 July and 6 Dec. 1990).

[43] The EOC was created by a government in haste and started to operate with only a skeleton staff seconded from the civil service. A dispute with the Home Office about the grading of the post of chief legal officer took three years to resolve and effectively delayed the establishment of the legal department. The EOC was also deluged with individual enquiries which diverted its attention from the task of evolving a general strategy.   [44] *Supra* n. 40.

[45] Case 96/80 [1981] ECR 911, discussed further below.

phrase 'test case strategy' was applied only later.' (Prosser, 1983: 21.)

Some of the earliest references funded by the EOC—*Garland*[46] (travel facilities granted after retirement), *Worringham*[47] (payments made by an employer to cover the costs of a male employee's contributions to an occupational pension scheme), and *Burton*[48] (discriminatory ages in a voluntary redundancy scheme)—were loosely related to retirement and pensions. Consequently, by the mid-1980s the EOC started to develop a 'litigation strategy' on the consequences of the discriminatory state pension age. It funded two complementary cases, *Marshall (No. 1)*[49] and *Roberts*,[50] in order to establish the appropriate comparator in respect of a discriminatory retirement age. It also funded references in *Newstead*,[51] challenging the legality of requiring all male civil servants to make contributions to a widow's pension fund; *Barber*,[52] concerning contracted out occupational pensions, redundancy pay, and *ex gratia* payments; *R v. Secretary of State for Social Security, ex parte* EOC,[53] testing the compatibility of discriminatory National Insurance contributions with Directive 79/7/EEC; and *Neath*,[54] concerning sex-based actuarial factors. It also eventually funded the reference in *Marshall (No. 2)*[55] to secure an effective remedy for Miss Marshall who had been forced to retire before her male colleagues.

Having funded these test references, the EOC and other organizations then supported cases before the national courts in order to capitalize on the Court's decisions. For example servicewomen unlawfully dismissed from the armed forces because of pregnancy have been relying on *Marshall (No. 2)* to secure an effective remedy.[56] The EOC also funded *Duke* v. *GEC Reliance*[57] before the English courts, and *Finnegan* v. *Clowney Youth Training Scheme*[58] before the Northern Irish Courts, in an effort to extend the

[46] Case 12/81 *Garland* v. *British Rail Engineering* [1982] ECR 359.
[47] Case 69/80 *Worringham* v. *Lloyds Bank* [1981] ECR 767.
[48] Case 19/81 *Burton* v. *British Railways Board* [1982] ECR 555.
[49] *Supra* n. 8.   [50] Case 151/84 *Roberts* v. *Tate & Lyle* [1986] ECR 703.
[51] Case 192/85 *Newstead* v. *Department of Transport* [1987] ECR 4753.
[52] *Supra* n. 11.   [53] Case C-9/91 [1992] 3 All ER 577.
[54] Case C-152/91 *Neath* v. *Hugh Steeper* [1993] ECR I-6935.
[55] *Supra* n. 9.
[56] See e.g. *Ministry of Defence* v. *Cannock* [1994] IRLR 509.
[57] [1988] 2 WLR 359.   [58] [1990] 2 WLR 1305.

decision in *Marshall (No. 1)* to non-state bodies. On that occasion the House of Lords was not prepared to interpret national law consistently with EC law.

In 1990 the EOC's legal section announced that it would pursue a two-fold strategy for the future:[59] firstly, it would continue to test EC law by making references to the Court of Justice, especially concerning pensions; secondly, it wanted to place more emphasis on litigating in the public interest in judicial review proceedings, using EC law directly to strike down national law.[60] Judicial review offers several advantages. It enables the EOC to select precisely the issue it wishes to challenge and to tackle the source of the problem directly—the offending statute and the relevant government department. Further, since the challenge is on a point of law the facts are usually not in dispute and so the issues are clear. In addition, the case is heard at first instance by senior judges in the Queen's Bench Division rather than by an Industrial Tribunal. There is also no need to put individual litigants through the stress of litigation against their employers. The EOC has full control over the case, without the risk of the applicant withdrawing at any stage or the case being settled with no publicity.

Judicial review proceedings could benefit a very large number of women. For example as a direct consequence of the House of Lords' ruling in *R* v. *Secretary of State for Employment*, ex parte *EOC*[61] that the provisions of the Employment Protection (Consolidation) Act 1978 unlawfully discriminated against women who worked part-time, the UK Government was forced to change the law.[62] This is estimated to have benefitted five million women. In earlier judicial review proceedings, *R* v. *Ministry of Defence*, ex parte *Leale and Lane*, the Ministry of Defence settled the case, admitting that its policy of dismissing pregnant women from the armed forces contravened the Equal Treatment Directive.[63] This led to a very large number of

---

[59] Alan Lakin, The EOC's Chief Legal Officer, Equality Lawyers' Network Meeting, 24 Apr. 1990.

[60] The EOC has sufficient *locus standi* to bring an action in its own name by virtue of its statutory functions. The High Court and the Court of Appeal cast doubt on this position in *R* v. *Secretary of State for Employment*, ex parte *EOC* [1992] 1 All ER 545 and [1993] 1 All ER 1022 respectively, but the House of Lords confirmed that the EOC does have sufficient standing, [1994] 1 All ER 910.

[61] [1994] 1 All ER 910.

[62] SI 1995/31, Employment Protection (Part-time Employees) Regs. 1995.

[63] Not reported, see EOC, 1993: 25.

claims from ex-servicewomen. The Government has admitted that it has paid £30 million to over 2,700 women.[64] At the time of writing, a further 2,000 cases still had to be resolved (Equal Opportunities Review, 1994: 5). The EOC liaises with the Armed Forces Pregnancy Dismissal Advisory Group and has issued a series of newsletters and information packs to advise the women of their rights.

The EOC has also appeared in the national arena as a quasi-*amicus curiae* in *R* v. *Secretary of State for Social Security*, ex parte *Thomas*,[65] a social security case which raised issues of the compatibility of national law with an EC directive. The Court of Appeal held that the EOC was deemed to have sufficient interest in the case by reason of 'its statutory duty to work towards the elimination of discrimination. It has a legitimate interest in the proper interpretation, application and implementation of EC law in that field'. However, the Master of the Rolls, Lord Donaldson, emphasized the unusual facts of the case and underlined his reluctance to allow third parties to intervene generally. The EOC is not, however, permitted to submit *amicus* briefs to the Court of Justice in cases in which it has no involvement.[66] It can only pass on its views to the European Commission which is under a duty to represent the views of the EC in each case in which it appears. This procedure is inefficient for two reasons: firstly, it seems that communication between the Women's Bureau in DG V (Social Affairs) and the legal service is poor; secondly, there is often a lack of awareness of the cases currently before the Court. Attempts are being made to remedy this situation through the establishment of an information network funded by DG V and operated by the EOC.

---

[64] Hansard HC, 18 Oct. 1994, col. 181.

[65] *Thomas* v. *Adjudication Officer* [1991] 3 All ER 315 (Court of Appeal). On 5 July 1990 the Court made an order pursuant to RCS Ord. 15 r. 6, joining the EOC as party to the proceedings. The House of Lords referred the case to the Court of Justice, Case C-328/91 *Secretary of State for Social Security* v. *Thomas* [1993] 3 CMLR 880. The EOC also appeared as *amicus curiae* in *Shields* v. *Coomes Holdings Ltd.* [1978] 1 WLR 1408.

[66] However, in Cases 25-26/84 *Ford of Europe Inc. and Ford-Werke AG* v. *Commission* ([1985] ECR 2725), two consumer groups, Bureau Européenne des Unions des Consommateurs (BEUC) and the British Consumers' Association, were given permission to intervene because the case had originated in complaints made by them to the Commission. In this way the groups were able to inform the Court directly of their views on cartels instead of being restricted to indirect representation by the Commission (Harlow, 1992: 348).

4. TACTICS COMPLEMENTING THE LITIGATION STRATEGY

Although the EOC's strategy has a strong legal bias, North American practice indicates that a litigation strategy does not occur in isolation and is often accompanied by other forms of action in the political arena. At EC level interest groups devote a considerable amount of energy to lobbying the institutions, in particular the Commission, which has proved highly receptive to input from non-governmental sources (Greenwood and Ronit, 1994: 33; Butt-Philip, 1980; Kirchner and Schwaiger, 1981a, 1981b). A symbiotic relationship exists between interest groups and the Commission.[67] From the Commission's perspective, interest groups fulfil a valuable function in providing to the Commission's officials independent or corroborative information against which official data and explanations from national governments can be checked. They also express the views of a constituency of interests at a level below that of national government.

For interest groups, the Commission, as a relatively open bureaucracy, is a source of information about current policies, operations, and future plans. Access to the Commission represents a mark of recognition, serving to legitimize the group itself as well as the interests it seeks to represent. Most importantly, by opening bilateral relations interest groups hope to be able to influence first, the attitudes and behaviour of the relevant Commission officials and secondly the content of new legislation proposed by the Commission.

The EOC has not ignored this potential source of influence. It has worked to develop relations with DG V and particularly its Women's Bureau. Its position may well be helped by its official status: the Commission probably deals more willingly with a respected, representative agency rather than with just another interest group. It could even be argued that parallels exist between the situation of the EOC and the Women's Bureau in DG V: both are administrative agencies, burdened with broad duties and high expectations. The empathy existing between the two can only strengthen their relationship.

---

[67] See further the Commission's White Paper on the Future of Social Policy, encouraging the involvement of voluntary groups, COM(94) 333 at 57.

Given its legal powers and funding, its expertise and longevity, the EOC has played an influential role in the evolution of an EC policy on equality, particularly in the 1980s. Following its early contacts with the Commission, the EOC organized a conference entitled 'Equality for Women—progress, problems and European perspectives', held in Manchester in May 1980 and sponsored by the Commission and the European Parliament. The value of this conference lay in the opportunity it provided for experts to meet and talk. The conference resulted in the establishment of an Advisory Committee on Equal Opportunities, chaired during its first year by Baroness Lockwood, then Chair of the EOC.[68] It has, however, been suggested that the EOC's 'high level, low profile' policy was not necessarily the most appropriate approach to Euro-lobbying and placed some restraint on the Advisory Committee on Equal Opportunities, which has never been as influential as might have been expected.[69]

The EOC is also actively involved in the EC's network of other committees. The Chair continues to sit on the Employment Advisory Committee (EOC(NI) enjoys only observer status); EOC representatives have also participated in the Equality Law Network, the Women's Rights Committee of the European Parliament, and the Economic and Social Committee. The Women's Bureau is in regular contact with the EOC's research department and relies heavily upon it for information. In addition, the EOC provides the co-ordinator for the network on positive action and also a national co-ordinator for the IRIS working group on vocational training for women.

In September 1993 the EOC, in conjunction with the TUC, took the unusual step of formally notifying the European Commission that it considered national legislation on equal pay to be incompatible with EC law (EOC 1993: 25). This followed from the Article 169 enforcement proceedings on equal value brought against the UK in

---

[68] The EOC's seventh Annual Report states that 'The Chair of the Advisory Committee was held, by unanimous election, by the Chairman (sic) of this Commission, and we have noted this fact as a token of the regard in which the EOC is held by within the European Community.' The EOC continues to attach great importance to its membership of this committee (EOC, 1994: 15). The EOC continues to organize conferences and seminars with a European theme. For example, in December 1993 the EOC organized a seminar for UK representatives of the European Commission's Equality Networks to discuss women's information needs (EOC, 1994: 15).   [69] Letter from Catherine Hoskyns, 22 May 1995.

1981.[70] They have also complained to the Commission about the abolition of the Wages Councils which, they argue, has had a discriminatory impact on women.

5. IS A EUROPEAN COMMUNITY LITIGATION
STRATEGY WORTHWHILE?

The EOC's pioneering use of references to the Court of Justice has identified an alternative point of access to the decision-making process. Although the EOC has primarily used EC law to strike at the heart of British law and practice, the consequence of Court of Justice decisions has been to precipitate a change in EC—and ultimately national—legislation. For example the derogations to Directive 86/378[71] may now be *ultra vires* Article 119, in the light of the pension cases[72] and the Commission has now proposed amendments to this Directive.[73]

There has also been a degree of cross-fertilization of ideas as a result of the EOC's strategy. For example it was thought from the decision in *Jenkins* v. *Kingsgate* that the Court of Justice had only a narrow understanding of the concept of indirect discrimination: that an action was only discriminatory when it was intended to be so.[74] The notion of indirect discrimination in s. 1(1)(b) of the British Sex Discrimination Act 1975, itself based on the decision of the American Supreme Court in *Griggs* v. *Duke Power Company*,[75] is much broader. It covers measures which have a disparate impact on women, whether or not the employer intends to discriminate. When *Jenkins* returned to the British Employment Appeal Tribunal, the Chair, Browne-Wilkinson J, stated that the Court's judgment was so unclear that he chose to apply national law. Such criticism seems to have prompted the Court of Justice to reconsider its approach. In

---

[70] Case 61/81 *Commission* v. *UK* [1982] ECR 2601.
[71] OJ 1986 L 225/40.
[72] E.g. *Barber, supra* n. 11. See also Curtin, 1990: 475.
[73] See Press Release IP 486, not yet published in OJ.
[74] Case 96/80 [1981] ECR 911, para. 14: 'Where the hourly rate of pay differs according to whether the work is part-time or full-time, it is for the national court to decide . . . whether, regard being had to the facts of the case, its history, *and the employer's intention*, a pay policy . . . is or is not in reality discrimination based on the sex of the worker' (emphasis added).   [75] 401 US 424 (1971).

subsequent references from Germany, *Bilka-Kaufhaus*[76] and *Rinner-Kühn*,[77] the Court made no mention of the requirement of intent. It therefore seems to have adopted the broader approach.

However, it is difficult to provide a comprehensive assessment of the EOC's success since, as the above discussion indicates, litigation is used to achieve a variety of objectives. If it is accepted that the EOC is both an outcome-oriented and a publicity-oriented litigant then its success must be measured against these yardsticks. As far as successful outcomes are concerned, equality has now been achieved in respect of retirement age[78] and occupational pension age;[79] men and women must now receive the same redundancy pay and *ex gratia* payments;[80] and both men and women must receive a genuine and effective remedy when they have been discriminated against.[81] These cases are significant successes for the EOC and represent substantial rewards for its determination and persistence. These cases have also generated considerable media and academic attention which has served to raise the profile of equality issues and increased awareness of the importance of EC law in the national system. EC law is now pleaded regularly before national courts and tribunals and judges are showing themselves more at ease with deciding cases on this basis. More generally, repeated references to the Court have afforded the EOC a high degree of respectability. This practical experience before the Court has strengthened the EOC's position to participate fully in European discussions and proposals on equal opportunities.

However, as with any learning experience, mistakes have been made. The EOC has been slow to fund certain types of cases. In *Marshall (No. 2)* for example, the EOC refused to fund the early stages of the case, leaving Helen Marshall to represent herself before the Court of Appeal.[82] It also did not fund Mrs Webb in the difficult case of *Webb* v. *EMO Air Cargo*.[83] Further, it is not especially pro-active in finding suitable test cases. Unlike the Child Poverty Action Group, which formed part of an alliance of poverty and disability organizations to campaign against discriminatory social security

---

[76] *Supra* n. 72.
[78] *Marshall (No. 1)*, *supra* n. 8.
[80] Ibid.
[82] [1991] ICR 136.

[77] Case 171/88 [1989] ECR 2743.
[79] *Barber*, *supra* n. 11.
[81] *Marshall (No. 2)*, *supra* n. 9.
[83] Case C-32/93 [1994] ECR I-3567.

provisions,[84] the EOC has never advertised for a suitable plaintiff. Instead applicants must make the first approach to the EOC.

The EOC has also discovered that relying on the Court to deliver a favourable judgment can be a risky strategy: the expense and risks of taking a case to the Court of Justice are not always rewarded. The Court has been criticized for its judgments in *Burton*,[85] *Worringham*,[86] and *Newstead*[87] on the grounds that it did not answer the questions referred, that it misunderstood the points at issue, and that its understanding of the law was incorrect. In *Barber* the Court was notoriously unclear as to the meaning of the temporal limitation imposed on the application of the principle of equality. It took an amendment to the Treaty on European Union[88] and four subsequent references to the Court[89] to clarify the scope of the *Barber* principle. Perhaps more seriously for many thousands of women, the Court has striven so hard to achieve equality for men that the long-term interests of women have suffered. In *Smith* v. *Advel Systems*[90] the Court said that it was compatible with EC law for pension schemes to raise the pensionable age for women to the same age as for men in order to achieve equality. As a result women may now have to pay contributions for up to an extra five years to attain the same level of pension.

Consequently, undertaking a European litigation strategy by no means guarantees success. The EOC has been fortunate in being able to rely on Article 119, a fundamental treaty provision, and a body of legislation. However, it must now contend with factors largely beyond its control: a changing political climate, increasingly hostile to EC matters, and a less enthusiastic Court. The EOC does, however, intend to continue to seek references to the Court of Justice, in particular to test the right of part-time workers to claim access to occupational pension schemes in the light of the Court's decisions in

---

[84] The Alliance advertised for a suitable plaintiff in its bulletins. Mrs Drake, a former lollipop lady, came forward. Her case (Case 150/85 *Drake* v. *Chief Adjudication Officer* [1986] ECR 1995) concerned the Invalid Care Allowance which was payable to married men but not to married women. [85] *Supra* n. 48.
[86] *Supra* n. 47. [87] *Supra* n. 51.
[88] Protocol No. 2 was added to the Treaty on European Union which clarified the temporal limitation of *Barber*.
[89] Case C-109/91 *Ten Oever* [1993] ECR I-4879; Case C-152/91 *Neath* [1993] ECR I-6935; Case C-200/91 *Coloroll* [1994] I-ECR 4389; and Case C-110/91 *Moroni* [1993] ECR I-6591. [90] *Supra* n. 18.

Vroege and *Fisscher*.[91] However, given its recent success in judicial review proceedings before the national courts, the EOC may continue to focus where possible on constitutional challenges to national law and wait until after the Intergovernmental Conference in 1996 to see if the Court of Justice will reconsider its approach.

[91] Case C-57/93 *Vroege* v. *NCIV Instituut* [1994] ECR I-4541; Case C-128/93 *Fisscher* v. *Voorhuis Hengelo* [1994] ECR I-4583.

The Court of Justice: taking taxes seriously?*

PETER CROWTHER

Article 12 EC prohibits customs duties and charges having an equivalent effect (CEEs) between member states. It is located in the EC Treaty provisions concerning free movement of goods and allows for no derogations from this prohibition, either within the Treaty itself or through the jurisprudence of the Court of Justice. It is commonly stated that an exception is made in the context of charges for services rendered. Strictly speaking, however, where a charge is both legitimate and in accordance with the principle of proportionality, such a charge will not be vindicated under Article 12, but simply it is not classed as a CEE. The reason for this is that the removal of customs duties lies at the very heart of the EC Treaty, as part of the fundamental principle of the free movement of goods within the internal market. This absolute prohibition may be contrasted with the requirement of Article 95 EC, located in the tax provisions of the EC Treaty, that taxation imposed by member states must not discriminate between domestic and imported goods. As the case-law under Article 95 has demonstrated, exceptions are permissible where the tax system can be objectively justified and the tax is the most appropriate means of achieving the particular end.[1] However, there are occasions where a 'tax' might legitimately be considered to operate in practice as a CEE, by reason of the purpose of the tax. Where for example a tax levied on both domestic and imported products is used specifically to benefit the domestic product alone, or where the tax is reimbursed to domestic producers, it might be considered that the tax amounts to a charge on the imported product. In fact such taxes, the nature of which is

* I owe a debt of gratitude to Martin Cave, Sally Wheeler, and an anonymous referee, who all provided extremely helpful comments on this paper. The opinions expressed within the paper are however entirely my own, as are any remaining errors.
[1] See e.g. Case 21/79 *Commission* v. *Italy (ecological grounds—recycling)* [1980] ECR 1. See also Barents, 1986.

examined below, do not merely beg the question of the relationship between Articles 12 and 95. Depending on how any given tax is used, it may well fall to be assessed as state aid under Articles 92–4 EC, included in the Treaty provisions concerning the rules on competition. Unless it falls within one of the exceptions under Article 92, state aid which affects trade between member states is 'incompatible with the common market'.

Quite apart from the substantive scope of these provisions, there are also significant procedural differences between the operation of the provisions. Both Articles 12 and 95 are directly effective[2] and thus may be relied upon by individuals before a national court as against the relevant tax authority. On the other hand, the state aids provisions are subject to the exclusive review by the Commission under stringent procedural requirements (Winter, 1993) and the Court has consistently affirmed that Article 92 does not have direct effect.[3] Furthermore, the existence of a CEE depends on whether a charge is present on the import or export of a product. Article 95, on the other hand, engenders a much more sophisticated form of (economic) analysis, to determine whether the goods are similar or in competition. Where goods are in competition, the applicant must show that the tax policy causes some protective effect.[4]

Despite the importance of deciding which Article is more appropriate in circumstances where the tax does not clearly fall within either provision, this question has been ignored by the legal literature. Therefore this essay is a first step towards determining how, if at all, the Court regulates the levying of international taxes[5] by member states. This will be done in two parts: the first section opens by considering the appropriate theoretical elements as regards the optimal level of levying and monitoring tax policies, and aims to provide some useful criteria with which to assess the approach taken by the Court. It continues by discussing which of the policy

[2] Art. 12: Case 26/62 *Van Gend en Loos* v. *Nederlandse Administratie der Belastingen* [1963] ECR 1; Art. 95(1): Case 57/65 *Lütticke GmbH* v. *HZA Saarlouis* [1966] ECR 205; Art. 95(2): Case 27/67 *Fink-Frucht GmbH* v. *HZA München-Landsbergerstraße* [1968] ECR 223.

[3] See e.g. Joined Cases C-78/90 to C-83/90 *Compagnie commerciale de L'Ouest* v. *Receveur principal des douanes de La Pallice-Port* [1992] ECR I-1847; Joined Cases C-149/91 and C-150/91 *Sanders Adour et Guyomarch nutrition animale* [1992] ECR I-3899.

[4] Case 170/78 *Commission* v. *UK* [1983] ECR 2265; Case 356/85 *Commission* v. *Belgium* [1987] ECR 3299.

[5] In this context an international tax should be understood as a tax which is raised on both domestic and imported goods.

instruments open to the Court might be more suitable in the light of the theoretical arguments advanced. Section two examines the relevant case-law, to assess the extent to which the Court's approach mirrors the theoretical framework set out.

Before going any further, however, we should consider exactly what kind of taxes might come within the ambit of Articles 12, 92–4, and 95. Most taxes which are subject to the application of those Treaty provisions will be regionally based taxes. That is a tax levied by member state authorities on both domestic and imported goods which serves a purpose which is confined to a particular geographical area. This area may be the whole of a member state or, as in many cases, a region of a member state. Consider the following hypothetical scenario:

member state Z enjoys a healthy production of product x, manufactured in a region significantly dependent upon the production of x for its well-being. Product x is substitutable for y, a product manufactured in other member states and imported into Z. Z, fearing an increase in unemployment in the affected region due to increased competition between the products, decides to impose a tax on both x and y. The revenue from the tax is used in ways which benefit the domestic manufacturing industry.

This exemplifies a situation with which the Court is frequently faced. We shall consider this example in the light of theoretical arguments and also modify it at a later stage in the light of the case-law of the Court. The theoretical arguments should be understood within the following context. As Community law currently stands, very little harmonization has taken place in the area of direct taxation (Bureau and Champsur, 1992). Therefore member states are still free to levy taxation as long as the Treaty provisions are not offended. However, it is the task of the Commission, and in some cases of individuals, to ensure that member states do not infringe these provisions. Therefore it will invariably be the case that the member state levies and spends the tax, subject to the two types of control mentioned. In the last analysis, of course, the Court has the final word on the interpretation of Articles 12, 92, and 95.

1. THEORETICAL ISSUES

Although this paper is principally concerned with how regionally based taxes are regulated, it is appropriate for the sake of completeness to consider the theoretical elements of both raising and scrutinizing taxes.

1.1 Levying taxes from domestic and imported goods: decentralization

The economic literature points unambiguously to a theoretical presumption in favour of decentralization in levying taxes, arguing that the closer a decision is taken to the affected area, the more likely the policy is to reflect the preferences of the affected individuals (Tiebout, 1956; Seabright, 1994), not least because the costs of obtaining information are then at their lowest. Indeed, according to Tiebout, it is in precisely these conditions that social welfare is theoretically maximized. If the population can be split into homogeneous sub-groups in terms of their willingness to pay for certain services then the optimal level and nature of regulation should be reached. It is expected that those who do not like the local regulatory system will move to an area which conforms with their own preferences. However, this portrays a highly contrived state of nature (Ogus, 1994: 101) and ignores empirical realities such as the facts that citizens do not have the information about different regulatory regimes (Myers, 1990), and are not perfectly mobile, and that the supply of public goods is not the only influential factor in the deciding where to live (Sauerland, 1994).

Nevertheless, the fact that the assumptions for the maximization of social welfare are not met in reality does not mean that a strong case cannot be made for decentralization, in the same way that the perfect competition model fails to explain real world phenomenon but nonetheless provides a useful starting point for analysis. Regulators who are closest to the area being regulated are in a much better position to determine not only the suitability of any given tax, but also the most effective means of levying (and restoring) it. There are many economic, social, political, and cultural differences between the various regions in the EC. The nature and scope of tax policies must of course take account of these differences and it is simply not the case that a uniform set of criteria implemented by centralized authorities is automatically in the best interests of the Community. On the contrary, Keen (1993: 16) points out that centralization 'would almost certainly be as unwise as a matter of economic principle as it is unthinkable politically, at least for the foreseeable future'.

Where a uniform set of rules *is* advisable there may be efficiency gains to be had from centralizing such rule-making. By avoiding heterogeneous regulatory regimes a more level playing field is created and barriers to trade between member states are reduced. However, the point here is precisely that in many instances homogeneity in tax rules is neither desirable nor politically feasible. The very fact that the Community is made up of differing groups of populations with their own preferences and problems means that a uniform, centrally controlled policy is not likely to be suitable. The linguistic difficulties, differing national regulatory regimes, and historical features of tax administration at member state level all suggest that, intuitively at least, the efficiency gains (if any) are likely to be slight. Indeed, of the limited studies which have been undertaken with respect to centralizing tax regimes in the US it seems that efficiency gains are slight (Netzer, 1974) and the US does not suffer from the same heterogeneity problems, or at least not to the same extent (Smith, 1994).

In fact the theoretical position is mirrored in the division of powers between Community and member states in respect of raising taxation (de Pitta e Cunha, 1994). Indeed, as Tömmel (1992) records, within member states there has been (with the exception of the United Kingdom) a clear move in the last decade from national centralized decision-making to local government in respect of regional policy measures.

1.2 Scrutinizing international taxes: centralization.

1.2.1 Why centralization?

The strongest economic argument for centralized scrutiny of taxes is based on the existence of any externalities generated by the taxation. An externality is defined as a cost or benefit imposed on another party without their consent. A common example of this is pollution, which in the absence of legislation imposes a cost on the population which is not compensated. Since governments are responsible in the first instance only to their own electorate, and not to that of the European Union as a whole, it is foreseeable that the wider effects of a tax in this context on the rest of the Community will not be taken into account (Oates, 1972). For instance a regionally based tax

concession which attracts investment from other parts of the
European Union will be beneficial to citizens of a particular area but
will mean that certain costs are imposed elsewhere as either
production is shifted or investment is attracted to a different
purpose. Although those exact effects can obviously only be
determined with reference to individual cases, some general
comments may be made. Where the externality created by the policy
is pecuniary rather than technological, in the sense that resources
are diverted rather than put to a more efficient use, theoretically at
least any costs imposed are cancelled out by the benefits. The
difficulty with this is that it assumes that distributional concerns are
irrelevant (more precisely, that the marginal utility derived from
increments in income is equal across the entire population of the
European Union (Bromley, 1989)). It may well be that the benefits
to the recipients of the tax policy are outweighed by the costs to
those who suffer from it in other parts of the Union. Even where the
tax policy envisages an improvement in production, a broader
picture must be gained in order to ascertain the overall effects of the
tax within the Union. Clearly, a member state which operates a
regionally based tax system is unlikely to assess the effects of the tax
on areas outside its own jurisdiction. Such concerns are, however,
the precise reasons for implementing a policy which is regionally
based. In terms of the distribution of income within the European
Union, external effects must be taken very seriously, especially given
the fact that spending on regional aid (and regional incentives for
investment) is proportionally higher in stronger economies
(Vanhoven and Klaasen, 1987).

1.2.2 *The appropriate type of control*

The theoretical arguments suggest that some form of Community
scrutiny is required where the effects of a tax may extend beyond the
borders of the member state, but that member states (or regional
authorities) are likely to be in the best position to determine the type
of taxation policy suitable for the areas which they control. This
would suggest that some form of co-ordination of international tax
policies might be the most suitable way of ensuring this. However,
the potential success of attempts at co-ordination turns on two
related issues: (a) what incentives an authority would have for co-
operating; and (b) what sanctions are available to punish an
authority which does not co-operate.

Incentives to co-operate

The starting point is to assume that member states might agree not to implement policies which entail substantial negative external effects. This could be because each might be a victim in the future. If this were the case the monitoring tasks of the Commission would obviously be reduced, with equally obvious benefits. But how likely is it that member states will co-operate? One answer to this question is provided by the Prisoner's Dilemma.[6] Each member state knows that the optimal overall approach is co-operation, since each knows only what it stands to gain from a protectionist tax, not what it stands to lose. However, if a member state decides to co-operate, it cannot effectively monitor the activities of others without incurring prohibitive costs. This means that if it does co-operate and others do not, then it stands to lose. On the other hand, since each individual policy cannot easily be monitored a member state will be tempted not to co-operate even if it thinks that the others are doing so. The upshot of this is that each member state's rational strategy is not to co-operate, whatever the purported strategy of the others might be.

Therefore the basic theoretical problem with co-ordination appears to rest in the likelihood that some tax policies which involve substantial negative externalities will be undetected. It is precisely these policies which should be of most concern to the Community. Moreover this concern will extend not only to the Commission (as the watchdog of the Community) but member states will naturally be concerned about other member state policies which may have negative effects on their particular market.

Sanctions available against a non-cooperating authority

An implicit assumption in the conclusion of the previous section was the inability of any member state to make a credible commitment to co-operate. It might be thought that *ex post* detection of non-cooperation would have severe political consequences and these may themselves serve to ensure *ex ante* compliance. The effectiveness of such (political) sanctions is, however, debatable. The fact that member states do not interact solely on regional policy issues suggests that we should be sceptical about the effectiveness of such

---

[6] The economic literature on this subject is immense. For an excellent application to environmental economics see Seabright, 1993.

implicit threats, as evidenced by the 'spirits' litigation of the 1980s.[7] In addition, since there may at any given time be a number of defections over various issues, this may simply mean that political alliances are adjusted over time.

It should be clear therefore that an effective sanction is required to provide an efficient co-ordination process. One obvious means would be to attach a financial sanction in respect of the levying of an undisclosed regionally based tax which has negative external effects, which would fall within the powers of the Court under Article 171 EC (a fine may however only be imposed where a member state has not complied with a previous judgment of the Court). This would require the member state to undertake some further cost–benefit analysis of whether to implement the policy and, depending on the severity of the penalty, would deter some member states from levying such a tax. Additionally, it will be seen below that the provision under which the Court of Justice chooses to assess the regionally based tax will also have significant effects upon the initial decision of the member state in respect of the levying of a regionally based tax.

1.2.3 The Treaty Articles: how the Court should proceed

The starting point is to assume that litigation costs are irrelevant to a member state tax authority in the absence of an additional penalty set out by the Court. If the Court of Justice chooses the Article 95 approach and finds the levy to be protectionist the practical effect is that the member state is allowed to reconstruct the tax policy in a way which does not offend Article 95. In this scenario there is no incentive for the member state to inform the Commission of the tax policy. In so far as the tax policy goes undetected, the member state has won. If the Commission becomes aware of the tax and it is successfully challenged in the Court of Justice, then the member state must simply alter its policy. The second possibility open to the Court of Justice is to classify the tax as a charge having an effect equivalent to a customs duty under Article 12, which may provide a reasonably efficient sanction. One important effect of this would,

---

[7] E.g. Case 170/83 *Commission* v. *UK* [1983] ECR 2265; Case 356/85 *Commission* v. *Belgium* [1987] ECR 3299; Case 243/84 *John Walker and Sons Ltd.* v. *Ministeriet for Skatter og Afgifter* [1986] ECR 875. For discussion of these cases see Lonbay, 1989; Danusso and Denton, 1990.

however, be that the potential benefits to the local electorate would be lost, even if the policy were not to impose significant costs on other member states. The third option would be to construe the tax as a form of state aid. This would give the Commission jurisdiction to monitor the tax and order any amendments it thought necessary. If this approach were adopted it would be unfortunate for the member state but it would not affect its decision whether or not to notify. If it notifies, it simply makes Commission intervention inevitable whereas in the absence of notification, this remains only a possibility.

The inference is therefore that the probability of notification looks bleak, and more significantly, it seems reasonable that the highest valued regionally based taxes, perhaps with the most significant external effects will not enter the discussion arena at the Community level. If the Court of Justice construes a regionally based tax as a state aid then the use of uniform criteria in respect of state aids should ensure an outcome which is in the interests of the Community as a whole. However, given the fact that member states have a natural wish to retain autonomous control of levying such taxes, there does not seem to be a sufficient incentive on the part of member states to notify.

We return therefore to the issue of how the Court of Justice might adopt an approach which serves to facilitate the notification of potentially damaging taxes, but still ensures that an outright prohibition does not follow without considering the appropriate costs and benefits to the Community as a whole. The most attractive solution may be to impose sufficiently severe financial sanctions against non-notification. A regionally based tax levied on both domestic and imported goods which is not notified should be faced with an outright prohibition as a CEE. The fact that the member state would have no opportunity to argue the relative merits of the tax,[8] coupled with its responsibility to its electorate, should ensure a relatively high degree of compliance. Where a tax is notified it is submitted that, within the existing institutional constraints, Article 92 provides the most appropriate forum for assessment.

It is convenient to summarize these findings in respect of the

---

[8] It is possible to draw an analogy with the inability of an undertaking to be exempted under Art. 85(3) unless the agreement in respect of which exemption was sought is previously notified.

hypothetical example set out at the beginning of this essay. The tax, if not notified as a state aid, should be classed as a CEE and struck down accordingly. However, it should be observed that such a finding by the Court is heavily dependent upon the Court also finding a direct connection between the raising of the tax and the distribution of the revenue. In other words, had the funds in our case been paid into the general Treasury, neither Article 12 nor Article 95 would apply because the tax would be neither a CEE in the strict sense nor discriminatory. The fact that the tax is used in a 'discriminatory' way does not render the tax system itself discriminatory (this point is elaborated below).

Therefore the Court should *not* construe the tax as a form of discriminatory taxation, for the following important reason: the facts in our case indicate clearly that there is a direct connection between the raising and the restoring of the tax. If the Court chooses the Article 95 approach member states will continue to maintain this link, since otherwise the aid would fall to be classed under the state aids provisions. Allowing the tax to be reconstructed means that member states will deliberately construct such tax policies to fall foul of Article 95, if detected.

2. THE CASE-LAW[9]

2.1 The Court's distinction between Articles 12 and 95

Whilst a levy on both domestic and imported goods may fall within any of the three Treaty articles, it is clear that Articles 12 and 95 cannot be used in combination.[10] Most commentaries cite *Inter-zuccheri* v. *Ditta Rezzano e Cavassa*[11] as providing the test for the applicability of Article 12 to a tax system. According to that case, a general system of taxation applicable to both domestic and imported products can only fall within Article 12 if 'it has the sole purpose of financing activities for the specific advantage of the taxed national

---

[9] For legal analyses of the cases, see Green, Hartley, and Usher, 1991; Danusso and Denton, 1990; Hancher, 1994c.

[10] See e.g. Case 57/65 *Lütticke GmbH* v. *HZA Saarlouis* [1966] ECR 205.

[11] Case 105/76 [1977] ECR 1029.

product; if the taxed product and the domestic product benefiting from it are the same; and if the charges imposed on the domestic product are made good in full'.[12]

This case must now, however, be read in the light of *Compagnie commerciale de l'Ouest ('Petrol')*.[13] Here the Court of Justice was asked by the Cour de Cassation to consider, *inter alia*, the basis for classification of a parafiscal charge[14] levied on both domestic and imported petroleum products under procedures which were not discriminatory. The Court declined to mention the so-called *Interzuccheri* test, relying instead on the older, less stringent test established in *Capolongo* v. *Maya*.[15] At paragraph 14 of the judgment in that case the Court stated that: '. . . a duty within the general system of internal taxation applying systematically to domestic and imported products according to the same criteria, can nevertheless constitute a charge having an effect equivalent to a customs duty on imports, when such contribution is intended exclusively to support activities which specifically benefit the taxed domestic product.'

While noting that there was a difference in the wording of the cases, AG Tesauro in his Opinion in *Petrol* merely paid lip-sevice to the distinction:

Although there are some differences in the wording of the relevant decisions, the fundamental characteristic which distinguish [sic] a [CEE] from discriminatory internal taxation is clear; it is necessary to establish whether, by virtue of the particular use to which the revenue from the charge is put, the taxed national product—and not the imported product—benefited from a total or partial set-off of the burden.[16]

According to the Court's judgment, the current position appears to be that Article 12 will apply where any domestic advantages *entirely* offset the burden borne by domestic products. Ultimately this will be a matter for the national court in Article 177 proceedings, yet the Court declined to direct the national court as to how it might make such a finding of fact. This raises potential difficulties, in particular

---

[12] Para. 12.
[13] Joined Cases C-78/90 to C-83/90 *Compagnie commerciale de l'Ouest* v. *Receveur principal des douanes de La Pallice-Port* [1992] ECR I-1847.
[14] A charge designed to finance the activities of a public or quasi-public body which engages in activities beneficial to the domestic product.
[15] Case 77/72 [1973] ECR 611.   [16] [1992] ECR I-1847, 1870.

the question of whether indirect benefits might suffice to compensate the domestic manufacturers. AG Tesauro suggested that in the present case the task for the national court would be to compare 'the proceeds resulting from the marketing of domestic petroleum products and the advantages accruing to the undertakings which marketed them as a result of the action taken for their benefit by the [public authority].'[17] This is certainly a good deal wider than the *Interzuccheri* test, but the lack of guidelines from the Court suggests that widely differing interpretations of this rule could well materialize at national level.

On the other hand, where the benefit only *partially* offsets the burden borne by the domestic product, Article 95 will be applicable. In the *Petrol* case the Court developed a highly suspect line of reasoning to arrive at this conclusion. It referred to its previous decision in *Italy* v. *Commission*[18] which stated[19] that where a tax which is levied in a non-discriminatory way is neutralized by the advantages accruing to the domestic product, this will nonetheless constitute discriminatory taxation. The Court used this authority in support of its own ruling that where the advantages *partially* offset the burden imposed on the domestic product, the levy is subject to Article 95. With respect, this is a difficult argument to sustain for two main reasons. First, if the effect of a tax is neutralized then the burden has been fully offset. It is therefore an inappropriate authority for the proposition that a partially compensated tax falls within Article 95. Secondly, although the purpose of a tax has long been taken into account when deciding whether it is discriminatory,[20] it is submitted that this is a consideration which should be irrelevant for the purposes of Article 95. Levying taxation and spending the revenue are two separate issues, and the fact that the revenue is applied in a discriminatory way does not mean that the taxation procedure itself is discriminatory.

In any case it is inimical to the absolute prohibition contained in Article 12 to adopt this distinction between a partially and a wholly restored tax. Where a tax which supports a domestic industry is raised in a non-discriminatory way there are two logical ways to approach the issue. The first is to attack the tax itself from the

---

[17] [1992] ECR 1847, 1871.   [18] Case 73/79 [1980] ECR 1533.
[19] Para. 15.
[20] For discussion see Danusso and Denton, 1990, and the cases discussed below.

perspective of the imported product. A CEE (however small)[21] is sufficient to trigger Article 12; therefore even if the domestic product benefits only partially from the revenue the practical effect is that there is a net burden on the imported product 'by reason of the fact that [it] cross[es] a frontier'.[22] The alternative approach is to address the manner in which the revenue is used under the state aids provisions. For these reasons, notwithstanding that the Court appears once again to have widened the ambit of Article 12 in this context, it is submitted that the present use of Article 95 is misplaced.

What are the implications of the Court's pronouncements for our hypothetical example? It will be seen that the question turns on the extent to which the domestic industry benefits from the tax. Where all the tax on the domestic product is recuperated Article 12 will apply. However, it is of course questionable whether many circumstances will arise where such a finding of fact may easily be made. The lack of guidelines given by the Court means that national courts are given a *de facto carte blanche* to determine which Article applies. We may comfortably expect more questions on the relationship of these two Articles to surface in Article 177 proceedings. Perhaps the most unfortunate aspect of this situation is that in our hypothetical example a national court might seek to adopt an approach which appears fair to both parties but is unlikely to be in the interests of the Community as a whole. By choosing to assess the tax under Article 95 (the most likely approach due to evidential constraints) the court might consider itself to be choosing the most suitable outcome. The individual succeeds because he or she has the tax declared unlawful as contrary to Article 95,[23] and the national government succeeds because it can continue the policy but

---

[21] Case 24/68 *Commission* v. *Italy* [1969] ECR 193, 201: '. . . any pecuniary charge however small and whatever its designation and mode of application which is imposed unilaterally on domestic or foreign goods by reason of the fact that they cross a frontier and which is not a customs duty in the strict sense constitutes a charge having an equivalent effect within the meaning of Articles 9, 12, 13 and 16 of the Treaty; even if it is not imposed for the benefit of the State, is not discriminatory or protective in effect and if the product on which the charge is imposed is not in competition with a domestic product.' [22] *Supra* n. 21.

[23] This is not actually very clear. In the *Petrol* case AG Tesauro stressed that such a tax was not inherently unlawful, but only unlawful to the extent to which it was discriminatory. Following this, it would be for the national court to determine the *extent to which* importers are entitled to claim a reimbursement.

in a way which does not offend Article 95. A national action which effectively orders the member state to break the link between raising the tax and spending it will not automatically attract the attention of the Commission, yet the regional aid may still continue.

2.2 When does a restored tax constitute a state aid?

This section considers predominantly, but not only, cases involving taxes which have an identifiable regional aspect. Where the use of the tax might be construed as a state aid but the taxation itself is *prima facie* discriminatory Article 95 will still apply.[24] However, the meaning of discriminatory has not been interpreted in a consistent manner, as the following cases illustrate. In *France* v. *Commission* (*Textiles*),[25] the French Government levied an equal charge on both domestic and imported textile products for the purpose of financing both the French Textile Union and research into the textile industry. The Commission decided that the aid was contrary to Article 92 and sought a Court ruling to this effect. The French Government argued that a fiscal measure should be assessed solely in the light of Articles 12 and 95, especially since the charge in question was levied on both national and imported products. The Court rejected this argument and stated that even if Article 95 were complied with Article 92 could still apply.[26] It ruled: '. . . whatever might be the rate of the said charge, [it] has the effect, *because of the method by which it is financed*, of adversely affecting trade to an extent contrary to the common interest within Article 92(3).'[27]

The Court held that paying the proceeds of a tax into a general fund would not fall within Article 95 but could still be caught: 'If such a system whereby an aid is serviced by a charge designed for that purpose, were to become general, it would have the effect of opening a loophole in Article 92 of the Treaty and of reducing the Commission's opportunities of keeping the position under review.'[28] This seems the logical approach, for the reasons already outlined. The fundamental flaw in using Article 95 to determine the validity of a taxation policy on the basis of how the revenue is spent is

---

[24] Case 17/81 *Pabst & Richarz* v. *HZA Oldenburg* [1982] ECR 1331.
[25] Case 47/69 [1970] ECR 487.   [26] Para. 13.
[27] Para. 23; emphasis added.   [28] Para. 18.

highlighted perfectly in *Commission* v. *Italy (Sugar)*.[29] The facts are directly comparable to the *Textile* case: the Italian Government decided to finance aid to the sugar industry and beet producers by means of charging a levy on both domestic and imported products. The Commission took the view that this was contrary to Article 95 and brought an Article 169 action against the Italian Government, in addition to instituting a review under Article 93. The Italian Government's argument was based on the ruling in the *Textile* case, namely that the method of financing the aid could not be isolated from an assessment of the aid itself and that the proper provision under which to test the aid was Article 92. The Court of Justice repeated its finding in the earlier case that Articles 92 and 95 can apply independently as they have different legal consequences. However, it then decided that to assess whether Article 95 had been breached it was necessary to take into account the use to which the revenue would be put. However, as the Italian Government argued, if it paid the revenue into the general budget of the state Article 95 would not be breached but the practical effect would be the same. The Court agreed with the Italian Government's argument, but stated that it had no effect on the present case as it was a purely hypothetical scenario.

This begs the question of why the Court should wish to extend the ambit of Article 95 in such a contorted way. The Court is saying that if the tax appears to be for the purpose of an aid then the taxation itself is discriminatory, even if it is raised in a non-discriminatory way. One way to justify the ruling is that the Court in the *Sugar* case believed the aid was justified but was not agreeable to the transparent way in which the imported product was supporting a state aid. Finding the tax contrary to Article 95 would allow the Italian Government to break the clear link between the raising and spending of the revenue by channelling the funds through the General Treasury.

The same line of reasoning can be seen in *Hansen* v. *Hauptzollamt Flensburg*.[30] The Court was asked by the Finanzgericht Hamburg, *inter alia*, by what criteria state aids should be distinguished from reductions in charges whose compatibility should be assessed under Article 95. The Court avoided the issue and stated:

---

[29] Case 73/79 [1980] ECR 1533.   [30] Case 148/77 [1978] ECR 1787.

It ... appears preferable to consider the question raised by the national court from the point of view of Article 95 rather than in the light of the provisions on aid contained in Articles 92–94, *since the latter also rest on the same basic idea as Article 95,* namely the elimination of State interventions—including tax abatements—which might have the effect of distorting the normal conditions of trade between Member States.[31]

Therefore the state aids provisions appear very much inferior in their relationship with Article 95. The significance of such a pronouncement should not be underestimated. If one agrees with the Court's statement that the two provisions rest on the same basic idea[32] then surely this is as far as the analogy may be drawn. The mere fact that two sets of provisions rest on the same basic idea is a weak justification for stating that one should be applied in favour of the other. In the context of the state aids provisions the choice is not simply between which provisions to apply. If the regionally based tax in *Hansen* had been construed as a state aid a different result would probably have followed. Why then was the Court eager to find this tax within Article 95? One possible reason was suggested by the Court itself in a statement which it has continually reiterated in Article 95 cases:

At the present stage of its development and in the absence of any unification or harmonization of the relevant provisions, Community law does not prohibit Member States from granting tax advantages, in the form of exemption from or reduction of duties, to certain types of spirits or to certain classes of producer ... Indeed tax advantages of this kind may serve legitimate economic or social purposes, such as the use of certain raw materials by the distillery industry ... or the continuance of certain classes of undertakings such as agricultural distilleries.[33]

A similar policy approach may also be discerned in *Regenerated Oil.*[34] A tax concession was given to Italian manufacturers of regenerated

---

[31] Para. 14; emphasis added.
[32] This is slightly suspect. The Articles refer to two types of intervention by member states: Art. 92 refers to the grant of aids, whilst Art. 95 refers to imposing discriminatory taxation. They are only comparable in the sense that the broad aim is to ensure that competition is not distorted. Indeed, in the *Sugar* case the Court made this very point, but went on to state that the 'application of those provisions presupposes distinct conditions peculiar to the two kinds of State measure which they are intended to govern and they *differ furthermore as to their legal consequences*' (para. 8: emphasis added).   [33] Para. 16.
[34] Case 21/79 *Commission* v. *Italy* [1980] ECR 1.

oils which, in their final state of manufacture, are impossible to tell from oils of primary distillation. Despite the Commission's arguments that the only way to remove the distortion of competition was to remove the offending legislation the Court took a different approach. It followed in substance the decision of the Court in *Hansen*, by allowing Article 95 its widest possible application: '[Article 95] does not . . . impose upon Member States the duty to abolish as regards internal taxes on domestic products differences which are objectively justified and which may be introduced by domestic legislation unless such abolition is the only way of avoiding direct or indirect discrimination against imported products.'[35]

In the event the Court construed the relevant Directive narrowly[36] by stating that it did not apply, even though the indemnity granted by the Italian Government fell squarely within Articles 13 and 14 of the Directive.[37] The Court stated that those provisions did not affect the rights of member states to introduce favourable taxation, but simply determined that if such taxation were introduced, it must not fall within the prohibition contained in Article 95. That Italy was found on the facts to have breached Article 95 is of little significance; the importance rests with the implications of the judgment. As a result of the decision Italy could modify the measure to render the tax no longer discriminatory. This can be compared to the abolition of the measure which was sought by the Commission. In this respect, therefore, the Court effectively decided in favour of an uncertain rather than a certain outcome. The rationale of the Court's decision may be explained in two ways, which may be linked: first, it is likely that the Court was impressed by the ecological issues surrounding the case and secondly, it is significant that the case was concerned with national fiscal autonomy. In effect the Court stated that if a member state can set out its charge as a measure of general economic policy it will not fall to be assessed either as a CEE or a state aid, and will be subject only to the less stringent scrutiny of Article 95. There is no reason other

---

[35] Para. 16.

[36] Dir. 75/439/EEC of 16 June 1975, OJ 1975 L194/23.

[37] Art. 13: 'As a reciprocal concession for the obligations imposed on them . . . indemnities may be granted to collection and/or disposal undertakings for the service rendered . . .' Article 14: 'The indemnities may be financed, among other methods, by a charge imposed on products which after use are transformed into waste oils, or on waste oils.'

than such policy concerns why the Court could not have required the abolition of the system as sought by the Commission.

It seems from these cases that the Court has recognized the limitations placed on Community law by the continuing the national fiscal autonomy of member states (Shaw, 1993). There is another possible reason for this policy approach, strongly hinted at in the above statement by the Court, and which runs through the whole series of cases in this field. It is arguably no coincidence that the one area where the Court fails to take a pro-interventionist stance concerns agriculturally based products, typically a highly sensitive issue to many member states. Member states use their powers of taxation on spirits (for example) not only as an expression of social or economic objectives but also, quite rationally, in support of national industries.

An interesting rationale can be gleaned from the case-law without reference to policy considerations. The original view of the Court appeared to be that Article 95 could not be used as a vehicle for circumventing the provisions on state aids. The Court has since clearly changed its position by broadening the scope of Article 95 with respect to regionally based taxes.[38] The distinction to be drawn therefore appears to depend on whether or not the measure falls foul of Article 95. If it does it cannot be justified as a legitimate state aid. If, however, the measure is held compatible with Article 95 there are only narrow circumstances in which the measure may be classed as a state aid.

4. CONCLUSION

The aim of this paper has been to initiate a necessary debate on the appropriate scope of Articles 12, 92, and 95. I argued in the theoretical section that Article 12 is the most appropriate instrument for assessing non-notified taxes,[39] if only to encourage member states to notify, whilst Article 92 is most suited to assessing those taxes which are notified. However, the case law reveals that the Court has

---

[38] See also Case 196/85 *Re Natural Sweet Wines: Commission* v. *France* [1988] 2 *CMLR* 851.

[39] Given the fact that Article 92 is not directly effective, as *per* the Court in the *Petrol* case.

taken a different approach. It is submitted that the expansive interpretation of Article 95 extends beyond its true and proper meaning, which is to determine the compatibility of an internal tax *ex ante* rather than *ex post*. The *ex post* issue falls squarely within the provisions on state aids.

The conclusions in respect of our hypothetical example are unsettling. It is simply a state aid and is in some way discriminatory, irrespective of how it is classified. Moreover, what incentive does member state Z have to notify it when such a measure can be vindicated (if necessary) under Article 95 without the need for the intervention of the Commission? Moreover, if the benefits of decentralization are to be realized a binary question of (a) is it discriminatory? and (b) is it a CEE? is not the proper way to approach the issue. The flexibility inherent in the state aids procedure allows for a weighing up of the relative worth of the tax from the Community perspective.

A final point is that national fiscal autonomy means much more than an ability to conduct an independent regional policy. Arguably the real difficulty for the Community lies not with the restrictive interpretation given by the Court to the relevant provisions but with jealously guarded national fiscal autonomy. The application of a simple version of the Prisoner's Dilemma would however suggest that member states might not necessarily be acting in their collective interest.

Political Theory, Law, and European Union*

DANIEL WINCOTT

Until recently, legal and political science analyses of European integration took place more or less in isolation from one another. Moreover, lawyers and political scientists came to opposite conclusions about the character of the European Community and the prospects for its future development: the former made grand claims about the existing achievements of and future possibilities for the Community, whereas political scientists were modest about both. There have, of course, always been a few hardy souls who have wandered into the territory of the other discipline, but it is only in the past few years that signs have appeared of a more general and consistent interest in the development of an interdisciplinary understanding and explanation of the range of legal and political phenomena which constitute European Community. This essay provides a brief account of traditional political and legal understandings of the European Community, which highlights the distance between their respective understandings of the history of European integration.

Any attempt to provide an overall account of the integration process in Europe would have to make sense of both the political and the legal character of the European Community, as well as the impact of the political and legal institutions on European society/societies. Traditionally, political scientists have ignored the influence of Community law; equally, many lawyers have understood the Community in purely legalistic terms. Legal scholars have played down the significance of the political institutions of the Community, provided no systematic account of the role of the member states, and more or less ignored the impact of forces

* The author would like to thank participants in the Edinburgh workshop for their comments on this paper. ESRC Award No. R45126421793 has supported this research.

external to the European Community (at least outside the obligatory introductory chapter in European law textbooks on the historical origins of the Community) such as the tendency towards economic globalization. Any interdisciplinary account of the integration process would have to illustrate how the logics of legal and political development of the Community interact with one another and how the internal logic(s) interact with external factors.

Before illustrating some ways in which legal and political analyses might be brought together, a brief 'reading' of traditional political and legal approaches to the study of European integration is presented. For politics and law in turn this will involve the presentation of the dominant view of the integration process (in the case of the political literature, a brief discussion of the 'tussle' between theoretical perspectives, and the manner in which a particular theory came to be the common sense of political science), followed by a sketch of Community history as viewed through the lens of the discipline.

1. POLITICAL SCIENCE

Political science analysis of European integration has been preoccupied with questions of sovereignty and power. The two main theoretical frameworks which have been used by political scientists to understand the European Community are neo-functionalism and a version of realism. These theories made quite different predictions about what would happen to national sovereignty through the process of integration. Neo-functionalism predicted a more or less automatic transfer of sovereignty from the states to the Community. For neo-functionalists the integration of 'functions' and the creation of a technocratic elite in Europe would unleash a dynamic, self-sustaining process of integration, which would eventually create a new European polity. In particular, various processes of 'spillover' would take place if one functional sector was integrated and a supranational agency created to administer it. Subsequent analysts have distinguished a number of different kinds of 'spillover' (functional, political, and 'cultivated': Tranholm-Mikkelsen, 1991), although they were not fully differentiated from one another in the original formulations of the theory (George, 1991: 21).

In the early formulations of neo-functionalism, once the first step had been taken the process of integration was broadly expected to be spontaneous (George, 1991: 24), gradual, incremental, and automatic (Moravcsik, 1993: 476). This expectation that the process of integration would be automatic arose partly as a result of the emphasis on functional spillover as a *process*. Although it postulated an internal dynamic of Community development, neo-functionalism was really grounded in the peculiarly apolitical approaches to the study of politics prevalent in the USA in the 1950s and '60s, rather than in any peculiarity of the Community institutions. Instead, a generic model of interest groups activity and assumptions about the efficiency of large-scale technocracy were adapted to the European context. Haas himself has acknowledged the biasing influence of 'end of ideology' theory on neo-functionalism (see Tranholm-Mikkelsen, 1991: 7).

De Gaulle's 'policy of the empty chair' was the beginning of the end for neo-functionalism. It led Haas explicitly to reject the 'automacity' of spillover (Tranholm-Mikkelsen, 1991). Following the partial resolution of the Gaullist 'problem' by the Luxembourg compromise, the pattern of policy-making 'in the shadow of the veto' (Weiler, 1991) resulted in a gradual proliferation of alternative mechanisms of integration (and disintegration) which watered down the theoretical distinctiveness of neo-functionalism. By the mid-1970s Haas had effectively abandoned neo-functionalism by assimilating it within general interdependence theories of international relations (Tranholm-Mikkelsen 1991: 7).

Perhaps more importantly, the traditional 'realist' critique of the distinctiveness of the European Community was asserted in the mid-1960s. Stanley Hoffmann developed a critique of neo-functionalism in the aftermath of the Gaullist crisis. He argued that the neo-functionalists had not considered the international environment of the EC adequately. Moreover, of most significance, the neo-functionalist had failed to distinguish 'high' from 'low' politics. Hoffmann asserted that integration could occur on matters of 'low' politics, but on matters of 'high' politics (the essence of state sovereignty) integration would be blocked. Moreover, if it ever threatened sovereignty, even as a result of low political issues, integration would give way (Hoffmann, 1966). This approach came to dominate the conventional political science of European integration. It represents the member states as being both in control of the Community and 'external' to it. In a pure form, it depicts the interaction of states as a structural consequence of the states system, and includes the Community as a form of interaction of fully sovereign states. Intergovernmentalism has been used to explain the development of the internal market programme and '1992' as an initiative of the member states which remained wholly under their control (Moravcsik, 1991).

There has been a partial revitalization of neo-functional theory as an explanation of the phenomenon of '1992' (Tranholm-Mikkelsen, 1991). However, it is not clear that the approach can deal adequately with the Gaullist phenomenon, except by radically downgrading its theoretical ambitions. Thus '. . . neo-functionalism remains a partial theory in the current dynamic phase of European integration' (Tranholm-Mikkelsen, 1991: 18). The 'automacity' of the process and therefore its predictive power have been given up. Instead a 'dialectic' is postulated between logics of integration and of disintegration. There remains little to distinguish this sort of analysis from the theoretically less ambitious attempt to provide an account which situates European integration within a general interpretation of international and domestic politics, while recognizing that supranational institutions might play important parts (Sandholtz and Zysman, 1989).

2. A POLITICAL HISTORY OF EUROPEAN INTEGRATION

As a consequence of the dominance of 'realist' and intergovern-mentalist theories of integration political scientists have tended to understand the history of European integration as riven by conflict and unlikely to produce significant supranational institutions or policies. According to this view, a period of abnormal development occurred during the late 1950s and early 1960s, which might be accurately characterized by neo-functional theory. 1965 takes on a vast importance in the conventional wisdom of political science. It marked the end of abnormality and the (permanent) return to inter-national relations as usual.

The emergence of 'summitry' in the late 1960s and 1970s, particularly its institutionalization in the form of the European Council, was taken as decisive evidence of the international and intergovernmental character of the Community after 1965. This interpretation was buttressed by evidence of the failure during the 1970s of the most ambitious projects supported by the European

Council, including the plans for Economic and Monetary Union ('EMU') by 1980, as embodied in the Werner Report.[1] The conventional wisdom in political science was that policy sectors such as social policy were characterized as failures during the 1970s. Moreover, the European Council's most important 'successes', initially European Political Co-operation and subsequently the European Monetary System, were actually outside the framework of the Treaty. The economic difficulties of the 1970s compounded these problems by producing a protectionist atmosphere (see in general Urwin, 1991: 150–85).

The revitalization of European integration based on the Programme for the Completion of the Internal Market and '1992' came as a complete surprise to most political scientists. One of the longest established specialists in European integration published a book in 1985, when the internal market programme was already relatively well developed, in which he claimed: 'The Community is most likely to face a future of constant compromise, papering over successively more frequent crises . . . the prospects for the creation of more common policies are not good' (George, 1985). (This inaccurate prediction notwithstanding, the book was sufficiently well received to go into a second edition in 1991, in which George gallantly acknowledged his earlier mistake). George's 'mistake' was the result of the general theoretical expectations of political scientists about European integration. The cluster of events signified by '1992' came as a shock to political scientists, particularly those of an 'intergovernmentalist' or 'realist' bent. Nevertheless, attempting to recover quickly, some political scientists analysed the Single European Act (SEA) as a confirmation of the traditional 'intergovernmentalist' theory (grounded in 'realist' or 'liberal' international relations), presenting the SEA as wholly a product of negotiaton between the member states giving no significant role to the Commission nor to the Court of Justice (Moravcsik, 1991). This has contributed to a tendency to attribute the development of policies in such areas as the environment to the SEA, ignoring their earlier roots. Nevertheless, one of the main theoretical consequences of the '1992' process has been the revitalization of other theoretical approaches to integration, including neo-functionalism (Tranholm-Mikkelsen, 1991), although with a downgrading of its theoretical ambitions.

[1] Bull. EC Supp. 11/70.

3. LEGAL ANALYSIS

Legal analysis of European integration has focused heavily on the role of the Court and on the nature of the law's contribution to European integration. There has been little legal analysis explicitly concerning the causes of the development of the Community, yet implicit causal explanations have ranged from a teleological assertion of the inevitability of the constitutionalisation of Community law to a hagiographic attribution of heroic qualities to the European Court of Justice. The first position removes any real trace of agency from the Court, as well as writing all politics out of the development of the constitutional and substantive law of the Community. One legal commentator, writing in the United States, argued that this: '. . . presents the Community as a juristic idea; the written constitution as a sacred text; the professional commentary as a legal truth; *the case law as the inevitable working out of the correct implications of the constitutional text*; and the constitutional court as the disembodied voice of right reason and constitutional theology' (Shapiro, 1981: 238, emphasis added).

In short, it is '. . . constitutional law without politics . . .'; the development of the Court's case-law leaves no room for politics of any kind. This view lies behind a good deal of the 'black letter' analysis of Community law, and even when authors explicitly consider the political or policy-making role of the Court a background assumption is often made that the development of the Community has followed a linear progression towards ever closer union.

Some legal scholarship gently writes a kind of politics back into the role of the Court. Legal analysis of confrontation between recalcitrant member states, or institutions within the member states and the Court, which should not occur, according to the first image, tends to adopt an heroic idiom to discuss the role of the Court. For example in relation to its human rights jurisprudence the Court has been described as pursuing its position 'courageously and coherently' (Dauses, 1985:419).

Not all legal analysis has taken this form. Hartley suggests that

A common tactic is to introduce a new doctrine gradually: in the first case that comes before it, the Court will establish the doctrine as a general principle but suggest that it is subject to various qualifications; the Court may even find some reason why it should not be applied to the particular facts of the case. The principle, however, is now established. If there are not too many protests, it will be re-affirmed in later cases; the qualifications can then be whittled away and the full extent of the doctrine revealed (Hartley, 1988: 78–9).

Hartley's analysis depicts the Court as a political institution, which could highlight the political role of the Court of Justice. The traditional image of the role of a court is that it should interpret the law. The court must impartially apply a general rule to a specific factual situation. On the other hand many, perhaps most, legal scholars would agree that in practice either courts exceed this interpretive role, or that courts' interpretation contains a significant political element (for example Dworkin, 1986: 271–2).

However, even this approach tends to assume that the statement of a legal principle by the Court is tantamount to the constitution of a new reality, rather than understanding it as part of a policy-making process. In general, legal analysis has been weak in its analysis of the creation of European legislation (rather than the description of the formal characteristics of the legislative process). In other words, and perhaps understandably, academic law has generally been more concerned with making sense of the internal development of Community law, as if legal doctrine distilled the essence of the Community. It has failed to consider the interaction of the legal order with the Community polity, never mind the impact of external factors on integration.

Very few legal scholars have attempted to analyse the Court in the context of the other Community institutions, although the most intriguing studies of the Community have come from this perspective (Weiler, 1991; Snyder, 1993a). Snyder's recent work can be understood as a kind of contextualist manifesto for the study of EC law. He has argued that '. . . from a contextual standpoint, any analysis of these institutions and relations between them requires that each institution should be taken seriously, for example both as a legal and as a political institution' (Snyder, 1993b: 26).

4. THE HISTORY OF THE EUROPEAN COMMUNITY IN LEGAL PERSPECTIVE

In contrast to the variability implicit in a political analysis of Community history, from a legal perspective the Community is usually pictured as a more or less continuous and undifferentiated process of ever closer union, constitutionalization, or federalization. In as much as qualifications are allowed to the image of general linear evolution, they are a consequence of political interventions in the judicial process of constitutionalization. These political interventions can even have an illegal or 'alegal' quality. Thus the crisis of 1965 and the Luxembourg Accords, or many of the 'bits and pieces' of the Maastricht Treaty (Curtin, 1993), are sometimes perceived simply as irrational political interferences in a legally rational constitutional scheme designed by the Court. Although from the point of view of a constitutional analysis of the EC/EU this interpretation makes sense, the law might benefit from a perspective on the member states which depicted them as more than petulant, short-sighted, and self-serving. In particular, a richer understanding of the part played by the states might render their impact on the Community in general, and especially its judicial structure, more predictable.

We have seen that the general consensus among political scientists is that the Single European Act was a major fillip to the integration process. It is ironic that (although generally better received by legal scholars than the Treaty on European Union, for example) even the Single European Act has been interpreted as political destruction of legal order (Pescatore, 1987). Pescatore's (admittedly rather formalistic) critique of the SEA tends therefore to be misunderstood by the majority of political scientists. My view is that they tend to assimilate Pescatore to the intergovernmentalism of traditional international relations theory.

5. UNITING LEGAL AND POLITICAL ANALYSIS

Each of the main traditions in law and politics identifies a primary locus of integration. For example legal analysts typically concentrate on the internal dynamics of the development of the jurisprudence of the Court of Justice: 'neo-functionalist' political scientists (Haas, 1958; Tranholm-Mikkelsen, 1991) direct their attention towards the development of a pattern of interest group activity around the supranational Commission, a pattern which can be conceived of as internal to the Community; and 'realist' (Hoffman, 1966) or 'intergovernmentalist' (Moravcsik, 1991; 1993) political scientists downgrade the distinctiveness of the Community, comprehending it using almost unmodified international relations models. This latter approach implies that change in the European Community is caused by factors which are more or less external to it, either by treating the Community as merely the creature of the member states (and conceiving of the member states as external to the Community) or by treating it as a product of the international system of states.

To state the issue in its most general form: the process of integration can be understood in terms of the internal logic(s) of development of the European Community, the impact of external factors on it, and the interaction of the internal and external. However, moving from this general form to a more specific analysis immediately presents difficulties. For a start, the issue of where the boundary between the internal development of the Community and external forces rests needs to be addressed. For example, to what extent should we consider the member states as part of the Community system? In many discussions the member states are depicted in opposition to the Community, a characterization which carries over into the image of the states as (partially) bound or constrained by the Community. Yet in another sense the member states, as well as the Community institutions, actually constitute the Community.[2] Even in the area of Community law, where the European Court of Justice has developed doctrines which 'fetter' the member states, a closer look at the relationship shows that some national institutions, for example national courts, may have been empowered by the relationship with the Community. Of course the Court of Justice has needed the co-operation of all branches of the various states in order to achieve its objectives. Ultimately, the Court could only cajole acquiescence from the states, as it has not had the capacity to coerce them.

Despite these difficulties, the attempt to draw legal and political analyses together remain a prerequisite for a full account of the

---

[2] A number of other questions must also be asked. For example although a focus on European Community institutions is likely to be fruitful, this analytic effort ought also to consider whether the various sectors of activity which the Community system seeks to regulate would make an appropriate unit of analysis. Space constraints prevent me from doing justice to this issue here, but see Colin Scott above for an analysis concerned with the relationship of institutions and policy sectors. In principle, of course, the process of integration as a whole may have some emergent properties which cannot be adequately comprehended analytically.

integration process. At least as far as the interaction of legal and political logics within the Community is concerned, the 'new institutionalism'[3] (set out by Bulmer, 1994a) seems likely to provide a fruitful framework for analysis, especially its emphasis on the sequence of historical development, 'path dependence', and the manner in which particular institutional settings condition the sense which actors make of changes to their environment.

6. TOWARDS AN INTEGRATED HISTORY OF THE COMMUNITY I: THE 1960S AND 70S

The first statements of the direct effect and supremacy of Community law and the resolution of the Gaullist boycott by the 'Luxembourg Accords' are the events usually identified as turning points of the Community in the 1960s. Without necessarily subscribing to the view that the logic of Community law development from the case of *Van Gend en Loos*[4] (or indeed from the signing of the Treaty of Rome) was ineluctable, there *is* nevertheless a clear logic to the development from direct effect of Treaty provisions to supremacy to, variously, human rights protection, direct effect of secondary legislation, and so on. These developments were clearly centred on the Court. In addition to their significance as legal developments they also transformed the context within which the Commission was operating by providing it with the law as a resource for integration. The political context within which the Commission found itself operating meant that the surprising effectiveness of supranational law became one of the most important available tools for promoting integration, although this reality only became clear gradually.

The constraints within which the Commission was operating are frequently attributed to fallout from de Gaulle's boycott of the Council of Ministers in 1965. De Gaulle's boycott should serve to remind us that, at the very least, (some) member states must adopt a permissive attitude for integration to proceed effectively. However, the impact of the boycott and the Luxembourg compromise on the political decision-making process in Europe has been overstated in the political science literature. It is possible to see portents of the

---

[3] See Armstrong above.   [4] Case 26/62 [1963] ECR 1.

Gaullist attitude in earlier negotiations between the states, and not only in the approaches of French politicians. For example negotiations in the Council of Social Affairs had completely broken down well before the Gaullist intervention, and were only resumed after a radical reappraisal of the character of Community social legislation embodied in the so-called Veldkamp Agreement.[5] This Agreement foreshadowed the change from centralization to co-ordination of rules which later become the strategy for integration. It is also important to note that the Gaullist boycott served to block the demise of unanimous voting rather than actually replacing unanimity with some form of majority voting, albeit blocking a change mandated by the Treaty. The Gaullist intervention probably took the Community further away from the legislative method set out in the Treaty than might otherwise have occurred, but to view it as a bolt from the blue would be misleading.

Be that as it may, by the end of the 1960s the Commission was acting within a tight set of constraints, including in particular the direct concern with sovereignty on the part of some states and the rather limited, overwhelmingly state-granted, budget within which the Community operated. The Commission gradually learnt how to exploit the resources it did have in order to promote both its own role and the integration process generally. A particularly significant lesson which the Commission was starting to learn was that it was relatively effective at the development of regulatory policies because of its position at the centre of a web of information about the European economy and the manner in which it could exploit the interests of businesses from the various member states (Majone, 1989, 1991; Cram, 1993). An additional factor, not generally emphasized by the regulation theorists but which an interdisciplinary perspective highlights, is the impact of the developing strength of Community law on the position of the Commission. By contrast, the lack of either a coercive apparatus at the Community or a 'tax and spend' capacity meant that the Community was likely to be relatively ineffective at, for example, developing social policy of the sort developed by European states after 1945. However, the strength of the legal order made the development of regulatory policies a possibility. As a consequence of

---

[5] This has been largely ignored in the analysis of the development of Community social policy. (Discussed briefly in Kapteyn, 1987: 629).

these 'regulatory' developments the traditional political interpretation of the 1970s as a completely stagnant period has had to be
modified (Cram, 1993).

If a legal perspective can add something to the political theory of
regulation then, likewise, political theory can provide important
additional support for even the best developed interdisciplinary
account of the historical development of the Community provided
by a legal scholar. This account, provided in Weiler's 'The
Transformation of Europe', also identifies the 1970s as a period of
profound, but subterranean, Community development—a period
described as the 'mutation' of competences (Weiler, 1991: 2437–47;
also Weiler, 1981). A good deal of this account of the 1970s is
actually concerned with the ongoing process of legal integration, in
other words with the rendering of the Community legal order more
like that of a state in terms of its effectiveness.[6] The variety of
mutation which Weiler himself identifies as the most radical—that
is, the 'extension' (Weiler, 1991: 2442) of Community competence
into new fields—did presuppose the occurrence of certain legal
developments (an example of the importance of the historical
'sequence' of events, emphasized by 'new institutionalism').
However, it was largely caused by *non-legal* factors. The role of the
Court in the 'extensions' of Community competence was merely
permissive, and therefore secondary. As late as 1990 it could be
argued in relation to environmental policy that '[t]o date, the ECJ
has dealt with only a relatively small number of environmental
matters' (Sands, 1990: 693). The Court had to accept that Article
235 EC could be used in an expansive manner (Weiler, 1991:
2443–6): only after laws had been passed by the Council was the
Court called upon to judge whether they had been made on an
adequate Treaty base.[7] In particular, the Court confirmed that the
Council could produce environmental legislation on the basis of
Article 100 EC (see Sands, 1990: 694).

Similar developments took place in policy areas where the Treaty
did give the Community some substantive competence (these sorts

---

[6] These changes are very important and Weiler's discussion of them is fruitful
(especially where he insists that the 'internal interplay of the various actors' is crucial
'in pushing forward the frontiers of Community jurisdiction', Weiler, 1991: 2442).

[7] The Court had accepted a wide use of Art. 235 in Case 8/73 *Hauptzollamt
Bremerhaven* v. *Massey-Ferguson GmbH* [1973] ECR 897.

of developments might be analysed by reference to the category of 'absorption' used by Weiler, 1991: 2438–41). However, in these areas the Court did play a larger and highly political role. Expansive rulings by the Court were often quickly followed by proposals for legislation, or by the Council's acceptance of legislation which it had previously blocked. In effect, the Court's rulings changed the terms of the legislative debate. Developments of this sort can be seen in the areas of sex discrimination law, competition, and education among others, and are not temporally restricted to the 1970s.

Weiler identifies three elements in an explanation of why new policies could be introduced successfully during the 1970s. First, the changes were incremental; no single moment marked their development. Secondly, directly challenging the intergovern-mentalist logic of mainstream political analysis, he sets some store by 'the strategy of revival' of the Community, pursued by the European Council. The European Council lent its substantial political prestige to the increased use of Article 235 EC (Weiler 1991: 2445) and to a number of specific policy programmes, such as environmental, consumer, and regional policies. The European Council provided opportunities for the Commission to pursue its strategies of integration more effectively. In addition, the role of the European Council should serve as a reminder that the acquiescence of the member states is important for the effective operation of the Community. Finally, Weiler suggests that the fact that each member state retained an effective veto over the Community's legislative process allowed them to extend the competence of the Community because they perceived the EC 'more as an instrument in the[ir] hands . . . than as a usurping power' (Weiler, 1991: 2449).

These factors do not account for the fact that some policies supported by the European Council did develop incrementally within the Community, while others did not develop effectively at all. Thus the plans for EMU to be completed by 1980 received the general support of the heads of government at the Hague Summit in 1969, but the monetary union did not develop incrementally from that position. This is where the political account of 'Regulatory Federalism' in the Community may help (Majone, 1992). Depicting the Commission as a learning institution with an interest in expanding its competence, Majone has found that 'regulatory' policies developed much more successfully than other policies during the 1970s. The development took place despite the fact that many of the regulatory policies possessed no Treaty base, or an inadequate base, while some other policies with a clear Treaty base, such as transport policy, failed to develop at all.

The 'regulatory' approach attributes the failure of the development of 'other' policies to the fact that the Community simply did not have the financial resources to develop wide-ranging and costly policies, and could not extract them from the member states. In these circumstances the Commission would have to find policy techniques which imposed their primary costs elsewhere (on the member states and the private sector). In addition, extension took place in areas regarded as peripheral by many states: much of the legislation in these areas was constructed in such a way as not to impose significant short-term costs on the member states; the legislation was often in areas with comparatively little existing national legislation; and the policy areas enjoyed increasingly popular support. This both motivated the Commission to develop policies to gain general support and made it more difficult for national governments to oppose these developments.

Overall, these developments seem to have occurred as a result of an internal dynamic, or rather the interplay of internal dynamics within the European Community. One of the characteristics of this period is the way in which the member states became increasingly entangled in European politics to the point where it becomes increasingly appropriate to identify the member states as a part of the internal operation of the Community, rather than as part of the environment in which the Community institutions operate. However, it is possible to imagine historical alternatives which did not actually materialize in which external factors might have had a much more powerful influence. Indeed the history of monetary policy in the Community may be an example of both the initiation of a policy partly under the influence of international forces (that is, an attempt to restore some monetary stability) and the failure of a policy as a result of those forces (the failure of the 'EMU by 1980' objective as a result of extreme exchange rate fluctuation during the 1970s). If, however, the objective set out in the Werner Report of 1970 had been achieved[8] the Community would by 1980 have had quite a different character.

[8] Bull. EC Supp. 11/70.

7. TOWARDS AN INTEGRATED HISTORY OF THE COMMUNITY II:
THE INTERNAL MARKET AND '1992'

Analysis of the origins of the internal market could begin by
exploring the internal development of either the jurisprudence of the
Court of Justice, or the unfolding logic within the European polity.
In each of these areas deep roots can be found for the internal
market project. Earlier developments can be regarded as the
foundations on which subsequent ones were built. Although such
claims should be made with care because of the risk of reading
history selectively in the light of subsequent events, the internal
market programme can be seen as exhibiting the 'path dependence'
which 'new institutionalist' analysts emphasize.[9] In order to understand adequately the internal causes of the development of the
internal market it is crucial to articulate the Court's jurisprudential
and political developments, particularly the strategy of the
Commission (Wincott, 1995b and 1995c).[10]

In my view the understandable tendency of academic lawyers to
trace the development of the internal market through the *Cassis de
Dijon* line of cases implicitly overemphasizes the Court's role in these
developments.[11] In fact the Commission picked up the *Cassis de Dijon*
ruling and took it in a different direction from that apparently
indicated by the Court. This was subsequently followed to some
extent by the Court (Alter and Meunier-Aitsahalia, 1994: 543).
After the Commission had adopted/adapted the *Cassis de Dijon*
ruling a new dynamic of interest group activity developed both in
Brussels and at state level, which, while not wholly supportive of the
position taken by the Commission, on balance provided it with more
support than discouragement (Alter and Meunier-Aitsahalia, 1994).
Of course the developing case-law on Article 30 EC remained as a
source of pressure on member states throughout the period of the
negotiation of the internal market and the Single European Act.

Although this approach to the development of the internal market
is enormously fruitful it does not capture the whole meaning of
'1992'. Part of the cause of the internal market was 'external' to the
European Community, rooted in economic and political changes in

---

[9] See Armstrong above.   [10] Ibid.
[11] Case 120/78 *Rewe Zentrale AG* v. *Bundesmonopolverwaltung für Branntwein* [1979]
ECR 649.

the rest of the world. By bringing these external factors into play the contingency of the integration project of the 1980s is emphasized. Ironically, however, these external factors also reveal the full extent of the creativity of the Commission.

Sandholtz and Zysman (1989) argue that changes in the international environment, particularly the declining hegemony of the USA in international affairs and the growing economic strength of Japan, conditioned the process of integration in the European Community. In addition, the technological changes which caused, or at least facilitated, the globalization of economic activity required European industry to reappraise its production techniques, and meant that it did so under conditions of growing international competition. As a result of these factors European business leaders and national politicians were increasingly on the lookout for European solutions to the economic and political problems they faced, especially as 'Atlantic' solutions were becoming less attractive. In other words they provided the circumstances within which a relaunch of European integration was possible.

The globalization of economic activity also meant that national solutions to policy problems were no longer credible. Arguably, globalization also influenced the general shift in European national politics towards market solutions, particularly where socialist governments abandoned traditional nationalization programmes in favour of more market-oriented alternatives. In any event, the shift towards market-oriented governance provided an important precondition for the acceptance of the basically neo-liberal and deregulatory thrust of the internal market programme. Within this international context, and given these national conditions, the activism of the Commission and the impact of interest groups, particularly the Roundtable of European Industrialists, allowed these bodies to play crucial 'creative' roles (Sandholtz and Zysman, 1989). These arguments can be recast in policy analytic terms. For example Majone seems to suggest that European Community style regulation is based on a general acceptance of the market as the fundamental mechanism for social organization: something which has only recently come to be accepted in Europe, he argues (Majone, 1992).

The creativity of the Commission and key interest groups can be seen in the manner in which they constructed the idea of a European integration project around globalization and the economic crisis in the early 1980s. This construction would have influenced European political and business elites to some extent, although presumably not all of them identically. Rather than simply lobbying for this or that alternative, based on pre-existing and determined preferences, they played an active part in helping to construct a common understanding of the condition of Europe and of paths out of the European crisis. Thus the manner in which the Commission picked up on the Court's *Cassis de Dijon* ruling resulted not only in a mobilization of interests but also in the focusing of the existing preferences of the Member States (Garrett and Weingast, 1993). Arguably, Community institutions and EC level groups also contributed to the reconstruction of the preferences of the national executives.

The hostility of the Council to this new approach (Alter and Meunier-Aitsahalia, 1994: 552) suggests that it was not within the initial preference-set of the national executives. The European Roundtable of Industrialists, created in 1983 with the express purpose of doing something about Europe, rapidly came to focus on the 'unification' of the European market (Green, 1993: 11–16). The Commission, aided by some other European institutions, followed a strategy of persuasion, using soft law in the hope of 'conquering the objections of the member states' (Majone, 1994: 264–266, my translation).

The Commission and key groups, such as the European Roundtable, *constructed* a European project out of international pressures and existing resources within the Community system. In doing so they (re-)interpreted the pressures of globalization, certainly giving them a particular form in the European context, and possibly influencing the meaning of globalization in other parts of the world. Understanding '1992' as a project can also assist interpretation of the choices made at national level. Thus the '1992' project played a part in constructing the alternatives facing the governments and political parties of the member states. So, while the existence of a minimal consensus on the role of 'the market' for organizing society was probably a pre-condition for the success of '1992', a dynamic European project facilitated the switch of a number of European Socialist and Labour parties from traditional Keynesian/socialist policies towards a more market-oriented approach, creating a kind of reinforcing feedback for a market-oriented project for European integration.

Although the internal market programme cannot be adequately understood without taking into account the interaction of the European institutions, neither can it be understood unless placed in the context of developments in international relations. 'New institutionalism' provides a useful framework for understanding developments within the Community polity and legal order, and for understanding the interaction of these developments. It can also further an understanding of how international changes impinge on and are interpreted by the Community. However, international events still exercise unpredictable external influences on the Community within this framework.

8. CONCLUSION

An interdisciplinary politico-legal approach to European integration needs to take into account the interaction of the institutions of law and politics within the Community. We have seen that this sort of account can bring together innovative work from both disciplines and provide a richer understanding of developments in Europe during the 1970s. The 'new institutionalism' provides a helpful framework for this sort of work.[12] Although the interaction of the Community institutions can provide the basis for an understanding of the integration process, the internal interactions and dynamics of the Community themselves need to be placed in a wider context if they are to be properly understood. In particular, the European institutions must be understood in the context of developments in both the domestic politics of the member states and the global political economy.

A sensitive use of the 'new institutionalist' approach is compatible with these broader concerns. It may be more interesting to explore how individuals working in institutionally defined roles in the Community make sense of developments in the domestic politics of member states, or of global economic trends, than to depict these institutions as buffeted by, say, international economic developments wholly beyond their control. The Commission is likely to interpret a particular 'global trend' in terms of 'standard operating practices', a process which might well change the 'standard practice'

[12] See Armstrong above.

but which would also create a particular construction of the meaning of the 'global trend' in Europe. How, and how far, pressures for economic globalization were transformed into a programme for European integration by the Commission and other Community institutions in the 1980s is an example of such development. Moreover, European developments may have unpredictable effects on the process of globalization itself. The creation of the North American Free Trade Area can be partly understood as a reaction to the successes of the European Community.

It is difficult to present an account of European integration which simultaneously provides an adequate discussion of particular developments, institutions, or policies and also places them in the context of influences from global and domestic politics. In other words, there is great scope for analyses which focus on developments in a particular sector, or on the role of a particular institution. However, unless wider factors are kept in mind misleading conventional wisdoms can build up, which may even organize the sorts of questions asked in research. As a corrective to the conventional wisdom of politics a strong emphasis on the role of the Court of Justice is required, and as a corrective to the legal conventional wisdom (at least as I see it), an emphasis on the other Community institutions, and especially on factors 'external' to the Community, is necessary. This essay has attempted to provide a brief example of what this sort of 'counterbalancing' might look like.

Bibliography

Agh, A. (1994), 'Citizenship and Civil Society in Central Europe', in van Steenberg (1994).

Ackers, L. (1994), 'Women, Citizenship and European Community Law: The Gender Implications of the Free Movement Provisions', 16 *JSWFL* 391–406.

Allan, T. (1983), 'Parliamentary Sovereignty: Lord Denning's Dexterous Revolution', 3 *OJLS* 22–33.

Allison, J. (1994), 'Fuller's Analysis of Polycentric Disputes and the Limits of Adjudication', 53 *CLJ* 367–83.

Alter, K. (1994), 'Legal Integration in the European Community and Integration Theory: A Focus on the National Judiciaries of the Member States—the Case of Germany', Paper delivered to the 2nd ECSA World Conference, Brussels, May 5–6 1994.

—— and Meunier-Aitsahalia, S. (1994), 'Judicial Politics in the European Community: European Integration and the Pathbreaking *Cassis de Dijon* Decision', 26 *Comparative Political Studies* 535–61.

Amory, B. (1990), 'Monopoly and Competition', in S. Schaff (1990).

Andersen, S. and Eliasen, K. (1993) (Eds.), *Making Policy in Europe* (London: Sage).

Anonymous (1990), 'Article 90', *ELR Competition Checklist* 63.

Appleby, G. and Ellis, E. (1984), 'Formal Investigations: the Commission for Racial Equality and the Equal Opportunities Commission as law enforcement agencies', (1984) *PL* 236–76.

Arendt, H. (1972), *Crises of the Republic* (New York: Harcourt Brace Jovanovich).

Argyris, N. (1993), 'Regulatory Reform in the Electricity Sector: An Analysis of the Commission's Internal Market Proposals', 9 *Oxford Review of Economic Policy* 31–44.

Artis, M. and Lee, N. (1994) (Eds.), *The Economics of the European Union: Policy and Analysis* (Oxford: Oxford University Press).

Atkins, S. and Luckhaus L. (1987), 'The Social Security Directive and UK Law', in McCrudden (1987).

Atkinson, J. (1984), 'Manpower Strategies for Flexible Organisations', *Personnel Management*, August, 28–31.

—— (1990), 'Management Strategies for Flexibility and the Role of Trade Unions', in J. Philpott (1990).

Avendaño, M. (1994), 'The further development of European telecommunications; Telecom operators' view', Conference Paper, *Implementing European Telecommunications Law*, November 21–2, 1994.

Bailey, J. (1992) (Ed.), *Social Europe* (London: Longman).

Balkin, J. (1987), 'Deconstructive Practice and Legal Theory', 96 *Yale LJ* 743–86.

Bamforth, N. (1995), 'Sexuality and Law in the New Europe', 58 *MLR* 109–20.

Barents, R. (1986), 'Recent case law on the prohibition of fiscal discrimination under Article 95', 23 *CMLR* 641–660.

—— (1990), 'The Community and the Unity of the Common Market' 33 *German Yearbook of Intl. Law* 9.

—— (1993), 'The internal market unlimited: some observations on the legal basis of Community legislation' 30 *CMLR* 85–109.

Barker, A. (1982) (Ed.), *Quangos in Britain: Governments and the Networks of Public Policy-Making* (London: Macmillan).

Barnard, C. (1992), 'A Social Policy for Europe: Politicians 1: 0 Lawyers', *IJCLLIR* 15.

Barrington, D. (1992), 'Emergence of a Constitutional Court', in O'Reilly (1992), 251.

Barry, A. (1994), 'Harmonization and the art of European government', in C. Rootes and H. Davis (1994).

Barry, N. (1989), 'Political and Economic Thought of German Neo-Liberals', in A. Peacock and H. Willgerodt (1989a).

Bartlett, K. and Kennedy, R. (1991) (Eds.), *Feminist Legal Theory* (Boulder: Westview Press).

Bauer, J.H. (1994), 'Outsourcing Out? Anmerkung zum Urteil des EuGH vom 14.4.1994', BB 21, 1433–6.

Bellamy, R., Bufacchi, V. and Castiglione, D. (1995) (Eds.), *Democracy and Constitutional Culture in the Union of Europe* (London: Lothian Foundation Press).

Bengoetxea, J. (1993), *The Legal Reasoning of the European Court of Justice: Towards a European Jurisprudence* (Oxford: Clarendon Press).

Bercusson, B. (1990a), 'The European Community's Charter of Fundamental Social Rights of Workers', 53 *MLR* 624–42.

—— (1990b), 'Fundamental Social and Economic Rights in the European Community', in Clapham *et al.* (1990), 195.

—— (1993), 'A Fundamental Change in European Labour Law', *IRJ* 177.

—— (1994), 'The dynamic of European Labour Law after Maastricht', 23 *ILJ* 1.

Bercusson, B. and van Dijk, J.J. (1995), 'The Implementation of the Protocol and Agreement on Social Policy of the Treaty on European Union', *IJCLLIR* 3.

Bhabha, J. and Shutter, S. (1994), *Women's Movement* (London: Trentham).

Bieber, R. (1988) (Ed.), *1992: One European Market?* (Baden-Baden: Nomos).

Birnbaum, P., Lively, J., and Parry, G. (1978) (Eds.), *Democracy, Consensus and Social Contract* (London: Sage).

Bishop, M., Kay, J., and Mayer, C. (1995) (Eds.), *The Regulatory Challenge* (Oxford: Oxford University Press).

Blackburn, R. (1993), *Rights of Citizenship* (London: Mansell).

Bliner, A., Solow, R., Break, G., Steiner, P., and Netzer, D. (1974), *The Economics of Public Finance* (Washington DC: The Brookings Institution).

Böhning, W. (1973), 'The Scope of the EEC System of Free Movement for Workers: A Rejoinder', 10 *CMLR* 81–6.

Bottomley, A. and Conaghan, J. (1993) (Eds.), *Feminist Theory and Legal Strategy* (Oxford: Blackwell).

Bourgoignie, T. and Trubek, D. (1987) (Eds.), *Consumer Law, Common Markets and Federalism in Europe and the United States* (Berlin/New York: Walter de Gruyter).

Boyron, S. (1992), 'Proportionality in English Administrative Law: A Faulty Translation?', 12 *OJLS* 237–64.

Bradley, K. (1994), ' "Better Rusty Than Missin' "?: The Institutional Reforms of the Maastricht Treaty and the European Parliament', in D. O'Keeffe and P. Twomey (1994).

Brah, A. (1992), 'Black Women and 1992', in Ward, A., Gregory, J., and Yural-Davis, N. (1992).

Brewster, C. and Hegewisch, A. (1994) (Eds.), *Policy and Practice in European Human Resource Management* (London: Routledge).

—— and Mayne, L. (1994), 'Flexible Working Practices: The Controversy and the Evidence,' in Brewster and Hegewisch (1994), 168–93.

Brown, P. and Crompton, R. (1994) (Eds.), *Economic Restructuring and Social Exclusion* (Series: A New Europe?) (London: UCL Press).

Buggy, P. (1994), 'TUPE after Schmidt', *NLJ* 23 Dec. 1994, 1771–2.

Bulmer, S. (1994a), 'Institutions and Policy change in the European Communities: The Case of Merger Control', 72 *Public Administration* 423–44.

—— (1994b), 'The Governance of the European Union: A New Institutionalist Approach', 13 *JPP* 351–80.

Bureau, D. and Champsur, P. (1992), 'Fiscal Federalism and European Economic Unification', May, *AEA Papers and Proceedings*, 88.

Burley, A-M. and Mattli, W. (1993), 'Europe Before the Court: A Political Theory of Legal Integration', 47 *IO* 41–76.

Butt-Philip, A. (1983), 'Pressure Groups and Policy Making in The European Community', in Lodge (1983).

—— (1985), *Pressure Groups in the European Community*, University Association for Contemporary European Studies, Occasional Paper No. 2.

Byrne, P. and Lovenduski, J. (1978), 'Sex Equality and the Law in Britain', 5 *JLS* 148.

Cafruny, A. and Rosenthal, G. (1993) (Eds.), *The State of the European Community. Volume 2: The Maastricht Debates and Beyond* (Boulder/Harlow: Lynne Rienner/Longman).

Cairns, A. (1992), *Charter* versus *Federalism: The Dilemmas of Constitutional Reform* (Montreal: McGill-Queens University Press).

Camus, A. (1975), *The Myth of Sisyphus* (Harmondsworth: Penguin).

Cane, A. (1995), 'European map is being redrawn slowly', *Financial Times* 20 Jan. 1995.

Capotorti, F., Ehlerman, C., Frowein, J., Jacobs, F., Joliet, R., Koopmans, T., and Kovar, R. (1987) (Eds.) *Du Droit International au Droit de l'Intégration* (Baden-Baden: Nomos, 1987).

Cappelletti, M. (1989), *The Judicial Process in Comparative Perspective* (Oxford: Clarendon).

—— Seccombe, M., and Weiler, J. (1986) (Eds.), *Integration Through Law: Volume 1: Methods, Tools and Institutions* (Berlin/New York: Walter de Gruyter).

Carroll, D. (1984), 'Rephrasing the Political with Kant and Lyotard: From Aesthetic to Political Judgments', 14 *Diacritics* 74–88.

Cass, D. (1992), 'The Word that Saves Maastricht?: The Principle of Subsidiarity and the Division of Power Within the European Community', 29 *CMLR* 1107–36.

Chalmers, D. (1993), 'Free Movement of Goods Within the European Community: An Unhealthy Addiction to Scotch Whisky', 42 *ICLQ* 269.

—— (1994), 'Repackaging the Internal Market—The Ramifications of the *Keck* Judgment', 19 *ELR* 385–403.

Chamoux, J. (1990), 'The Role of National Government in the Regulation of Telecommunications', in S. Schaff (1990).

Charnovitz, S. (1993), 'Environmentalism Confronts GATT Rules: Recent Developments and New Opportunities', 27 *JWT* 37.

Charny, D. (1991), 'Competition among Jurisdictions in Formulating Corporate Law Rules: An American Perspective on the "Race to the Bottom" in the European Communities', 32 *Harv. J. of Intl. Law* 423.

Cheyne, I. (1994), 'International Agreements and the European Legal System', 19 *ELR* 581–98.

Christensen, B. (1993), 'European Social Dialogue: Overview and Prospects', in ETUI (1993a).

Chung, C. (1994), 'Recent Developments in EC Postal Liberalization', (1994) *ECLR* 4, 217–24.

Clapham, A. (1990), 'A Human Rights Policy for the European Community', 10 *YBEL* 309.

—— Cassese A., and Weiler, J.H.H. (1990) (Eds.), *Human Rights and the European Community* (Nomos: Baden-Baden).

—— and Emmert, F. (1990) (Eds.), *Collected Courses of the Academy of European Law*, Volumes 1–2 (Dordrecht: Martinus Nijhoff).

Clune, W. (1992), 'Implementation as Autopoietic Interaction of Autopoietic Organizations', in G. Teubner and A. Febbrajo (1992) (Eds.) 485–513.

Cockbourne, J-E. (1995), 'The Pipeline, Plans and Investigations', in *Implementing European Telecommunications Law*, Proceedings of a European Commission conference held in Brussels, Nov. 1994, 132–40.

Collins, H. (1990), 'Independent Contractors and the Challenge of Vertical Disintegration for Employment Protection Laws', 10 *OJLS* 353–80.

Cooper, J. and Dhavan, R. (1986) (Eds.). *Public Interest Law* (Oxford: Blackwell).

Coote, A. (1978), 'Equality and the Curse of the Quango', *New Statesman* 734.

Coppel, J. and O' Neill, A. (1992), 'The European Court of Justice: Taking Rights Seriously?', 12 *LS* 227.

Cornell, D. (1992), *The Philosophy of the Limit* (London: Routledge).

—— (1993), *Transformations* (London: Routledge).

Cox, S. (1993), 'Equal Opportunities,' in Gold (1993).

Craig, P. (1991), 'Constitutions, Property and Regulation' (1991) *PL* 538–54.

Craig, P. and de Búrca, G. (1995), *EC Law: Text, Cases and Materials* (Oxford: Clarendon Press).

Cram, L. (1993), 'Calling the Tune without Paying the Piper? Social Policy regulation: the role of the Commission in European Community Social Policy', 21 *Policy and Politics* 135–46.

—— (1994), 'Breaking Down the Monolith: The European Commission as a Multi-Organization: Social Policy and IT Policy in the EC', 1 *JEPP* 195–218.

Crenshaw, K. (1988), 'Race, Reform and Retrenchment: Transformation and Legitimation in Antidiscrimination Law', 101 *Harv L Rev* 1331–87.

Cullen, B. and Blondeel, Y. (1994), 'Union Measures Taken in the Telecoms Area and the Results Achieved', Conference Paper, *Implementing European Telecommunications Law*, 21–22 Nov. 1994.

Curtin, D. (1990), 'Scalping the Community Legislator: Occupational Pensions and Barber', 27 *CMLR* 475–506.

—— (1993), 'The Constitutional Structure of the Union: A Europe of Bits and Pieces', 30 *CMLR* 17–69.

Curzon, G. (1989), 'International Economic Order: Contribution of Ordo-Liberals', in A. Peacock and H. Wilgerodt (1989a).

Dahrendorf, R. (1992), *Der Moderne Soziale Konflikt* (Stuttgart: DVA).

Danusso M. and Denton, R. (1990), 'Does the European Court of Justice look for a protectionist motive under Article 95?', *LIEI* 1990/1 67.

Darian-Smith, E. (1995), 'Law in Place: Legal Mediations of National Identity and State Territory in Europe', in P. Fitzpatrick (1995).

Dauses, M. (1985), 'The Protection of Fundamental Rights in the Community Legal Order', 10 *ELR* 398–419.

Deakin, S. and Wilkinson, F. (1994), 'Rights vs. Efficiency? The Economic Case for Transnational Labour Standards', 23 *ILJ* 289–310.

Dehousse, R. (1992), 'Integration *v.* Regulation? On the Dynamics of Regulation in the European Community', 30 *JCMS* 383–402.

—— (1994) (Ed.), *Europe After Maastricht: An Ever Closer Union?*, (Munich: Law Books in Europe/C.H. Beck).

—— Joerges, C., Majone, G., Snyder, F., and Everson, M. (1992), *Europe after 1992—New Regulatory Strategies* EUI Working Paper 92/31 (Florence: EUI.).

—— and Weiler, J. (1990), 'The Legal Dimension', in W. Wallace (1990).

Demiray, D. (1994), 'The Movement of Goods in a Green Market', *LIEI*, 1994/1, 73–110.

Department of Employment (1979), *New Earnings Surveys* (London: HMSO).

Deringer, A. (1965), 'The Interpretation of Article 90(2) of the EEC Treaty', 2 *CMLR* 129–38.

Derrida, J. (1989), *Of Spirit: Heidegger and the Question* (Chicago: University of Chicago Press).

—— (1990), 'The Force of Law: "The Mystical Foundation of Authority" ', 11 *Cardozo L. Rev.* 920–1045.

—— (1992), *The Other Heading: Reflections on Today's Europe* (trans. P-A. Brault & M. Naas) (Bloomington: Indiana University Press).

Diver, C. (1981), 'Policymaking Paradigms in Administrative Law', 95 *Harv. L. Rev* 393–434.

Douzinas, C. and Warrington R., with McVeigh, S. (1991), *Postmodern Jurisprudence: The Law of Text in the Texts of the Law* (London: Routledge).

—— Goodrich, P., and Hachamovitch, Y. (1994), *Politics, Postmodernity and Critical Legal Studies* (London: Routledge).

Düerkop, M. (1994), 'Trade and Environment: International Trade Aspects of the Proposed EC Directive Introducing a Tax on Carbon Dioxide Emission and Energy', 31 *CMLR* 807–844.

Dummett, A. (1991), 'Europe? Which Europe?', 18(1) *New Community* 167–175.

Dummett, A. (1994), 'Objectives for Future European Community Policy', in Spencer (1994).

Durkheim, E. (1893), *The Division of Labour in Society* (London: Macmillan, 1984).

Dworkin, R. (1986), *Law's Empire* (London: Fontana).

Dyson, K. (1992), *The Politics of German Regulation* (Aldershot: Dartmouth).

Edwards, G. and Spence, D. (1994) (Eds.), *The European Commission* (London: Longman).

El-Agraa, A. (1994) (Ed.), *The Economics of the European Community* (4th edn.) (London: Harvester Wheatsheaf).

Elkin, S.L. and Soltan, K.E. (1994) (Eds.), *A New Constitutionalism* (Chicago: Chicago University Press).

Ellwein, T., Hesse, J.J., Mayntz, R. and Scharpf F.W. (1989) (Eds.), *Jahrbuch zur Staats- und Verwaltungswissenschaft* (Nomos: Baden-Baden).

Emiliou, N. (1992), 'Subsidiarity: An Effective Barrier Against the Enterprises of Ambition?', 17 *ELR* 383–407.

—— (1993), 'Treading a slippery slope: the Commission's original legislative powers', 18 *ELR* 305–14.

Emmert, F. (1993), 'The Family Policy of the European Community', in Waaldijk and Clapham (1993).

Empel, M. van (1992), 'The 1992 Programme: Interaction between Legislator and Judiciary', *LIEI*, 1992/1, 1.

EOC (1979), *1978 Annual Report* (London: HMSO).

—— (1980), *1979 Annual Report* (London: HMSO).

—— (1993), *1992 Annual Report* (London: HMSO).

—— (1994), *1993 Annual Report* (Manchester: EOC).

Equal Opportunities Review (1994) Volume 58, 5.

Esch, B. van der (1970), 'L'Unité du Marché Commun dans la jurisprudence de la Cour' 6 *CDE* 303.

Escott, K. and Whitfield, D. (1995), *The Gender Impact of CCT in Local Government* (Manchester: Equal Opportunities Commission).

Eucken, W. (1950), *The Foundations of Economics* (London: William Hodge).

European Trade Union Institute (1992), *The European Dimensions of Collective Bargaining after Maastricht* (Brussels: ETUI).

—— (1993a), *The Social Architecture of Europe put to the Test: Trade Union Ideas for a European Model of Development* (Brussels: ETUI).

—— (1993b), *The European Industry Committees and Social Dialogue: Experience at sectoral level and in multinational companies* (Brussels: ETUI).

—— (1994), *Bargaining in Recession: Trends in Collective Bargaining in Western Europe 1993–1994* (Brussels: ETUI).

Everling, U. (1992), 'Reflections on the Structure of the European Union', 29 *CMLR* 1053–77.

Everson, M. (1995) 'Economic Rights within the European Union', in R. Bellemy *et al.* (1995).

Faraday, F. (1994), 'Dealing with Sexual Harassment in the Workplace: The Promise and Limitations of Human Rights Discourse', 32 *Osgoode Hall LJ* 33.

Finer, S. (1966), *The Anonymous Empire* (London: Pall Mall).

Fitzpatrick, B. (1992), 'Community Social Law after Maastricht', 21 *ILJ* 199.

Fitzpatrick, P. (1987), 'Racism and the Innocence of Law', 14 *JLS* 119–32.

—— (1995) (Ed.), *Nationalism, Racism and the Rule of Law* (Dartmouth: Aldershot).

Forbes, I. and Mead, G. (1992), *Measure for Measure: A Comparative Analysis of Measures to Combat Racial Discrimination in the Member Countries of the European Union* (London: Department of Employment).

Foster, D. (1993), 'Industrial Relations in Local Government: the Impact of Privatisation', 64 *Pol. Q* 49–59.

320   *Bibliography*

Freedland, M. (1994), 'Government by Contract and by Public Law', (1994) *PL* 86–104.

Foreman-Peck, J. and Millward, R. (1994), *Public and Private Ownership of British Industry 1820–1990* (Oxford: Clarendon Press).

Frowein, J. (1986), 'Fundamental Human Rights as a Vehicle of Integration in Europe', in Cappelletti, Seccombe, and Weiler (1986), Vol. 1, Bk. 3, 231.

—— (1990), 'The European Convention of Human Rights as the Public Order of Europe', in Clapham and Emmert (1990), 358.

Fuchs, G. (1992), 'Integrated Services Digital Network: The Politics of European Telecommunications Network Development', 16 *JEI* 63.

—— (1994), 'Policy-Making in a System of Multi-Level Governance—the Commission of the European Community and the Restructuring of the Telecommunications Sector', 1 *JEPP* 27–44.

Fuller, L. (1978), 'The Forms and Limits of Adjudication', 92 *Harv. L Rev.* 353–409.

Gaete, R. (1993), *Human Rights and the Limits of Critical Reason* (Aldershot: Dartmouth, 1993).

Galanter, M. (1974), 'Why the "Haves" Come Out Ahead: Speculations on the Limits of Legal Change', 9 *Law and Soc. Rev.* 95–106.

—— (1986), 'The Day after the Litigation Explosion', *Maryland LR* 3.

Garrett, G. (1995), 'The politics of legal integration in the European Union', 49 *IO* 171.

—— and Weingast, B. (1993), 'Ideas, interests and institutions: constructing the EC's internal market', in Goldstein and Keohane (1993).

Gava, J. (1994), 'Scholarship and Community', 16 *Sydney LR* 442.

George, S. (1985), *Policy and Politics in the European Community* (Oxford: Oxford University Press).

—— (1991), *Policy and Politics in the European Community* 2nd edn. (Oxford: Oxford University Press).

Gerardin, D. (1993), 'The Belgian Waste Case', 18 *ELR* 144–53.

Gerber, D. (1994a), 'The Transformation of European Community Competition Law', 35 *Harv. Intl. LJ* 97–147.

—— (1994b), 'Constitutionalizing the Economy: German Neo-liberalism, Competition Law and the "New" Europe', 42 *AJCL* 25.

Geyer, F. and van der Zouwen, J. (1986) (Eds.), *Sociocybernetic Paradoxes: Observation, Control and Evolution of Self-Steering Systems* (Beverly Hills: Sage).

Glasner, A. (1992), 'Gender and Europe: Cultural and Structural Impediments to Change', in Bailey (1992).

Gold, M. (1993) (Ed.), *The Social Dimension: Employment Policy in the European Community* (London: Macmillan).

Goldstein, J. and Keohane, R. (1993) (Eds), *Ideas and Foreign Policy* (Ithaca: Cornell University Press).

Golub, J. (1994), *Rethinking the Role of National Courts in European Integration: A*

Political Study of British Judicial Discretion EUI Working Paper 94/12 (Florence: EUI).

Glasner, A. (1992), 'Gender and Europe: cultural and structural impediments to change', in Bailey (1992).

Goodrich, P. (1992), 'Critical Legal Studies in England: Prospective Histories', 12 *OJLS* 195–236.

Gormley, L. (1985), *Prohibiting Restrictions on Trade Within the EEC* (Amsterdam: North Holland).

—— (1994), 'Reasoning Renounced? The Remarkable Judgment in *Keck* & *Mithouard*', (1994) *EBLR* March, 63–7.

Goyder, D. (1993), *EC Competition Law* (2nd edn.) (Oxford: Oxford University Press).

Greaves, R. (1986), '*Locus standi* under Article 173 When Seeking Annulment of a Regulation', 11 *ELR* 119–33.

—— (1991), *Transport Law of the European Community* (London: Athlone).

Green, M. (1993), 'The Politics of Big Business in the Single Market Program' Paper presented for the European Community Studies Association', 27 May Washington DC.

Green, N., Hartley, T., and Usher, J. (1991), *The Legal Foundations of the Single European Market*, (Oxford: Oxford University Press).

Greenwood, J. and Ronit, K. (1994), 'Interest Groups in the European Community: Newly Emerging Dynamics and Forms' 17 *West European Politics* 31.

Gregory, J. (1993), 'Racial Discrimination and the European Community', 22 *ILJ* 59–62.

Groot, C. de (1993), 'The Council Directive on the Safeguarding of Employees' Rights in the Event of Transfers of Undertakings', An Overview of the Case Law *CMLR* 331–50.

Gunsteren, H. van (1978), 'Notes on a Theory of Citizenship', in Birnbaum *et al.* (1978), 162–90.

—— (1994), 'Four Conceptions of Citizenship', in van Steenberg (1994), 36–48.

Gyselen, L. (1994), 'Anti-Competitive State Measures under the EC Treaty: Towards a Substantive Legality Standard', 19 *ELR Competition Law Checklist* 55.

Haas, E. (1958), *The Uniting of Europe* (London: Stanford Univ. Press).

Haas, P. (1992), 'Introduction: Epistemic Communities and International Policy Co-ordination' 46 *IO* 1–35.

Habermas, J. (1994), 'Citizenship and National Identity', in van Steenberg (1994), 16–35.

Hall, E. (1993), *The Electronic Age: Telecommunications in Ireland* (Dublin: Oak Tree Press).

Hall, P. (1986), *Governing the Economy: The Politics of State Intervention in Britain and France* (Oxford: Oxford University Press).

—— (1986), *Governing the Economy* (Cambridge: Polity).

Hallstein, W., Goetz, H., and Narjes, K. (1969), *Der unvollendete Bundesstaat: Europäische Erfahrungen und Erkenntnisse* (Düsseldorf: Econ).

Hancher, L. (1991), 'European Utilities Policy: The Emerging Legal Framework', 1 *Utilities Policy* 255–66.

—— (1992), *EC Electricity Law* (London: Chancery).

—— (1994a), 'Case Note—*Corbeau*', 31 *CMLR* 105–22.

—— (1994b), 'Guidelines for the Development of Community Postal Services', 5 *Utilities LR* 121–24.

—— (1994c), 'State Aids and Judicial Control in the European Community' (1994/3) *ECLR* 134.

—— and Moran, M. (1989a), 'Organizing Regulatory Space', in L. Hancher and M. Moran (1989b).

—— and Moran, M. (1989b) (Eds.) *Capitalism, Culture and Regulation* (Oxford: Oxford University Press).

—— and Sevenster, H. (1993), 'Note on Case C-2/90 *Commission* v. *Belgium*', 30 *CMLR* 351.

Harden, I. (1992), *The Contracting State* (Buckingham: Open University Press).

Harlow, C. (1986), 'Public Interest Litigation in England: The State of the Art', in Cooper and Dhavan (1986).

—— (1992), 'A Community of Interests? Making the Most of European Law', 55 *MLR* 331–50.

—— and Rawlings, R. (1992), *Pressure Through Law* (London: Routledge).

Harris, A. (1991), 'Race and Essentialism in Feminist Legal Theory', in Bartlett and Kennedy (1991).

Harris, A. (1994), 'The Jurisprudence of Reconstruction', 82 *Calif L Rev* 741–785.

Hartley, T. (1988), *The Foundations of European Community Law* (1st edn.) (Oxford: Clarendon Press).

—— (1994), *The Foundations of European Community Law* (3rd edn.) (Oxford: Clarendon Press).

Heater, D. (1990), *Citizenship: The Civic Ideal in World History, Politics and Education* (London: Longman).

Hecq, C. and Plasman, O. (1991), *La mobilité européenne des travailleurs feminins dans la communauté* (Brussels: Commission of the EC).

Heller, A. and Feher, F. (1988), *The Postmodern Political Condition* (Cambridge: Polity).

Helm, D. (1989) (Ed.), *The Economic Borders of the State* (Oxford: Oxford University Press).

—— (1993), 'The Assessment: The European Internal Market: The Next Steps', 9 *Oxford Review of Economic Policy* 1–14.

Henry, C. (1993), 'Public Service and Competition in the European Community Approach to Communications Networks', 9 *Oxford Review of Economic Policy* 45–66.

Hepple, B. (1977), 'Community Measures for the Protection of Workers against Dismissal', 14 *CMLR* 489–500.

—— (1990), *Main Shortcomings and Proposals for Revision of Council Directive 77/187*, Report for Directorate-General V of the Commission of the EC.

—— and Szyszczak, E. (1992) (Eds.), *Discrimination: The Limits of Law* (London: Mansell).

Herman, D. (1993), 'Beyond the Rights Debate', 2 *Social & Leg. Studies* 25.

Hicks, C. (1994) (Ed.), *Regulating Telecommunications—An International Assessment of Prospects and Strategies* (London: Centre for the study of Regulated Industries).

Hilf, M., Jacobs F., and Petersmann, E-U. (1986) (Eds) *The European Community and the GATT* (Deventer: Kluwer).

Hill, A. (1995), 'Italian telecoms giant roars as tiny challenger scores a hit', *Financial Times* 20 Jan. 1995.

Hindess, B. (1993), 'Citizenship in the Modern West', in Turner (1993a).

Hindley, B. (1988), 'Dumping and the Far East Trade of the European Community' (1988) *World Economy* 445.

Hix, S. (1994), 'The Study of the European Community: The Challenge to Comparative Politics', 17 *West European Politics* 1–30.

Hoffman, S. (1966), 'Obstinate or Obsolete? The fate of the Nation State and the Case of Western Europe', *Daedalus* No. 95

—— (1982), 'Reflections on the Nation-State in Western Europe Today', 21 *JCMS* 21.

Hoskyns, C. (1985), 'Women's Equality and the European Commission', 20 *Fem. Rev.* 71.

Hunt, A. (1990), 'The Big Fear: Law Confronts Postmodernism', 35 *McGill LJ* 508–17.

Hurwitz, (1981) (Ed.), *Contemporary Perspectives on European Integration: attitudes, nongovernmental behaviour and collective decision making* (London: Aldwych Press).

Hutchinson, A. and Monahan, P. (1984), 'The "Rights" Stuff: Roberto Unger and Beyond', 62 *Texas LR* 1477.

Hutsebaut, M., 'State of Implementation of the European Social Charter and the European Social Action Programme', in ETUI (1993a), 23.

Ingram, A. (1993), 'The Empire Strikes Back: Liberal Solidarity in a *Europe des Patries*', in M. Karlsson (1993).

Ipsen, H.P. (1972), *Europäisches Gemeinschaftsrecht* (Tübingen: J.C.B. Mohr).

Jackson, P.C. (1990), *The Impact of the Completion of the Internal Market on Women in the EC* (Brussels: Commission of the EC).

Jadot, B. (1990), 'Environnement et Libre Circulation', 26 *CDE* 403.

Jepperson, R. (1991), 'Institutions, Institutional Effects, and Institutionalism', in W. Powell and P. DiMaggio (1991) 143–63.

Jobert, B. (1994) (Ed.), *Le tournant Neo-Liberal en Europe: Idées et recettes dans les pratiques gouvernementales* (Paris: L'Harmattan).

Joerges, C. (1994), 'European Economic Law, the Nation-State and the Maastricht Treaty', in R. Dehousse (1994).

—— (1995) (Ed.), *ERPL* Special Issue on The Europeanization of Private Law: The Case of the Directive on Unfair Contract Terms (August 1995) (forthcoming).

Joint Council for the Welfare of Immigrants (JCWI) (1993), *The right to family life for immigrants in Europe* (Report of international meeting organised by Coordination Européene pour le Droit des Etrangers à Vivre en Famille, Brussels, 1993).

Judge, D., Earnshaw, D., and Cowan, N. (1994), 'Ripples or Waves: The European Parliament in the European Community Policy Process', 1 *JEPP* 27–52.

Kapteyn, P.J.G. and Verloren Van Themaat, P. (1987), *Introduction to the Law of the European Communities* 2nd edn. (Ed. L.W. Gormley) (London: Graham and Trotman).

Karlsson, M. (1993) (Ed), *Law, Justice and the State* (Berlin: Duncker & Humblot).

Keeling, D. and Mancini., G.F. (1994), 'Democracy and the European Court of Justice', (1994) 57 *MLR* 175–90.

Keen, M. (1993), 'The Welfare Economics of Tax Co-ordination in the European Community: A Survey' 14 *Fiscal Studies* 15.

Kelman, M. (1988), 'On Democracy-Bashing: A Skeptical Look at the Theoretical and "Empirical" Practice of the Public Choice Movement', 74 *Va. L Rev.* 199–273.

Kennedy, D. (1979), 'The Structure of Blackstone's Commentaries', 28 *Buffalo L. Rev.* 205.

Keohane, R. and Hoffman, S. (1990), 'Community Politics and Institutional Change,' in W. Wallace (1990).

—— (1991) (Eds.), *The New European Community* (Boulder: Westview Press).

—— and Nye, J. (1977), *Power and Interdependence: World Politics in Transition* (Boston: Little, Brown).

Kilroy, B. (1995), 'Judicial Independence or Politically Constrained Court: The Integrative Role of the European Court of Justice', paper presented at the Fourth Biennial Intl. Conference of the European Community Studies Assn., Charlston, SC, 11–14 May 1995.

Kilroy, B. (1995), 'The Agenda-Setting Role of the European Court of Justice', Paper delivered to the Fourth Biennial International Conference of the European Community Studies Association, 11–14 May, 1995, Charleston, SC.

Kingdom, E. (1991), *What's Wrong with Rights?: Problems for Feminist Politics of Law* (Edinburgh: Edinburgh University Press).

Kirchner, E. and Schwaiger, K. (1981a), *The Role of Interest Groups in the European Community* (Aldershot: Gower).

—— (1981b), 'Interest Group Behaviour at Community level', in Hurwitz (1981).

Knieps, G. (1990), 'Deregulation in Europe: Telecommunications and Transportation', in G. Majone (1990b).

Koelble, T. (1995), 'The New Institutionalism in Political Science and Sociology', (1995) *Comparative Politics* 231–43.

Kohler-Kock, B. (1989) (Ed.), *Regime in Internationalen Beziehungen* (Baden-Baden: Nomos).

Kohnstamm, M. (1990), 'Conflicts Between International and European Network Regulation: An Analysis of Third Parties' Rights in European Community Law' *LIEI* 1990/1 49–100.

Koopmans, T. (1992), 'Federalism: The Wrong Debate', 29 *CMLR* 1047–52.

Krämer, L. (1990), 'Environmental Protection and Article 30 EEC Treaty', 29 *CMLR* 111–43.

—— (1993), *European Environmental Law Case Book* (London: Sweet and Maxwell).

Kymlicka, W. and Norman, W. (1994), 'Return of the Citizen: A Survey of Recent Work on Citizenship Theory', 104 *Ethics* 352–81.

Lacey, N. (1987), 'Legislation against Sex Discrimination: Questions from a Feminist Perspective', 14 *JLS* 411–21.

—— (1995), 'Normative Reconstruction and Socio-Legal Studies', Paper delivered to the Socio-Legal Studies Association Annual Conference, March 1995, Leeds.

Ladrech, R. (1993), 'Parliamentary Democracy and Political Discourse in EC Institutional Change', 17 *JEI* 53–69.

Lake, W. (1990), 'Monopoly or Competition: The legal framework in the European Communities', in S. Schaff (1990).

Langan, M. and Ostner, I. (1991), 'Gender and Welfare', in Room (1991).

Lange, P. (1992), 'The Politics of the Social Dimension', in Sbragia (1992), 225.

—— (1993), 'Maastricht and the Social Protocol: Why Did They Do It?', 21 *Politics and Society* 5.

Latham, E. (1965), *The Group Basis of Politics* (New York: Octagon Press).

Lauwaars, R. (1972), *Lawfulness and Legal Force of Community Decisions* (Leiden: Martinus Nijhoff).

—— (1990), 'Note on Cases 46/87 and 227/88 *Hoechst AG* v. *Commission*', 27 *CMLR* 355–70.

Lenaerts, K. (1991), 'Fundamental Rights to be Included in a Community Catalogue', 16 *ELR* 367–90.

—— (1992), 'Some Thoughts about the Interaction between Judges and Politicians in the European Community', 12 *YEL* 1–34.

Lenel, H. (1989), 'Evolution of the Social Market Economy', in A. Peacock and H. Wilgerodt (1989a).

Levi, M. (1988), *Of Rule and Revenue* (Berkeley: University of California Press).

Lindblom, C. (1968), *The Policy-Making Process* (New Jersey: Prentice Hall).

Lindemann, M. (1995a), 'Runners and riders poised for the off', *Financial Times* 12 Jan. 1995.

—— (1995b), 'Bonn stands firm on phone monopoly', *Financial Times* 1 Feb. 1995.

Lodge, J. (1983) (Ed.), *Institutions and Policies of the European Community* (1st edn.) (London: Pinter).

—— (1994), 'Transparency and Democratic Legitimacy', 32 *JCMS* 343–68.

Lonbay, J. (1989), 'A review of recent tax cases—wine, gambling, fast cars and bananas' 14 *ELR* 48–56.

Lorenz, D. (1992), 'Economic Geography and the Political Economy of Regionalisation: The Example of Western Europe' 82 *AEA Papers and Proceedings* in *American Economic Review*, Issue no. 2, 85.

Loughney, D. (1995), *A Trade Union Response to the Proposed Revision of the Acquired Rights Directive*, MA Thesis, Leicester University, 1995.

Lowenfeld, A. (1994), 'Remedies Along with Rights: Institutional Reform in the New GATT', 88 *AJIL* 477.

Luhmann, N. (1986), 'The Autopoiesis of Social Systems', in F. Geyer and J. van der Zouwen (1986) 179–92.

Lukes, S. (1991), 'The Rationality of Norms', XXXII *Archives Européennes de Sociologie* 142–49.

Lyotard, J-F. (1984a), *The Postmodern Condition: A Report on Knowledge* (Manchester: Manchester University Press).

—— (1984b), 'The Differend, the Referent, and the Proper Name', 14 *Diacritics* 4–14.

—— (1988), *The Differend* (Manchester: Manchester University Press).

—— (1993), 'Heidegger and the 'jews': A Conference in Vienna and Freiburg', in *Political Writings* (trans. B. Readings and K. Geiman) (London: University College Press).

MacCormick, N. (1993), 'Beyond the Sovereign State', 56 *MLR* 1–18.

McCrudden, C. (1987) (Ed.), *Women, Employment and European Equality Law* (London: Eclipse).

McCubbins, M., Noll, R., and Weingast, B. (1989), 'Structure and Process, Politics and Policy: Administrative Arrangements and Political Control of Agencies', 75 *Va. L Rev.* 431–82.

McGee, A. and Weatherill, S. (1990), 'The Evolution of the Single Market—Harmonisation or Liberalisation', 53 *MLR* 578–96.

McGowan, F. (1993a), 'Ownership and Competition in Community Markets', in C. Pitelis and T. Clarke (1993).

—— (1993b), 'Trans-European Networks: Utilities Infrastructures. Editor's Introduction', 3 *Utilities Policy* 179–86.

—— (1994), 'EC Transport Policy', in A. El-Agraa (1994).

—— and Seabright, P. (1995), 'Regulation in the European Community and its impact on the UK', in M. Bishop *et al* (1995).

McGowan, L. and Wilks, S. (1994), 'Competition Policy in the European

Union', Paper presented at The Evolution of Rules for a Single European Market Conference, Exeter University, September 1994.

McMullen, J. (1994), 'Contracting Out and Market Testing—the Uncertainty Ends?', 23 *ILJ* 230–40.

Macey, J. (1992), 'Organisational Design and Political Control of Administrative Agencies', 8 *Journal of Law, Economics and Organization* 93–110.

Machlup, F. (1977), *A History of Thought on Economic Integration*, (London: Macmillan).

Majone, G. (1989), 'Regulating Europe: Problems and Prospects', in Ellwein *et al.* (1989), 159–77.

—— (1990a), 'Introduction', in G. Majone (1990b).

—— (1990b) (Ed.), *Deregulation or Reregulation—Regulatory Reform in Europe and the United States* (London: Pinter).

—— (1991), 'Cross-National Sources of Regulatory Policymaking in European and the United States', 11 *JPP* 79–106.

—— (1992), 'Regulatory Federalism in the European Community', 10 *Government and Policy*.

—— (1993), 'The European Community between Social Policy and Social Regulation', 31 *JCMS* 153–70.

—— (1994), 'Communauté Economique Européenne: Déréglementation ou re-réglementation? La conduite des politiques publiques depuis L'Acte Unique', in Jobert (1994).

March, J. and Olsen, J. (1984), 'The New Institutionalism: Organizational Factors in Political Life', 78 *American Political Science Review* 734–49.

—— (1989), *Rediscovering Institutions: the Organisational Basis of Politics* (New York: Free Press).

—— and Simon, H. (1958), *Organizations* (New York: John Wiley & Sons).

Marenco, G. (1983), 'Public Sector and Community Law', 20 *CMLR* 495–527.

—— (1991), 'Legal Monopolies in the Case-Law of the Court of Justice of the European Communities', (1991) *Fordham Corporate Law Institute* 197–222.

Maresceau, M. (1986), 'The GATT in the Case-Law of the European Court of Justice', in M. Hilf, F. Jacobs, and E-U. Petersmann (1986).

Marks, G. (1993), 'Structural Policy and Multilevel Governance in the EC', in A. Cafruny and G. Rosenthal (1993).

Marshall, T.H. (1950), *Citizenship and Social Class and Other Essays* (Cambridge: Cambridge University Press).

Mayer, C. (1989), 'Public Ownership: Concepts and Applications', in D. Helm (1989).

Mazey, S. and Richardson, J. (1993a), 'Introduction: Transference of Power, Decision Rules, and Rules of the Game', in Mazey and Richardson (1993b).

—— (1993b) (Eds.), *Lobbying in the European Community* (Oxford: OUP).

—— (1994), 'The Commission and the Lobby', in G. Edwards and D. Spence (1994).

Meehan, E. (1983), 'Priorities of the EOC', 54 *Pol. Q.*69.

—— (1993), *Citizenship and the European Community* (London: Sage).

Milward, A. (1992), *The European Rescue of the Nation State* (London: Routledge.

Minow, M. (1990), *Making All the Difference: Inclusion, Exclusion and American Law* (New York: Cornell University Press).

Mitchell, M. and Russell, D. (1994), 'Race, citizenship and "Fortress Europe" ', in P. Brown and R. Crompton (1994).

Monar, J. (1994),'Interinstitutional Agreements: The Phenomenon and its new Dynamics after Maastricht', 31 *CMLR* 693–719.

Montagnon, P. (1990), *European Competition Policy*, (London: Pinter Publishers).

Moore, S. (1994), 'Re-visiting the Limits of Article 30 EEC', 19 *ELR* 195–201.

Moravcsik, A. (1991), 'Negotiating the Single European Act: National Interests and Conventional Statecraft in the European Community', 45 *IO* 19–56.

—— (1993), 'Preferences and Power in the European Community: A Liberal Intergovernmentalist Approach', 31 *JCMS* 473–524.

More, G. (1993), 'The Acquired Rights Directive and its Application to Public Sector Contracting-out', 18 *ELR* 442–8.

Morokvasic, M. (1991), 'Fortress Europe and Migrant Women', 39 *Fem. Rev.* 69–84.

Mueller, M. (1993), 'Universal Service in Telephone History', 17 *Telecommunications Policy* 352–69.

Maller-Armack, A. (1989), 'The Meaning of Social Market Economy', in Peacock and Wilgerodt (1989b).

Muller, J. (1990), 'Natural Monopoly, Deregulation and Competition', in S. Schaff (1990).

Musgrave, R. (1989), *The Theory and Practice of Public Finance* (5th edn.) (New York: McGraw-Hill).

Mückenberger, U. and Deakin, S. (1989), 'From deregulation to a European floor of rights: Labour law, flexibilisation and the European single market', 3 *Zeitschrift für ausländisches und internationales Arbeits- und Sozialrecht* 153.

Mutimer, D. (1989), '1992 and the Political Integration of Europe: Neofunctionalism Reconsidered', 13 *JEI* 76–101.

Myers, G. (1990), 'Optimality, Free Mobility, and the Regional Authority in a Federation', 43 *Journal of Public Economics* 107.

Naftel, M. (1993), 'The Natural Death of a Natural Monopoly', *ECLR* 105.

Napier, B. (1993), *CCT, Market Testing and Employment Rights* (London: Institute of Employment Rights).

Netherlands Scientific Council (1986), *The Unfinished European Integration* (the Netherlands).

Netzer, D. (1974), 'State-local finance and intergovernmental fiscal relations', in A. Bliner *et al.* (1974).

Nielsen, R. and Szyszczak, E. (1993), *The Social Dimension of the European Community* (Copenhagen: Handelshojskolens Forlag).

Noam, E. (1992), *Telecommunications in Europe*, (New York: Oxford University Press).

Oates, W. (1972), *Fiscal Federalism* (London: Harcourt Brace).

O'Connor, B. and van de Ven, A. (1995), 'Trade and Environment: An Update on the GATT Agenda', 5 *European Environmental Law Review* 20.

O'Connor, K. (1980), *Women's Organisations' Use of the Courts* (Lexington: Heath).

OECD (1994a), *The OECD Jobs Study: Evidence and Explanations. Part I—Labour Market Trends and Underlying Forces of Change* (Paris: OECD).

—— (1994b), *The OECD Jobs Study: Evidence and Explanations. Part II—The Adjustment Potential of the Labour Market* (Paris: OECD).

Offe, C. (1987), 'Democracy against the Welfare State?: Structural Foundations of Neoconservative Political Opportunities', 15 *Political Theory*, 501–37.

Ogus, A. (1994), *Regulation: Legal Form and Economic Theory* (Oxford: Clarendon Press).

O'Higgins, T.F. (1990), 'The Family and European Law', 140 *NLJ* 1643–46.

O'Keeffe, D. and Twomey, P. (1994) (Eds.), *Legal Issues of the Maastricht Treaty* (Chichester: Chancery).

d'Oliveira, H.U.J. (1994), 'Citizenship: Its Meaning, Its Potential', in Dehousse (1994), 126–48.

Olsen, F. (1984), 'Statutory Rape: A Feminist Critique of Rights Analysis', 62 *Texas LR* 387.

—— (1993), 'Employment Discrimination in the New Europe: A Litigation Project for Women', in Bottomley and Conaghan (1993).

O'Reilly, J. (1992) (Ed.), *Human Rights and Constitutional Law: essays in honour of Brian Walsh* (Dublin: Round Hall Press).

Page, A. (1982), 'Member States, Public Undertakings and Article 90', 7 *ELR* 19.

Pahl, R.E. (1991), 'The Search for Social Cohesion: From Durkheim to the European Commission", *Archives Européennes de Sociologie* XXXII, 345.

Painter, C. (1994), 'Public Service Reform: Reinventing or Abandoning Government?', (1994) *Pol. Q.* 242–62.

Paul, R. (1991), 'Black and Third World peoples' citizenship and 1992', 32 *Critical Social Policy* 52–64.

Peacock, A. and Willgerodt, H. (1989a) (Eds.), *German Neo-liberals and the Social Market Economy* (Basingstoke: Macmillan).

—— (1989b) (Eds.), *Germany's Social Market Economy* (Basingstoke: Macmillan).

Pelkmans, J. (1980), 'Economic Theories of Integration Revisited', 18 *JCMS* 333.

—— and Robson P. (1987), 'The Aspirations of the White Paper', 25 *JCMS* 181.

Perry, M. (1984), 'Taking Neither Rights Talk nor the "Critique of Rights" too Seriously', 62 *Texas LR* 1405.

Pescatore, P. (1987), 'Some Critical Remarks on the Single European Act', 24 *CMLR* 9–18.

Peters, G. (1992), 'Bureaucratic Politics and the Institutions of the European Community', in A. Sbragia (1992).

—— (1994), 'Agenda-Setting in the European Community', 1 *JEPP* 9–26.

Petersmann, E-U. (1991), 'Strengthening the Domestic Legal Framework of the GATT Multilateral Trade System: Possibilities and Problems of Making GATT Rules Effective in Domestic Legal Systems', in E-U. Petersmann and M. Hilf (1991).

—— (1992), 'National Constitutions, Foreign Trade Policy and European Community Law', 5 *EJIL* 1.

—— (1993), 'Application of the GATT by the Court of Justice of the European Communities', 20 *CMLR* 397.

—— (1994), 'The Trade Dispute Settlement System of the World Trade Organisation and the Evolution of the GATT Dispute Settlement System Since 1948', 31 *CMLR* 1157.

—— and Hilf, M. (1991) (Eds.), *The New GATT Round of Multilateral Trade Negotiations: Legal and Economic Problems* (2nd edn.) (Deventer: Kluwer).

Peterson, J. (1991), 'Technology practice in Europe: Explaining the framework programme and Eureka in theory and practice', 29 *JCMS* 269.

—— (1994), 'Subsidiarity: A Definition to Suit any Vision?', 47 *Parl. Aff.* 116–133.

Phelan, D. (1992), 'Right to Life of the Unborn v. Promotion of Trade in Services: the European Court of Justice and the normative shaping of the European Union', 55 *MLR* 670–89.

Philpott, J. (1990) (Ed.), *Trade Unions and the Economy into the 1990s* (London: Employment Institute).

Pieterse, J. N. (1991), 'Fictions of Europe', 32(3) *Race and Class* 3–10.

Pillinger, J. (1992), *Feminising the Market* (London: Macmillan).

Pitelis, C. and Clarke, T. (1993) (Eds.), *The Political Economy of Privatization* (London: Routledge).

Pitta e Cunha, P. de (1994), 'Tax harmonisation and monetary union requirements within the European Community', Paper presented to 2nd ECSA-World Conference, Brussels, 5–6 May 1994.

PLC (1993), 'Outsourcing: Contracting out to save costs', *PLC* 1993, 4(6).

Plender, R. (1990), 'Competence, European Community Law and Nationals of Non-Member States', 39 *ICLQ* 599–610.

Pollard, D. and Ross, M. (1994), *European Community Law: Text and Materials* (London: Butterworths).

Pollert, A. (1990), 'The Mystique of Flexibility', in Philpott (1990), 67–85.

Poullet, Y. (1990), 'The Belgian Telecommunications Case', in S. Schaff (1990).

Powell, W. and DiMaggio, P. (1991) (Eds.), *The New Institutionalism in Organizational Analysis* (Chicago: Chicago University Press).

Preuị, U.K. (1994), *Concepts, Foundations and Limits of European Citizenship*, ZERP-Diskussionspapier (Bremen: Zentrum für Europäische Rechtspolitik) (forthcoming).

Prosser, T. (1983), 'Test Cases for the Poor: Legal Techniques in the Politics of Social Welfare', *CPAG Poverty Pamphlet No. 60*.

—— (1994), 'Privatization, Regulation and Public Services' 3 *Juridical Review* 3–17.

Puchala, D. (1972), 'Of Blind Men, Elephants and International Integration', 10 *JCMS* 267.

Ramsey, L. (1995), 'The Implications of the Europe Agreements for an Expanded European Union', 44 *ICLQ* 161–71.

Rasmussen, H. (1986), *On Law and Policy in the Court of Justice*, (Dordrecht: Martinus Nijhoff).

Ravaioli, P. and Sandler, P. (1994), 'The European Union and Telecommunications: Recent Developments in the Field of Competition (Part I)', 2 *International Computer Lawyer* 2–24.

Rawlings, R. (1993), 'The Eurolaw Game: Some Deductions from a Saga', 20 *JLS* 309–40.

Raworth, P. (1994), 'A Timid Step Forwards: Maastricht and the Democratisation of the European Community', 19 *ELR* 16–33.

Rehbinder, E. and Stewart, R. (1985), *Integration through Law (Volume 2): Environmental Protection Policy* (Berlin/New York: Walter de Gruyter).

Reich, N. (1994), 'The November Revolution of the European Court of Justice: *Keck, Meng* and *Audi* Revisited', 31 *CMLR* 459–92.

Rex, J. (1992), 'Race and ethnicity in Europe', in Bailey (1992).

Rhodes, M. (1993), 'The Social Dimension after Maastricht: Setting a new Agenda for the Labour Market', *IJCLLIR* 297.

Riccardi, F. (1994), 'A Look Behind the News—Foundations for a European Doctine of Public Service', *Agence Europe* 16 Nov. 1994.

Richardson, J. (1995), 'EU Water Policy: Uncertain Agendas, Shifting Networks and Complex Coalitions', 3 *Environmental Politics* 139–67.

Riesenberg, P. (1992), *Citizenship in the Western Tradition: Plato to Rousseau* (Chapel Hill: University of Carolina Press).

Room, G. (1991) (Ed.), *Towards a European Welfare State?* (Bristol: SAUS Publications).

Rootes, C. and Davis, H. (1994) (Eds.), *Social Change and Political Transformation* (Series: A New Europe?) (London: UCL Press).

Röpke, W. (1989), 'Interdependence of Domestic and International Economic Systems' in A. Peacock and H. Wilgerodt (1989b).

Rorty, R. (1989), *Contingency, Irony and Solidarity* (Cambridge: Cambridge University Press).

Rosenberg, G. (1991), *The Hollow Hope: Can Courts Bring About Social Change?* (Chicago: University of Chicago Press).

Sacks, V. (1986), 'The EOC—Ten Years On', 43 *MLR* 560–92.

—— and Maxwell, J. (1984), 'Unnatural Justice for Discriminators' 47 *MLR* 334.

Sally, R. (1994), 'The Social Market and the Liberal Order' (1994) *Government and Opposition* 461–76.

Sandalow, T. and Stein, E. (1982) (Eds.), *Courts and Free Markets: Perspectives from the United States and Europe*, (Oxford: Clarendon Press).

Sandholtz, W. and Zysman, J. (1989), '1992: Recasting the European Bargain', 42 *World Politics* 95–128.

Sandholtz, W. (1992), 'ESPRIT and the Politics of International Collective Action', 30 *JCMS* 1.

Sands, P. (1990), 'European Community Environmental Law: Legislation, the European Court of Justice and Common-Interest Groups,' 53 *MLR* 685–98.

Sauerland, D. (1994), 'Federalism and Constitutional Economics', Paper presented to 2nd ECSA-World Conference, Brussels, 5–6 May 1994.

Sauter, W. (1994a), 'The ONP Framework: Towards a European Tele-communications Agency', 5 *Utilities Law Review* 140–6.

—— (1994b), 'The Rejection of the ONP Voice Telephony Directive by the European Parliament', 5 *Utilities Law Review* 176–8.

Sbragia, A. (1992) (Ed.), *Euro-Politics: Institutions and Policymaking in the 'New' European Community* (Washington DC: Brookings Institution).

Schaff, S. (1990) (Ed.), *Legal and Economic Aspects of Telecommunications*, (North-Holland: Amsterdam).

Scheingold, S. (1974), *The Politics of Rights: Lawyers, Public Policy and Political Change* (New Haven: Yale University Press).

Schermers H. (1975), 'Community Law and International Law', 12 *CMLR* 77–90.

—— (1990), 'The European Communities bound by Fundamental Human Rights', 27 *CMLR* 249–58.

—— and Waelbroeck, D. (1991), *Judicial Protection in the European Communities*, (5th edn.) (Deventer: Kluwer).

Schindler, P. (1970), 'Public Enterprises and the EEC Treaty', 7 *CMLR* 57–71.

Schneider, V., Dang-Nguyen, G., and Werle R. (1994), 'Corporate Actor Networks in European Policy-Making: Harmonizing Telecommunic-ations Policy', 32 *JCMS* 473.

—— and Werle, R. (1989), 'Vom Regime zum Korporativen Akteur: Zur institutionellen Dynamik der Europäischen Gemeinschaft', in B. Kohler-Kock (1989).

Schoenbaum, T. (1992), 'Free Trade and Protection of the Environment: Irreconcilable Conflict?', 86 *AJIL* 700.

Schott, J. (1990), *Completing the Uruguay Round: A Results Oriented Approach to the GATT Trade Negotiations* (Washington DC: Institute for International Economics).

Schuster, G. (1992), 'Rechtsfragen der Maastrichter Vereinbarungen zur Sozialpolitik', *EuZW* 178.

Schwarze, J. (1992), *European Administrative Law* (London: Sweet and Maxwell).

Schweie, K. (1994), 'EC Law's Unequal Treatment of the Family: The Case Law of the European Court of Justice on Rules Prohibiting Discrimination on Grounds of Sex and Nationality', 3 *Social and Legal Studies* 243–65.

Scott, C. (1994), 'The Development of a European Telecommunications Policy', in C. Hicks (1994).

Scott, J. (1995), *Development Dilemmas in the European Community: Rethinking Regional Development Policy* (Buckingham: Open University Press).

—— and Mansell, W. (1993), 'European Regional Development Policy: Confusing Quantity with Quality', 18 *ELR* 87–108.

Seabright, P. (1993), 'Managing Local Commons: Theoretical Issues in Incentive Design', 7 *Journal of Economic Perspectives* 113.

—— (1994), *Accountability and Decentralisation in Government: An Incomplete Contracts Model*, Discussion Paper No. 889 (London: Centre for Economic Policy Research).

Séché, J.-C. (1993), 'L'Europe sociale après Maastricht', *CDE* 509.

Shanks, M. (1977), *European Social Policy, Today and Tomorrow* (Oxford: Pergamon).

—— (1978), *A New Social Action Programme for Europe* (Brussels: European Cooperation Fund).

Shapiro, M. (1981), 'Comparative Law and Comparative Politics', 53 *S. Ca. L. Rev.* 537–42.

—— (1992), 'The European Court of Justice', in A. Sbragia (1992).

Shaw, J. (1993), *European Community Law* (Basingstoke: Macmillan).

—— (1994), 'Twin-Track Social Europe—the Inside Track', in D. O'Keeffe and P. Twomey (1994).

—— (1996), 'European Union legal studies in crisis? Towards a new dynamic', 16 *OJLS* (forthcoming).

Siebert, H. (1989a), 'The Harmonization Issue in Europe: Prior Agreement or Competitive Process' in H. Siebert (1989b).

—— (1989b) (Ed.), *The Completion of the Internal Market* (Tübingen: JCB Mohr).

—— and Koop, M. (1990), 'Institutional Competition. A Concept for Europe?' 45 *Außenwirtschaft* 439–62.

—— (1993), 'Institutional Competition *versus* Centralization: *Quo Vadis Europe?*', 9 *Oxford Review of Economic Policy* 15.

Sivanandan, A. (1988), 'The new racism', *New Statesman and Society*, 4 Nov. 1988.

Slaughter Burley, A-M. (1993), 'New Directions in Legal Research on the European Community', 31 *JCMS* 391–400.

Slaughter, A-M. and Mattli, W. (1995), 'Law and politics in the European Union: a reply to Garrett', 49 *IO* 189.

Smart, C. (1989), *Feminism and the Power of Law* (London: Routledge).

Smith, S. (1994), 'Subsidiarity and the Coordination of Indirect Taxes in the European Community', Paper presented to 2nd ECSA-World Conference, Brussels, 5–6 May 1994.

Snyder, F. (1985), *The Law of the Common Agricultural Policy* (London: Sweet and Maxwell).

—— (1990), *New Directions in European Community Law* (London: Weidenfeld & Nicholson).

—— (1993a), 'The Effectiveness of European Community Law: Institutions, Processes, Tools and Techniques', 56 *MLR* 19–54.

—— (1993b), 'Soft Law and Institutional Practice in the European Community', *EUI Working Paper (Law)* No. 93/5.

Soltan, K.E. (1994), 'Generic Constitutionalism', in Elkin and Soltan (1994), 70–95.

Sommers, M.R. (1994), 'Rights, Relationality and Membership: Rethinking the Making and Meaning of Citizenship', 19 *Law and Social Inquiry (Journal of the American Bar Foundation)* 63–112.

Sorauf, F. (1976), *The Wall of Separation: the Constitutional Politics of Church and State* (Princeton: Princeton University Press).

Spencer, S. (1994) (Ed.), *Strangers and Citizens* (London: Rivers Oram).

Springe, C. (1993), 'Women—Winners or Losers in the New Europe', in Templeton (1993).

Steenberg, B. van (1994), *The Condition of Citizenship* (London: Sage).

Stein, E. (1981), 'Lawyers, Judges and the Making of a Transnational Constitution', 75 *AJIL* 1–27.

Steiner, J. (1994a), *Textbook on EC Law* (London: Blackstone Press).

—— (1994b), 'Subsidiarity under the Maastricht Treaty', in O'Keeffe and Twomey (1994), 49–64.

Steinmo, S., Thelen, K., and Longstreth, F. (1992) (Eds.), *Structuring Politics—Historical Institutionalism in Comparative Analysis* (Cambridge: Cambridge University Press).

Stewart, R. (1993), 'Environmental Regulation and International Competitiveness', 102 *Yale LJ* 2039.

Stubbs, P. and Saviotti, P. (1994), 'Science and Technology Policy', in M.J. Artis and N. Lee (1994).

Sun, J-M. and Pelkmans, J. (1995), 'Regulatory Competition in the Single Market', 33 *JCMS* 67–89.

Szyszczak, E. (1992), 'Racism: The Limits of Market Equality', in Hepple and Szyszczak (1992).

—— (1994), 'Social Policy: a Happy Ending or a Reworking of the Fairy Tale?', in O'Keeffe and Twomey (1994), 313.

—— (1995), 'Future Directions in European Union Social Law', 24 *ILJ* 19.

Tatchell, P. (1992), *Europe in the Pink* (London: GMP).

Taylor, S. (1994), 'Article 90 and Telecommunication Monopolies', 6 *European Competition LR* 322.

Teasdale, A. (1993), 'Subsidiarity in Post-Maastricht Europe', 64 *Pol. Q.* 187–97.

Templeton, E. (1993) (Ed.), *A Woman's Place?* (Edinburgh: Saint Andrew Press).

Teubner, G. (1987a), 'Juridification—Concepts, Aspects, Limits, Solutions', in G. Teubner (1987b).

—— (1987b) (Ed.), *Juridification of Social Spheres* (Berlin: Walter de Gruyter).

—— (1991), 'Autopoiesis and Steering: How Politics Profit from the Normative Surplus of Capital', in R. 'T Veld *et al.* (1991).

—— (1993), 'Piercing the Contractual Veil? The Social Responsibility of Contractual Networks', in T. Wilhelmsson (1993), 211–38.

—— and Febbrajo, A. (1992), *State, Law and Economy as Autopietic Systems—Regulation and Autonomy in New Perspective* (Milan: Guiffre).

Thelen, K. and Steinmo, S. (1992), 'Historical Instiutionalism in Comparative Politics', in S. Steinmo *et al.* (1992).

Therborn, G. (1995), *European Modernity and Beyond* (London: Sage).

Thomas, C. and Tereposky, G. (1993), 'The Evolving Relationship Between Trade and Environment', 27 *JWT* 23.

Tiebout, C. (1956), 'A Pure Theory of Local Expenditures', 98 *Journal of Political Economy*, 1119.

Tömmel, I. (1992), 'Decentralisation of Regional Development Policies in the Netherlands—A New Type of State Intervention?', 15 *West European Politics* 107.

Toth, A. (1992), 'The Principle of Subsidiarity in the Maastricht Treaty', 29 *CMLR* 1079–105.

—— (1994), 'A Legal Analysis of Subsidiarity', in O'Keeffe and Twomey (1994), 37–48.

Tranholm-Mikkelsen, J. (1991), 'Neo-Functionalism: Obstinate or obsolete? A reappraisal in the light of the New Dynamism of the EC', 20 *Millenium* 1–22.

Tsoukalis, L. (1993), *The New European Economy; The Politics and Economics of Integration*, 2nd edn. (Oxford: Oxford University Press).

Tumlir, F. (1989), 'Franz Böhm and the Development of Economic-Constitutional Analysis', in A. Peacock and H. Wilgerodt (1989a).

Turner, B. (1994), 'Postmodern Culture—Modern Citizens', in van Steenberg (1994), 153–68.

—— (1993a) (Ed.), *Citizenship and Social Theory* (London: Sage).

—— (1993b), 'Contemporary Problems in the Theory of Citizenship', in Turner (1993a).

—— (1993c), 'Outline of the Theory of Human Rights', in Turner (1993a), 163–90.

Tushnet, M. (1984), 'An Essay on Rights', 62 *Texas LR* 1363.

Tweedy, J. and Hunt, A. (1994), 'The Future of the Welfare State and Social Rights: Reflections on Habermas', 21 *JLS* 288.

Twining, W. (1986a), 'Evidence and Legal Theory', in W. Twining (1986b).

—— (1986b) (Ed.), *Legal Theory and Common Law* (Oxford: Basil Blackwell).

Twomey, P. (1994), 'The European Union: Three Pillars without a Human Rights Foundation,' in O'Keeffe and Twomey (1994), 129.

Urwin, D. (1991), *The Community of Europe* (London: Longman).

Usher, J. (1994), 'The Commission and the Law', in G. Edwards and D. Spence (1994).

Vanhoven, N. and Klaasen, L.H. (1987), *Regional Policy: A European Approach*, (Aldershot: Avebury).

Vaubel. R. (1995), 'Social Regulation and Market Integration: A Critique and Public-Choice Analysis of the Social Chapter', 50 *Aussenwirtschaft* 111–132.

'T Veld, R., Schaap, L., Termeer, C., and van Twist, M. (1991) (Eds.), *Autopoiesis and Configuration Theory: New Approaches to Societal Steering* (Dordrecht: Kluwer).

Vickers, J. and Yarrow, G. (1988), *Privatization: An Economic Analysis* (Boston MA: MIT Press).

Vose, C. (1955), 'NAACP Strategy in the Covenant Cases', 6 *Western Reserve LR* 101.

Waaldijk, K. and Clapham, A. (1993) (Eds.), *Homosexuality: A European Community Issue* (Dordrecht, Martinus Nijhoff).

Waas, B. (1994), 'Betriebsübergang durch "Funktionsnachfolge"?', (1994) *EuZW* 528–31.

Waelbrock, M. (1982), 'The Emergent Doctrine of Pre-Emption—Consent and Re-delegation', in T. Sandalow and E. Stein (1982).

Wainwright, R. (1994), 'The Future of European Community Legislation in the light of the Recommendations of the Sutherland Committee and the Principle of Subsidiarity', 15 *Stat. L.Rev.* 98–107.

Wallace, W. (1990) (Ed.) *The Dynamics of European Integration*, (London: Pinter).

Ward, A., Gregory, J., and Yural-Davis, N. (1992) (Eds.), *Women and Citizenship in Europe: borders, rights and duties* (London: Trentham).

Ward, H. (1994), 'Trade and Environment in the Round—and After', 6 *Journal of Environmental Law* 263.

Ward, I. (1993), 'Making Sense of Integration: A Philosophy of Law for the European Community', 17 *JEI* 101–36.

—— (1994a), 'The Anomalous, the Wrong, and the Unhappy: UK Administrative Law in a European Perspective', 45 *NILQ* 46–52.

—— (1994b), 'In Search of a European Identity' 57 *MLR* 315–29.

Watson, P. (1991), 'The Community Social Charter', 28 *CMLR* 37–68.

—— (1993), 'Social Policy after Maastricht', 30 *CMLR* 481–513.

Weatherill, S. (1994), 'Beyond Preemption', in D. O'Keeffe and P. Twomey (1994).

—— (1995), 'Prospects for the Development of European Private Law in the European Court—The Case of the Directive on Unfair Terms in Consumer Contracts', in Joerges (1995).

—— and Beaumont, P. (1993), *EC Law* (Harmondsworth: Penguin).

Webber, F. (1991), 'From ethnocentrism to Euro-racism', 32(3) *Race and Class* 11–17.

Weiler, J. (1981), 'The Community System: The Dual Character of Supranationalism', 1 *YEL* 267–306.

—— (1982), 'Community, Member States and European Integration: Is the Law Relevant?' 21 *JCMS* 39.

—— (1986), 'Eurocracy And Distrust', 61 *Washington LR* 1103.

—— (1987), 'The European Court at a Crossroads: Community Human Rights and Member State Action', in Capotorti *et al.* (1987), 821.

—— (1991), 'The Transformation of Europe', 100 *Yale LJ* 2405–83.

—— (1992), 'Thou Shalt Not Oppress a Stranger: On the Judicial Protection of the Human Rights of Non-EC Nationals—A Critique', 3 *EJIL* 65–91.

—— (1993), 'Journey to an Unknown Destination: A retrospective and prospective of the European Court of Justice in the Arena of Political Integration', 31 *JCMS* 417.

—— (1994a), 'Fin-de-Siècle Europe', in R. Dehousse (1994), 203–16.

—— (1994b), 'A Quiet Revolution: The European Court of Justice and its Interlocutors', 23 *Comparative Political Studies* 510.

Weinberger, O. (1993), 'Institutional Theory of Action and its Significance for Jurisprudence', 6 *Ratio Juris* 171–80.

Weir, M. (1992), 'Ideas and the Politics of Bounded Innovation', in S. Steinmo *et al.* (1992).

Weiss, M. (1992), 'The significance of Maastricht for European Community Social Policy', *IJCLLIR* 3.

Wellens, K. and Borchardt, G. (1989), 'Soft Law in European Community Law', 14 *ELR* 267–321.

Westin, A. (1975), 'Someone has to Translate Rights into Realities', 2 *Civil Liberties Rev.* 104.

Westlake, M. (1994), 'The Commission and the Parliament', in G. Edwards and D. Spence (1994).

White, N. (1994), 'Is ONP living up to its expectations', Conference Paper, *Implementing European Telecommunications Law*, 21–2 Nov. 1994.

Whiteford, E. (1993a), 'De sociale dimensie van de EG na Maastricht: oude

Bibliography

wijn in nieuwe zakke' 18 *Nederlands Tijdschrift voor de Mensenrechten NJCM-Bulletin* 110.

—— (1993b), 'Social Policy after Maastricht', 18 *ELR* 202–22.

Wilhelmsson, T. (1993) (Ed.), *Perspectives of Critical Contract Law* (Aldershot: Dartmouth).

Williams, S. (1991), 'Sovereignty and Accountability in the European Community', in R. Keohane and S. Hoffman (1991).

Williamson, O. (1988), *The Economic Institutions of Capitalism: Firms, Markets, Relational Contracting* (New York: Free Press/London: Collier Macmillan).

—— (1993), *The Economic Analysis of Institutions and Organisations* Working papers/OECD, Economics Department, no. 133, (Paris: Organisation for Economic Co-operation and Development).

Wils, W. (1993), 'The search for the rule in Article 30: much ado about nothing', 18 *ELR* 475–92.

—— (1994), 'Subsidiarity and EC Environmental Policy: Taking Peoples' Concerns Seriously', 6 *Journal of Environmental Law* 85.

Wilson, J. (1980a), 'The Politics of Regulation' in J. Wilson (1980b).

—— (1980b) (Ed.), *The Politics of Regulation* (New York: Basic Books).

Wilson, T. and Estellie Smith, M. (1993) (Eds.), *Cultural Change and the New Europe. Perspectives on the European Community* (Boulder/San Francisco/Oxford: Westview).

Wincott, D. (1995a), 'Institutional interaction and European integration: Towards an everyday critique of Liberal Intergovernmentalism', 33 *JCMS* (forthcoming).

—— (1995b), 'The Role of Law or the Rule of the Court of Justice? An "institutional" account of judicial politics in the European Community', 2 *European Journal of Public Policy* (forthcoming).

—— (1995c), 'The European Court of Justice in a policy perspective', Paper presented to the Fourth Biennial International Conference of ECSA, Charleston, SC, 11–14 May 1995.

Winter, J. (1993), 'Supervision of State Aid: Article 93 in the Court of Justice', 30 *CMLR* 311–29.

Witte, B. de (1991), 'Community Law and National Constitutional Values', (1992) *LIEI* 1–22.

Wolin, R. (1991), *The Heidegger Controversy: A Critical Reader* (New York: Columbia University Press).

Woolcock, S., Hodges, M., and Schreiber, K. (1991), *Britain, Germany and 1992: The Limits of Deregulation* (London: Pinter).

Woude, M. van der (1992), 'Article 90: "Competing for Competence" ', *ELR Competition Law Checklist* 60.

Wyatt, D. and Dashwood, A. (1993), *European Community Law* (London: Sweet and Maxwell).

Index

energy policy *see also* utilities law and
   policy
  Green Paper (1995) 203, 212
  liberalization 215
  third party access to energy
    networks 205
  universal service obligations 211–12
  Working Paper on the Internal
    Energy Market (1988) 201–2,
    203
environmental protection 12, 70, 304
  'drifting pollution' 160
  extra-territoriality of process
    regulation 159
  policy competence 171
  regulation and competitiveness 156–8
    GATT 1994, effects of 148, 158–64
  Trade Related Environmental
    Measures 162
  waste disposal 67, 70
environmental rights 38–9
epistemic communities 171
Equal Opportunities Commission
    (EOC) 13, 254
  annual grant 255
  formal investigations 256–7
  legal budget 256
  litigation strategy 254–5, 263–6
    amicus briefs 266
    effects 269–70
    judicial review proceedings 265–6,
     272
    mistakes 270
    references to Court under Article
     177 263–5, 269, 272
    tactics complementing 267–9
  litigator, as 258–63
    locus standi 265n, 266
  powers and functions of 255–8
  seventh Annual Report 268n
  staff 260
Equal Opportunities Commission
    (Northern Ireland) 254, 260n
equal pay 34, 47, 94, 254, 268–9
equal treatment 37
  Community law 91, 93, 94
  employment matters 34, 51–2
  EOC litigation strategy *see* Equal
    Opportunities Commission
Equality Law Network 268
Equipment Directive (88/301/
    EEC) 224, 225, 228–30, 230–31
Escott, K. and Whitfield, D. 141
Esprit Telecom 233

Estellie Smith, M. 6n
ethical relation 23n
ethnic rights 36
ETUC 121, 122
EU *see* European Union
EU nationals (EUNS)
  families, rights of 97
  migrant workers 95, 96
    third country nationals and,
     distinction between 96–8
Eucken, Walter 57, 58
EUNS *see* EU nationals
Euro-groups 253
Eurolobbying 171, 210–11, 253
Europe of the Regions 26
European Commission *see* Commission
European Convention on Human
    Rights 32, 33, 40, 45, 51, 75
European Council 248–9, 296, 305
  Edinburgh Summit (1992) 189, 201,
    237, 246
  summitry 296
European Court of Justice *see* Court of
    Justice
European Defence Community 55
European Federation 19
European identity *see* identity
European integration 11, 28, 293–4 *see
    also* European Union
  economic integration 55 *see also*
    internal market; single market
  history of
    internal market and '1992' 307–10
    legal history 299–300
    political history 296–7
    politico/legal analysis 302–10
  institutionalist approach 165–6
  internal market programme: '1992'
    process 297
  legal analysis 298–9, 300
  neo-functionalist theory 8, 294–5,
    300
  political science analysis 8, 294–6,
    300–1
  realist theory 294, 295, 296, 297, 300
  rights and 29–30
    rights as integrating force 41–3, 44–
     5, 47–9
    social impact of rights 50–52
  telecommunications and 217–20, 234
    see also telecommunications policy
  theory 6
  uniting legal and political
    analyses 300–2

Werle, R. 219n
Werner Report 297, 306
Westin, A. 262n
White, Nick 233
Whiteford, Elaine 4, 5, 6, 12
Whitfield, D. 141
Wilkinson, F. 142
Wilks, S. 205
Willgerodt, H. 56n
Williams, Shirley 22
Williamson, O. 195
Wils, W. 64, 161, 179
Wilson, J. 195
Wilson, T.
  and Estellie Smith, M. 6n
Wincott, Daniel 1n, 4, 5, 6, 8, 9, 10, 13, 166, 307
Winter, J. 274
Wolin, R. 16n
women
  Community's construct of 'family' and 105–6
  equal treatment *see* equal treatment; sex discrimination
  'market', and 107–8
  migrant workers 104–5, 107–8
  Community's construct of 'work' and 104
    family of 105–6
    gendered implications of EC law 104–8

third country nationals 107
pregnancy and maternity rights 34
protection for 92, 93, 94
single parent families 106
Woolcock, S. 225
words and phrases
  citizenship 80, 82
  European 98–102, 109
  family 105–6, 109
  institutions 167, 193–4, 196
  work 104, 109
  worker 104–5, 106
work *see also* employment
  Community's construct of 104, 109
workers 51
  Community's construct of 'worker' 104–5, 106
  free movement of 33, 47 *see also* migrant workers
working time directive 115, 125
works councils 122
WTO Agreement 151, 163, 164
  dispute settlement procedures 151–2
Wyatt, D. 8
  and Dashwood, A. 96, 97

xenophobia 94

Zysman, J. 296, 308